Reading the River in Shakespeare's Britain

Lisa: For my sister-in-law, Elaine Hopkins
Bill: For Lina Ou and Melody Wei

Reading the River in Shakespeare's Britain

Edited by Bill Angus and
Lisa Hopkins

EDINBURGH
University Press

Edinburgh University Press is one of the leading university presses in the UK. We publish academic books and journals in our selected subject areas across the humanities and social sciences, combining cutting-edge scholarship with high editorial and production values to produce academic works of lasting importance. For more information visit our website: edinburghuniversitypress.com

© editorial matter and organisation Bill Angus and Lisa Hopkins 2024
© the chapters their several authors 2024

Edinburgh University Press Ltd
13 Infirmary Street
Edinburgh EH1 1LT

Typeset in 10.5/13 Adobe Sabon by
Cheshire Typesetting Ltd, Cuddington, Cheshire, and
printed and bound in Great Britain

A CIP record for this book is available from the British Library

ISBN 978 1 3995 3448 2 (hardback)
ISBN 978 1 3995 3450 5 (webready PDF)
ISBN 978 1 3995 3451 2 (epub)

The right of Bill Angus and Lisa Hopkins to be identified as the editors of this work has been asserted in accordance with the Copyright, Designs and Patents Act 1988, and the Copyright and Related Rights Regulations 2003 (SI No. 2498).

Contents

List of Illustrations vii
Acknowledgements ix

    Introduction: Theologies, Economies and Ecologies of the River 1
    Bill Angus and Lisa Hopkins

Part I Conceptualising the River

1. Rivers of Milk, Honey, Tears and Treasures: Mapping Salvation in Early Modern English Devotional Poetry 21
   Brice Peterson

2. 'Plenteous Rivers': Waterways as Resources, Threats and the Heart of the Community in Early Modern England 42
   Daniel Gettings

3. Rivers and Contested Territories in the Works of Shakespeare 61
   Rebecca Welshman

Part II Writing the River

4. The Navigation of the Trent and William Sampson's *The Vow-Breaker* (1636) 83
   Lisa Hopkins

5. Ship of Fools and Slow Boat to Hell: The Literary Voyages of the Gravesend Barge 101
   Lindsay Ann Reid

6. Rivers, Monstrosity and National Identity in Izaak Walton's *The Compleat Angler* 124
   Melissa Caldwell

Part III Rivers and Money

7. 'Your Innes and Alehouses Are Brookes and Rivers': John Taylor and Free-flowing Rivers of Ale — 143
   Bill Angus

8. The Rose and the Riverside — 168
   Cecilia Lindskog Whiteley

9. 'As Water Mill, Made Rags and Shreds to Sweate': Fluvial Bodies and Fluminous Geographies — 187
   Jemima Matthews

Part IV Ecocritical Approaches

10. 'Insatiable [Gourmandize] Thus All Things Doth Devour': Reading the Threat of Human Greed along the Rivers of Early Modern England — 211
    Emily J. Naish

11. Powtes, Protest and (Eco)politics in the English Fens — 231
    Esther Water

12. Shakespeare's Waterways: Premonitions of an Environmental Collapse — 250
    Sophie Chiari

    Conclusions: Rivers of Life and Death — 269
    Lisa Hopkins and Bill Angus

Notes on Contributors — 273
Index — 277

List of Illustrations

Figure 2.1 A plan and explanation of 'the New River'. Used by permission of Warwickshire County Record Office, ref. CR136/D1/91.   45

Figure 5.1 Detail from John Norden's *View of London Bridge from East to West* (1597). STC 18643.5. Used by permission of the Folger Shakespeare Library.   103

Figure 5.2 Detail from John Norden's map of London in *Speculum Britanniae* (1593). STC 18635. Used by permission of the Folger Shakespeare Library.   104

Figure 5.3 Map of London entitled 'Londinum Feracissimi Angliae Regni Metropolis' from the 1635 edition of Georg Braun and Frans Hogenburg's *Civitates Orbis Terrarum* (first published 1574). MAP L85c no. 27. Used by permission of the Folger Shakespeare Library.   105

Figure 5.4 Detail from a 1625 imprint of Claes Visscher's *Londinum Florentissima Britanniae Urbs* (first published 1616). GA795.L6 V5 1625 Cage. Used by permission of the Folger Shakespeare Library.   105

Figure 5.5 Poem about John Day written into a manuscript of *The Prick of Conscience* between approximately 1562 and 1584. Ms. E Mus. 88, fol. 94v. The Bodleian Libraries, University of Oxford.   115

Figure 5.6 Title page of *Westward for Smelts* (1620). STC 25292. Used by permission of the Folger Shakespeare Library.   117

Figure 5.7 Title page of *The Tincker of Turvey* (1630). RB 81683. © The Huntington Library, San Marino, California.   118

Figure 7.1 Detail from *Taylors physicke has purged the divel* (1641). © British Library Board. E.163.(9) fol. 1r. 143

Figure 7.2 Map of London; illustration to Braun and Hogenberg's *Civitates Orbis Terrarum*. © British Library Board. 147

Figure 10.1 Frontispiece to William Iaggard's *A true report of Certaine wonderfull overflowings of water* (1607). © British Library Board 1103.e.58. 217

Figure 10.2 Cartographic etching for Song 15 of Michael Drayton's *Poly-Olbion* (1612/1622). Image used courtesy of the University of Sheffield Library, Special Collections and Archives. 225

Acknowledgements

Lisa would like to thank Chris Hopkins for yet again asking a ridiculous and annoying question that gave her an idea, Bill Angus for giving the idea a shape, Pat Griffin for her tireless editorial work on *The Vow Breaker*, and Emanuel Stelzer for thoughtful and incisive comments on the first draft of the essay. Bill would like to thank Lisa and Chris for initiating another interesting milestone in a mutual journey of letters.

Introduction: Theologies, Economies and Ecologies of the River

Bill Angus and Lisa Hopkins

Alongside the tectonic forces that define the shape of all land, the world's waterways, principally its rivers and in some places glacial rivers of ice which are themselves the fountainheads of great rivers, have literally formed the landscapes we inhabit.[1] Our essays herein represent the most contemporary historical and literary research in the cultural and literary geography of rivers. By now established as a critical genre of its own, literary or cultural geography of this kind should need no further introduction. As 'meaningful segments of space', rivers, like many other features of the natural and human-moulded world, are very much 'locations imbued with meaning and power', we may employ Tim Cresswell's designations to assert.[2] Following Joël Bonnemaison's dictum that 'no identity exists without a space that sustains it', to a significant extent these essays also explore the ways in which early modern human identities are defined and refined in relation to this enduring and sustaining feature of the landscape.[3]

With their immense presence and life-giving function, rivers have long been worshipped as entities in their own right. Karen V. Lykke Syse observes that most Celtic and Gallic river names are female or actually 'named after mother goddesses... [while] British rivers, like the Thames, for instance, were male deities'.[4] At the time such names were bestowed, there may have been genuine belief in the divinity of rivers; by the early modern period any such belief had long since vanished, but the idea of river gods and goddesses remained appealing. Claudia Lazzaro notes that in January 1512,

> when a colossal ancient statue of the Tiber River was unearthed in Rome, many people gathered to see it... Pope Julius II immediately acquired the work for his sculpture garden in the Vatican, already famous for such antiquities as the Laocoon and the Apollo Belvedere. A year or two later, a second statue representing the Nile River... also from the sanctuary of Isis, entered the Vatican Statue Court, and soon after a third river god. The Tiber

and Nile led to a clear understanding of the ancient type, the identification of other statues, and ultimately the tremendous popularity in the sixteenth century of river gods in fountains, festivities and triumphal entries, political propaganda, and much more.[5]

As Lazzaro's list indicates, the idea that rivers could be personified readily lent itself to the early modern passion for ostentatious display, shows and pageants, which typically had both a local and an allegorical flavour.

The idea of river deities was also congenial to devisers of other kinds of entertainments. In England, playwrights and poets both chose to play with the conceit of river gods. Edmund Spenser's *The Faerie Queene* (1596) describes a marriage of the Thames and the Medway whose divine guest list seems to delineate the contemporary topography of myth and legend surrounding rivers. This includes the Amazon, Nile, Tigris, Ganges, Euphrates, Indus and Orinoco rivers, the last, 'though but knowen late', having recently been encountered by Spenser's associate Walter Raleigh. Situated within this list also are the domestic rivers in a roll call which serves to define the parameters of the land as Spenser sees it. Some Irish rivers are mentioned (including the 'Blacke water', overlooking which he owned property, a typical English colonist of his era) but Scottish rivers (excepting the Tweed) are excluded as being beyond the 'Tyne, along whose stony bancke / That Romaine Monarch built a brasen wall'.[6] Aside from a few additional contextual comments about some of the rivers, this wedding guestlist remains within the realm of myth and its power is in associative iteration,[7] although Spenser does pay tribute to these 'famous riuers' by noting that they 'doe the earth enrich and beautifie'.[8]

Michael Drayton's *Poly-Olbion* (1612) again addresses a marriage of rivers, this time of Thame and Isis, placing this within a rich English pastoral that offers much more in the way of complex interrelations between physical phenomena. We are told for instance that Thame is 'old Chiltern's sonne' and that Isis is the heir of the Cotswolds (15.3–4).[9] The narrative this generates situates these rivers within more detailed geographical and economic contexts than Spenser's listing allows. In this mode, Thame's origins 'in the Vale of *Alsbury*, at the foot of the *Chilterne*' (15.3n.) are explored as if they were of genealogical significance:

> ... *Alsbury's* a Vale that walloweth in her wealth,
> And (by her wholesome ayre continually in health)
> Is lustie, frim, and fat, and holds her youthfull strength.
> Besides her fruitfull earth, her mightie breadth and length,

Doth *Chiltern* fitly match: which mountainously hie,
And beeing very long, so likewise shee doth lie. (15.27–32)

Drayton's epic pastoral aims at a fairly complex understanding of the functions of such geographical elements as rivers within both a local and national economy, and in something like what we call an ecosystem. This imagery seems to persist as a point of reference throughout the era, if not quite with Drayton's level of complexity. Maggie Kilgour notes the mythical figure of Sabrina, associated with the River Severn, in John Milton's *Ludlow Masque* (1634) as invoking 'both Spenser and also Drayton's revision of Spenser's marriage of the rivers in *Poly-Olbion*'.[10]

The continuing conceptual play with the idea of river gods did not please everyone, however, even when obviously intended as merely metaphorical. Following the Reformation, as Lykke Syse and Terje Oestigaard show, 'the Church aimed to abolish all belief in the magical powers of water, its ambition being to eradicate the traditional water cult, a cult that it viewed as diabolic and a testimony to the power of Satan'.[11] Nevertheless, despite the church's best efforts, water continued to be understood as an apt medium for supernatural phenomena and its significant bodies as sites in which these might be made manifest, even within the Christian mythos. Lowell Duckert records an instance in which an unusual double high tide on the Thames on 4 February 1641 was taken as a message from on high that 'people should put away their uncivil disputes and pray "for the joyfull Union, and prosperous harmony between King and Parliament, wherein consisteth the onely happiness of this Kingdome"'.[12] Despite the lack of practical efficacy of any such response, the Thames nevertheless continued to be perceived as a site of divine political commentary. Joseph P. Ward remarks that in general, seventeenth-century London, a 'focal point for both political crises and natural disasters', was also 'fertile ground for providentialist speculation' of this kind, and especially in this regard 'the River Thames, with its central location and pivotal role in the life of the city, served as something of a mirror for the metropolis'.[13] He recounts how God's approval of the recent dissolution of Parliament was indicated on 21 April 1659 by the appearance of two strange fish in the Thames, one resembling a bull and the other identified as a mermaid.

Rivers at this time also retained their ancient association with borders and liminality. Julius Caesar's decisive crossing of the Rubicon is remembered in Christopher Marlowe's translation of *Lucan's First Book*, and in Marlowe's hugely influential two-part play *Tamburlaine the Great* there are several references to rivers as both borders and markers of identity: Tamburlaine himself is 'the rogue of Volga' (Part Two, 4.1.4) and

Sigismond speaks of crossing the Danube (Part Two, 1.1.79).[14] Another momentous stretch of water treated by Marlowe, the Hellespont of his epyllion *Hero and Leander*, was humorously transposed by Ben Jonson in *Bartholomew Fair* into the familiar Thames. Roy Booth notes that this joke worked for contemporaries because

> at a basic level, 'Hero and Leander' was a story about a young man who crossed to the other side of a waterway to get sex. As the story was revisited by seventeenth century English writers, it mapped exactly onto their own urban geography. Abidos and Sestos became London and Southwark. Men in search of amusement seem to have preferred to travel by water across the Thames to the South Bank. Hero, 'Venus' nun', waiting at her tower, inescapably recalled one of the 'Winchester geese' whose working premises clustered around the theatres.[15]

But if young men in London crossed the river to get from a place of restraint and control to one of freedom, in other parts of the country rivers could sometimes be understood as policing the passage from life to death. Just as in classical mythology the Styx divided the land of the living from that of the dead, so in medieval Wakefield a chantry chapel built on a bridge over the River Calder invited pilgrims to stop and consider the fate of their souls, while in early modern York the recusant Margaret Clitherow was pressed to death on a bridge over the River Ouse in York. In both cases the riverine location may have been chosen partly for its visibility, but the crossroads-like liminality of a bridge over a river may also have been part of the appeal.[16] Ideas of mortality seem to hang about these Yorkshire rivers and, if not now quite divine in themselves, they figure still in the conceptual transition to an afterlife in divine or demonic company.

The river's association with divinity and transience was the spiritual counterpart to its fundamental connection to the physical practicalities of human living within a particular space. In her book *River Kings: The Vikings from Scandinavia to the Silk Road*, Cat Jarman notes that the Gough Map, 'the earliest map to show Britain in a geographically recognisable form', illustrates a 'vast network of rivers stretching across the landmass . . . tentacle-like and swirling, the rivers appear as arteries connecting towns and churches with the coast-line'. She notes that 'it is the rivers that strike you as the key to communication between one place and another'.[17] Rivers could also mark county boundaries, most famously in the case of the Tamar, which divided Cornwall from Devon, but also less prominently in that of the Shirebrook which divided Derbyshire from Yorkshire and still gives its name to a region of Sheffield. Such fundamental geographical significance may be enhanced by the fact that the attributes of rivers often determined the locations and indeed the characters of the early settlements that grew up around them. The first may be clearly perceived in the ancient origins of the place names of old towns like Doncaster, Oxford and Cambridge, but even without such obvious designation it is clear that this is the case for many settlements. Ward notes John Stow suggesting in the early seventeenth century that London was England's capital city primarily because of its location on the Thames: it was 'far enough inland that it was protected from foreign invasion and yet close enough to the sea for ships to take advantage of the tides'.[18] Such determinism, of basic egress and ingress as much as of the intricacies of its hinterland, may extend to anything from a settlement's primary defensive capabilities to the trade that the river facilitates and in turn ultimately to the economics and conditions of life for all its inhabitants. These factors to a greater extent have established and maintained the identities and ideologies of the lived 'spaces' which emerge from the human occupation and use of mere 'places' like riverside localities.[19]

The fundamental historical connection between London and the Thames might, *pace* Ward, be described as a 'mirroring' in that the city reflects, or it might be more accurate to say 'manifests', the attributes of the river. In the early modern period, more than operating as a main thoroughfare for traffic of various kinds, the river functioned as the city's main life-giving artery (this vascular symbolism is persistent in river imagery, especially that concerning the economic life of a nation). When the Thames froze, as it did around one year in ten throughout the 'Little Ice Age' of the time, so did the majority of the city's trade. During the Great Frost of 1683–4, the river was frozen over for two months, with the ice in London reaching almost a foot thick. As Ward notes, this frozen state 'brought consequences that varied from episode to episode' but in some cases 'ice could prevent ships from passing under the London Bridge to the tackle houses of the City for unloading'.[20] The narrow passages between the bridge's piers may actually have exacerbated the problem by contributing to the river's sluggish flow and hence its congealability. Although, as Ward notes, there were those who saw a significant river freeze as 'an opportunity for frivolity', it would also cause 'considerable economic dislocation' (although the ensuing 'frost fairs' suggest the city's commerce was not completely arrested).[21]

Not only is the river fundamental to the identity of the city in its underlying practical conditions of existence, providing water supply and waste outlet, defence, trade and means of travel, but it is also essential to the city's organising ideologies. In the early modern era, the Thames provided a convenient setting for the regal pageantry of Queen Elizabeth I. In the popular drama of the time a very different river provided a similar spectacular backdrop for the self-dramatisation of Shakespeare's Cleopatra as 'The barge she sat in, like a burnish'd throne, / Burned on the water' while its 'oars were silver, / Which to the tune of flutes kept stroke, and made / The water which they beat to follow faster, / As amorous of their strokes' (*A&C*, 2.2.235–9). Besides providing an ever-moving stage for royal spectaculars, London's other formal occasions often 'acknowledged the river's central role in metropolitan life', Ward noting that during the annual Lord Mayor shows the Thames served as 'a ceremonial thoroughfare in . . . London, as its streets were far too narrow for the purpose'.[22] Maria Shmygol too observes its historically crucial role in elaborate civic festivities. It served as 'both a means of passage and a watery stage during occasional royal processions and annual Lord Mayor's Day celebrations', which might include 'a vibrant flotilla of vessels accompanied by trumpets, drums, and the thundering gunfire of the galley-foist, as well as symbolic and allegorical devices'.[23] She describes two of these spectacles, the first occurring in June 1610 for Prince Henry's investiture as Prince of Wales and the second in February 1613 celebrating the marriage of the Princess Elizabeth. Unfortunately, the latter ended badly, as Shmygol tells: 'The conquest of the "castle" never took place, and quotes a report suggesting that combat was ultimately terminated because

> divers [were] hurt in the former fight, (as one lost both his eyes, another both his handes, another one hande, with divers other maymed and hurt) so that to avoyde further harme, yt was thought best to let yt alone.

The perilous nature of this riverine performance is confirmed by one involved, who notes that in such 'jesting business I ran more danger than if it had been a sea service in good earnest'.[24]

Besides contributing to these commercial, cultural and ideological functions of the life of a society, rivers could of course also pose mortal dangers to both individuals and their communities. Lykke Syse notes coroners' records from the sixteenth century showing that of all accidental deaths 53 per cent were by drowning.[25] Flooding was also an ever-present danger and Oestigaard notes that in the seventeenth century these might be regarded as 'God's chosen instruments for cleansing the corrupt earth' (even more implausibly it was also claimed locally that 'the area beside Dagenham near the Thames was the site of the original Deluge').[26] There were other ways too in which the river might be a destabilising presence. Lykke Syse shows how the river was not only very obviously 'physically unstable' but it furthermore 'eluded social control' and to an extent therefore contemporary moral norms; the example given is the phenomenon that on the river 'everyone felt free to swear, and a term for swearing was actually "water-language", comparable to "gutter language"'.[27]

Rivers were particularly important for early modern London's poets and playwrights. Duckert points out that on the various occasions that Shakespeare and other playwrights required characters to 'enter wet', it was probably the Thames that supplied the water, and he also notes that the 'Water Poet' John Taylor was one who 'staged river pageants of sea battles', and describes how Richard Brome, in order to 'bring flouds o' gaine to th'watermen', imagined a dramatic aquarium unreachable by the sedan-driving fad in 1632: 'a new Theatre or Playhouse / Upon the Thames on Barges or flat boats'.[28] Even if no actual theatres were on boats, many were close enough to the Thames which Duckert argues is both 'local' and simultaneously 'tied to the global hydrosphere'.[29] Even when spectators at the Globe or the Rose had disembarked from the boats in which they had probably reached the south bank of the Thames and entered the theatres, they could probably still smell and hear the social and commercial activities surrounding the river. The river not only brought the theatres their customers but also energised and informed the plays they put on. Just as the river conveyed its passengers and conducted its commerce, the theatres welcomed the world of the river.

Shakespeare in particular seems to go out of his way to mention rivers in his plays. The Thames is an important presence in *The Merry Wives of Windsor*.[30] In *Julius Caesar*, Cassius tells Brutus about how Caesar once got into difficulties in the Tiber.[31] And *Antony and Cleopatra* works in several mentions of the Nile which contribute nothing to the plot but plenty to the atmosphere and to the characterisation of Cleopatra herself where she is Antony's 'serpent of old Nile' (1.5.30). In *Cymbeline*, the Roman envoy Lucius is sent on his way with an escort who are instructed by the king, 'Leave not the worthy Lucius, good my lords, / Till he have cross'd the Severn'.[32] Geoffrey of Monmouth had identified the Severn as dividing England from Wales, and this idea retained sentimental even if not political currency in the early modern period.[33] Leah Marcus therefore suggests that this reference to it is designed to present the Wales of the play as a completely separate country from the one which Cymbeline rules (either from his historic capital of Maldon or, Shakespeare may have thought, from the hillfort known as Cymbeline's Castle near Aylesbury).[34] This heightens the sense that the place to which Belarius has fled with Guiderius and Arviragus is a remote and lawless one, but it also introduces an important river to sit alongside the play's reference to Milford Haven whose Welsh name, Aberdaugleddau, meaning 'mouth of the two Cleddau(s)', comes from the names of two rivers, the Eastern Cleddau and the Western Cleddau. Shakespeare, it seems, likes to discuss rivers, and his plays express something of the range of symbolic values and practical uses they had in his society.

This book aims to investigate the multiplicity of meanings that attach to the river in Shakespeare's Britain, to elucidate how rivers help to determine not only how that society functions but also some of its organising ideas. The book has twelve chapters and is divided into four parts, 'Conceptualising the River', 'Writing the River', 'Rivers and Money' and 'Ecocritical Approaches'. In these chapters we hope to do justice to the complexity of interactions between the human populace and the rivers that sustain them both physically and in their ways of understanding their world.

In Part I, 'Conceptualising the River', the first chapter is Brice Peterson's 'Rivers of Milk, Honey, Tears and Treasures: Mapping Salvation in Early Modern English Devotional Poetry'. As interest in early modern literary geographies has burgeoned over the past twenty years, critics have begun to explore the literary intersections between the environment and conceptions of the soul. Peterson's chapter investigates how Protestant theologians discuss salvation in terms of potamology: rivers literalise the abstract phenomenon of receiving God's grace. For example, clergymen imagine believers being reborn by drinking water from a river of grace. They also metaphorise the regenerate union with Christ as producing spiritual rivers of good works that flow from believers. In effect, theologians envision salvation making believers become spiritually riverine. Devotional poets take up this discourse and interrogate the implications of becoming part of such a river ecosystem in ways that theologians never quite reach. The chapter examines three case studies: Aemilia Lanyer's *Salve Deus Rex Judaeorum*, George Herbert's *The Temple* and Thomas Traherne's 'Circulation'. Lanyer teases the sensorial implications of imaging grace in riverine terms by imaging what rivers of grace taste like and the phenomenological mode of living they may consequently inspire. Herbert imagines spiritual rebirth as an affective experience that produces tears and physiologically changes the body into a fluvial world. Traherne depicts regeneration as a hydrologic cycle that transforms a believer's visual acuity, enabling them to properly interact with the material world. Charting the physical phenomenology of grace in these ways, devotional poets push doctrinal boundaries by imagining themselves and their poetry as crucial elements in riverine soteriology.

The second chapter in this section, Daniel Gettings's '"Plenteous Rivers": Waterways as Resources, Threats and the Heart of the Community in Early Modern England', focuses on the interrelationship between rivers and the communities which lived close to them. Waterways provided a bounty of resources in the form of fish, waterfowl, clay and of course the water itself, but living near a river in this period was complicated by the threat of flooding that loomed large in the early modern mind, supported by a print culture that ensured such events were widely publicised. Gettings describes how despite these ever-present dangers communities still tended to regard the river as a source of comfort and a feature of the land that had been there for their ancestors and would be there for them so long as other responsible parties maintained a requisite balance between its exploitation and potential profits. This chapter explores how the multifaceted relationship between early modern people and their waterways changed when new ideas about the landscape and industry saw attitudes toward the river shift faster than ever before.

Finally in Part I, Rebecca Welshman's 'Rivers and Contested Territories in the Works of Shakespeare' focuses on rivers' significance as sites of battle. Rivers featured in a number of battles during the medieval period, such as Otterburn (1388), fought beside the River Rede, Boroughbridge (1322) and the battle of Stirling Bridge (1297) on the River Forth. Riverside battlefield sites in the early modern period include Shrewsbury (1403) and Tewkesbury (1471), both of which figured in early modern drama. Conflicts might take place near rivers because they marked the edge of a contested territory and were natural borderlands, or they might result from an attempt to gain control of a strategic river crossing. Welshman explores how Shakespeare's use of rivers as settings was informed by his awareness of the military significance of riverside battlefield sites in London, Tewkesbury and Shrewsbury, and expressed through his depiction of prominent noblemen of different historical time periods. In particular, she considers the textured meanings and military associations of certain terms used by Shakespeare in riverine settings which had been absorbed into the language of the time through the influence of military culture. She argues that in his implicit recognition of riverside sites as theatres of war, Shakespeare reimagined these locations as gendered sites of conflict – arenas in which to revisit past political and social tensions in ways which passed commentary on contemporary states of affairs, including the tensions between crown and community, and the Elizabethan system of government.

In Part II, 'Writing the River', the first chapter is Lisa Hopkins's 'The Navigation of the Trent and William Sampson's *The Vow-Breaker* (1636)'. Cat Jarman notes that 'the name "Trent" derives from a Celtic word meaning "the wanderer": a wonderfully poetic name reflecting its ability to move and change course rapidly'.[35] Sampson and his contemporaries would not have been able to deduce that derivation, but they would have been well aware that rivers could and did move, and that the Trent in particular had shifted its course. *The Vow Breaker* itself could also be said in a sense to shift its course, because its first four acts focus on the story of a girl who jilts her lover while he is away at the siege of Leith. When he returns and discovers what has happened he commits suicide, and she is subsequently driven by his ghost to follow suit. We appear to have reached the end of the narrative, but the fifth act introduces an entirely new motif when a visit by Queen Elizabeth to Nottingham prompts an impassioned plea by the mayor for the Trent to be made navigable. Hopkins argues that in fact the play has been interested in the Trent all along, and that the ways in which it figures the river allow us to see some of the reasons why the Trent mattered and how it was thought about in the early part of the seventeenth century.

The next chapter is Lindsay Ann Reid's 'Ship of Fools and Slow Boat to Hell: The Literary Voyages of the Gravesend Barge'. At the opening of *The Cobler of Caunterburie* (1590), the narrator makes a momentous decision: though he arrived at Billingsgate intending to hire a tilt boat, he instead decides to join the 'crue of madde companions' he spots waiting aboard the two-penny Gravesend barge. Their subsequent journey eastward on the Thames sparks a tale-telling competition à la *Canterbury Tales*, with Chaucerian pilgrims reimagined as passengers travelling along one of early modern London's most trafficked waterways. Though the journey from Billingsgate to Gravesend might be made aboard other vessels, this common barge shuttled back and forth in continuous motion along this twenty-some-mile stretch of river. Leaving Gravesend at low water and London at high water, the barge moved with regular irregularity at the turn of every tide. On occasion, the Gravesend barge also ventured into the realm of imagination and this chapter charts its most significant literary voyages. That people of all estates might rub shoulders on the Gravesend barge makes it a suitable setting for the neo-Chaucerian tale-telling contests that feature not only in *The Cobler of Caunterburie*, but also in the highly derivative *Tincker of Turvey* (1630); this same social variegation provokes conflict rather than merriment, however, in John Foxe's *Book of Martyrs* (1570, expanded 1583) when John Browne sits too close to a priest. Sometimes, the Gravesend barge is a veritable ship of fools and/or floating den of inequity – as attested, for example, by the title page to John Awdelay's *Fraternitye of Vacabondes* (1575) where the legendary Cock Lorel affirms that his 'knaves' can be found aboard. At other times, it provides the stage for literary transactions: it is from this vessel that one 'Pasquil' (quite possibly Thomas Nashe, who mentions the barge with some frequency throughout his writings) purportedly penned *A Countercuffe*

Given to Martin Junior (c. 1589), and an undated manuscript poem playfully reports of the stationer John Day that 'The grave consell of gravesend barge / Gevethe [him] a privilege large' to print the text of *The Prick of Conscience*. Elsewhere, this public ferry becomes the slow boat to hell. In Thomas Dekker's *Newes from Hell* (1606; later expanded as *A Knights Conjuring*, 1608), the Knight of the Post begins a journey to the underworld in the Gravesend barge, and this same vessel later reappears on the Acheron, where it is equated with Charon's boat (an image apparently so apt that Dekker could not resist recycling it in *If It Be Not Good, the Divel Is in It*, c. 1610).

Finally in this section we have Melissa Caldwell's 'Rivers, Monstrosity and National Identity in Izaak Walton's *The Compleat Angler*'. Rivers here offer Walton a calculus – and an ecology – of national identity. Though most remember Walton's description of fish and the art of angling, the English waterways that are the natural backdrop for Walton's main subject are just as significant to Walton's nostalgic vision of Englishness. Walton's Socrates, the loquacious if somewhat overbearing Piscator, elevates water to the highest place among the four elements, conferring upon it the paradoxical distinction of being the most physically productive and spiritually moving of elements: it is the perfect blend of action and contemplation, which is to say, action *in* contemplation. For Walton, rivers are distinctly English, the site of Piscator's pleasure and holy recreation, and the very juncture that connects England to the outside world. Echoing Aristotle, Pliny, traditions of depicting the ocean and its dangers in the *Physiologus* and the medieval bestiary, and William Camden among others, Walton's pastoral setting never entirely exorcises the potential dangers of the water. Even the most celebrated of England's rivers, the Thames, is subjected by its connection to the ocean to both physical and metaphorical inconstancy: as the ocean affects the rise and fall of the Thames, it becomes a site of spiritual and epistemological disruption as it brings strange fish, or monsters as Walton also calls them, begetting wonder and unbelief. Written in a post-civil war context, these sites of connection and conflict between England and the outside world, the known and the unknown, the normative and the unnatural, reflect both England's borders and its battlegrounds within: they mark a physical boundary of Englishness, while also housing strangers in the midst of England. This chapter considers how, as Walton attempts to instruct his reader in the art of the good life, his discourse returns again and again to waterways and their relationship to monstrosity.

In Part III, 'Rivers and Money', the first chapter is Bill Angus's '"Your Innes and Alehouses are Brookes and Rivers": John Taylor and

Free-flowing Rivers of Ale'. This explores the writing of John Taylor the 'Water Poet', contemporary of Shakespeare and friend of Ben Jonson. Taylor was a waterman employed on the Thames who wrote on many topics, including his wager-journeys and his career as a ferryman, and became one of the most popular writers of his time. Not always a controversial character, on one count at least Taylor leaves himself open to easy criticism from his would-be detractors: he spent what some thought to be an inordinate amount of energy in the praise, promotion and partaking of the benefits of traditional ale. He was a stereotypical waterman in this respect perhaps. Surveying his publications, including *A very Merry-Wherry-Ferry Voyage* (1623), *Drinke and Welcome* (1632), *Taylor's Travels And Circvlar Perambulation* (1636) and *Ale-Ale-vated* (1651), this chapter explores his representation of his river journeys, the commercial aspects of river-improvement projects that arose from his lifetime's experience on the river and the way he connects all of this to the beneficial drinking of ale. Taylor's abiding metaphor for the place of rivers in the health of the nation is that of the body's vascular system. In his most commercially driven writing, he relates this further to alcohol flowing through the national body and imparting health to all its parts. From his position of expertise in the traffic of both river and ale, the key to the healing of a nation riven by religious and political ideologies and heading for civil war seems to Taylor to be found in commercial rivers of ale flowing ever more freely through its veins.

The second chapter in this section is Cecilia Lindskog Whiteley's 'The Rose and the Riverside'. Towards the end of the 1580s, a symbiotic relationship developed between theatrical entrepreneurs and the local economy in which the river was central. When the playing companies were banned from performing in London, the company of watermen petitioned the Privy Council for Strange's Men to be allowed to resume playing at the Rose, the practice having provided 'much relief for us, our poor wives and children'. In their turn, Strange's Men also brought up the plight of the watermen in their own petition to be allowed to return to the Rose. The watermen depended economically on the steady stream of playgoers seeking to cross the river, just as the playhouse could only operate outside of the geographical demarcation provided by the Thames but also needed their audiences to traverse it. This chapter traces the winding of rivers through the plays performed in the vicinity of the Thames from the perspective of this interdependency. The ways in which the contexts of local economy and cultural geography shaped the plays appearing in this riverside community are best explicated by the playhouse at the centre of the pleas. At the Rose, George Peele's *The Battle of Alcazar* was performed at the playhouse by Strange's Men around the time of the joint petitions. It is a play that abounds with rivers real and mythological. Portugal and Morocco are associated with contemporary London through references to rivers, and the act of river crossing becomes a moment of importance that links with the journey of players and playgoers across the Thames by way of the watermen. Meanwhile, the mythological rivers of Hades are invoked as sites of stagnation where Muly Mahamet vows to entrench his traitorous uncle, preventing his crossing and fixing him forever at the river's side. Testament to the importance of the river as simultaneously demarcation and liminal is the fact that Peele's play is the first recorded use of 'river shore', a compound that grounds the flowing body of water in its landlocked surroundings. As a contrast to this river-bound duality, the chapter will conclude by reading the figure of a ferryman in another riverside play, John Lyly's *Sapho and Phao*, noting how Phao facilitates (social) movement but is denied his own social mobility. Whether north or south of the Thames, what we discover is that crossing the river is an act of flux that temporarily unites the interests of the disparate groups that meet through it, although ultimately this symbiosis remains class-bound.

The final chapter of this section, Jemima Matthews's '"As Water Mill, Made Rags and Shreds to Sweate": Fluvial Bodies and Fluminous Geographies', considers poetic petitions by watermen John Byshop and John Taylor alongside a poem praising the erection of a paper mill at Dartford. These poets frame the river's 'work' as a service to the state but the labour these writers each have in mind is incompatible. Matthews considers how river water is worked and reworked by these writers and these two different industries. Thomas Churchyard's poem *Sparke Of Frendship*, published in 1588, takes delight in the mill's engineering and creates an energy narrative of water in which water itself is controlled, rechannelled and harnessed. It is human labour which provides the kinetic energy and Churchyard describes the rags and raw materials tossed and pounded through the water in the mill. By contrast, in John Byshop's poetic petition in 1585 it is the bodies of the watermen and their goods which are tossed, spoiled and drowned by the water; Byshop emphasises the vulnerability of working bodies and the force of artificial alterations in the riverine environment. Despite their opposing views, both writers make surprisingly similar assertions concerning the public good, charitable work and the universal right to water. This chapter traces the entangled histories of bodies, river-water, paper and sweat, charting how these poems map fluvial geographies of location and dislocation.

In Part IV, 'Ecocritical Approaches', Emily J. Naish's '"Insatiable [Gourmandize] Thus All Things Doth Devour": Reading the Threat of

Human Greed along the Rivers of Early Modern England' investigates poetic and cartographic representations of rivers during the sixteenth and early seventeenth centuries in order to understand the ways in which the river was often anthropocentrically idealised in this period, whilst also paying attention to anxieties about unmanaged water. Naish takes a historicist ecocritical approach, drawing on the discipline of environmental history, to examine the narratives that resist (but also uphold) this human-centric thinking about the landscape. Naish builds on previous ecocritical attention to the literary river of the period by pulling together different environmental and socio-economic contexts, leading to a more cohesive account of the represented river in early modern literature. She focuses on an established body of river poetry, homing in on the works of John Taylor and Michael Drayton's *Poly-Olbion*. It is *Poly-Olbion* that calls into question cartographic representations of rivers. Comparative analysis between the poetic river, its cartographic counterpart and the river itself (via topographic accounts) will reveal moments of romanticisation or excessive anxiety. After outlining factors such as the appearance of blockages and the problem of burst banks that informed the representation of rivers, the chapter explores how the represented river might elude the grievances of watermen. The final section focuses on William Hole's etchings in *Poly-Olbion*, which appear to expose anxieties about unmanaged water, and leads to a conclusion that considers this mesh of idealisation and anxiety: the river could represent anthropocentric opportunity whilst also sparking some ecophobia. However, there are moments where poets reconfigure the human relationship to the river, allowing a more sympathetic representation of nature to prevail.

Esther Water's chapter, 'Powtes, Protest and (Eco)politics in the English Fens' takes as its starting point the proposal to significantly alter the landscape of the fens in the sixteenth century, a project which was met with strident opposition in the form of legal challenges and direct protest. Opposition to this is reflected in poems, plays and protest songs of the time, including Ben Jonson's *The Devil is an Ass* (1631) and Penny of Wisbech's *The Pout's Complaint Upon the Draining of the Fens in Cambridgeshire, Ely and Wisbech* (1619). This chapter explores what these texts tell us about the nature of the resistance against the project, and examines how this reflects prevailing attitudes to, and relationships with, the fens. At this time, the fens encompassed an area of 3,850 square km of land between East Anglia and the eastern Midlands and formed an integral part of the drainage system of several major rivers in the region, including the Great Ouse, the Nene and the Welland. Michael Drayton's 'Holland Fen' (1622) describes the fen landscape in glowing terms. His careful enumeration of the myriad species living in the fens demonstrates their diversity, and his descriptions of fen-dwellers reflect a fens culture that was mediated and maintained through a system of customary use rights and local regulatory institutions. Not all of Drayton's contemporaries shared his appreciation of the fens and the culture associated with it: the low-lying fen area was described by an anonymous traveller in 1635 as an 'unhealthful, raw, & muddy land', occupied by 'debauched' men who were 'Lazy and intemperate' and 'half fish, half flesh'.[36] In 1605, several factors contributed to Crown approval of the new, large-scale drainage network which would result in the modification of the fens. These included the difficulty of managing increased flooding, a desire to increase the navigability of waterways to facilitate commerce and the desire to capitalise on tracts of Crown land within the fens. The plan indicated mounting state control over resources, and Ben Jonson and Penny of Wisbech both opposed these unprecedented changes. Their reasons were similar. Jonson's comedy suggests that widescale modification of the fens would disadvantage and displace the fen-dwellers: this perspective is revealed through the scheming Merecraft, and his attempted manipulation over the guileless Fitzdotterel, whose name links him to a fenland species of plover. Penny of Wisbech's ballad, told from the perspective of a fish, deplores the destruction of fenland ecology and fen-dwellers' livelihoods, and advocates for direct resistance. The use of humour, strident language and attention to local ecology within these texts make them a compelling frame through which to understand the conflict over the fens and what it signified.

Sophie Chiari's 'Shakespeare's Waterways: Premonitions of an Environmental Collapse' focuses on the waterworld of early modern England: its streams, rivers, channels and brooks, as one of the kingdom's most strategic networks of economy, exchange and transportation. She notes how waterways and their productive riverside pasturages were usually praised for their utilitarian dimension rather than for their beauty or their rich riparian ecosystems. In *The Tempest*, Caliban shows his master '[t]he fresh springs, brine pits, barren place and fertile' of the island (1.2.339): with the arrival of the settler Prospero, fresh water has suddenly become a tradable commodity. Whether or not the commodification of water could help improve access to freshwater supplies and conserve water as a resource was already an issue in Shakespeare's time. The topic of fresh water diversion is especially highlighted in two plays, namely in *1 Henry 4*, where it serves a political agenda, and in *Coriolanus*, when the eponymous hero contemptuously refers to an 'officer' ready to turn the senators' 'current in a ditch' and make their channel his (3.1.94–8). The playwright here possibly had in mind a project aimed at bringing fresh water from the River Lea to Central London between 1608 and 1613, and if so this testifies to the local population's concerns about the project. More generally speaking, the word 'ditch' often appeared in connection with drainage issues and riverine pollution in the literature of the period. In *The Merry Wives of Windsor*, the well-named Mistress Ford famously orders her servants John and Robert to take the buck basket in which Falstaff has hidden himself under a heap of dirty linen, to carry it among the whiteners, and to 'empty it in the muddy ditch close by the Thames' (3.3.12–14). The polluted waters of the English realm, and especially those of its burgeoning capital, were then raising serious health concerns and, despite its resolutely comic tones, Shakespeare's comedy alerted its audience to the condition of rivers which tended to become open sewers as they crossed the cities. By shedding light on three environmental issues represented in Shakespeare's plays and involving the waterscape of the period (the exploitation of rivers, ditch digging and the increasing pollution of fresh water) Chiari unpacks the specific implications of the use of fresh water and puts forward an early modern aesthetics of riverine collapse.

These chapters elucidate a complex of interactions between rivers and the early modern communities that rely on them and represent them in their literature. They offer a window with a river view onto the doings and writings of those concerned with the life of the nation's waterways and so of the nation as a whole.

Notes

1. Rivers originating in glaciers include the Ganges, the Indus, the Mekong, the Yangtze and the Yellow River.
2. Tim Cresswell, *On the Move* (Abingdon: Routledge, 2006), 2.
3. Joel Bonnemaison, *Culture and Space: Conceiving a New Cultural Geography* (London: I. B. Tauris, 2005), 81. See also Randall Martin, *Shakespeare and Ecology* (Oxford: Oxford University Press, 2020); Leona J. Skelton, *Tyne after Tyne: An Environmental History of a River's Battle for Protection 1529–2015* (Winwick: White Horse Press, 2017).
4. Karen V. Lykke Syse, 'Ideas of Leisure, Pleasure and the River in Early Modern England', in *Perceptions of Water in Britain from Early Modern Times to the Present: An Introduction*, ed. Karen V. Lykke Syse and Terje Oestigaard (Bergen: University of Bergen, 2010), 35–57, 35. While not quite a god, New Zealand's Whanganui River was granted legal personhood in 2017 reflecting its relationship with indigenous Maori iwi; see https://www.parliament.nz/en/get-involved/features/innovative-bill-protects-whanganui-river-with-legal-personhood/ (last accessed 13 March 2023).

5. Claudia Lazzaro, 'River Gods: Personifying Nature in Sixteenth-Century Italy', *Renaissance Studies* 25.1 (February 2011), 70–94, 70.
6. Edmund Spenser, *The Faerie Queene*, ed. A. C. Hamilton (London: Longman, 1977), Book IV, Canto XI, stanzas 21, 36 and 41.
7. This section of *Faerie Queene* echoes a passage in William Camden's *Britannia* (1586) in which Isis is the male partner and marries the Tame to unite as Thamisis.
8. Spenser, *The Faerie Queene*, Book IV, Canto XI, stanza 20.
9. Michael Drayton, *Poly-Olbion* (1623), https://poly-olbion.exeter.ac.uk/the-text/scholarly-edition/ (last accessed 19 October 2022).
10. Maggie Kilgour, 'Writing on Water', *English Literary Renaissance* 29.2 (Spring 1999), 282–305, 284.
11. Syse and Oestigaard, *Perceptions of Water*, 1–15, 12.
12. Lowell Duckert, *For All Waters: Finding Ourselves in Early Modern Wetscapes* (Minneapolis: University of Minnesota Press, 2017), 26.
13. Joseph Ward, 'The Taming of the Thames: Reading the River in the Seventeenth Century', *Huntington Library Quarterly* 71.1 (March 2008), 55–75, 55–6.
14. Christopher Marlowe, *Tamburlaine the Great*, in *Christopher Marlowe: The Complete Plays*, ed. Mark Thornton Burnett (London: J. M. Dent, 1999).
15. Roy Booth, 'Hero's Afterlife: *Hero and Leander* and "lewd unmannerly verse" in the Late Seventeenth Century', *Early Modern Literary Studies* 12.3 (January 2007). Online: http://purl.oclc.org/emls/12–3/bootber2.htm.
16. See Bill Angus, *A History of Crossroads in Early Modern Culture* (Edinburgh: Edinburgh University Press, 2022), 21, 49.
17. Cat Jarman, *River Kings: The Vikings from Scandinavia to the Silk Roads* (London: William Collins, 2021), 82.
18. Ward, 'The Taming of the Thames', 57.
19. A seminal resource for this kind of thinking is Henri Lefevbre, *The Production of Space*, translated by D. Nicholson-Smith (Cambridge, MA: Blackwell, 1991).
20. Ward, 'The Taming of the Thames', 60.
21. Ward, 'The Taming of the Thames', 60.
22. Ward, 'The Taming of the Thames', 58.
23. Maria Shmygol, 'Jacobean Mock Sea-Fights on the River Thames: Nautical Theatricality in Performance and Print', *The London Journal* 47.1 (2022), 13–35, 13–14 and 23.
24. Shmygol, 13–14 and 23.
25. Syse, 'Ideas of Leisure', 36.
26. Terje Oestigaard, 'The Topography of Holy Water in England after the Reformation', in Syse and Oestigaard, *Perceptions of Water*, 15–34, 31.
27. Syse, 'Ideas of Leisure', 37.
28. Duckert, *For All Waters*, xx and 19.
29. Duckert, *For All Waters*, 20.
30. See Jemima Matthews, 'Inside Out and Outside In: The River Thames in William Shakespeare's *The Merry Wives of Windsor*', *Shakespeare* 15.4 (2019), 410–27.

31. William Shakespeare, *Julius Caesar*, ed. David Daniell (London: Thomas Nelson and Sons, 1998), 1.2.100–15.
32. William Shakespeare, *Cymbeline*, ed. J. M. Nosworthy (London: Methuen, 1955), III.v.16–17.
33. See for instance Philip Schwyzer, 'A Map of Greater Cambria', *Early Modern Literary Studies* 4.2 (September 1988). Online: https://extra.shu.ac.uk/emls/04-2/schwamap.htm (last accessed 12 August 2023).
34. Leah Marcus, *Puzzling Shakespeare* (Berkeley: University of California Press, 1988), 134–5.
35. Jarman, *River Kings*, 81.
36. Quoted in Ash, *The Draining of the Fens*, 17.

I. Conceptualising the River

Chapter 1

Rivers of Milk, Honey, Tears and Treasures: Mapping Salvation in Early Modern English Devotional Poetry

Brice Peterson

In *The First Sermon of R. Sheldon Priest* (1612), the newly recanted minister Richard Sheldon explicates the crucified body of Christ by drawing on a seemingly unrelated practice: chorography. He compares Christ's blood to a fountain, meaning the headspring of a river, declaring, 'Oh that we would, with all Saints, comprehend the altitude, longitude, latitude, and profoundnes [depth] of this bleding fountaine of this bleding Christ.'[1] While Sheldon clearly borrows from the biblical image of Christ as a fountain of the water of life (Revelation 21:6), his use of chorographic terminology to conceptualise the salvific power of Christ's blood raises the following question: how does one map the altitude, longitude, latitude and profundity of a spiritual river of grace? Rather than charting an allegorical terrain to delineate a pathway to heaven, Sheldon leverages chorography to anatomise the origin and nature of salvation. He asserts that grace comes from Christ who lacked 'pride' (altitude) and, with 'body proportioned to the length of the Crosse' (longitude), gave his blood for 'all sorts of persons' (latitude) as an example of the 'inestimable charitie of God' (profundity) (26, 30, and 33). Sheldon's ostensible purpose in mapping Christ's blood is to help readers avoid the 'puddles of Egypt' (31), which he drank from as a Roman Catholic, and to encourage them to drink from the true source of salvific water – a Protestantised Christ. More importantly, however, his sermon reveals an impulse to expand a biblical riverine metaphor as an index for searching out deeper questions about salvation: if Christ is a fountain or a river, where is its source? Where does it flow? What is the quality of its waters? And how does one, as Sheldon says, 'sucke of this fountaine' (31)?

Sheldon's use of chorographic language in thinking about grace speaks to a greater trend among early modern theologians of turning to riverine metaphors to conceptualise salvation. Beyond the geographic dimensions of rivers, theologians draw upon riverine ecosystems, riparian vegetation, water quality, hydrologic cycles and human–river interaction to chart the contours of salvific processes. Rivers act as natural symbols that reveal the origin and nature of God's grace: how it operates, how a believer accesses it, and what it is like to experience it. This theological discourse provides important context for the way early modern devotional poets limn salvation. Poets such as Aemilia Lanyer, George Herbert and Thomas Traherne rely on riverine images in their poetry to explore what the experience of receiving divine grace entails.

When examining rivers in early modern English poetry, critics primarily discuss how they crisscross the landscape of poets' national imagination. Andrew McRae, Maggie Kilgour, Richard Helgerson and Wyman H. Herendeen demonstrate how poets employ fluvial imagery to rethink cultural and national identity.[2] For instance, Edmund Spenser, John Leland, William Camden, Michael Drayton and John Milton look to the river, as Herendeen observes, 'to outline a national image in terms of the rivers and their historical and topographical associations'.[3] Specifically in their capacity both to unite and divide regions, rivers become apt metaphors for meditating on Britain's nuanced identity: a unified island nation with competing Welsh, Scottish and English constituents.[4] A nation in such an intricate situation demands a poet to fashion it. Rivers therefore serve as crucial metaphors for poets in delimiting their own poetic identity, legacy and puissance.[5] Although critics have helpfully charted the influence of fluvial bodies in developing a national poetics, they have yet to explore how rivers do the same for a theological poetics. As much as national poets turn to the river to rethink their identity and that of the nation, devotional poets take it up to explore their identity and that of the regenerate – those who have been spiritually reborn or regenerated through God's grace. For Lanyer, Herbert and Traherne, the ways in which rivers hydrate, irrigate and circulate manifest not only the nature of God's grace but more specifically what it is like to experience it. As we shall see, the need for a poet to explicate the phenomenological implications of such fluvial grace elevates the soteriological role of a devotional poet from an observer to a mediator of salvation.

I will begin this chapter by investigating the way in which early modern Protestant theologians discuss salvation in terms of potamology, the study of rivers.[6] While Donald R. Dickson has helpfully charted how theologians turn to subterranean and atmospheric hydrologic cycles as symbols of baptismal regeneration, I will examine how they specifically use geographic, ecological and hydrologic aspects of rivers to delineate the nature of God's grace in spiritual regeneration.[7] Indeed, they develop a riverine soteriology that characterises the experience of salvation as that of becoming like a river: as grace flows into believers, good works flow from them unto others. Devotional poets take their cue from theologians by scrutinising the phenomenology of becoming spiritually riverine. However, where theologians discuss the experience of grace largely in spiritual and moral terms, Lanyer, Herbert and Traherne describe it in material and corporeal ones. In *Salve Deus Rex Judaeorum* (1611), Lanyer considers how believers experience grace through gustatory sensation; thus, grace changes the way a person engages with and 'tastes' the mortal world. Herbert in his poem 'Grief', from *The Temple* (1633), figures grace as an internal hydrologic system that transforms a believer's physiology and affective state, physically altering the body's veins to produce rivers of tears. And Traherne in his poem 'Circulation', from the Dobell Folio (c. mid- to late-seventeenth century), pictures grace as a hydrologic cycle that transforms a believer's eyes and speech, enabling the believer to properly see the material world and vocalise praise unto God. Charting the physical phenomenology of grace, devotional poets imagine themselves and their poetry as crucial elements in riverine soteriology. Consequently, I will conclude by examining how Lanyer, Herbert and Traherne border on heresy by expanding Protestant soteriology to include devotional poets and their poetry. They each take up the task of explicating rivers of grace not as *mimesis* but as *poesis*, situating themselves as facilitators of salvation by composing poetry that acts as a medium through which believers receive grace and as a mode by which they textually experience it.

The potamology of salvation and riverine soteriology

Continuing a religious tradition that began in the twelfth century, early modern Protestant theologians turned to the 'Book of Nature' as a means for understanding God.[8] Like scripture, nature could be read and interpreted to reveal divine truth. As the anonymous writer of the theological text *Two Guides to a Good Life* (1604) indicates,

> God doth reveale, and as it were make himselfe visible unto us after two manner of waies: first, in the booke of his word, by the mouthes of his holy prophets, Apostles, and Patriarches: and secondly, by the book of nature, in the whole frame of heaven and earth.[9]

It is no surprise, then, that theologians evaluate rivers and other fluvial bodies (streams, brooks, fountains, springs) to better comprehend the abstract phenomenon of God's grace. In 'reading' rivers of grace, theologians craft a hermeneutics that we might think of as a potamology of salvation: they scrutinise the river of God's grace (its source, where and how it flows, its surrounding ecosystems) to delimit the origin and nature of salvation and how grace is spiritually experienced. By studying rivers in this way, then, theologians develop a riverine soteriology that imagines the phenomenology of salvation as a process in which the regenerate commune with a fluminous God to become fluvial themselves.

Theologians primarily use the river to emphasise the divine source of grace. Drawing on the early modern hydrologic theory that rivers originate from underground sources of water (fountains, springs or wells), they assert that Christ is the springhead of grace, the fountain of the waters of life. However, they also demarcate specific aspects of grace by portraying salvific rivers issuing from different locations: the word of God; the throne of God; God's love; Christ's body; and the Holy Spirit which resides in the heart of the regenerate.[10] Although these rivers of grace are often likened to water, they also comprise milk and honey (from the scriptures), crystal streams (from the throne of God) and blood (from Christ's body).

But how does one access these waters? One of the most common biblical metaphors that theologians use is that of a tree being planted by a river (Psalm 1:3). For instance, the Oxford college head Thomas Anyan indicates that a regenerate believer 'is likened to a tree planted by the rivers of waters' and therefore 'receive[s] juyce into his veynes from the waters of life, by which hee is planted'.[11] Believers first access God's river of grace by being 'planted' along the river's banks through their spiritual regeneration or rebirth. They become one with God as a tree becomes one with a river by receiving 'juyce' from its waters.

Theologians use riparian ecosystems to describe the experience of receiving grace and becoming one with God via rebirth. Thomas Sparke, a doctor of divinity, describes spiritual rebirth as 'rivers of water of life flowing over the bankes, for the force it shall have in all such effectually to wash them, to soften them, . . . and to quench in them the flames and heate of sinne'.[12] Grace is experienced as a spiritual cleansing that exonerates a believer of sin; softens the obduracy of pride; and douses fiery, sinful desire. Anyan also describes the experience of receiving grace as gaining a new spiritual capacity to speak and act differently: like a tree planted by a river of water, a regenerate believer brings forth new green leaves and fruit – 'his words are the leafes, his workes the fruit'.[13] And other theologians, borrowing from a metaphor in Psalm 42, suggest that rivers of grace induce spiritual thirst: 'a gracious heart growes more and more into a longing for Christ: *As the Hart brayeth for the rivers of water, so panteth his soule after Christ.*'[14]

In effect, theologians describe how believers experience grace as a new mode of spiritual being that makes them like rivers themselves. Anthony Anderson declares to his readers that after they receive grace, 'abundant rivers of spirituall goodnes flowe out of you, that all men seeing your good workes, may bee provoked to prayse the Lorde'.[15] Samuel Hieron indicates that believers receive graces – Christian virtues such as mercy, compassion, or patience – from the Holy Spirit and those graces flow from their belly, 'issu[ing] out to the refreshing of others'.[16] And John Cotton similarly avers that a believer

> shall have a spring of grace in his soule, that shall ever be like a running river cleansing his heart and way, and making him fruitfull in all places, cooling and refreshing his owne and others soules with the experience of Gods favour to him in Christ.[17]

For clergymen such as Anderson, Hieron and Cotton, the reception of grace transforms believers into fluvial conduits of righteousness. As they receive rivers of grace in their souls, believers then emit rivers of good works, virtuous graces and God's favour that 'cool' and 'refresh' others. Salvation for the regenerate means not only drinking from the river of God's grace but also becoming spiritually riverine themselves.

By explicating salvation in potamological terms, theologians craft a riverine soteriology that delineates what Cotton describes above as 'the experience of Gods favour'. In other words, they turn to the river to articulate the phenomenology of grace. They emphasise how the soul experiences grace as a spiritual cleansing, softening, purging, thirsting, altering, cooling, and refreshing. Devotional poets mimic theologians by adopting riverine soteriology to explore the phenomenology of grace, but with one difference: devotional poets examine how the 'experience of Gods favour' registers on a corporeal scale. That the hydrologic vocabulary of grace should lead poets to re-evaluate the human body is unsurprising since even before William Harvey's discovery of circulation in 1615, early modern theories of Galenic humoralism imagined the body and its humoral balance in terms of liquid ebbs and flows. As we shall see presently, devotional poets tease the metaphor of grace as a river to explore the physical implications of riverine soteriology: what does it look like for a believer who inhabits a corporeal body and material world to become like a river?

Rivers of milk and honey

In her lengthy devotional poem, *Salve Deus Rex Judaeorum*, the poet Lanyer spends considerable time not only praising God for his benevolent grace but also examining the phenomenological consequences of believers receiving it.[18] She reflects on the experience of salvation by engaging in the Protestant rewriting of medieval cartography. Medieval maps such as the thirteenth-century Map Psalter and Ranulf Higden's fourteenth-century *mappa mundi* picture the four rivers of Eden flowing throughout and around the world. Depicting the world in this way, these maps illustrate the divine origin of geographic order by charting the precise location of paradise.[19] Early modern Protestant theologians reinvent this cartographic tradition by imagining rivers originating not from Eden but from Christ and ordering not the world but Christ's invisible church – the worldwide body of elect believers. For instance, the clergyman John White indicates that four rivers of divine virtues (mercy, truth, righteousness and peace) flow from Christ, who is 'the head fountaine of Eden' and so 'the head of Paradise, of the Church'.[20] Similarly, Sheldon declares that Christ's crucified body emanates rivers of eucharistic blood that extend salvation worldwide:

> Foure-fold were the rivers, which issued from one fountaine, in the earthly Paradise, and watered the whole earth, making the same fruitfull: not foure fold onely, but manifold are the rivers, which issued from the fountaine in the spirituall Paradise, where Christ Jesus was placed with his spouse, his wife, his Church. (25)

Sheldon clarifies how the rivers that water the Church issue from Christ's 'head', 'feet', 'hands', 'face' and 'whole body' (26). In *Salve Deus*, Lanyer also reimagines the medieval *mappa mundi* tradition, resembling Sheldon in the way that she portrays four rivers flowing from specific body parts of the crucified Christ: 'His hands, his feete, his body, and his face, / Whence freely flow'd the rivers of his grace'.[21] However, where White and Sheldon turn to Christ's river-emitting body to emphasise the ordering of a global elect, Lanyer uses the same metaphor to illustrate the individual phenomenon of receiving grace and how grace orders the way a regenerate believer inhabits the mortal, material world. Consequently, instead of delineating the spiritual ramifications of paradisical rivers, as White and Sheldon do, Lanyer teases the sensorial implications of imagining grace in fluvial terms: if salvation is akin to drinking from a river, what does the river water *taste* like?

Lanyer suggests that a believer accesses rivers of grace through the gustatory experience of reading Christ's body. Critics such as Julianne Sandberg and Femke Molekamp have demonstrated how Lanyer conceptualises her poetry as a eucharistic feast.[22] As Molekamp asserts,

Lanyer reverses the doctrine of incarnation – 'the Word made flesh' – in order to access Christ as the Word, presenting the crucified Christ as the body made text, and her book as constructed of the materials of Christ's body. Lanyer's bold claim to her readers is that Christ is not merely represented but actually incarnated in her text.[23]

Readers thus partake of Christ's body by reading its poeticised image. Yet, Lanyer suggests that her poetry offers access to more than the body of Christ. It makes available the 'rivers of his grace' that 'freely flow' from 'His hands, his feete, his body, and his face' (1727–8). These rivers are not composed of blood, as we might expect. Instead, they contain 'sweet milke' (1738) and 'hony' (1737). In riverine soteriology, milky and mellifluous rivers are associated with the word of God. For example, White affirms that God's word comes from 'all holy Scripture' and 'floweth with milke and hony, of one savour and power of life'.[24] Rivers of milk and honey are the scriptural conduits through which flows the 'savour and power' of grace. Depicting in *Salve Deus* milk and honey issuing from Christ's body instead of blood, Lanyer adopts a common Protestant doctrinal stance by conflating the salvific powers of the Eucharist with those of God's word.[25] If Lanyer equates reading to eating the Eucharist, and if she conflates the Eucharist with textual conduits of grace, then Lanyer presents reading as a way to 'taste' (1736) the 'sweet holy rivers' (1729) and 'swift sugred currents that salvation brings' (1731). The metaphor of reading as eating, of course, was common in early modern England.[26] However, as Molekamp demonstrates, Lanyer views reading her poem as engaging with the 'actually incarnated' Christ, which invites us to consider how the tasting of grace constitutes for Lanyer an actual as well as metaphoric sensorial experience. She blurs the distinction between metaphor and reality, spiritual and physical. If spiritual rivers of grace are made accessible through the material, written word, then the spiritual experience of grace can be 'savour[ed]' through the physical sense of tasting.

The gustatory experience of salvation elevates how regenerate believers engage with the mortal world. Grace, it turns out, makes earthly experiences *taste* differently. Lanyer makes this clear when she compares regenerate believers to historical martyrs:

Who drinkes thereof, a world can never move,
All earthly pleasures are of them abhorred;
This love made Martyrs many deaths to prove,
To taste his sweetnesse, whom they so adored[.] (1739–42)

Believers 'who drinke' of Christ's grace resemble martyrs who 'taste[d] his sweetnesse' in death. This comparison has two phenomenological implications. First, as martyrs of old, the regenerate find 'all earthly pleasures are of them abhorred'. And, second, as Lanyer describes Christ doing for the martyr Stephen, the regenerate discover that the 'short sowre of Life' is 'sweet'ned': 'Making all bitternesse delight ... [the] taste' (1769–70). In other words, rivers of milk and honey make the tempting pleasures of the flesh unappetising and the bitter hardships of life sweet. Both 'earthly pleasures' and the 'sowre of Life' denote aspects of the physical world: material, sensual things that bring enjoyment or the pains, injuries or death of a mortal body. To be regenerate is to experience inversely the pleasures and sorrows of 'earthly' 'Life'. Indeed, the term 'taste' in early modern England, besides referring to the perception of flavour, meant to experience or to feel.[27] In drinking and 'tast[ing]' lacteal and honeyed rivers, regenerate believers interact with and 'taste' the earthly world in a fundamentally different way. Martyrdom, for Lanyer, is not merely a model of Christian piety but more particularly the regenerate mode of experiencing mortality.

By imagining how Christ's body issues rivers of milk and honey that transform the way the regenerate inhabit the world, Lanyer remaps Paradise. As we saw above, medieval cartographers strove to identify the specific geographic location of Eden and its rivers. Early modern Protestant theologians continued this quest by locating paradise – which White and Sheldon describe as Christ's invisible church – existing throughout the world. Although their aims differed, medieval cartographers and early modern theologians mapped Paradise on a global scale. Lanyer, however, charts Paradise not somewhere on the earth but within individual believers. She declares that the 'sweetnesse' (1774) that Stephen received as a martyr is 'The Paradise of our celestiall pleasure' (1776) that the regenerate ingest via rivers of grace. For Lanyer, Paradise is neither a place nor a spiritual organisation. It is instead the lived experience of the saved: the phenomenological mode catalysed by tasting rivers of milk and honey that, in turn, enables a believer to taste their earthly life in new ways.

Rivers of tears

While Lanyer uses the image of the river to represent Christ's grace, the pastor and poet Herbert employs it to scrutinise a believer's response to grace, namely their tearful reaction to salvation. In the poem 'Grief', from his collection of devotional poetry entitled *The Temple*, Herbert meditates on the weeping galvanised by spiritual rebirth.[28] Critics have primarily discussed 'Grief' for its intervention in what Louis L. Martz identifies as the Counter-Reformation 'literature of tears'.[29] Whereas Martz suggests that Herbert engages seriously in this Catholic literary tradition, Gary Kuchar, Elizabeth Clarke and Richard Strier argue that Herbert parodies, ironises or rejects it.[30] Clarissa Chenovick has recently reconsidered these claims. She illustrates how early modern Protestant theologians (both Calvinist and anti-Calvinist) often characterise tearful contrition as a part of salvation and how Herbert seriously engages in this Protestant discourse.[31] Chenovick's argument is corroborated by riverine soteriology. Drawing on biblical verses such as Jeremiah 9:1 and Psalm 119:136 that portray prophets weeping, Protestant theologians depict rivers of tears as an integral component of regeneration. For instance, William Cowper, the Bishop of Galloway, tells believers that they must pray and ask God to 'fill my head with water, and make mine eyes a fountaine of teares, that I may weepe both night and day'.[32] Where Cowper and other clergymen identify how grace induces the lachrymal 'fill[ing]' of a believer's head, Herbert explores the affective and physiological experience of such 'fill[ing]' and how fluvial grace then transforms a believer into a watery world themself.

In 'Grief', Herbert uses riverine imagery to describe the affective phenomenology of grace. Wishing for rivers of tears to fill his head, Herbert crafts a soteriological paradigm in the subjunctive mood, describing a regeneration that he has yet to undergo himself. He imagines spiritual rebirth in terms of terranean and atmospheric hydrologic systems:[33]

> O who will give me tears? Come all ye springs,
> Dwell in my head & eyes: come clouds, & rain:
> My grief hath need of all the watry things,
> That nature hath produc'd.[34]

Here, Herbert identifies two sources of water: springs and clouds. As we saw above, theologians associate Christ, the source of grace, with springs. They also sometimes describe Christ's grace as rain,[35] whose origin Herbert specifies as 'clouds'. Depicting the hydrologic sources of grace, Herbert then describes what happens downstream. Springs and clouds actuate an affective response from a believer: they catalyse grief ('My grief hath need of all the watry things'), which then produces 'river[s]' (5), 'foords' (9) and 'spouts' (9) of tears. The comparison of affect to water is an early modern *locus communis*.[36] As Gail Kern Paster demonstrates, early modern people understood affective states in terms of, and resonant with, the natural world.[37] By linking grief with soteriological springs, clouds and rivers, Herbert characterises the experience of rebirth as the activation of a hydro-affective system: fluvial grace stimulates grief, which then triggers rivers of tears. Moreover, to feel affect in the early modern world was not a wholly mental experience. Emotions, or what early moderns called the 'passions', were operations of the soul that influenced and were influenced by the body's humoral balance. Depicting grace transforming a believer's affective state, then, Herbert underscores how the salvific phenomenon can be experienced on a corporeal level.

Indeed, Herbert portrays grace-inspired grief altering the body's physiology. Early modern physicians and natural philosophers characterised crying as physiologically transformative because it balances the body's humours by excreting superfluities via tears.[38] Clergymen drew on such physiological theory as a spiritual metaphor: as crying physically purges the body, it also spiritually cleanses the soul.[39] Yet, Herbert depicts grace as inducing more than a spiritual cleansing. After demanding for springs and clouds to dwell in his head, Herbert pleads,

> . . . Let ev'ry vein,
> Suck up a river to supply mine eyes,
> My weary weeping eyes too drie for me,
> Unlesse they get new conduits, new supplies
> To bear them out, and with my state agree. (4–8)

On the one hand, the term 'vein', meaning a rivulet, continues Herbert's conceit of the hydro-affective system that actuates regenerate grief.[40] On the other hand, 'vein' denotes a blood vessel, suggesting that Herbert asks God to let his blood vessels 'supplie' tears to his 'drie' eyes.[41] The intravenous transportation of tears aligns with early modern medical theory. In his medical manual *Mikrokosmographia* (1615), the royal physician Helkiah Crooke indicates that tears are a 'moisture' that 'together with the blood is transported unto the braine'.[42] In the head, this blood/tear moisture is disaggregated, as 'whay [whey] is separated from the milk', and then the remaining lachrymal moisture is excreted through the corners of the eyes.[43] Crying for 'new supplies' and 'new conduits' so that they 'with my state agree', Herbert asks God to change the lachrymal liquid in his blood ('supplies') and his physical veins ('conduits') so that they match his sorrowful and hopefully regenerate state. The adjective 'new', meaning enhanced, suggests that grace can augment the quality or quantity of tears and restore the functionality of his veins. Herbert therefore imagines the hydro-affective experience catalysed by spiritual springs and clouds as having powerful transformative capabilities to alter the bodies of the regenerate.

Picturing grace as restructuring the affective and physiological hydrology of the body, Herbert imagines the experience of salvation as that of embodying a fluvial world. In early modern England, the human body was often viewed as a microcosm of the earth. In particular, veins were described as rivers coursing through the geography of the *corpus naturale*.[44] By depicting salvific clouds and springs issuing new affect throughout and revitalising the moisture and veins of a believer's body, Herbert highlights how grace is experienced, as it were, as a corporeal terraformation. He implies as much when he characterises regenerate eyes as 'two shallow foords, two little spouts / Of a lesse world' (9–10). The 'lesse world' within a regenerate believer is characterised by hydrologic features: 'all the watry things, / That nature hath produc'd' (3–4). His emphasis that the regenerate possess 'all' the 'watry things' reveals how the unregenerate lack such hydrology. On one level, the unregenerate might internalise an arid world: their 'heart and soule' being 'drie' 'earth' that lacks the 'moysture' of grace, as the Whittington College lecturer William Jackson describes.[45] On another level, as Herbert outlines, the unregenerate might embody a watery world, but one that is the wrong kind of watery: their tearful sorrow derives not from divine clouds and springs but rather from mortal 'griefs and doubts' of the 'greater' world (10–11). To become regenerate is for the internal hydrology of the body to be initiated or corrected. Thus, Herbert underscores how the phenomenology of grace is the experience of becoming a fluvial world: spiritual rivers of grace cause physical rivers of tears to flow within and issue from believers.

Rivers of treasures

In 'Circulation', from *Poems* in the Dobell Folio, the poet and clergyman Traherne contemplates the physical phenomenology of salvation by rethinking the common early modern comparison of God's grace to the water cycle. The early modern theory of hydrologic circulation – based on classical sources, like Plato and Aristotle, and biblical sources, specifically Ecclesiastes 1:7 – maintained that rivers flow into oceans whose waters then travel in subterranean springs back to the rivers. Theologians frequently draw on this theory to conceptualise the effect of God's grace on humans. For instance, the Pitminster clergyman William Sclater affirms that 'seeing our rivers flowe all from this sea, they should thether return[;] . . . the guifts we have receaved from Christ, we should use all to the honour of him from whome we have receaved them'.[46] The 'guifts' believers receive from Christ are what clergymen often call *graces* or *virtues*. As God's grace descends on a believer, it cultivates graces or virtues within them that they then use in good works to return honour to God. In 'Circulation', Traherne charts a similar circulatory process.[47] However, where Sclater and other clergymen emphasise the spiritual nature of the circulation of God's grace, Traherne accentuates the sensorial experience of being a part of such a salvific cycle.

Traherne depicts the hydrologic cycle of grace in terms of maritime economy. As McRae illustrates, rivers in the early modern imagination represented the potential 'to facilitate social and economic flows' because, in part, 'they imply directions and connections'.[48] Traherne leverages the economic flow of commodities between rivers and oceans to highlight the spiritual flow of salvific treasures between God and believer:

> He [God] is the Primitive Eternal Spring
> The Endless Ocean of each Glorious Thing.
>   The Soul a Vessel is
>   A Spacious Bosom to Contain
>   All the fair Treasures of his Bliss
> Which run like Rivers from, into the Main,
> And all it doth receiv returns again.[49]

As an 'Ocean', a 'Primitive Eternal Spring' and a 'Main', God is the origin from whence flow rivers of 'Treasures of his Bliss', meaning those celestial 'Joy and Glories' (82) promised to the regenerate. Regenerate believers receive these salvific treasures in their 'Bosom' as a 'Vessel' does commodities in its hold. The depiction of a soul as a ship carrying treasures figures grace as an economic exchange: the soul receives treasures from God, which it then 'returns again'. The quid quo pro nature of trade gives considerable free will to humans in Traherne's conceptualisation of the economy of salvation. This prioritising of free will evinces his vision of election articulated in his treatise *A Sober View of Dr Twisses His Considerations* where he describes salvation for some believers as an irresistible election and for others as a product of their own choice.[50] A ship can be propelled by a current, or it can navigate its own course by oar, rudder and sail. However, the socio-economic flow of rivers, as McRae demonstrates, 'impl[ies] direction'. Despite a ship's potential volition to follow the river as it will, Traherne is careful to emphasise the direction in which rivers of treasure flow: they issue from God and actuate those that come from the regenerate. While a person might seek out regeneration, the power to be spiritually reborn nonetheless resides with God. The poem's first and second stanza clarifies that just as a person 'breaths out' air that 'he before suckt in', so too does a believer breathe out 'Joys and Praises' (17–19) that originate from the Divine: 'No Prais can we return again, / ... / But what derived from without we gain' (12–14). In effect, God's rivers of treasures ('Joy and Glories') can either stimulate or be voluntarily returned by encomiastic rivers of treasure ('Joy and Praise') that stream heavenward from believers' mouths.

Dickson characterises this cycle of grace that Traherne charts in 'Circulation', and the rest of the Dobell *Poems*, as cerebral in nature. Dickson states that according to Traherne, God's grace enables a believer to perceive the world anew and that 'when the world is perceived rightly, *thoughts* flow back to the abyss of the godhead'.[51] While Traherne does depict the noetic nature of perception and praise in 'Circulation', what Dickson does not acknowledge is that for Traherne perception and praise in the circulatory economy of salvation are also physical, sensory activities.[52]

Traherne charts the sensory nature of grace by first describing spiritual unregeneracy in terms of bodily sensation. Describing the praise that one ought to render God, he avers that ''tis a Sin / To bury [Praise], in a Senceless Tomb' (20–1). If grace evokes rivers of praise from the regenerate, its absence in unregenerate believers then corresponds with their inability for panegyric. The phrase 'a Senceless Tomb' highlights the corporeal ramifications of such speechlessness: a sinner's body is refractory to worship, a tomb for praise since it cannot 'Sence' properly. Traherne identifies two specific sensory modes that fail to work in the unregenerate. First, he indicates that sinful silence derives from the inability to see: '*Tis Blindness Makes us Dumb*' (26). And, second, assuming that blindness makes someone '*Dumb*', Traherne implies that sin impacts the sense of speech. Why Traherne associates speech with sensorial 'Senceless[ness]' is helpfully explained by Crooke's theory of speech in *Mikrokosmographia*. In his medical treatise, Crooke describes speech as a sense.[53] He indicates that the tongue is the 'instrument both of the Sense of Tasting and of the Speech'.[54] While we think today of sensing only in terms of receiving sensory data, Crooke characterises it as conveying sensory information. He therefore implies that the tongue senses by communicating 'those things that fall under the Sense, as when wee crie for paine, or for Foode and succour'.[55] For Traherne, then, the inability to see and to speak renders a body 'Senceless'. Such ocular deficiency and phonal incapacity consequently require divine rectification.

Traherne imagines grace altering the eyes and organs of speech. In answer to the 'Senceless Tomb' concomitant with unregeneracy, he suggests that

> Had we but those Celestial Eys,
>   Whereby we could behold the Sum
> Of all his Bounties, *we should overflow*
> With Praises[.] (27–30)

To be sure, Traherne here references a noetic awakening of the understanding: if an individual could see with 'Celestial Eys', they could understand the 'Sum' of God's 'Bounties', meaning his benevolence. Yet, the 'Sum / Of all his Bounties', which Traherne enumerates in his poem, is manifest in circulatory cycles found in the physical world. He describes these cycles in ocular terms: 'Colour', 'a Glimps of Light', 'The Sparcle of a Precious Stone' and 'a lovly Sight' cannot 'shew' – meaning to be made visible – unless they 'borrow Matter first, / Before they can communicat' (34, 36–8 and 41–2). God's benevolence is 'communicat[ed]' to humans through sensory apprehension of the visible manifestation, or 'shew[ing]', of an object's 'Matter' or material composition.[56] Traherne therefore identifies circulation occurring throughout the material world as evidenced by trees, rain, streams, springs, sunlight, fruit and earth. These material objects play an important soteriological role: they 'shew that we must some Estate / Possess, or never can communicate' (44–5). Early modern theologians frequently use the term 'Estate' to refer to a believer's salvific status. Thus, Traherne describes the regenerate 'Estate', by which a believer gains 'Celestial Eys', as resembling the circulatory cycles by which colour, light, a sparkly stone and a lovely sight are made visible. Just as these objects cannot 'shew' unless they 'borrow Matter first', the regenerate cannot 'shew', meaning to gaze or behold, unless they 'borrow [grace] first'. The regenerate must 'possess' sight-enabling grace; else they 'never can communicate' or articulate praise. And such praise is not wholly noetic. In stanza two, Traherne aligns the physiology of breathing – 'No Man breaths out more vital Air, / Then he before suckt in' – with the 'Joys and Praises' the regenerate 'must repair' (17–19). Breath is vital for speech, as Crooke indicates, for 'breath' is 'the matter of the voyce', which the 'mouth and the tongue' change into 'speech'.[57] If grace allows the regenerate to communicate, then it must enable their lungs, elevating them from the '*Dumb*' (26) state of unregeneracy. For Traherne, then, the experience of grace registers in the eyes and lungs, in vision and in speech.

The regeneration of the body's ocular and phonal faculties makes a believer riverine. Illustrating the effects of acquiring 'Celestial Eys', Traherne uses fluvial terminology to explain how the regenerate will '*overflow / With Praises*' (29–30). As God sends rivers of treasures into a believer's soul, the believer is enabled to gaze on the natural world and understand that 'All Things to Circulations owe / Themselvs' (32–3); such understanding then causes them to overflow with encomiastic rivers of treasures in praising the ubiquity of divine circulation. Theologians in riverine soteriology sometimes attribute a state of *overflowing* to Christ: 'Christ is an ever-over flowing fountain, continually streaming forth into the souls of his people.'⁵⁸ In this way, Traherne imagines the regenerate echoing God's fluminous state.⁵⁹ To experience grace is to sensorially engage with the world; to perceive and participate in divine circulation; and thus to resemble and become one with God by overflowing with rivers of treasure.

The devotional poet and rivers of grace

Although devotional poets draw primarily on hydrologic rather than geographic aspects of rivers to metaphorise the phenomenology of grace, I return now to chorography because it captures the theological stakes of charting rivers of grace in devotional poetry. Identifying the relationship between chorographer and landscape, Helgerson indicates that

> the chorographical traveler [is not] a mere passive observer of what most readily presents itself to his eyes. Rather he actively seeks out information that will make the land known[.] . . . The chorographic project is a project in self-description – and, indeed, in self-making.⁶⁰

To describe the world is to fashion it and, in so doing, fashion oneself. Spenser and Milton therefore style themselves national poets by poeticising and thereby mastering the nation's fluvial waters.⁶¹ Devotional poets do not attempt to master God as national poets do England's rivers. But devotional poets do envision themselves exercising significant influence in the divine riverscape of salvation. By charting rivers of grace, they picture themselves playing a crucial role in salvific processes: they produce a poetic medium through which readers access and experience grace. Lanyer, Herbert and Traherne consequently push doctrinal boundaries by attributing to poetry the spiritual efficacy of scripture and by fashioning themselves as creators of riverine conduits of grace.

Lanyer articulates her soteriological role as a devotional poet in the dedicatory poem to Lucy Russell, Countess of Bedford, that prefaces *Salve Deus*. She tells Bedford to 'entertaine', meaning to receive or admit, Christ, 'The Ocean of true grace, whose streames doe fill / All those with Joy, that can his love recover' (16–18). Lanyer here again portrays Christ's grace making the regenerate riverine, but with a caveat: they will be 'fill[ed]' with 'streames' of grace only if they 'recover' his 'love'. To receive Christ's love or the promise of salvation, Lanyer suggests that Bedford needs to *read* the rivers that flow from his body: 'In whose most pretious wounds your soule may reade / Salvation, while he (dying Lord) doth bleed' (13–14). As we saw above, Christ's 'wounds' issue more than blood: they also issue 'sweet milke' (1738) and 'hony' (1737). To properly 'reade' rivers of grace as both eucharistic blood and soteriological milk and honey, Bedford needs Lanyer and her poetry. *Salve Deus* not only 'reverses the doctrine of incarnation', as Molekamp demonstrates, but also reimagines the doctrine of salvation: the poem is the flesh made word, rivers of grace made legible.[62] Lanyer therefore presents her poem as a medium to understand and access salvific rivers of milk and honey. As clergymen depict rivers of grace flowing from scripture, so too does Lanyer imagine them issuing from her poetry.

Herbert formulates a similar role for himself and his poetry by charting rivers of tears. In *The Temple*, he maintains the significant agenda of spiritually reforming the people of England.[63] He highlights this project in the collection's dedication by indicating that 'Lord, my first fruits present themselves to thee' (1) and then asks for God to 'Turn their [English believers'] eyes hither, who shall make a gain' (5). While Herbert elucidates his purpose in turning the 'eyes' of the nation 'hither' (to his poetry) so they might 'make a gain', he does not clarify in the dedication what such 'gain' entails. In 'Grief', however, he does. After mapping how the regenerate become riverine through tearful sorrow, Herbert then curiously turns his discussion to poetry:

> Verses, ye are too fine a thing, too wise
> For my rough sorrows: cease, be dumbe and mute,
> Give up your feet and running to mine eyes,
> And keep your measures for some lovers lute[.] (13–16)

By the end of 'Grief', he seemingly forsakes poetry for its uselessness in capturing his feelings. Yet, in light of the dedication's poetic agenda, this final sentiment is more indicative of his own salvific anxiety rather than a disavowal of poetry. In fact, these last lines include a tacit endorsement of devotional poetry's (and the poet's) role in salvation. Punning on the term 'running', which refers both to poetic metre and to a river's flow, Herbert seems to imply that he should forsake lyrical 'running' in favour of the lachrymal 'running' of his 'eyes'. That Herbert does not abandon poetry to 'some lovers lute' and instead pens 181 other poems demonstrates that he does not 'give up', meaning to relinquish, poetry but rather 'give[s] up', meaning to devote entirely, the running of poetry to making 'eyes' cry. He produces poetry to help the 'eyes' that look 'hither' spout streams themselves. In fact, the initial question that begins his poem – 'O who will give me tears?' (1) – has a bold answer: a devotional poet and their poetry. Thus, the poems of *The Temple* will provide readers a 'gain' in that they can help catalyse rivers of tears by allowing readers to embody and 'gain' a fluvial world within.[64]

Traherne similarly imagines his poetry granting readers access to rivers of grace. In his wistful yearning for 'Celestial Eys' (27), he highlights how grace-enhanced vision would come to readers if they did '*Know*' the '*Causes*' of all God's 'Bounties' (29–30). Traherne laments for readers who cannot laud God because they lack the '*Know*[ledge]' of God's benevolence that derives from properly seeing circulation throughout the world. Yet, as Jane Partner argues, Traherne uses his poetry 'to enable the reader to have an experience of seeing'.[65] For this reason, he maps out the '*Causes*' of circulation in his poem so that 'Mortal Man can take Delight to *know*' (83, emphasis added). By the poem's own logic, the causal knowledge of circulation that it describes can make blind eyes see and mute mouths speak. In this way, Traherne imagines himself playing a vital role in actuating God's circulatory grace: his poetry enables believers to know, see and therefore receive rivers of treasures so they can produce their own in panegyrical reply.

Considering how devotional poets depict the phenomenology of grace in physical terms, we should not be surprised that they also imagine their poetry enabling readers to access rivers of grace through physical means: via the eyes. Lanyer helps readers 'reade' the wounds of Christ; Herbert turns 'eyes' and makes them cry; and Traherne promises to make the blind see. For these poets, devotional poetry is a crucial element of salvation: it provides a textual medium through which flow rivers of grace. The salvific puissance of such poetry resembles that of scripture, which, as the preacher Theodore Herring indicates, constitutes the 'channels' or 'pipes' that convey rivers of grace to believers that they 'may sucke, and be delighted'.[66] In this way, then, Lanyer, Herbert and Traherne flirt with heresy. They envision their poetry operating as 'channels' or 'pipes' of grace, not unlike divinely inspired scripture. Moreover, they characterise their poetry not only as channelling grace but also as the textualised experience of grace itself. Lanyer's poetry brings readers to the incarnated fountain of rivers of milk and honey; Herbert's opens lachrymal conduits and supplies; and Traherne's actuates the redemptive perceptive faculty it describes. Devotional poetry becomes a visual mode through which believers might immerse themselves in and be immersed by rivers of grace. If grace is experienced sensorially, physiologically and affectively, then why might it not be experienced in the physical act of reading poetry?

Lanyer, Herbert and Traherne thus rearrange the contours of Protestant soteriology by fixing the devotional poet as a prominent feature in the riverscape of salvation. Ministers, to be sure, play a significant salvific role in guiding believers to scriptural conduits of riverine grace through preaching and admonishing. Yet, they do not claim to create conduits of grace themselves. Lanyer, Herbert and Traherne do, however. By depicting rivers of grace, they *ipso facto* craft poetic conduits for those same rivers. Mimesis then becomes an act of *poesis*; in making rivers of grace legible, the devotional poet makes them accessible. To echo Helgerson in theological terms: the devotional poet then is not a mere passive observer of salvation – he or she actively facilitates salvation by seeking to make rivers of grace known and thereby opening conduits to them. By charting rivers of grace poetically, devotional poets become mediators of salvation, allowing believers to access and to experience rivers of milk, honey, tears and treasures as and because of what they read.

I am grateful to Jason Kerr, Sharon Harris and Julianna Chapman for their advice on early drafts of this chapter and to my research assistant Tin Yan Grace Lee, who helped me comb through theological treatises and gather secondary criticism.

Notes

1. Richard Sheldon, *The First Sermon of R. Sheldon Priest* (London, 1612), 26; subsequent quotations appear parenthetically. I have preserved the original spelling of quotations from early modern texts, except for silently expanding abbreviations, replacing w for vv, and modernising u/v and i/j.
2. Andrew McRae, *Literature and Domestic Travel in Early Modern England* (Cambridge: Cambridge University Press, 2009), 21–66 and 'Fluvial Nation: Rivers, Mobility and Poetry in Early Modern England', *English Literary Renaissance* 38.3 (2008), 506–34; Maggie Kilgour, 'Writing on Water', *English Literary Renaissance* 29.2 (1999), 282–305; Richard Helgerson, *Forms of Nationhood: The Elizabethan Writing of England* (Chicago: University of Chicago Press, 1992), 107–47; and Wyman H. Herendeen, *From Landscape to Literature: The River and the Myth of Geography* (Pittsburgh: Duquesne University Press, 1986), 140–338.
3. Herendeen, *Landscape to Literature*, 289.
4. Ibid., 225–338.
5. Kilgour, 'Writing on Water', 282–305; and Herendeen, *Landscape to Literature*, 161–2 and 181–338.
6. Although *potamology* was not coined until the nineteenth century, the term nonetheless helpfully highlights theologians' concern with rivers beyond their geographic and topographical features, including their hydrologic processes, ecological impact and water quality.
7. See Donald R. Dickson, *The Fountain of Living Waters: The Typology of the Waters of Life in Herbert, Vaughan, and Traherne* (Columbia: University of Missouri Press, 1987). I also differ from Dickson by focusing on rivers and soteriology rather than water circulation more generally and biblical typology.

8. Lindsay J. Starkey, *Encountering Water in Early Modern Europe and Beyond: Redefining the Universe through Natural Philosophy, Religious Reformations, and Sea Voyaging* (Amsterdam: Amsterdam University Press, 2020), 194–5; and Peter Harrison, 'The "Book of Nature" and Early Modern Science', in *The Book of Nature in Early Modern and Modern History*, ed. Klaas van Berkel and Arjo Vanderjagt (Leuven: Peeters, 2006), 1–15.
9. Anonymous, *Two Guides to a Good Life* (London, 1604), sig. B5r.
10. On the word of God, see Robert Barrell, *The Spirituall Architecture* (London, 1624), 11–12. On the throne of God, see John White, *English Paradise* (London, 1612), 9. On Christ's love, see William Cowper, *The Anatomie of a Christian Man* (London, 1611), 5. On Christ's body, see Henry Smith, *A Treatise of the Lords Supper in Two Sermons* (London, 1591), 10–11. On the Spirit, see Niels Hemmingsen, *The Faith of the Church Militant* (London, 1581), 287.
11. Thomas Anyan, *A Sermon Preached at S. Maries Church in Oxford* (London, 1612), 3–4 and 12.
12. Thomas Sparke, *A Sermon Preached at Cheanies* (Oxford, 1594), 31.
13. Anyan, *A Sermon*, 9.
14. Adam Harsnett, *A Touch-Stone of Grace* (London, 1630), 62.
15. Anthony Anderson, *A Godlie Sermon* (London, 1576), sig. B1v.
16. Samuel Hieron, *The Abridgement of the Gospell* (London, 1609), 6.
17. John Cotton, *The Way of Life* (London, 1641), 97.
18. While here I consider *Salve Deus* as a devotional poem, other critics have categorised it as one of many genres; see my 'Aemilia Lanyer, Edmund Spenser, and the Literary Hymn', *Early Modern Women: An Interdisciplinary Journal* 15.2 (2021), 4–5.
19. Herendeen, *Landscape to Literature*, 94 and 112–13.
20. White, *English Paradise*, 1.
21. Aemilia Lanyer, *Salve Deus Rex Judaeorum*, ll. 1727–8, in *The Poems of Aemilia Lanyer*, ed. Susanne Woods (Oxford: Oxford University Press, 1993), 124; subsequent quotations from *Salve Deus* and its prefatory poems come from this edition and appear parenthetically.
22. Julianne Sandberg, 'Book, Body, and Bread: Reading Aemilia Lanyer's Eucharist', *Philological Quarterly* 96.1 (2017), 1–25; and Femke Molekamp, 'Reading Christ the Book in Aemilia Lanyer's *Salve Deus Rex Judaeorum* (1611): Iconography and the Cultures of Reading', *Studies in Philology* 109.3 (2012), 311–32.
23. Molekamp, 'Reading Christ', 312.
24. White, *English Paradise*, 9.
25. On the Protestant conflation of Eucharist and Bible, see Sandberg, 'Book, Body, and Bread', 12–13.
26. Katharine A. Craik, *Reading Sensations in Early Modern England* (Basingstoke: Palgrave Macmillan, 2007), 94.
27. *OED* online, s.v. 'taste, v.', I.3.a.
28. I consider 'Grief' as a snapshot of Herbert's phenomenological paradigm of grace rather than articulating a consistent theology of tears across his poems as Clarissa Chenovick does in 'A Balsome for Both the Hemispheres: Tears as Medicine in Herbert's *Temple* and Seventeenth-Century Preaching', *ELH* 84.3 (2017), 559–90.

29. Louis L. Martz, *The Poetry of Meditation: A Study in English Religious Literature of the Seventeenth Century* (New Haven, CT: Yale University Press, 1954), 199.
30. Martz, *Poetry of Meditation*, 202–3. See also Gary Kuchar, *The Poetry of Religious Sorrow in Early Modern England* (Cambridge: Cambridge University Press, 2008), 77; Elizabeth Clarke, *Theory and Theology in George Herbert's Poetry: 'Divinitie, and Poesie, Met'* (Oxford: Clarendon Press, 1997), 121–3; and Richard Strier, 'Herbert and Tears', *ELH* 46.2 (1979), 221–47.
31. Chenovick, 'A Balsome', 559–90.
32. Cowper, *The Anatomie*, 151.
33. I use the term *system* rather than *cycle* to describe how Herbert portrays grace because he pictures only an input (spring/clouds) and output (rivers) rather than a circulatory movement from spring/clouds to rivers and back again. On early modern understanding of terranean and atmospheric water cycles, see Dickson, *Fountain of Living Waters*, 11–28.
34. George Herbert, 'Grief', ll. 1–4, in *The English Poems of George Herbert*, ed. Helen Wilcox (Cambridge: Cambridge University Press, 2007), 560; all subsequent quotations from *The Temple* come from this edition and are cited parenthetically.
35. For example, see Arthur Lake, 'Sundrie Sermons de Tempore', in *Sermons with Some Religious and Divine Meditations* (London, 1629), 19.
36. Gail Kern Paster, *Humoring the Body: Emotions and the Shakespearean Stage* (Chicago: University of Chicago Press, 2004), 2.
37. Paster, *Humoring the Body*, 9–10.
38. Chenovick, 'A Balsome', 576.
39. Ibid., 576.
40. *OED*, s.v. 'vein, n.', I.1.b.
41. Ibid., II.4.a.
42. Helkiah Crooke, *Mikrokosmographia* (London, 1615), 538.
43. Ibid., 538–9, esp. 538.
44. Lowell Duckert, *For All Waters: Finding Ourselves in Early Modern Wetscapes* (Minneapolis: University of Minnesota Press, 2017), 37–8.
45. William Jackson, *The Celestiall Husbandrie* (London, 1616), 8.
46. William Sclater, *The Christians Strength* (Oxford, 1612), 14.
47. He also borrows from Neoplatonism and its emphasis on *circuitus spiritualis* (Dickson, *Fountain of Living Waters*, 166).
48. McRae, 'Fluvial Nation', 507 and 509.
49. Thomas Traherne, 'The Circulation', ll. 84–90, in *The Works of Thomas Traherne*, vol. 6, ed. Jan Ross (Cambridge: D. S. Brewer, 2014), 47; all subsequent quotations are from this edition and are quoted parenthetically.
50. Thomas Traherne, *A Sober View of Dr Twisses His Considerations*, 26.84–96, in *The Works*, vol. 1, 184–5.
51. Dickson, *Fountain of Living Waters*, 166–89, esp. 174.
52. On the imbricated relationship of the senses and spiritual knowledge in Traherne's poetry, see Jane Partner, *Poetry and Vision in Early Modern England* (Cham, Switzerland: Palgrave Macmillan, 2018), 93–9.
53. Although Crooke does not classify speech as a sixth sense, he nonetheless discusses it as a companion sense, as it were, of taste; see Elizabeth L. Swann,

Taste and Knowledge in Early Modern England (Cambridge: Cambridge University Press, 2020), 80.
54. Crooke, *Mikrokosmographia*, 629.
55. Ibid., 629.
56. See Partner, *Poetry and Vision*, 94–5.
57. Crooke, *Mikrokosmographia*, 633.
58. George Hopkins, *Salvation from Sinne by Jesus Christ* (London, 1655), 43.
59. See Dickson, *Fountain of Living Waters*, 167.
60. Helgerson, *Forms of Nationhood*, 143.
61. Kilgour, 'Writing on Water', 282–305.
62. Molekamp, 'Reading Christ', 312.
63. Brice Peterson, 'George Herbert's Literary Career as a Holy Laureate', *SEL, 1500–1900* 59.1 (2019), 113–34.
64. Chenovick also sees Herbert espousing an agenda in *The Temple* of helping believers access grace ('A Balsome', 583–4).
65. Partner, *Poetry and Vision*, 90.
66. Theodore Herring, *Panacea Christiana* (London, 1624), 14.

Chapter 2

'Plenteous Rivers': Waterways as Resources, Threats and the Heart of the Community in Early Modern England

Daniel Gettings

> LEAR:
> Of all these bounds, even from this line to this,
> With shadowy forests and with champains rich'd,
> With plenteous rivers and wide-skirted meads,
> We make thee lady: to thine and Albany's issue.
> – William Shakespeare, *King Lear* (1.1.65–8)

The idea of the 'plenteous river' of King Lear would have been all too familiar to the early modern audience watching the play. Waterways provided the communities that lived on them with a bounty of resources in the form of fish, waterfowl, clay and of course the water itself. Living near a river in this period, however, was far from a simple affair. The threat of flooding loomed large in the early modern mind, supported by a print culture that ensured such events were widely publicised. Despite this ever-present danger, however, many saw the river as a sort of comfort, a feature of the land that had been there for their ancestors and would be there for them, so long as other people maintained a balance.[1] This multifaceted relationship between early modern people and their waterways is the focus of this chapter, and I explore how these feelings changed across a period when new ideas about the landscape and industry saw attitudes toward the river shift faster than they ever had before.

With that said, the term 'river' was not necessarily as discrete for those in early modern England as it is for us today. Some of the watercourses that early modern peoples quite happily labelled as 'rivers' are rather divorced from the term in modern understanding; thus, an ancient natural watercourse and a new, human-built canal were both 'rivers' in early modern parlance.[2] For the purposes of this chapter, this problem has been solved by deciding that if early modern people called something a river, then we should consider it one. To attempt to distinguish between waterways based on modern definitions would be both anachronistic and damaging to an attempt to read the river from an early modern perspective. It matters little whether we agree that what contemporaries were talking about was a river, only that they did. Additionally on this issue, the sources being utilised, which range from popular print and ballads, to petitions, court cases and land disputes, do tend to favour examples of 'the river' which we would recognise as such today.

This chapter will explore the evolution of the 'plenteous' river in three sections. First it will examine the degree to which a river served as a resource or a source of resources for those that lived alongside it, and how attitudes changed with the coming of the capitalist and commercialist age. Second it will explore the idea of the threat that living near rivers posed and how this changed as English people became preoccupied with 'improving' the world around them. Finally, it will interrogate the place of rivers in local communities and how this too changed as the era progressed.

Rivers as resource

Access to a river provided a whole host of opportunities to early modern people. Fast-flowing water meant not only a steady and relatively safe supply for the daily tasks of cooking and cleaning without the need to resort to a well, but also provided other benefits in the form of a waste removal system into which otherwise dangerous products could be disposed and would flow away from a community. This is in addition to the other resources found around and in rivers which could provide sustenance and profit to those willing to exploit them.

The most important resource rivers provided was water itself. Early modern people had a solid idea of water quality, and that some sources of water were safer to drink or use than others. This is evident from the writings of individuals such as William Harrison, Tobias Venner and Thomas Tryon that described a very similar hierarchy of waters in which spring water, rainwater and river water were all consistently rated as the best for human consumption in various orders, far superior to human sources such as the well or pump and clearly preferable to unhealthy natural sources such as the bog or pond.[3] Those who drew their water from the river took this access seriously. When Frances Humphreys's access to the Thames was blocked by the scaffolding of Peter Marsh in 1630, we see how individuals would argue and fall into slandering one another if they felt their right to collect from a river had been impeded rather than move to another source like a well.[4] This is because access was a right, and frequently tied to property so it would not be surrendered lightly. River water was therefore an important resource for its physical uses, in cooking, cleaning or drinking, but it was also significant for its mechanical use as a source of water power. In this seventeenth-century plan for the design of the 'New River' (a canal to provide London with additional fresh water) we see the location of water mills on the river Coln which have been marked in the region around the canal (Figure 2.1).[5]

From the explanation, it appears that the plan was produced both to highlight the intended course of the project, as well as to emphasise that the mill owners around St Albans would either benefit, or not feel the effects of the changes in water flow.[6] In this helpfully scaled map, we see that in less than five miles of river around St Albans, there are eleven watermills. This demonstrates the level to which waterpower was being utilised by the late seventeenth century.[7] As watermill usage increased, so too did complaints surrounding them. Here we see an aspect of the change the river resource was undergoing in this period. In the sixteenth and seventeenth centuries, millers were fined when their mills disrupted the water flow upstream. We see evidence of this in the lists of accusations made by county 'water bailiffs' in charge of safe river management as well as in petitions to the House of Commons or county courts. For just one example, George Browne, Roger Price and Widow Morgan were all charged in the same Warwickshire court of April 1653 for not having water gates on their mills, causing flooding in their surrounding areas, and thereby 'great damage to the inhabitants'.[8] The penalties were severe: a seemingly standardised fine of just over two pounds was imposed upon all three, a sizeable figure for the time. As the eighteenth century dawned, central government appears to have become less concerned over these issues. In many of the petitions of the seventeenth century, issues with millers are a common feature, but by the eighteenth, their absence is shockingly apparent given the increasing number of mills on English rivers.[9] This does not mean that people stopped having issues with millers but their cessation of petitions on this issue suggests an acceptance that they will do no good. This new paradigm is demonstrated perfectly in a letter exchange from the 1710s. Landowner Edward Willes repeatedly tries to convince a Mr Fisher to engage with him over a mill with 'high Dammes' which keep overflowing into the meadow. Willes refers repeatedly to the importance of 'peace between neighbors' but is totally ignored by Fisher who simply insists he either is not aware of the problem or that it is not his to fix.[10] Where sixty years earlier Fisher would have faced a two pound fine for his actions and might well have been more amenable, there is no evidence in the letters

'Plenteous Rivers' 45

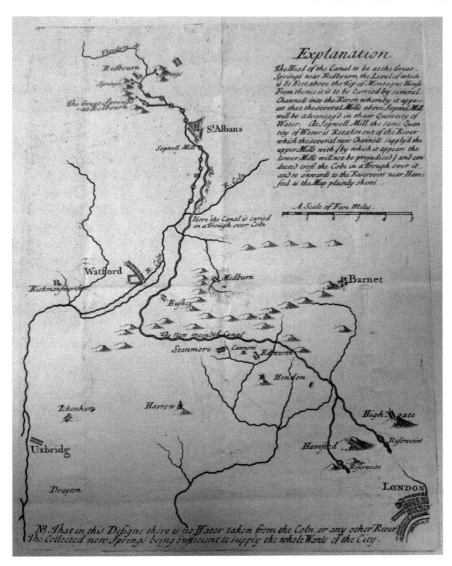

Figure 2.1 A plan and explanation of 'the New River'. Used by permission of Warwickshire County Record Office, ref. CR136/D1/91.

that he sees any reason he should change his ways and Willes's attempts to resort to the law prove futile.[11] As the economic need to demand 'energy rent' from the rivers increased, it appears that some of the older, more communal regulation of this resource fell by the wayside.

In addition to the river water's motion as a resource for energy, water flow offered another service by enabling the disposal of waste which needed to be removed from human presence quickly. In large cities like London, there seemed to be no way to dispose of the huge amount of waste produced by that many people without using the river, but the result of this by as early as 1603 was what Bruce Boehrer has called 'a discontinuous belt of fetid water so foul that even the local river life had abandoned it'.[12] Attempts had been made from the late fifteenth century on to provide for 'the conservation of the water and river of Thames' and some seventeenth-century commentators including Thomas De Laune and James Howell were eager to point out some of the measures the city had taken, commenting that 'There is a watchful eye, that no carren, or dead carkasses be thrown into the River to pollute, or infect the stream.'[13] Even when there were not so many people that an excess of human waste was the problem, various industries produced pollution too dangerous not to be disposed of and many were permitted to use the river under certain circumstances.[14] Despite the regulations however, cases of industries flouting the laws were common as seen in tracts such as Ralph Gardiner's *England's grievance discovered*, a treatise on the crimes of the Newcastle coal industry which included testimony on the 'great damages' done to the river through the 'dirt cast' into it.[15] Even if industries complied they could occasionally still be sanctioned with sufficient public outcry. A factory for processing alum in Wapping in 1626 received sufficient local complaints for both the smell of boiling urine and the pollution the factory waste was causing to the river to be suppressed by the royal council.[16] As the period progresses, however, cases in which river pollution by industry seems to be met with a sort of local acceptance appear more noticeable. In her travels around England in the reign of William and Mary, Celia Fiennes looked to taste various water sources for health reasons and, on more than one occasion, had to be warned off by locals from drinking the water of their local river or stream due to the likes of 'mine runoff'.[17] It seems that the growing proto-industry of early modernity demanded not only an increasing energy toll upon English rivers but also a greater acceptance of their waste content.

Another key resource associated with early modern rivers were the animals that lived in or around them. The most important and the most discussed of these were fish as the issue of fishing rights proved a complex aspect of English river management. Fish were a valuable commodity. A judgement case against John Coton by Westminster's Upper Bench in 1653 laid out the value of the fish Coton had 'stolen' as he trespassed on Richard Higgins's land. This shows us that, for example, ten 'fishes called Pikes' were priced at thirteen shillings and four pence, a tidy sum. Even smaller fish like roach were priced at ten shillings for two hundred.[18] Clearly, an able fisherman on a plentiful stretch of river had opportunity to make a fair wage. Due to this value, complaints about abuses of fishing rights, much like issues with mills, also appear in large numbers in both petitions and county courts documents. Through these documents, the relationship between fish extraction and the river becomes clear. In the simplest cases, some land-transfer documents make it clear that the right to fish a particular section of a river came with the ownership of the land around it. When William Shuttleworth purchased Broad Meadow in 1627, we see that the meadow comes with the 'libertie and power of fishe and fishing in the water on River called Blythe runinge by on alonge the said meadowe'.[19] When his descendant leases the meadow again forty years later, the same rights transfer again with the property.[20] Where matters were less codified or there were multiple layers to the lease, things became far more complicated. A petition of Richard Marryot in 1679 explains a very unusual and complex situation in which the Duke of Norfolk had granted fishing rights on part of his lands through Marryot to a third party but the third party's former tenants had become angry that their tenancy agreements did not extend them a portion of these rights.[21] The right to fish therefore was most frequently connected to land and its associated rights, hence the tenants felt their land commitments represented a stake in the new fishing. The significance of this separation is that it highlights how, in many cases, while landowners had the right to exploit the resources of a river this did not automatically grant a total 'ownership' over it in the same way documents did to the land around it. This is also demonstrated by the limits to these fishing rights. While landowners could fish a section of river they had right to, overfishing it, fishing it in such a manner as to prevent others downstream from doing so, or altering a river to fish it, were crimes. George Marshall of Warwick was fined over two pounds in 1653 as he 'usually doth fish with an unlawfull net called a draught net or dragg' which was destroying too many of the Avon's fish.[22] Peter Mills was fined the larger sum of six pounds at the same session for diverting the Leame into several channels or gorges that he had made in which he installed 'severall sluces' to trap fish while 'Many hundreds' of fishermen signed a petition in Worcestershire in 1613 to protest against five men upstream who were all using river-wide draught nets resulting in 'the said river being thus destroyed for fishing' and, they claimed, the threat of total starvation in the region.[23] The issue of fish and fishing was clearly a vital aspect of the early modern river.

Looking at the river as a resource begins to illuminate some of the peculiarities of the early modern river but also how things were beginning to change. Rights to river produce and river ownership could be legally distinct from one another, but often entangled in these legal rights was significant communal negotiation. Much of this communality seems to have begun to wear down by the eighteenth century with an increasing demand on rivers for energy and as disposal sites with less action taken (either intentionally or through inability) by regulatory powers. Turning to rivers as a threat will enable us to further explore this changing paradigm.

Rivers as threat

Perhaps the most apparent threat facing communities around waterways was flooding. Like many early modern disasters, floods represented the kind of newsworthy occurrence that London publishers took note of, providing us with a plethora of print on early modern floods across the country. Despite the number of these documents to survive, many of them possess a very similar quality to one another. To take one example for comparison: *A true report of certaine wonderful overflowings of waters* is an anonymously authored pamphlet from 1607, describing flooding in 'Summerset-shire, Norfolke, and other places of England'.[24] The pamphlet first reminds readers that events such as these have happened before, in this case in 1570, and makes an immediate reference to the relative weakness of this most recent flood in comparison to the previous one and how this is a sign of God's mercy. The pamphlet then proceeds to tell the story of the flood (in this case multiple floods with the Somerset flood first) including the names of specific rivers known to have flooded, the place names of key areas that are known to have been affected, and then finally, the damage done. This damage involves the destruction and damage of property ('the Foundations of the buildings being washed away'), the death of livestock ('Oxen in great numbers were caryed away with the streame') and finally several specific stories of human tragedy (in this case a man who left his children to die to save himself is the main feature).[25] Throughout this description, the language of divine providence is rich and frequently intertwined with water and flooding metaphors. 'Sinne ouerflowes our soules: the Seas of all strange impieties haue rusht in upon us: we are couered with the waues of abhomination and uncleanness: we are drowned in black puddles of hellish iniquity.'[26] This formula of event reporting in combination with the language of providential destruction in response to sin can be seen in almost all flood pamphlets of this period. William Jones's pamphlet of the same year, *Gods vvarning to his people of England*, makes clear its providential message from the title and again provides the same kind of details to support it: both factual reporting with the likes of 'Many Gentlemen, Yeomen and others had great losses of cattle' and water-based language of providence with the 'late swellings of the outrageous Waters'.[27] *Sad news from the country* came some seventy years later in 1674 and yet still we see that the waters were 'bearing away Bridges and Cattel' and can only be 'stopt for the future by Floods of Repentant Tears'.[28]

The strength of this association between God and disaster has not escaped the notice of historians and in her work on religion and the landscape Alexandra Walsham makes clear this link between disaster and the calls within pamphlets like these to reflect on the situation in broader English society that might be responsible for it. Was the 'Great and Lamentable flood' of the 1650s, for example, a judgement from God upon the actions of Oliver Cromwell?[29] Walsham also notes that inherent popular awareness of the biblical 'Great Flood' played into many of these depictions.[30] Indeed, within the pamphlets already listed we see such references with William Jones reminding readers at the end of his tract that, 'had it not binne for the mercyfull promise of God, at the last dissolution of the World, by Water, by the signe of the Rainbowe', humanity would have already been destroyed in this manner. The millenarianism of the period after the Reformation appears to be a major factor here and, in a world that seemed at such odds with itself, disasters like these could only herald the coming end of days.

While it is clear that this early modern print material on flooding presents us with a distinctly apocalyptic and providential viewpoint, some historians of this topic have rightly suggested that this source does not represent the totality of early modern views on the subject. John Morgan in his extensive work on flooding and flood management in early modern England has demonstrated that providential flooding narratives such as these, while useful, actually represent a very specific point of view. Morgan points out that flooding pamphlets are an example of a 'public, commercial genre'.[31] The reason the narrative in so many of these pamphlets seems to be so similar is because this is what sells. Furthermore, London authors and printers often had other agendas beyond simply reporting saleable news. Morgan also points out that, for all events such as these, public discussion tends to focus on 'exhortation and blame', perhaps explaining why, in addition to fitting an expected narrative, so many of these documents needed to find an explanation for these disasters, and to fit that into the public politics of the time. To contrast this view, Morgan examines an account of the flood produced in a local community, not intended for mass publication and for primarily local reflection upon recent events. He finds that, while 'occasionally' local records of this kind do entertain providential narratives similar to print, they are generally much smaller in scope.[32] Where the print focuses on the flood of Genesis, community narratives focus on local memories of flooding; rather than widespread destruction and death the concern is with bonds of kin and damage to local landmarks and, perhaps most significantly, localised records such as commissions of sewers show a far greater concern for, and understanding of, the human relationship to, and impact on, 'hydrologic systems'.[33] Flood management, Morgan shows, was something that those who lived near rivers were inherently very aware of, and the aftermath of disasters such as these was often concerned with what had gone wrong and what could be improved.[34]

Morgan's analysis suggests a more nuanced view of flooding in which the response of local communities cannot accurately be judged from the readily available print literature produced in the wake of floods, much of which took a very providential view of disaster (specifically, print that claimed floods and similar events represented a punishment from God for recent sins of either the local populace, or the kingdom at large). Local accounts of other floods seem to support many of his conclusions. A narrative of a flood of 1588 written into the back of a parish register for St Peter's, Welford-on Avon seems concerned, as Morgan suggests, with the local memory of the event rather than with some providential judgement being levelled upon the parishioners.[35] The parish priest compared the height of the flood waters 'a yard and a half and something more' to something he remembered 'viii years past'. There are concerns over local issues, a woman almost drowned and a mill damaged and even some of the more practical issues that Morgan saw in his commissions of sewer records, such as a bridge that has been damaged and must be repaired.[36] The threat of flooding demonstrates how rivers could be seen differently on the local and national level. For both, flooding was a serious concern, but on a national level the river was a sensationalised weapon of God's judgement acting upon an unworthy people. To those that lived near them, in contrast, rivers represented a threat to be managed and a flood was a far more complicated, and indeed more locally tragic, event than the sensational press surrounding it might suggest.

While floods represented perhaps the most extreme danger of a river's presence, it is worth noting that the presence of a body of water did inherently enable death by drowning, both accidental and intentional. Early modern drowning is a subject on which only limited work has been done, and often quite tangentially, but it is clear from both the existing literature and references to it in early modern works that this was an understood and relatively sizeable threat. In his work on accidental death in London, Craig Spence notes that, while deaths in fires dominate the publicised accidents of the period, drowning was by far the most common accidental fate to befall citizens of the capital in actual mortality records. Just under half of all sudden deaths reported were drownings, and Spence suggests this frequency led to drowning being seen as 'nothing out of the ordinary' and unworthy of print space compared to more unusual accidents like fires.[37] The appearance of a drowned body was unpleasant, as a particular graphic description by early modern physician Alexander Read illustrates:

> ... an unusual swelling and flabbiness of the whole Body cannot be hid; the Belly also will swell; some mucous Excrements will come out of the Nose, and froathy stuff out at the Mouth; the Fingers ends are worn: for they that are drowned, endeavour to get out, and scrabble in the Sand, and so wear their Fingers.[38]

The horror of the drowned body was clearly a culturally understood aspect of the fate. In *The Merry Wives of Windsor*, Falstaff comments on it specifically, joking 'I had been drowned, but that the shore was shelvy and shallow, – a death I abhor; for the water swells a man; and what a thing should I have been when I had been swelled! I should have been a mountain of mummy.'[39]

Death by drowning was also not a danger exclusive to London or other urban centres. While more work must be done on non-urban drowning, Josephine Billingham in her work on infanticide does demonstrate that this was still a serious problem in rural settings. From her investigation of Sussex inquests, she states that 'drowning was common' and that 'around a third of the accidental deaths of young people and infants which are recorded in the inquests were caused by water'.[40] If Billingham had been interested in older adults as well, one could imagine her numbers would be relatively close to Spence's. Drowning therefore was an ever-present threat in early modern life, particularly for those who lived near waterways. This threat adds another layer to the image of the early modern river, a source of life, of food and of new industry that could be managed in times of crisis but also something to which every riverside community in England would likely lose members on a yearly basis. With this duality in mind, we move to examine the relationship more specifically between communities and their waterways.

River and community

This section will look to expand upon some of the elements of community that have already appeared in many of the sources examined in the first two sections. For many waterside communities, rivers had value and meaning beyond their usable resources or inherent dangers. In her groundbreaking work on how the early modern environment structured the everyday lives of those who lived within it, Nicola Whyte notes that rivers, along with roads and crossroads, were a key feature in the construction of a community space. Parish rituals like the 'beating of the bounds' integrated these elements and 'helped structure and gave spiritual context to the ordinary aspects of everyday life'. The parish community and the environment it consisted of were made one and the landscape 'structured people's cognitive maps' of who they were as individuals and community.[41] This allowed communities not only to define themselves in the present, but to connect to a shared past as they walked the same paths along the same riverbanks that their parents and grandparents had. The river was an important part of a parish's history. We see elements of these ideas reflected in the language of some of the kinds of sources already examined. The charges by county governments against those who disrupted the flow of the rivers, for example, were framed in terms of community disruption both through breach of the peace but also through the disturbance of an ancient order. The actions of innholder Richard Swame of Anstey in 1653 were criminal both because he had disturbed the 'water mills belonging to the major Aldermen and citizens' of Coventry but also because he had 'turned part of the river of Shirburne . . . out of the ancient channel and current'.[42] This emphasis on the violation done to the river's 'ancient' course illustrates some of the history that waterways were imbued with. The same element was present in the charge against Peter Mills for his sluicing of fish, that he had turned the Leame out of 'the ancient channel' and was also being mobilised by numerous petitioners looking for parliamentary support against those they saw as taking unjust action against their waterways.[43]

Beyond a communal connection to a river through parish rituals, the river site itself could also serve as a location for more active community creation. In his work on London, Mark Jenner discusses 'conduits', the large, manmade water sources that served a large number of London inhabitants. Jenner makes the compelling argument that the conduit site, much like the market site in the work of E. P. Thompson, involved a 'moral economy' in which morality was regulated and community bonds created and reinforced.[44] This model cannot be simply transplanted to the local river for a number of reasons. Alternative water sources to the river mean that the presence of a 'critical mass' of local inhabitants at the riverside would be unlikely, and the river's physical size and scope mean that unlike the conduit or the market, there would be no obvious need to crowd around a single area. With that said, there are parallels we can draw between the two scenarios. Riverbanks are not uniform, meaning that access to the waterway would likely be somewhat limited to a number of sites at which access was safest or easiest – shallows without a sharp drop between bank and river for example. This would facilitate some community interaction. On this matter, Kathleen Brown in her work on cleanliness identifies the growth of river bathing in the eighteenth century, a relatively risky activity and one that would likely have only been conducted in specific, safe areas of the river. She also discusses a 1744 cleanliness act which required each citizen to clean the dirt from their house and dispose of it in 'the river or some other convenient place' every Friday.[45] These two examples demonstrate the capacity for riverside meetings at both spatially and chronologically specific sites. Individuals could meet one another at the river when heading to the same spot to bathe, or when cleaning their house out at the mandated time of day. Further support for this idea is provided through the work Brown and others have done on laundry. The need for fresh water and to dispose of dirty water quickly meant that the most efficient place to wash clothes was at a water source like a river. Brown suggests that many women preferred to bring kettles of water into the home due to the potential risks of being away for an extended period, but she also notes that new laws for cleanliness increasingly cracked down on this practice which resulted in dirty water being dumped out of the window and into the streets.[46] Additionally, the work that historians such as Laura Gowing have done on female servants demonstrates that while women could find themselves in danger outside the home, they still ventured out as part of their labours.[47] All of these aspects support the concept that community members could meet up at the river side in the course of their daily business, and while the case for a moral economy of the riverside is not as clear cut as Jenner's case for the conduit, it seems fair to argue that, at least for those near the river, some aspect of community creation and maintenance was performed here.

Despite the significance of river sites in the shaping of community spatial and social relations, there is also evidence here that, in a similar manner to the river's status as a resource, these aspects too were changing as the period progressed. In a petition to Parliament in 1679, Sir Nicholas Stoughton laid out a story that illuminates this change. Stoughton claimed that his family had held milling rights on the river Wye near Guildford but that he had been stripped of these by the 'pretended parliament' of the Commonwealth government in 1651. In the years since, Stoughton describes a tyrannical new rule over the river by one James Piston, setting enormous limitations on what he and others were allowed to do with the waters. Most significantly, he complains that from 25 December, Parliament had declared the river a 'private river' and made legal Piston's 'cutting of any bancks or locks' and general 'hindering' of the river.[48] This seems to be a far cry from the 'ancient channels' of the water bailiff's court, and represents a changing attitude to rivers as part of the natural world. No longer was the river to be preserved in its ancient manner, instead it was to be 'improved' to increase its economic capacity. In 1696, Parliament was in the process of passing a bill to make the rivers of the Wye and Lugg 'navigable or portable'. The idea was that making a river more navigable to boats meant increased trade, though this often-involved major works like dredging the river or cutting away sections of the bank. This particular bill produced a number of petitions for and against from both urban and rural communities. What is striking in these petitions is what is absent from all of them. Regardless of whether the petitioners are arguing for or against the change, all argue in economic terms.[49] The idea of using the concept of an 'ancient river' to defend against these plans, it seems, will no longer stand against the tide of change. Even those rural petitioners of Saint Briavels who seem the most upset of any group at the idea of physically altering the river implore against the change by suggesting that the 'tilladge' on the banks being removed will cause great impoverishment to their agriculture.[50] It is impossible to know if this group still saw the river as an 'ancient' and important part of their communities in need of protection and merely adopted the language of economics, or if the physical river mattered far less to them by this point and the monetary losses were their greatest concern. Regardless, it seems clear that, as the period progressed, similarly to how central government no longer appears interested in regulating the 'unneighbourly' violations of those utilising the river, the concept that rivers were important to communities and should be preserved for this reason alone also no longer held weight.

This chapter has sought to tease out some of the complexities of the relationship between people and the river in early modern England and how this was beginning to change. Rivers were of major importance for both economic and social reasons to the communities around them, and subject to major regulation from central government for a large portion of the early modern period. They also represented an ever-present threat at the heart of the community, both on the macro level with flooding and on the micro level with individual accidental death. They therefore occupied an unusual and rather unique space in the communities that surrounded them, a natural feature in a constant state of negotiation, exploitation, preservation and management.

As time progressed, however, a change began to appear in how English people saw their rivers. The external forces of economics and proto-industry forced rivers to bear new and increasingly heavy burdens under which older systems of regulation no longer seemed sufficient. These burdens included making physical alterations to rivers themselves, both to extend their economic benefit and, at times, to better protect the community against dangers like floods. As this became more accepted, aspects of the 'ancient river' as a fundamental part of the landscape upon which communities had constructed themselves through generational memory was lost. In its place came arguments for and against 'progress' and 'economic benefit', but no longer was the preservation of a waterway simply for its own sake a concept with much weight.

This chapter has focused on a change in attitudes to the river as it emerges from a wide variety of primary sources in order to sketch conceptions of rivers in everyday early modern understandings. Through their petitions, legal records and travel logs, this chapter has explored people's changing experience of the early modern waterway. In later chapters of this volume, a great many of the themes discussed here will reappear in a variety of texts and contexts, highlighting the relevance of this change in attitudes and experience to how early modern people wrote about rivers. In Chapter 10, for example, Emily J. Naish explores the literary side of rivers as exploited resources, contrasting a similar dichotomy to this chapter of idealised space versus the imperfect realities of these waterways.[51] Similarly, Esther Water in Chapter 11 explores the large-scale draining of early modern English fenland and narratives of resource improvement therein, as well as those who stood against such changes.[52] Shifting physical realities both inform and are informed by literary discussions of the same subjects, hence the significance of the insight to be gained by reading the river through multiple source bases across this volume. This chapter therefore suggests that its conclusions are to be read in tandem with many of those from the rest of this volume exploring the subject from a more literary dimension.

In 1797, Edward Hasted published *The History and topographical survey of the county of Kent*. The work spans multiple volumes, each around six hundred pages, and includes the history of the county as well as information on the geography and people as well as the 'present state of it, civil and ecclesiastical'.[53] Like many similar surveys (Hasted's own preface describes Kent as perhaps the county in England to have received 'a greater share of attention than any other in the Kingdom' in similar descriptions), the relationship to the subject is positive, describing the 'valor and intrepidity' of 'the Kentishmen' as well as the great beauty of the county generally.[54] It also describes the county's rivers, and within this description, underneath the general veneer of beautiful, ancient countryside that permeates Hasted's words, we can see that the waterways are perhaps not as well off as they once were. 'The river Medway is plentifully stored with fish', Halsted states, though he quickly notes that 'about once a year there is a salmon caught . . . there were formerly great numbers of this fish in the Medway.'[55] Similarly, 'Sturgeon, in former times, used to be so exceedingly plenty in this river . . . but there has been hardly any fish of this kind in the river for many years, which is imputed to the largeness and frequency of the men of war in it, which, disturbing the fish, have driven them from it.'[56] The smaller rivers faced even more obvious issues. Halsted describes the course of the River Darent nicely enough, injecting pleasant details as 'it continues its course, and so goes on to Eynsford, where it runs by the old castle there on to Faringham', and eventually it 'empties itself into the Thames'.[57] Still, we see that along the way there are changes to this 'old river' which now 'supplies a gunpowder manufactory' and later 'supplies the iron-mill'.[58] These changes have taken their toll:

> The Darent, or Darford-creek, as it is called, below Darford town, is navigable for small boats . . . though not at all tides, the channel being of late years much choaked up with sulliage &c. which drives into it, as it is said, from the above manufactory, insomuch, that it is feared this navigation, so useful to this town and neighbourhood, will be by this means, before many years are elapsed, entirely destroyed.[59]

By Halsted's time, the altered attitudes toward the river in early modern society, and the broader shift in the viewpoints of early modern people that this chapter has highlighted had made noticeable and frequently permanent changes to England's waterways, changes we are often still fighting to undo. There is more work to be done on these shifting attitudes to the English river, and perhaps with a sufficiently long study, one could attempt to better understand how we reached our present situation of habitat collapse and pollution. As Hasted demonstrates though, whatever the course we took, the seeds of that future were most certainly planted in early modernity.

Notes

1. James Brome, *An historical account of Mr. Roger's three years travels over England and Wales* . . . (London: J. Moxon and B. Beardwell, 1694). Brome writes up the travel accounts of Mr R. Rogers, which talk about many rivers in friendly terms: the 'Noble River *Thames*', 'a very good River, called *Newbury* River', 'gentle Rivers', 'murmuring Rivers' and

'a pretty River' to name but a few. This is not universal praise (a river in Dorset is 'neither very large nor beautiful, being much decayed'), but he is more positive about the majority of rivers than negative (see 3, 6, 55, 69, 49, 41). J. Childrey, *Britannia Baconica: or, The natural rarities of England, Scotland, & Wales* (London: Printed for the author, 1662) is very similar with 'fresh Rivers' and the 'goodly River of *Thames*' (see 17, 89). Both works were written by Londoners who made special note of the Thames as a 'goodly' and 'Noble' River. Samuel Pepys also spoke favourably of the Thames, particularly in how it had been damaged and it would be 'better for the River' if actions were taken to repair it. He also noted that it was a 'sad sight' to see the river with 'no houses nor church near it', highlighting this idea of local comfort. Pepys is comforted by a Thames surrounded by buildings as others would be comforted by their own local waterways which might be far less busy. Samuel Pepys, *The Diary of Samuel Pepys* (1660–1669), https://www.pepysdiary.com/diary/ (last accessed 21 September 2023). Entries for Wed. 3 July 1667 and Thu. 6 September 1666 are of note here.

2. London's 'New River' would be a prime example here which today we would describe as a canal.
3. William Harrison, *Description of England* (1577) part of Holinshed's *Chronicles*, https://sourcebooks.fordham.edu/mod/1577harrison-england.asp (last accessed 21 September 2023). Harrison is particularly concerned with the quality of water for brewing and explains that rivers that 'run by clalk or cledgy soil be good', though the Thames was the best. Tobias Venner, *Via recta ad vitam longam, or A plaine philosophical discourse of the nature, faculties, and effects, of all such things ...* (London: Edward Griffin for Richard Moore, 1620), 9. Venner famously tried to provide medical information to the average person with a plainly written style. He rates spring water first, then rainwater, then rivers. Thomas Tryon, *A discourse of waters* (London: T. Sowle, 1696), 7–21. Tryon was obsessed with the importance of drinking water as a health cure. He rated rainwater first, then rivers, then springs.
4. Mark Jenner, 'From Conduit Community to Commercial Network? Water in London: 1550–1725', in *Londinopolis: Essays in the Cultural and Social History of Early Modern London*, ed. Paul Griffiths and Mark S. R. Jenner (Manchester: Manchester University Press, 2000), 250.
5. 'Plan and explanation of the New River design', Warwickshire County Record Office, CR0136/D1/91.
6. It is significant to mention that this is not the route that the New River followed upon its completion in 1613. The plan is undated, so could be an example of either an alternative route option, or a possible plan for expansion. Regardless of why it was created, the plan clearly wants to portray this construction as only positive for mill owners.
7. On watermill increase generally see Stefania Barca, *Enclosing Water: Nature and Political Economy in a Mediterranean Valley, 1796–1916* (Cambridge: The White Horse Press, 2010), particularly 27. Barca is looking at Italy where they eloquently frame the idea of increasing water mill numbers with the rise of proto-industry under the term 'energy rent' and the increasing 'energy rent' demand on rivers.

8. Writ from Oliver, the Lord Protector to the Sheriff of Warwickshire ordering the collection of various fines (1653) Warwickshire County Record Office, CR4141/4/16.
9. Some examples of seventeenth-century petitions on this issue would be a Petition to the House of Lords: 1661, HL/PO/JO/10/1/303 in which Freeholders complain about 'malicious persons' who have dammed the river for profit. Petition to the House of Lords: 1679, HL/PO/JO/10/1/286/141. An extensive petition in which various issues with a river and the millers upon it over some twenty years are expounded. By contrast, from the eighteenth-century petitions there are no mentions of mills whatsoever. Again on the increasing number of mills refer to the concepts in Barca, *Enclosing Water*.
10. Correspondence concerning a water mill in Leamington Priors (1714–18). Warwickshire County Record Office, CR4141/5/290/1-6. Willes eventually contacts a lawyer but seems to have no luck convincing Fisher who insists that what he does on his own property is his business.
11. Ibid. CR4141/5/290/6.
12. Bruce Boehrer, *Environmental Degradation in Jacobean Drama* (Cambridge: Cambridge University Press, 2013), 18.
13. Boehrer, *Environmental Degradation*, 19. James Howell, *Londinopolis an historicall discourse or perlustration of the city of London* (London: J. Streater, 1657), 14; Thomas De Laune, *The present state of London: or, Memorials comprehending a full and succinct account* (London: George Larkin, 1681), 199. Both comment on the same measure.
14. Both Howell and De Laune for example discuss that serious measures have been taken in the western part of the river due to the fact that anything done here would flow downstream to the rest of the city.
15. Ralph Gardiner, *Englands grievance discovered, in relation to the coal-trade with the map* (London: R. Ibbitson, 1655), 103.
16. Boehrer, *Environmental Degradation*, 131.
17. This happened to Fiennes multiple times but for one example from Derbyshire in 1697 see Celia Fiennes, *Through England on a side saddle in the Time of William and Mary*, https://www.visionofbritain.org.uk/travellers/Fiennes/14 (last accessed 15 August 2022).
18. Exemplification of judgement in favour of Richard Higgins against John Coton, Warwickshire County Record Office, CR2981/4/2/39.
19. Documents concerning Broad Meadow with the fish and fishing (1627). Warwickshire County Record Office, CR121/62/1.
20. Documents concerning Broad Meadow with the fish and fishing (1668). Warwickshire County Record Office, CR121/62/3.
21. Petitions to the House of Lords: 1679, HL/PO/JO/10/1/385/109. The situation was made all the more complex by the Duke of Norfolk not being in the country and the disgruntled tenants choosing to arrest their former landlord rather than continue to argue with him.
22. Writ from Oliver (1653) Warwickshire County Record Office, CR4141/4/16.
23. Writ from Oliver (1653) Warwickshire County Record Office, CR4141/4/16; Worcestershire Quarter Sessions: 1613, Many hundreds of fishermen of Worcestershire and Shropshire. Ref. 110 BA1/1/21/74. The river in question was the Severn and the petitioners claimed they were taking out sixty salmon and turning the rest back, resulting in the issue.

24. Anonymous, *A true report of certaine wonderful ouerflowings of waters* (London: William Laggard, 1607), 1.
25. Anonymous, *1607 A true report*, 1–7.
26. Ibid., 4.
27. William Jones of Usk, *Gods vvarning to his people of England By the great ouer-flowing of the vvaters* (London: R. Blower, 1607), 4–6.
28. Anonymous, *Sad news from the countrey, or, A true and full relation of the late wonderful* (London: s.n, 1674), 3–8.
29. Alexandra Walsham, *The Reformation of the Landscape: Religion, Identity & Memory in Early Modern Britain & Ireland* (Oxford: Oxford University Press, 2011), 345–6.
30. Ibid.
31. John Emrys Morgan, 'Understanding flooding in early modern England', *Journal of Historical Geography*, Vol. 50 (2015), 3.
32. Ibid., 23.
33. Ibid., 18–26.
34. Ibid., 24–8.
35. Register of baptisms, 1561–1687; Register of marriages, 1561–1689; Register of burials, 1561–1687, Parish of St Peter, Welford-on-Avon, Warwickshire County Record Office, DR0892/1. The description is on the very last page.
36. Ibid.
37. Craig Spence, *Accidents and Violent Death in Early Modern London 1650–1750* (Woodbridge: The Boydell Press, 2016), 78–9.
38. Alexander Read, *Chirurgorum comes, or The whole practice of chirurgery* (London: Edw. Jones, 1687), 437–8.
39. *The Merry Wives of Windsor* (3.5.5).
40. Josephine Billingham, *Infanticide in Tudor and Stuart England* (Amsterdam: Amsterdam University Press, 2019), 87–8.
41. Nicola Whyte, *Inhabiting the Landscape: Place, Custom and Memory, 1500–1800* (Barnsley: Windgather Press, 2009), 65.
42. Writ from Oliver (1653) Warwickshire County Record Office, CR4141/4/16.
43. Writ from Oliver (1653) Warwickshire County Record Office, CR4141/4/16; Anonymous, *A brief remembrance when the report concerning the pretended ryot* (London: s.n, 1653), 2. This is one example in which petitioners complain, amongst other things that the course 'of an ancient Navigable River called Idle' has been diverted.
44. Jenner, 'From Conduit Community to Commercial Network?', 254.
45. Kathleen Brown, *Foul Bodies: Cleanliness in Early America* (New Haven, CT: Yale University Press, 2009), 41, 124. The book does turn to America, but its early sections establish the existing English and British practices.
46. Brown, *Foul Bodies*, 62.
47. Laura Gowing, *Domestic Dangers: Women, Words and Sex in Early Modern London* (Oxford: Clarendon Press, 1998), 21. Gowing shows that most women displayed through testimony a knowledge of their local area and would leave the house for a destination within that area relatively frequently. Trips further afield were rarer.
48. Petition to the House of Lords: 1679, HL/PO/JO/10/1/386/141.

49. Petition to the House of Lords: 1696, HL/PO/JO/10/1/482/1017. There are four petitions in this set.
50. Ibid.
51. Emily J. Naish, '"Insatiable [Gourmandize] Thus All Things Doth Devour": Reading the Threat of Human Greed along the Rivers of Early Modern England', chapter 10 herein.
52. Esther Water, 'Powtes, Protest and (Eco)politics in the English Fens', chapter 11 herein.
53. Edward Hasted, *The history and topographical survey of the county of Kent. Containing the antient and present state of it, civil and ecclesiastical; Collected From Public Records, And Other Authorities*, vol. 1 (Canterbury: W. Bristow, 1797).
54. Ibid., v for the preface, 2.
55. Ibid., 218.
56. Ibid.
57. Ibid., 284.
58. Ibid.
59. Ibid.

Chapter 3

Rivers and Contested Territories in the Works of Shakespeare
Rebecca Welshman

As natural boundaries, which afforded strategic advantage, rivers have been sites of conflict since at least the Bronze Age.[1] Rivers featured in a number of battles during the medieval period, such as Otterburn in 1388, set beside the River Rede, Boroughbridge (1322) and the Battle of Stirling Bridge in 1297 on the River Forth. Riverside battlefield sites continued to be used into the early modern period at Shrewsbury (1403), Tewkesbury (1471) – when the Yorkists hemmed in the Lancastrians between the rivers Severn, Avon and Swilgate – and Culloden (1746), the last pitched battle fought in Britain. Conflicts often took place near rivers because they marked the edge of a contested territory and were natural borderlands.[2] In some cases, a river crossing could itself become the field of battle, as was the case at Boroughbridge where forces fought for control over a narrow bridge and ford where the Great North Road crossed the River Ure.

Due to their prominence in historical texts, in the popular imagination and local folk memory, such sites naturally attracted the attention of writers who explored their potential as dramatic settings. According to Charles Edelman, the military action and imagery in Shakespeare's plays and poems convey an 'extraordinarily detailed knowledge of warfare, both ancient and modern'.[3] Writing in 1859, William J. Thoms concluded that the detailed knowledge of military affairs in Shakespeare's works, particularly in *Troilus and Cressida*, indicated that the poet had served in the military.[4] While Fortescue, writing in 1916, observed that in *Othello* Shakespeare confused military ranks, Draper later concluded that it was the 'psychology' and 'human' aspects of military life not the 'institutional' that mattered to him.[5] Others have since argued that the detail of Shakespeare's military knowledge can only be explained by his own experience of the army at the rank of soldier,[6] while it has also been suggested that Shakespeare simply drew his knowledge from the plethora of military books published during the age.[7]

Yet whether or not Shakespeare was writing from experience, these military aspects have rarely, if ever, been discussed in the context of the real or figurative riverside settings in his works. This chapter thus explores how Shakespeare's use of rivers as settings was informed by his awareness of the military significance of riverside battlefield sites in London, Tewkesbury and Shrewsbury, and expressed through his depiction of prominent noblemen of different historical time periods. As discussed by Dong Ha Seo, military culture was not imposed upon Elizabethan society by military institutions, but by the elite, who took the lead in military fashion and contributed to formal and ceremonial occasions, with leading nobles essentially shaping the military culture of the time.[8] I consider the textured meanings and military associations of certain terms used by Shakespeare in riverine settings which had been absorbed into the language of the time through the influence of military culture. In his implicit recognition of riverside sites as theatres of war, Shakespeare reimagined these locations as gendered sites of conflict – arenas in which to revisit past political and social tensions in ways which passed commentary on contemporary states of affairs, including the tensions between crown and community, and the Elizabethan system of government.

While primarily focusing on works that involve the theme of rebellion, the essay also discusses the significance of military and riverine associations in *The Rape of Lucrece* and *The Merry Wives of Windsor*. I will consider how these associations are worked into imaginative landscapes – such as the 'turrets' of the body in *The Rape of Lucrece* – in order to create a conflict setting where the body becomes a contested territory. I draw attention to the military significance of imagery used in association with rivers as sites of contest – to include, for example, Hotspur's use of the half-moon image in *Henry IV* when he plans to manipulate the course of the River Trent. The body again becomes a site of conflict in *The Merry Wives of Windsor* when Falstaff, a knight, receives his comeuppance at the hands of two married women beside the Thames in Windsor Great Park. Into this riverside setting, where Falstaff is carried in a basket of dirty laundry to Datchet Mead, Shakespeare incorporates a landmark oak tree, known as the Herne (or Horne) Oak. In the landscape sites of battle were often located by a landmark such as a stone or oak, with oaks in particular bearing legendary stories attached to them. As the wood of warships, oak was a symbol of resilience; an association still present today in the Royal Navy's march 'the Heart of Oak'. In light of the royal associations of great oaks, some of which were named after kings or queens of England, I suggest that Shakespeare deliberately imbued the Herne Oak scene with courtly and military qualities.

Historically, Britain's rivers have been subject to erratic tidal activity and notoriously difficult to defend, making them vulnerable points of entry into the country. Saxon shore forts along Britain's coastlines date from the Roman period when the coastlines came under regular attack by Saxons and Franks. Along the Thames, where Renaissance theatre flourished in the mid-to-late sixteenth century, sites commemorated pivotal conflicts that prefigured the birth of the Elizabethan period. At Brentford, Edmund Ironside, King of England in 1016, defeated Cnut and the Danes, driving them across the Thames. London Bridge marked the site of the pivotal skirmish in Jack Cade's Kentish rebellion of 1450 against the government of Henry VI, where several hundred people lost their lives. This uprising, which threatened royal authority, ultimately led to the Wars of the Roses (1455–85) between the houses of York and Lancaster. These landmarks would have been permanent reminders to visitors and travellers of the roles that rivers played in shaping the contemporary world, and for playwrights, looking for material, furnished the literary imagination with new possibilities for dramatic settings. River settings as theatres of war were marked in the imagination not only by physical monuments, but by the historical sources used in the writing of dramatic texts. The 1587 edition of Raphael Holinshed's *Chronicles*, for example, a source employed by Shakespeare, draws upon the *Anglo-Saxon Chronicle* in the account of Alfred's strategic move against the Danes on the River Lea when freshly dug channels drained the Lea into the Thames, leaving the Danes' ships stranded and forcing them to flee.[9] The same Saxon chronicle alludes to Brentford where Ironside achieved his victory, and his later fording of the Thames at low water, which gained him significant advantage over the enemy in Kent. The Thames ran through the lives and workplaces of poets, playwrights and publishers alike, and offered an ever-present living metaphor familiar to audiences and readers. As noted by Brian Campbell, rivers have long attracted the attention of writers 'who used their continuous movement, sound, and power as illustrations and similes, as a context for philosophical speculation on the human condition'.[10] Plays for the royal court were enacted at 'Avon', an old name for Hampton Court meaning 'river', on the banks of the Thames.[11] The office of Richard Field, who published Shakespeare's first-known publication *Venus and Adonis*, was only a few doors away from Blackfriars, London's first indoor playhouse, also on Bankside. Poets of the era, including Edmund Spenser, Michael Drayton and Shakespeare, who lived in the vicinity of the Thames, celebrated its royal associations in their works and regularly used it as a form of transport.[12]

In Shakespeare's history plays rivers often feature as sites of contest. The events of *History of Henry VI* recall the insurrection of Jack Cade and his 5,000 followers in 1450 in which London Bridge played a central part. After two days of executions, looting and drinking, a battle between Cade's men and defenders of London took place on the bridge from 10 p.m. until the morning of the next day, which resulted in Cade's band being unable to cross, the bridge chains being drawn and the gateway bolted. Following a brief truce, more rebels joined him from Essex.[13] In *Henry VI*, Part Two, Cade instructs his men to 'first, go / and set London bridge on fire; and, if you can, burn / down the Tower too' (4.6.13–15), two of the most iconic structures of London, symbolic of the transport system, commerce and the law.[14] Within this riverside setting Shakespeare integrates the ancient monument known as the London Stone, situated a few hundred metres from the Thames, which gave its name to a former historic area of the city.[15] London Stone was a civic meeting point and a 'symbolic instrument of dispensing power'[16] – a tradition that Shakespeare recalls when Cade strikes his sword upon the stone and declares himself lord, as was custom for a new Mayor of London.

With Cade's rebellion having underscored key weaknesses in the court of Henry VI, paving the way for future resistance movements, the rivers Thames and Severn became theatres of war when the houses of York and Lancaster, both descended from King Edward III, began their thirty-year struggle for power in 1455.[17] King Edward IV's restoration in 1471 marked the end of the wars when the Lancastrians were defeated at Barnet, followed by a further battle between the armies a month later at Tewkesbury where Edward IV and his army decisively defeated the House of Lancaster. The Lancastrians had marched swiftly to reach the crossing of the Severn at Tewkesbury, where their leader Somerset deployed his army near the Abbey and Swilgate River. This was his preferred choice, rather than be attacked while making the difficult river crossing. When Edward deployed his army to the south, fleeing Lancastrians who made for the Severn were cut down before they got there in the adjacent water meadow, known today as Bloody Meadow.

In *Richard II*, the first in a series of plays that chronicles the rise of the house of Lancaster, the river becomes a metaphor for civil unrest and imminent rebellion. Known as the 'deposition play', a performance of *Richard II* may have been ordered by the Essex faction on the eve of the Essex rebellion in 1600.[18] In his warning to the King, Sir Stephen Scroop compares the swelling uprising under Bolingbroke, in which 'both young and old rebel' to 'an unseasonable stormy day':

> Which makes the silver rivers drown their shores,
> As if the world were all dissolved to tears,
> So high above his limits swells the rage
> Of Bolingbroke, covering your fearful land.[19] (3.2.106–19)

The image of land being flooded by a rising river, and associated power struggles, is returned to in *Henry IV* in which an organised rebellion is framed – in geographical terms – by the rivers Trent and Severn. In a discussion over a map between land-owners Mortimer, Worcester and Glendower, Hotspur believes he has the least prosperous share of the land. He thus suggests, upon their successful uprising, that they divide their spoils of land according to the natural boundaries of the Trent and Severn – two rivers that become pivotal to the events of the Battle of Shrewsbury:

> Methinks my moiety, north from Burton here,
> In quantity equals not one of yours:
> See how this river comes me cranking in,
> And cuts me from the best of all my land
> A huge half-moon, a monstrous cantle out.
> I'll have the current in this place damm'd up;
> And here the smug and silver Trent shall run
> In a new channel, fair and evenly;
> It shall not wind with such a deep indent,
> To rob me of so rich a bottom here.[20] (3.1.94–103)

Mortimer and Worcester agree that 'a little charge' to the Trent to make it 'run straight and even' would benefit them all.[21] However, their plan to redirect the Trent north of Burton, so confidently proposed here, is nullified when news of their rebellion reaches the King at Burton-on-Trent, while he was marching his army north to support the Percys against the Scots. Upon hearing the news Henry immediately changes direction westwards for Shrewsbury and arrives before the Percys can take hold of Shrewsbury. Hotspur's plan to manipulate the Trent – to change its course and maximise his opportunity – again seems foolish in the later battle scenes when he finds himself on the wrong side of the Severn to gain support from his Welsh allies, and the river's presence ultimately leads to his demise.

Hotspur's reference to the 'half-moon' shape cut out of his proposed share of the lands by the river is worthy of further consideration. Godwyn, summarising the work of Johannes Rosinus (1550–1626),[22] noted that half-moon–shaped clasps on Roman shoes were a token of nobility, given that only senators were allowed to wear that kind of shoe, with the half-moon resembling the Roman 'C' signifying a hundred, and possibly a hundred senators.[23] Alternatively, the mooned clasp 'put them in minde that the honour to which they had attained, was mutable and variable as the moon'.[24] These *lunaticalcei* were not only tokens of nobility at Rome, but in other places too.[25] According to John Cruso, who collected his material from the Italian general Giorgio Basta (1550–1607), and other authors, the lunarie was a term for a wedge of cavalry, one of four forms of ordering the cavalry in battle.[26] In *Pharsalia*, which depicts a 'universal struggle between Caesarism and liberty',[27] the Roman military poet Lucan refers to the half moon formation of Caesar's fleet:

> The horns of Cesar's fleet Gallies that bore . . .
> Liburnian Gallies with two Oars content.
> Conjoyn'd in form of an half Moon they went.[28]

In *Edward III*, considered by some to have been part-authored by Shakespeare, the 'proud armado of King Edward's ships' sail in Medina Sidonia's crescent formation of 31 July 1588: 'Majestical the order of their course / figuring the horned circle of the moon' (3.1.71–2),[29] which is taken by Edelman as a veiled allusion to the Spanish Armada, 'disguised' in the play as the Battle of Sluys.[30]

Hotspur's use of 'cantle', in the context of the River Trent, is another term with wider military connotations, and one that was employed by contemporary poets of the time. The word originates from the medieval Latin *cantellus* (descended from 'cant'), meaning 'corner', 'piece' or 'fragment', and was used by several other poets in a military context. The English translation of Italian poet Torquato Tasso's *Godfrey of Bulloigne: Or, The Recovery of Jerusalem* (1581), depicts large fragments of armour falling to the ground – 'huge cantles flies' – during battle.[31] In its discussion and etymology of 'cantle', the *Encyclopaedia Metropolitana*, first edited by Samuel Taylor Coleridge, includes this example from Tasso along with two further examples, both of which appear in military contexts. In his historical poem 'The Battle of Agincourt', Michael Drayton refers to how 'the English without all remorce . . . cut into cantels all that them withstood', and in his translation of Ovid's *Metamorphoses*, John Dryden writes of a warrior who 'Raging with high disdain, repeats his blows; / Nor shield, nor armour can their force oppose; / Huge cantlets of his buckler strew the ground'.[32]

Significantly, the only other appearance of 'cantle' in Shakespeare's works is found in *Antony and Cleopatra*, in the battle scene at Actium[33] between Antony and Octavian (Caesar Augustus). When Cleopatra's ship leaves the sea-battle, Antony follows, and the forces are thrown into chaos, giving victory to Caesar. Scarus regrets that 'the greater Cantle of the world, is lost / With very ignorance, we have kist away / Kingdomes, and Provinces'.[34] Rivers had long been celebrated as sites of heroism and valour in battle through the writings of Julius Caesar – great-uncle to Octavian – which 'show the salient points of mobile military campaigns, in which rivers feature prominently and were exploited by an alert tactician',[35] and demonstrate an unmatched record of victory in water-based battles. During a campaign against the Andes, one of Caesar's lieutenants found a way to reach a river bridge before the enemy, the only crossing point of the wide Liger. On another occasion Caesar had to use ingenious ways to work around the force of a stormy melting River Sicori (Segre) which destroyed two bridges. His troops crossed in light wickerwork vessels which enabled them to build a new bridge. In 52 BCE Caesar's attempt to cross the Elaver (Allier) was thwarted when the enemy destroyed the bridges and marched parallel to prevent him building any further bridges. At that point Caesar was cornered because the river could not be forded until autumn, and made his way across by means of a ruse whereby two legions went into hiding while the rest of the army continued, drawing the enemy along, and the legions could rebuild a bridge.[36]

In *Antony and Cleopatra* the river and nearby territories is the inciting setting that sets the events of the story in motion. Antony sees Cleopatra 'upon the River of Cydnus' (2.2.198), meaning the river and its vicinity.[37] Where the river opens out into the sea, 'A strange invisible perfume hits the sense / Of the adjacent Wharfes. The city cast / Her people out upon her' (2.2.223–5).[38] His love for her, kindled in the moment of this sighting, shapes how he responds to the political and military events which underpin the play, including his desire to fight, his decision to retreat and his final act of self-sabotage – the antithesis to the innovative heroism depicted in Caesar's writings.

In Shakespeare's *The Merry Wives of Windsor*, written c. 1596, the setting of Windsor Great Park bounded by the River Thames is used to explore a number of historical and military associations, and possibly as a means to pass commentary on the court. The character of Falstaff, of the early history plays, becomes central to the story of *Merry Wives*, which uses the river in a different way. Falstaff's oversized status is represented by the image of a beached whale stranded on the shore of the Thames. As Mistress Ford exclaims, 'What tempest, I trow, threw up this whale, with so many tuns of oil in his belly, ashore at Windsor?' (2.1.56–8).[39] Jemima Matthews draws attention to the Thames-side location of this beached whale that appears in the Folio as an alternative to the 'bladder' of the Quarto version.[40] Other commentators have interpreted the whale, floundering out of its usual habitat, as a symbol of Falstaff's 'helplessness and alien status' in the middle-class world of

Windsor, where his previous – and very different – roles in the history plays have become largely irrelevant.[41]

Yet the addition of the whale to the Folio version may also have been designed as a symbol of political change. Whales were considered threats to mariners at a time when the fortunes of England largely rested on successful overseas campaigns. Beached whales were powerful symbols of political unrest and sovereign power, particularly in the Netherlands where a concentration of beached-whale imagery appears in the later sixteenth to seventeenth centuries.[42] As expressed in a late sixteenth-century Latin inscription accompanying an engraving of a beached whale, 'What a terror of the deep Ocean is a whale, when it is driven by the wind and its own power on to the shore of the land and lies captive on the dry sand'.[43] In this context, the whale is no longer a threat but a spectacle that draws crowds of curious onlookers.

The Folio text of *Merry Wives* may have been the version performed at Whitehall, on the Thames, only a few years after the failed Essex Rebellion against Elizabeth I when the rebel earls Essex and Southampton (Shakespeare's patron) sought to regenerate what they saw to be an outdated system of government, and aimed to force the Queen to replace her advisors.[44] In poetry of the late sixteenth century, the 'beryl' Thames came to represent the 'glittering destiny' of England under the rule of Elizabeth, and for Shakespeare was 'one of the highways of his invention'.[45] According to Thomas Gainsford, the Thames was the glory of London – 'flowing twenty foot, and full of stately ships, that flie to us with marchandize from all the ports of the world, the sight yielding astonishment, and the use perpetuall comfort … the river westward matcheth Paris every way'.[46] As the Thames was a valuable arterial route through the country, upon which many fortunes depended, the appearance of a whale on its banks could have posed a symbolic threat to the stability of the crown and its interests. That Falstaff's humiliated body in *Merry Wives* is closely aligned with riverine imagery may point to his symbolising the political class of statesmen responsible for the corrupted body of England.

Shakespeare's decision to model the character of Falstaff upon Sir John Oldcastle aligns the character with the historic conflict setting of the River Wye on the English–Welsh border. Oldcastle, who took his name from the historic family home in Ameley, Herefordshire, close to the border, was associated with rebellion against the state and evasion of the usual persecution laws applicable to heretics. Peter Corbin and Douglas Sedge note that as the monarchy employed knights such as the Oldcastles for administration and defence of the border, it is probable that Sir John was known for his military role in border warfare.[47]

They further note that although Oldcastle was situated away from the administrative centres of the borders it was strategically important in the control of the Marches, and thus would have played an important role in containing the Welsh rebellion.[48] For Catholics, Oldcastle was 'a proclaimed outlaw, a rebel and a traitor', while Protestants, for whom he was a 'saint and martyr', had to find a way to justify his behaviour when he so consistently challenged the popular monarchy of Henry V.[49] In 1417 Oldcastle was burned over a fire in chains in St Giles in the Fields, less than a mile from the banks of the Thames, after his involvement in the failed Lollard rising planned to assassinate the King.

In changing the name of his thieving, dishonourable and cowardly figure from Oldcastle to Falstaff, Shakespeare developed Falstaff's political activity to include his involvement in a campaign to quash the rebellion that led to the Battle of Shrewsbury (1403). In *The Merry Wives* the comic and double-crossing Falstaff receives his comeuppance at the hands of the two married women he is pursuing when he is immersed in the Thames waters. Carried in a basket of dirty laundry, Falstaff is dumped in Datchet Mead, a 'muddy ditch close by the Thames side', an act that may have been intended to attract the attention of the court, not least because the path of Falstaff's embarrassing journey by laundry basket and his subsequent immersion occupies the historic setting where the Magna Carta was signed.[50] The spot known as Runnymede, a meadow by the Thames at the edge of the park, commemorates the Magna Carta that was signed by King John in 1215 under pressure from rebel barons. As this piece of legislation founded English civil liberties it is often considered to be the greatest step forward in the history of politics. Falstaff's immersion might thus symbolise the regression of courtly law, whereby the oppressive Elizabethan statesmen, deemed to be outdated, spelled the continued need for a revolution – a situation that had begun under Elizabeth but still rumbled beneath the surface under the rule of James I, who kept many of the former court advisors, including Robert Cecil, who had so enraged the youthful earls of Essex and Southampton. As noted elsewhere, in *Henry IV, Part 2*, a play that is 'urgently preoccupied with questions of disease and cure', the 'unruly, over-surfeited body' of Falstaff becomes 'a central figure for the diseased body of the state'.[51] The unstable political situation is further expressed by the unwholesome 'muddy' river waters. Ditches or drainage channels used for the removal of effluents and waste products were typically slow moving, and their stagnancy – with its associated corrupted air – posed an invisible health threat. As Leonardo da Vinci had noted earlier in the sixteenth century, in his idea for a multi-tiered city, 'One needs a fast flowing river to avoid the corrupt air produced by stagnation.'[52]

The 'unseen' presence of contagion in *The Merry Wives*, in the form of the dirty laundry and the potentially contaminated river waters would have chimed uncomfortably with an audience tired of years of plague, and the troublesome body of Falstaff, so unfit for the times, can thus be seen as representative of a decaying society that required new order.[53]

While the specific Thames-side location is pertinent to our reading, we might gather further insight into the political dynamic of the period by placing the river in the context of its royal and wartime associations. The Banqueting house, where *Merry Wives* was performed in 1604, became a site of the English Civil War when Charles I was beheaded there in 1649. Windsor Castle, built on the orders of William I, and home to over 900 years of royal history, was situated above the Thames for the purpose of guarding the western approach to London. On the eastern side, at Tilbury, the Thames became the site of the momentous speech delivered by Queen Elizabeth I to the land army in 1588 assembled at Tilbury Camp to defend against a Spanish invasion. On a practical level, the Thames facilitated military and naval operations. The transportation of troops and heavy military equipment to sites of battle was often the only viable option considering the state of some of Britain's roads. The Thames housed dockyards at Deptford and Woolwich, built on the orders of Henry VIII, as part of his founding of the Navy Royal. These dry-dock facilities and storage warehouses were located near Greenwich Palace to enable the King to visit and inspect them.[54] The Thames facilitated the transportation of oak timber to the dockyards, and upon construction was the route of passage for repaired or newly constructed warships to join the fleet at sea. The Thames was thus integral to the construction and support of the royal fleet, and it was here, and at the docks on the River Medway, where the fleet of British warships was expanded from five to fifty, an expansion that continued under Elizabeth.

The English oak, as the primary construction material of England's and Scotland's warships throughout the middle ages and the early modern era, played an important role in national defence. At Windsor the Thames ran along the edge of the former Saxon hunting ground known as Windsor Forest, populated with veteran oak trees bearing royal and legendary associations. Windsor Great Park is unusual for its concentration of ancient oaks named after kings and queens, including the Conqueror's Oak, Offa's oak and the Queen Elizabeth Oak, all over a thousand years old. The oak and the river had long been associated in the British imagination due to their shared function as territorial boundary markers. Oaks often stood on the shores of rivers or on the edges of Anglo-Saxon land units, and their function as navigation markers naturally imbued them with military significance. At East Tilbury, for example, a landmark oak known as 'The old round tree' stood on the marshy shore of the Thames, and appeared on Admiralty charts as 'oak tree'.[55] As a royal symbol, oaks were chosen throughout history as sites for synods, royal meetings, military musters and army look-outs. At Shrewsbury, the Shelton Oak, close to the banks of the Severn, was the alleged site of Owen Glendower's view of the battle before he decided not to support Percy's army. In 851 Aclea, meaning 'oak pasture' or 'oak field', was the site of a battle between the West Saxons and Danish Vikings in which the Thames was the main site of conflict.[56] While in Herefordshire, the Battle of Mortimer's Cross (1461) was marked by a Battle Oak and medieval stone at the crossroads, with the battlefield most likely lying between the oak and the nearby River Lugg,[57] and in Sussex, at the Battle of Hastings, the Watch-Oak was the legendary tree where King Harold's wife Edith watched the battle.[58]

According to the seventeenth-century etymologist Stephen Skinner, 'ac' or 'oak' meant 'strength' to the Saxons, much as 'robur' meant to the Latins.[59] In High Renaissance art, the oak was a symbol of strength, 'a byword for military and administrative firmness . . . an attribute of the strong-hearted hero'.[60] In 1651 an oak (known as the Royal Oak) was the alleged hiding place of the future Charles II when on the run from Parliamentarian forces,[61] and in 1660 when Charles wore oak leaves on his return from exile in France to claim the throne, the oak became an emblem of the Stuart Restoration. Echoing this historic association between oaks, royalty and strength, John Dryden described the British oak as 'The monarch oak, the patriarch of the trees, / Shoots rising up and spreads by slow degrees / Three centuries he grows, and three he stays / Supreme in state; and in three more decays'.[62]

With these affinities in mind we might now turn to consider Falstaff's disguise, as Herne, 'with huge horns on his head' beneath the Herne Oak, a legendary tree associated in folklore with Herne the Hunter, set amongst the trees of Windsor Great Park, beside the Thames.[63] It would seem that Shakespeare, by tapping into this predilection for large named oaks, was seeking imagery that would resonate with the courtly audience. The oak's traditional role as a symbol of royalty and military muster is inverted so that the tree becomes a gendered site of conflict – at once setting the scene for Falstaff's cuckolding, and the ultimate male disempowerment, while Mistress Page and Mistress Ford contrive the events of the meeting. As noticed in the nineteenth century, the Queen Elizabeth Oak – almost thirty feet in circumference – was situated only 200 yards from the Herne Oak.[64] Given its close proximity, there is little doubt that the presence of the Herne Oak in the play would have also brought to mind the larger tree named after Queen Elizabeth. Perry also noted that in the 1602 edition of the play, the oak is named 'Horne' rather than 'Herne'.[65] That the river and the oak – both symbols of courage and resistance – are so instrumental in *Merry Wives* in the lampooning of a character modelled upon an Elizabethan knight, formerly known for his prowess, might suggest an attempt to pass comment on the integrity and stability of the court and its governance.

While the shape of a horned headdress may also recall the aforementioned crescent or half-moon military formation, the appendage of the oak branches to Falstaff's body suggests a close alliance between the material riverine environment and the human body, a connection alluded to earlier in the image of a beached whale with 'tuns of oil' in its stomach. We might also note Sophie Chiari's chapter in this volume, where she alludes to Gail Kern Paster's 'leaky vessels' theory in relation to the 'eminently porous feminine body of the early modern era'. The solid, naturally robust oak, associated with military strength and endurance, is the antithesis to the liquidity and porousness of the early modern feminine body, and yet Falstaff is aligned with both. To see Falstaff himself as a form of 'leaky vessel' that permits the ingress of aqueous substances implies an affinity between the human body and the hull of a ship, as previously suggested by Mistress Page and Mistress Ford:

> Mistress Page: . . . hee would have boorded me in this furie.
> Mistress Ford: Boording, call you it? Ile bee sure to keepe him aboue decke.
> Mistress Page: So will I: if hee come vnder my hatches, Ile neuer to Sea againe.[66]

The number of maritime allusions in the play certainly would have chimed with an audience well versed in the protracted Anglo–Spanish war (1585–1604). One of England's greatest military achievements, the defeat of the Spanish Armada of 1588 signalled the decline of Spain as an imperial power.[67] Yet the Whitehall performance of *Merry Wives* in 1604 might, in this riverside setting, have resonated with the audience's knowledge of the fate of two English ships in the Battle of the Gulf of Cadiz earlier that year, which was seen as a significant humiliation to the English navy. The episode at Cadiz led to two English privateers being captured and damaged while plundering shipping lanes and villages. That the ingress of water into the hold signalled failure or imminent defeat might prompt us to look again at the scene where Falstaff's flawed vessel is discarded in the Thames waters. Here the heavy ungainliness of his capsized body, coupled with his macabre speculation that his drowned corpse would swell monstrously ('What a thing I should have been when I had been swelled!'),[68] not only evokes a comic contrast to a streamlined structure needed for navigating the water, but offers a strong visual reminder of former military success and prowess, now consigned to history.

In the century before Shakespeare was writing, Leonardo da Vinci had likened rivers to the veins of the body,[69] and such forms of personification are still traceable today in terms such as 'the arm of the estuary', and 'the body' and 'mouth' of the river. Some of the earliest mixed-language dictionaries also suggest an inherent connection between river imagery and the body. In Shakespeare's lifetime, the French word 'Mollet' meant 'the fleshie part of the hand between the thumb and middle finger', the 'tip, lug, or soft part of the eare', the calf of the leg and also 'a muddie place in a riuer'.[70] This early modern fluidity in meaning between places in rivers and parts of the body might reflect the deeper origin for the association between the river and the body that had its roots in Christian and pre-Christian tradition.[71]

These linguistic and imaginative intersections between the river and the body were employed by Shakespeare in some of his earliest works concerned with politics and nobility. In *The Rape of Lucrece*, the assault of the virtuous Lucretia, wife of the nobleman Collatinus, by Sextus Tarquinius, son of Tarquinius, King of Rome, is a version of the story recounted in Livy's *History of Rome* – an event that allegedly hastened the revolt that overthrew the Roman monarchy and led to the establishment of the Roman Republic. The rape takes place in the context of the siege of Ardea, prefiguring the intentionally close alignment between the rape of Lucrece and the invasion of enemy forces into defended territory. Peter J. Smith argues that Lucrece is both cityscape and besieged territory, noting her breasts as 'round turrets destitute and pale', and herself as a 'never-conquered fort', and a muddied fountain.[72] Smith also alludes to *Titus Andronicus* when Titus addresses Lavinia's attackers: 'the spring whom you have stained with mud'.[73]

The image of a steadily flowing river flooding a piece of land symbolises the final desecration of Lucrece by the means of her self-inflicted wound:

> And bubbling from her breast, it doth divide
> In two slow rivers, that the crimson blood
> Circles her body in on every side,
> Who, like a late-sack'd island, vastly stood
> Bare and unpeopled in this fearful flood. (Lines 1737–41)[74]

Here, the traditionally cleansing nature of the river is reversed in the image of rivers of blood – some tainted 'black' – encircling her body. The subsequent uprising in defence of her honour against the Tarquin family can thus be seen as an attempt to erase the dark stain of their tyrannical regime. Elsewhere in the poem clear waters tainted by outside sources are symbolic of dishonesty and treachery as we are invited to contemplate a series of possibilities:

> Or toads infect fair founts with venom mud?
> Or tyrant folly lurk in gentle breasts?
> Or kings be breakers of their own behests?
> 'But no perfection is so absolute,
> That some impurity doth not pollute.' (Lines 850–4)[75]

Here, 'fount', meaning spring, source or place of baptism, may also mean river source – the point at which a spring surfaces from the earth and begins its downward flow to become a river.[76] The idea of a water source being contaminated by toads – perceived in medieval times as venomous – becomes a metaphor not only for the defiled woman, but the condition of England, corrupted at its source by a dishonest state in which kings break their own oaths.

In *The Tragicall History of Romeus and Juliet* (1562), the source for Shakespeare's *Romeo and Juliet*, the deceiving nature of a river – whereby a beautiful surface masks a mysterious subterranean world – is suggested by the 'Silver streame with chanel depe, / that through the town doth flow'.[77] The enticing veneer of a river that concealed a treacherous nature was a well-known literary metaphor of the time. Indeed, Shakespeare has been credited with popularising the English version of the Latin proverb 'still waters run deep', meaning that someone who may appear calm and serene has passionate emotions or thoughts beneath the surface. In *History of Henry VI* the idea of 'tyrant folly' that 'lurk[s] in gentle breasts'[78] is returned to in the description of Gloucester's treacherous nature 'Unsounded yet and full of deep deceit' that poses a threat to the established order: 'Smooth runs the water where the brook is deep; / And in his simple show he harbours treason' (3.1.53–4).[79]

When considering rivers as sites of contest that could decide the fate of a territory and its people, pivotal to a conflict tradition that lasted until the eighteenth century, we are reminded of a largely forgotten perception of these geographical features. For early modern writers and readers, this perception was part of everyday consciousness, and as such endowed rivers with rich metaphorical possibilities. The imaginative interplay between the river and the body can be traced in the layered meanings of terms used by Shakespeare in these settings. In the turbulent political times of the early modern era, the powerful, slippery and erosive nature of a river – coupled with its smooth 'silver' surface – invited experimentation in metaphors that represented human nature.

These textured meanings and playful ambiguities invited early modern playgoers and readers to question the authority of the state, and reflect upon the undercurrents of feeling and hidden desires that 'lurk' within the deeper recesses of the mind.

Notes

1. See, for example, Andrew Curry, 'Slaughter at the Bridge: Uncovering a Colossal Bronze Age Battle', *Science*, 24 March 2016, http://www.science.org/content/article/slaughter-bridge-uncovering-colossal-bronze-age-battle (last accessed 21 September 2023).
2. In the Saxon period, for example, the River Frome formed the boundary between the three hundreds of Bere, Winfrith and Hasler. See Ryan Lavelle, *Royal Estates in Anglo-Saxon Wessex: Land, Politics and Family Strategies* (Oxford: Archaeopress, 2007), 32. One example of a river forming a natural boundary and borderland is the River Wye on the English–Welsh border, which was a conflict setting for centuries.
3. Charles Edelman, *Shakespeare's Military Language: A Dictionary* (London: Continuum, 2004), 1.
4. W. J. Thoms, writing in *Notes and Queries*. Cited in Edelman, *Shakespeare's Military Language*, 1.
5. Cited in Paul A. Jorgensen, 'Military Rank in Shakespeare', *Huntington Library Quarterly* 14.1 (1950), 17–41, 17–18.
6. See Duff Cooper (1949) cited in Jorgenson, 'Military Rank in Shakespeare', 18.
7. Jorgenson, 18.
8. Dong Ha Seo, 'Military Culture of Shakespeare's England', PhD thesis (University of Birmingham, 2011), 1.
9. Raphael Holinshed, *Holinshed's Chronicles of England, Scotland, Ireland*, vol. 1 (London: J. Johnson, 1807), 89.
10. Brian Campbell, *Rivers and the Power of Ancient Rome* (Chapel Hill: University of North Carolina Press, 2012), 1.
11. According to Alexander Waugh, lines by John Leland quoted by Camden in 1607 identified Avondunum as the Celtic-Roman name for Hampton Court, shortened to 'Avon', meaning a fortified place by a river. See Alexander Waugh, 'The True Meaning of Ben Jonson's Phrase "Sweet Swan of Avon"', *The Oxfordian* 16 (September 2014), 97–103 (99, 100).
12. Peter Ackroyd, *Thames: Sacred River* (London: Random House, 2008), 337.
13. Alexander L. Kaufman, *The Historical Literature of the Jack Cade Rebellion* (Farnham: Ashgate, 2013), 201.
14. William Shakespeare, *History of Henry VI: Part Two*. This, and all subsequent quoted works by Shakespeare, can be found in *The Arden Shakespeare: Complete Works*, ed. Richard Proudfoot, Ann Thompson, David Scott Kastan and H. R. Woudhuysen (London: Bloomsbury, 2022).
15. The account by John Stow locates the stone by the Thames: 'Some haue said this stone to be set, as a marke in the middle of the citie within the

walles: but in truth it standeth farre nearer vnto the riuer of Thames.' John Stow, *Stow's Survey of London*, in Kaufman, *The Historical Literature of the Jack Cade Rebellion*, 161.
16. Ibid., 162.
17. Cade's rebellion is described by John Ashdown-Hill as having been 'Yorkist in flavour'. See John Ashdown-Hill, *The Wars of the Roses* (Stroud: Amberley, 2015), vii.
18. For an assessment of the possibility that Richard II was the play commissioned on the eve of the Essex Rebellion, see Paul Hammer, 'Shakespeare's Richard II, the Play of 7 February 1601, and the Essex Rising', *Shakespeare Quarterly* 59 (2008), 1–35. For a discussion of Shakespeare's interest in insurrection, see Jonathan Bate, 'Was Shakespeare an Essex Man? Shakespeare Lecture', in *Proceedings of the British Academy*, vol. 162, ed. Ron Johnston (London: The British Academy, 2009; online edn, British Academy Scholarship Online, 31 Jan. 2012), https://doi.org/10.5871/bacad/9780197264584.003.0001 (last accessed 17 November 2022).
19. William Shakespeare, *King Richard II*, Arden Shakespeare.
20. Shakespeare, *King Henry IV, Part 1*, Arden Shakespeare.
21. Ibid.
22. Rosinus's work on Roman antiquity was first published in Latin, in Basel, in 1585.
23. Thomas Godwyn, *Romanae Historia Anthologia Recognita et Aucta: An English Exposition of the Roman Antiquities* (London: Robert White, 1648), 157.
24. Ibid.
25. Ibid.
26. John Cruso, *Militarie Instructions for the Cavalrie: or Rules and directions for the service of horse collected out of divers forrain authors ancient and modern* (Cambridge: University of Cambridge, 1632), 101.
27. David Norbrook, *Writing the English Republic: Poetry, Rhetoric and Politics, 1627–1660* (Cambridge: Cambridge University Press, 2000), 41.
28. Marcus Annaeus Lucanus, *Lucan's Pharsalia or the Civil-Wars of Rome, between Pompey the great, and Julius Caesar,* The whole ten books Englished by Thomas May, vol. 1 book 3 (London: William Bentley, 1650), 64.
29. Edelman, *Shakespeare's Military Language*, 18.
30. Ibid., 18.
31. See note 32.
32. *Encyclopaedia Metropolitana: Plates and Maps to the Historical and Miscellaneous Divisions*, ed. Edward Smedley, Hugh James Rose, Henry John Rose and B. Fellowes, vol. 16 (London: B. Fellowes and others, 1845), 261.
33. The Battle of Actium (31 BCE) was a naval battle off a promontory in the north of Acarnania, on the western coast of Greece.
34. Shakespeare, *Antony and Cleopatra*, Arden Shakespeare.
35. Campbell, *Rivers and the Power of Ancient Rome*, 164.
36. Ibid., 164—6.
37. Charles and Mary Victoria Cowden-Clarke suggested that 'upon the river of Cydnus' signifies the 'district on the shores of the river of Cydnus',

including the city and market-place where Antony sat. Elsewhere 'upon the Seine' or 'upon the Thames' is used to depict the nearby shores of those rivers and the country within their vicinity. Charles Cowden-Clarke and Mary Victoria Cowden-Clarke, *The Shakespeare Key: Unlocking the Treasures of His Style, Elucidating the Peculiarities of His Construction, and Displaying the Beauties of His Expression; Forming a Companion to* The Complete Concordance to Shakespeare (London: Sampson, Low and Marston, 1879), 21.

38. Shakespeare, *Antony and Cleopatra*, Arden Shakespeare.
39. Shakespeare, *The Merry Wives of Windsor*, Arden Shakespeare.
40. Jemima Matthews, 'Inside Out and Outside In: The River Thames in William Shakespeare's *The Merry Wives of Windsor*', Shakespeare 15.4 (2019), 410–27, 411.
41. Evelyn Gajowski and Phyllis Rackin, 'Introduction: A Historical Survey', in *The Merry Wives of Windsor: New Critical Essays*, ed. Evelyn Gajowski and Phyllis Rackin (London and New York: Routledge, 2015), 1–24, 7.
42. See Victoria Sears Goldman, 'Omen and Oracle: Dutch Images of Beached Whales', n.p., http://www.victoriasearsgoldman.com/16th-17th-century-dutch-images-beached-whales/ (last accessed 21 September 2023).
43. Ibid.
44. See Matthews ('Inside Out and Outside In', 411), who suggests that the increased 'liquidity' of the folio seems to bear the 'impression' of the 'event' of the 1604 performance.
45. Ackroyd, *Thames: Sacred River*, 337.
46. Thomas Gainsford, *The Glory of England, or, a true description of many excellent prerogatiues whereby she triumpheth over all the nations* (London: E. Griffin, 1620), 257.
47. Peter Corbin and Douglas Sedge (eds), *The Oldcastle Controversy: Sir John Oldcastle, Part I and The Famous Victories of Henry V* (Manchester: Manchester University Press, 1991), 1.
48. Ibid., 3.
49. Ibid., 2, 6.
50. Shakespeare, *The Merry Wives of Windsor*, Arden Shakespeare, 992, line 14.
51. See Rachel Falconer and Denis Renevey's discussion of Jennifer Richards's essay in Rachel Falconer and Denis Renevey, 'Introduction', in *Medieval and Early Modern Literature, Science and Medicine* (Tubingen: Narr Verlag, 2013), 11–17, 17.
52. *Notebooks of Leonardo Da Vinci, Manuscript B*, as cited in Martin Kemp, *Leonardo Da Vinci: The Marvellous Works of Nature and Man* (Oxford: Oxford University Press, 2007), 98.
53. For my discussion of the 'unseen' presence of contagion in Renaissance drama and its perceived relation to the corrupted body, or state, of England, see Rebecca Welshman, '"The Invisible Operator": Plague, Corruption, and Conspiracy in Renaissance Drama', in *Pandemics and Epidemics in Cultural Representation*, ed. Sathyaraj Venkatesan, Antara Chatterjee, A. David Lewis and Brian Callender (Singapore: Springer Nature, 2022), 49–62, 50.
54. Clayton Drees, *Henry VIII: A Reference Guide to His Life and Works* (Lanham, MD: Rowman and Littlefield, 2022), 172.

55. Albert Gravely Linney, *Lure and Lore of London's River* (London: Sampson Lowe, Marston & Co., 1932), 5.
56. In Anglo-Saxon documents, the place names Oakley (Hants), Ockley (Surrey) and Acley (Kent) are all called Aclea, meaning 'oak pasture'. See Isaac Taylor, *Names and Their Histories: Alphabetically Arranged as a Handbook of Historical Geography and Topographical Nomenclature* (New York: Macmillan, 1896), 210.
57. See Glenn Foard and Tracey Partida for their analysis of the site and reproduction of the Victorian O.S. map. Glenn Foard and Tracey Partida, 'The 2018–2022 Investigation of the 1461 Battle of Mortimer's Cross', February 2022, https://www.battlefieldstrust.com/media/820.pdf (last accessed 21 September 2023).
58. Notably, Falstaff's cowardly act at the battle of Shrewsbury, when he stabs the dead Hotspur in the thigh, echoes an alleged event at the end of the Battle of Hastings when a soldier wounded the already dead King Harold in the thigh, and possibly castrated him. For this dishonourable and emasculating act, he was penalised by the Duke of Normandy.
59. See Samuel Johnson, *A Dictionary of the English Language* (London: W. Strahan, 1755), n.p.
60. George L. Hersey, *High Renaissance Art in St. Peter's and the Vatican: An Interpretive Guide* (Chicago: University of Chicago Press, 1993), 44.
61. I discussed the significance of oak trees in theatres of war in 'The Hoar Apple Tree of the Battle of Hastings: A New Translation', paper presented at 'Theatres of War: British Commission for Military History New Researcher's Conference', 8–9 November 2019.
62. John Dryden, 'Palamon and Arcite', Book III, 1058–1061, *The Poems of John Dryden: Volume Five: 1697–1700*, ed. Paul Hammond and David Hopkins (London: Routledge, 2014), 184.
63. *The Merry Wives of Windsor, Arden Shakespeare*, 1000, line 42.
64. William Perry, *A Treatise on the identity of Herne's Oak* (London: L. Booth, 1867), 58–9. As noted by Frank Buckland, within the same park stood William the Conqueror's Oak, of around 1200–1500 years of age; see Gilbert White, *Natural History and Antiquities of Selborne* (London: Macmillan, 1887), 285.
65. Perry, *A Treatise on the Identity of Herne's Oak*, 4.
66. From the Folio version of 1623. Quoted in Jemima Matthews, 417.
67. Colin Martin and Geoffrey Parker, *The Spanish Armada*, rev. edn (Manchester: Manchester University Press, 1999), 246.
68. William Shakespeare, *The Merry Wives of Windsor* (Cambridge: Cambridge University Press, 2010), 119.
69. Kemp, *Leonardo Da Vinci*, 98.
70. Randle Cotgrave, *A Dictionarie of French and English Tongues* (London: Adam Islip, 1611), n.p.
71. In Christian tradition the connection between river waters and full-body baptism goes back to the time of Jesus and John the Baptist who were baptised on the banks of the Jordan river. The casting of weapons and personal items, such as ornaments and pins, into rivers during the Bronze Age might also suggest a ritual connection between rivers and the body. See, for example, patterns in the deposition of weapons, bracelets and pins in

major rivers of the Netherlands in the late Bronze Age in David R. Fontijn, 'Analecta Praehistorica Leidensia 33/34 / Sacrificial Landscapes: Cultural Biographies of Persons, Objects and "Natural Places" in the Bronze Age of the Southern Netherlands, c. 2300–600 BC', PhD thesis (University of Leiden, 2002), 175, https://hdl.handle.net/1887/33737 (last accessed 21 September 2023).
72. Peter J. Smith, 'Rome's Disgrace: The Politics of Rape in Shakespeare's "Lucrece"', *Critical Survey* 17.3 (2005), 15–26, 22.
73. Ibid.
74. William Shakespeare, 'The Rape of Lucrece', *Arden Shakespeare*, 81, lines 1737–41.
75. Ibid., 72, lines 890–905.
76. See John Florio's *Queen Anna's New World of Words* (London: Melch. Bradwood, 1611), 192 for these synonyms.
77. 'The Tragicall History of Romeus and Juliet', in William Shakespeare, *Sonnets. Passionate Pilgrim. Lover's Complaint. Titus Andronicus. Romeus and Juliet*, vol. 16 (Dublin: John Exshaw, 1794), 289–389, 290.
78. William Shakespeare, 'The Rape of Lucrece', *Arden Shakespeare*, 72, line 851.
79. William Shakespeare, *History of Henry VI, Part II*, *Arden Shakespeare*, 628, lines 53–4.

II. Writing the River

Chapter 4

The Navigation of the Trent and William Sampson's *The Vow-Breaker* (1636)

Lisa Hopkins

William Sampson's play *The Vow-Breaker, or, the Fair Maid of Clifton* (1636) tells the tragic story of a young woman from Clifton in Nottinghamshire, Anne Boot, who vows fidelity to Young Bateman, a departing soldier, but marries the rich and elderly Jermane while he is away fighting at the Siege of Leith (which dates this part of the plot to 1560). When Bateman returns from the siege and discovers Anne's perfidy, he hangs himself. Anne has a baby but is haunted by Bateman's ghost (although nobody else can see it) and drowns herself in the River Trent. The story is over and the play might well have ended at this point, but instead it moves in an unexpected new direction as the fifth act stages a visit to Nottingham by Queen Elizabeth, who is greeted by the mayor with a petition imploring her that the River Trent should be made navigable. Elizabeth accedes to the request, receives good news of the Siege of Leith, and then decides to go and tour the caves made famous by Isabella, wife of Edward II, and her lover Roger Mortimer.

This sequence of events may seem improbable in terms of both generic norms and factual probability. For one thing, Elizabeth never visited Nottingham, although it 'was a proposed venue for the planned meeting in 1562 between Elizabeth and Mary Queen of Scots';[1] for another, Julie Sanders notes that 'it is not clear whether full navigability of the kind envisaged by the Mayor in his motion had been achieved by the time this play was performed'.[2] Even if it had, it would have been no thanks to Elizabeth: Patricia Griffin, who edited the play for a doctoral thesis, reported that

> Although I have searched extensively through Acts of Parliament and Royal Charters covering the period of Elizabeth's reign and the first half of the seventeenth century, there is no evidence of any Charter that refers to the river Trent. The only connection that I have been able to find with the Trent's navigational system and Queen Elizabeth around 1560 was a long dispute at Hull docks and the Act subsequently passed in 1557, to the disadvantage of

the town, confirming that all vessels were to pass freely through the harbour without paying a toll.[3]

However, although *The Vow Breaker* may depart from historical fact and generic norms, it does seem to have attracted an audience. The title page rather ambiguously names the play as 'The Vow Breaker, or the Fair Maid of Clifton. In Nottinghamshire as it has been divers times acted by several Companies with great applause.' The period between 'Clifton' and 'In Nottinghamshire' makes it unclear whether we are being reminded that Clifton is in Nottinghamshire or whether the play has been acted there, but the latter seems more likely, and Emanuel Stelzer is confident that '*The Vow-Breaker* represents one of those few extant texts that the dramatists did not conceive for London performance, but intentionally directed at regional audiences.'[4] Local interest certainly seems likely to have been a strong part of the play's appeal. Boot was a common name in Nottinghamshire: Griffin notes a number of Boots and Germans in the parish records of Clifton,[5] and there has also been a famous modern bearer of the name in the shape of Jesse Boot, 1st Baron Trent, the founder of Boots the Chemist. It also seems clear that the story of the fair maid of Clifton was a genuine local legend which Nottinghamshire audiences would have recognised as part of their cultural landscape.

It is conceivable that local memories could also help explain *The Vow Breaker*'s interest in the Siege of Leith. Griffin observes, 'My research has not revealed any document that could suggest why he had such an interest in the battle at Leith.'[6] However, it is clear that Sampson connects the Siege of Leith with Mary, Queen of Scots, who had once planned to meet Queen Elizabeth in Nottingham and had spent long periods of captivity in Derbyshire and Staffordshire in the custody of the Earl of Shrewsbury and his wife Elizabeth, better known as Bess of Hardwick, whose grandson William Cavendish, Earl (later marquess and then duke) of Newcastle, was the most important local magnate at the time when *The Vow Breaker* was written. The play mentions Mary's mother Marie de Guise, 'the Queen Regent of Scotland' (1.2.53), of whom there was a portrait at Bess's former home Hardwick Hall; Monluc brings a message from Mary Queen of Scots herself, then in France (3.2.93–103); and one of the terms of the peace is that 'Francis and Mary, King and Queen of France / From henceforth bear not the arms of England' (5.1.51–2). Local memories of Mary's long imprisonment might well have made such references of interest, and I shall suggest later that other aspects of Mary's story might also have chimed with the play's concerns.

Above all, the play offers a remarkably comprehensive snapshot of early modern figurings and uses of the River Trent, which flowed through both Nottingham and Clifton. This is an emphasis entirely new to the story as Sampson found it, since the ballad mentions neither the river nor the fact that Anne was drowned.[7] The play, however, is so interested in the river that it even features in the illustration which precedes the title.[8] As Sampson would certainly have been aware, the Trent featured prominently in early modern literature, historiography and chorography. In *Poly-Olbion* Drayton calls it 'Princely Trent' and claims that the very word 'Trent' is distinguished because 'A more then usuall power did in that name consist, / Which thirty doth import';[9] Samuel Clarke's 1657 explanation of the relevance of the number thirty was the river was 'so called from thirty kindes of fish found in it', and Clarke also called it the 'christall Trent'.[10] Drayton too thought that the river was both clear and rich in fish, and he also connected it with fords: 'The cristall Trent, for Foords and Fish renowened'.[11] It may also have been important for Sampson that Ben Jonson had written about the Trent. Julie Sanders points out that 'In the months prior to his death in 1637, Jonson had been effecting his own dramatic engagement with the force and potency, cultural and literal, of a river, this time the River Trent, which flowed so suggestively through the landscapes and domains of his chief 1630s patron, William Cavendish, the Earl of Newcastle'; she observes that in *The Sad Shepherd* 'we see in Jonson's version of the Trent a gesture towards the chorographic enterprises of Drayton and to other dramatic precursors such as John Lyly in its regional setting and tone'.[12] Sampson too was interested in the Cavendishes and aware of their potential as patrons, and although *The Vow Breaker* was in print by the time Jonson was writing *The Sad Shepherd*, Sampson might have been aware of its gestation.

In some texts, such as *Gorboduc*, it is the Humber that is prominent rather than the Trent, and Thomas Dekker referred in *Britannia's Honor shining brightly in severall magnificent shewes or pageants* to 'our three famous Rivers, Humber, Trent, and Seuerne'.[13] However Holinshed's *Chronicles* declare that 'There is no River called Humber from the Heade', and perhaps that is one reason why the Trent, which Holinshed calls 'one of the most excellent ryuers in the lande',[14] begins to take precedence. There was also a well-understood division into 'this side Trent' (implicitly this side as viewed from London), a phrase that goes back at least as far as *Le Morte d'Arthur*,[15] and what Rowland Broughton amongst others calls 'the hether side of Trent'.[16] Henry Calthrop's 1632 *The liberties, usages and customes of the city of London confirmed by especiall acts of Parliament* refers to things being done 'as other Sheriffes have used on this side Trent';[17] John Brydall's 1676 *Camera regis, or, a short view of London* declares that 'in ancient time there were but two Escheators in England, the one on this side of Trent, and the other beyond Trent';[18] and Drayton observed in *Poly-Olbion* that

> In Brittane here we find, our Seuerne, and our Tweed,
> The tripartited Ile doe generally diuide,
> Trent cuts the Land in two, so equally, as tho
> Nature it pointed-out, to our great Brute to show
> How to his mightie Sonnes the Iland he might share.[19]

The Trent was considered a natural division by other writers too: Holinshed called it 'the riuer Trent, which passeth thorowe the middest of Englande'[20] and Patrick Gordon's 1615 *History of Robert the Bruce* speaks of 'Trent that pairteth England just in two'.[21]

Specifically, Trent divided the north from the south. In Edward Bowles's *Manifest Truth, or an Inversion of the truths manifest containing a narration of the proceedings of the Scottish army* (1646), the Scottish army debates whether to march 'southward, that is over the Trent'.[22] For twenty-first century Londoners the north may begin at Watford, but for their seventeenth-century counterparts the north of England was the area between Trent and Tweed, as established in Holinshed's *Chronicles*, which declares that the Romans established provinces between Trent and Tweed and between Trent and Thames.[23] Thus a sermon preached in York Minster in 1644 before William Cavendish (by then marquess of Newcastle), Charles I's commander in the North, spoke of 'all men betweene Trent and Tweede',[24] and Michael Drayton pairs the two rivers in *Poly-Olbion*, speaking of 'the land that lies betwixt the Trent and Tweed' and 'all the Townes that lay betwixt our Trent and Tweed'.[25] It is not clear whether *The Vow Breaker* is related to the lost two-part play *Black Bateman of the North*,[26] but if the Bateman of that play is indeed the same as in Sampson's story, it is no surprise that someone living by the Trent should be introduced to a London audience as being 'of the north'.

As the gateway to the north, the Trent was in a sense a frontier river. William Vallans might declare in *A tale of two swannes* that 'Trent is one of the most excellent rivers in England',[27] but it was also considered to be a place that marked the end of English excellence, for the territory beyond it was understood as wild, dangerous and savage. James Howell's *Epistolae ho-Elianae* thinks that the Picts lived between Trent and Tweed,[28] and many writers considered that when northerners came south of Trent they lost all inhibitions. Holinshed's *Chronicle* explained that during the Wars of the Roses 'These Northerne people, after they were once passed ouer the riuer of Trent, spoyled and wasted the Countrey afore them, in maner as if they had bin in the land of forayne enimies';[29] John Speed's version in *The theatre of the empire of Great Britaine* was that 'the *Northern* armie, (in which were *Scots*, *Welsh*, and *Irish* as well as *English*,) made bold by the way with what they liked, making small distinction of sacred or prophane, after they were once past the riuer of *Trent*';[30] and William Habington in his 1640 *The History of Edward the Fourth* referred to terrible behaviour by 'the Northerne troopes ... as soone as they had past Trent, as if they had there parted with all obedience to discipline'.[31] In Part II of *A Chronicle of the Kings of England*, Richard Baker declares that Margaret of Anjou, 'encouraged by the death of the Duke of *Yorke*, with a power of northern men marcheth towards *London*, but when her souldiers were once South of Trent, as if that river were the utmost limit of their good behaviour, they fell to forrage the Country in most barbarous manner'.[32] Richard Brome's 1653 play *The Damoiselle* similarly paints the region north of the river as uncivilised and unsafe: ''tis as bonny a Beggars name, as ever came from beyond Trent'.[33]

As this reference to naming suggests, even language was not the same on the other side of the Trent. Holinshed's *Chronicle* declared that

> The Scottish englische is much broader and lesse pleasaunt in utterance, then ours, because that nation hath not hitherto indeoured to bring the same to any perfit order, and yet it is such in maner, as Englishmen themselues doe speake, for the most part beyonde the Trent, whether the aforesayde amendement of our language, hath not as yet very much extended it selfe.[34]

John Cowell's 1607 *The Interpreter* assures its readers that the word wapentake 'is especially used at this day in the countries be north the river Trent',[35] and George Puttenham eschews language used beyond the river, leading Cathy Shrank to speak of 'Puttenham's "civill" frontiers of the River Trent'.[36] The area beyond Trent could also be considered a militarised zone: John Weever declares that in the reign of Henry VIII the Duke of Norfolk was put in charge of all the land 'from the Trent Northward, to defend the Realme agaynsts the kyng of Scottys'.[37] John Brydall's 1676 *Camera regis* declared that 'This Realm hath only three principal Rivers, whereon a Royal City may well be scituated: Trent in the North, Severne in the South-west, and Thames in the South-east',[38] but John Stow cautioned that 'for the prince of this realm to dwell upon Trent were to turn his back, or his blind side'.[39] In the *Compleat Angler* Izaak Walton wishes 'Let me live harmlessly, and near the bank of Trent or Avon have a dwelling place', but the Trent was generally thought of as far wilder and more dangerous than the Avon.[40]

Finally, the Trent could find itself tainted by an involuntary linguistic association with the Council of Trent. The two meanings collide at Newark where King John died, since English Reformers often presented him as a Protestant *avant la lettre*, and there is also an odd irony in that Henry Burton, whose 1636 *A divine tragedie lately acted* recounted how fourteen young men who played football on the frozen Trent near Gainsborough on a Sunday (25 January 1634) were drowned when the ice gave way,[41] also wrote *Truth's Triumph Over Trent*, where the Trent in question is the Council rather than the river. The Trent was, then, a difficult and dangerous river to which many meanings might accrue, and several of those meanings are in play in *The Vow Breaker*.

Even before the River Trent itself is mentioned in Sampson's play, there is a note of watery imagery. Old Bateman assures Old Boote that Young Bateman, whom he disdains as a suitor for his daughter, is a perfectly appropriate match for her:

> His purity of blood
> Runs in as sweet a stream and natural heat
> As thine, or hers.
> (I.i.101–3)

'Stream' obviously refers to the bloodstream, but the idea of it 'run[ing]' lends a riverine feel. Later Miles, a character from the Siege of Leith subplot, says of Anne's cousin Ursula, 'I will fly on her at my return with the verses out of new *Hero and Leander*' (2.1.66–8), a poem which tells the story of two lovers who live on opposite sides of the Hellespont; the fact that Leander drowns foreshadows Anne's fate. When Young Bateman realises that Anne is married, he too turns to aquatic language, and explicitly evokes drowning:

> such an overture and flood of woes
> Surrounds me that they almost drowned
> My understanding.
> (2.2.133–5)

Grey of Wilton may gesture at how rivers flow when he says, 'We'll keep the Frenchman keep within his bounds' (2.3.43), and when Anne laughs to see Young Bateman hanged his father turns to two creatures which live in water to express his disgust at her behaviour, calling her first a 'crocodile' and a 'swan' (2.4.89, 95). Finally the Ghost figures death in terms of crossing a body of water, first telling Anne, 'The ferryman attends thee at the verge / Of Cocytus and sooty Acheron' (4.3.199–200), and then warning her:

> I'll bring thee over turrets, towers and steeples,
> O'er shady groves, brinish meres and brooks;
> The slatt'ring sea to me is navigable.
> (4.3.205–7)

There is also a final, comic use of the water motif when Ball says Joshua is 'i'th' temper he was when he leaped into the Leen' (5.1.72–3) (he was drunk at the time).

The River Trent itself is first mentioned when Anne recounts a dream she has had, in a passage which I will quote in full because of its importance and because of the play's noncanonical status:

> Methought I walked along the verdant banks
> Of fertile Trent at an unusual time,
> The winter quarter, when herbs and flowers,
> Nature's choicest braveries, are dead,
> When every sapless tree sads at the root.
> Yet then, though contrary to nature,
> Upon those banks where foaming surges beat,
> I gathered flowers: roses red and damask,
> Love pansies, pinks, and gentle daffodils
> That seldom buds before the spring-time comes;
> Daisies, cowslips, harebells, marigolds,
> But not one bending violet to be seen.
> My apron full, I thought to pass away
> And make a garland of these fragrances.
> Just as I turned, I spied a lovely person
> Whose countenance was full of splendancy
> With such embelishings, as I may imagine
> Better than name them. It bade me follow it
> Then, methought, it went upon the water
> As firmly as on land. I, covetous
> To parley with so sweet a frontispiece,
> Leaped into th' water and so drowned myself.
> Pray watch me well this night for, if you sleep,
> I shall go gather flowers and then you'll weep.[42]

There is a lot going on this passage, including memories of Shakespeare (both *Hamlet* and *The Winter's Tale*), but there are two elements of its description of Trent which would have resonated particularly in early modern culture: its perhaps surprising identity as a *locus* of pastoral, and the disturbing instability of its waters.

Michael Drayton imagined the Trent as a home of nymphs – 'Neare to the Siluer Trent, / Syrena dwelleth'[43] – and in George Wither's *Epithalamia* for the marriage of Princess Elizabeth to the Palsgrave he says, 'We must have to fill the number All the Nimphs of Trent and Humber';[44] there had also been a Nymph of Trent at Prince

Henry's investiture, and the fact that this role was danced by his cousin Lady Arbella Stuart may perhaps explain why the Trent, often considered the third river of England,[45] was here listed second after the Thames.[46] In the first of Thomas Bancroft's *Two books of epigrammes, and epitaphs*, the epigram 'To Trent' similarly imagines it as almost Arcadian:

> Sweet River, on whose flowery Margin layd,
> I wist the slippery Fish have often playd
> At fast and loose: when ere th'enamour'd ayre
> Shall in soft sighes mine ecchoed accents beare,
> Gently permit the smoother verse to slide
> On thy sleeke bosome, and in tryumph ride
> Vnto the Mayne: where when it sounds along,
> Let Tritons dance, and Syrens learne my song.[47]

Another of Bancroft's epigrams, 'To old Sir John Harpur of Swarston, deceased' (Book 1, epigram 46), classicises and personifies the river:

> As did colde *Hebrus* with deepe grones
> The Thracian Harper once lament,
> So art thou with incessant mones
> Bewayled by thy dolefull Trent,
> While the astonisht Bridge doth show
> (Like an Arch-mouner) heaviest woe.

A 1649 collection of elegies on the death of Henry, Lord Hastings, *Lachrymae Musarum*, figured the Trent as 'adorn'd with swans'.[48] Richard Barnfield's 1595 *Cynthia* might speak deridingly of something excelling something else 'as much as Po in clearness passeth Trent',[49] but for poets such as Bancroft and Drayton the Trent was in fact as worthy of respect as the Po, while in the Prologue of *The Two Noble Kinsmen* we hear of 'Po and silver Trent',[50] where it is the Trent which attracts an epithet that might seem better fitted to the Po.

The second aspect of early modern ideas about the river to chime with Anne's dream is the idea that the waters of Trent might not always operate as waters usually did. John Cartwright's 1611 *The preachers trauels* explains that the Euphrates 'runneth very swiftly, almost as fast as the river of Trent',[51] but the fast flow of the Trent could sometimes slow to a trickle. John Hayward in *The Lives of the III Normans, Kings of England* declared that in the reign of Henry I there was an earthquake and 'the water of Trent was dried up at Nottingham the space of a mile';[52] Richard Baker's *A Chronicle of the Kings of England* slightly varies this by saying that 'the River of *Trent* at *Notingham* was dryed up a whole day'.[53] In Part II, he adds that in the reign of Mary I, within a mile of *Nottingham*, so mervailous a tempest of thunder happened, that it beat down all the Houses and Churches in two Towns thereabouts . . . the river of Trent running between the two Townes, the water with the mud in the bottom was carried a quarter of a mile, and cast against trees, with the violence whereof the trees were pulled up by the roots, and cast twelve score off.[54]

The Trent's waters move in mysterious ways, sometimes flowing with unusual violence and sometimes disappearing altogether.

Even the topography of the riverbank might seem treacherous. Nathen Amin notes that at the Battle of Stoke, when supporters of the pretender Lambert Simnel fought the troops of Henry VII, 'Bernard André suggests the rebels were waiting "on the ridge of a mountain", which was probably a plateau today known as Burnham Furlong'.[55] This unlikely mountain is only part of the nightmarish landscape which confronted the vanquished followers of Simnel: Charles Aleyn in *The historie of that wise and fortunate prince, Henrie of that name the seventh* figures the river itself as malevolent when he says that Francis Lovell tried to swim the Trent but 'Was swallow'd by the angry Element. / It seemes the streame out of a loyall sense / Would not support a Traytor to his Prince',[56] while Francis Bacon declared that Lovell 'could not recover the further side, by reason of the steepnesse of the ground'.[57] In George Buchanan's *The History of Scotland* the Trent becomes an impassable obstacle when the Dauphin of France invades in the reign of King John: 'John had broken down all the Bridges on the Trent, and had fastned sharp Pikes, or Pallisadoes, in all its Fords, removing away all Ships and Boats, so that it seemed to be so great an Impediment unto him that he could not avoid it, but must certainly be destroyed'; it is only because 'In the meantime, John was poysoned by an English Monk at Newark, a Town seated on the Trent' that the Dauphin's Scots allies can make progress.[58] The strategic importance of Newark is underlined by Margaret Cavendish, wife of the Earl of Newcastle, who notes in her life of her husband that when he was in command of all the royalist forces north of the Trent 'My Lord setled a Garison at *Newark* in *Nottingham-shire*, standing upon the River *Trent*, a very considerable pass, which kept the greatest part of *Nottingham-shire*, and part of *Lincoln-shire* in obedience.'[59] One would not now describe Newark as 'a very considerable pass' in geophysical terms, but it was certainly an important stronghold, and in that respect it has been a victim of its own success: the reason there is so little left of the castle to see today is that the Parliamentarians took special care to demolish it as thoroughly as possible.

One further aspect of Anne's dream is worth noting. Even before the Civil War, the banks of Trent had been the scene of several important battles. Holinshed notes that Polydore Vergil thought the Trent was the site of a battle between Britons and Saxons, and he himself is sure that

> a mightie battell was fought betwixt the sayd Ecgfrid, and Edilred King of Mercia, neere to the riuer of Trent, where Alswine ye brother of King Ecgfrid was slaine, with many other of the Northumbers, so that King Ecgfrid was constreyned to returne home with losse.[60]

Richard Baker's *A Chronicle of the Kings of England* declares that Edward II, with the earls of Atholl and Angus in his army, defeated the earls of Lancaster and Hereford at Burton upon Trent.[61] Patricia Griffin notes that Sampson's play was based on 'a local legend dating from the 15th century that had been published as a ballad in 1603' and that in at least one version of the legend the lover leaves to fight in the Wars of the Roses;[62] the play's explicit reference to the Siege of Leith has divorced it from this context, but Anne's vision of herself gathering 'roses red and damask' smuggles the idea of the Wars of the Roses back into the narrative, lending the story a timeless air but also connecting the Trent with recurrent conflict.

The particular issue in which *The Vow Breaker* is most urgently interested is the navigability of the river. Queen Elizabeth says to the Mayor:

>   to 'gratulate
> As a small token of our princely love
> On to your former motion made for Trent;
> You'd have it navigable to Gainsborough,
> So to Boston, Kingston, Humber, and Hull.
> But what are the causes?
>   (V.iv.9–14)

The causes about which the queen enquires were primarily economic, since towns along the Trent profited from being able to use it as a trade artery. Griffin notes that 'the Domesday Book records that the water of Trent was to be kept clear so that if anyone prevented progress of boats he should make amends'; she also observes that 'Gainsborough, still Britain's most inland port, is located at the highest navigable point on the Trent for seagoing vessels and during the seventeenth century, in particular, the town prospered greatly.'[63] Julie Sanders remarks that 'Navigability of inland waterways was certainly a pressing concern in the decade when Sampson's play was written and performed',[64] but there may also have been personal considerations at stake: Griffin discovered that

> There is an undated letter of Elizabeth's reign indicating that money was spent by a close relation of Sir Henry Willoughby, Sir Francis Willoughby

of Wollaton Hall, in an effort to make the Trent more navigable, perhaps to enable the easier transportation of coal from his own pits around Wollaton.[65]

The river could also be used to move wood as well as coal: in *The History of the Worthies of England* (1662), Thomas Fuller wrote that 'So indulgent is Divine Providence to England, that our four principal Forests lie either on the Sea, or Navigable Rivers; viz. New-Forest on the Sea, Shirewood on the Trent, Deane on the Severne, and this Windsor-Forest on the Thames.'[66] While the Trent might seem a pastoral feature to poets, to those who lived on its banks it represented the economic lifeblood of the region. It is also possible that the question seemed particularly urgent at the time *The Vow Breaker* was written: John Potter Briscoe notes that 'One of the middle arches of the Trent Bridge fell on the 10th August 1636. The rebuilding of it cost upwards of £100.'[67] *The Vow Breaker* was published in 1636, so was probably written before the collapse, but its discussion of the river would have sounded topical, especially when Joshua says, 'Commend me to my learnèd brother Spritchall, the cobbler of Nottingham bridge, and bid him look up and give me a coal' (2.1.75–7).

Making the river (more) navigable would have entailed work which would have affected how and where it flowed. The idea that it might be possible to effect change to the River Trent was one with a long and suggestive pedigree. Robert Burton declared in *The Anatomy of Melancholy* that 'Bishop *Atwater* of old, or as some will *Henry* 1st, made a channel from *Trent* to *Lincoln*, navigable; which now, saith Mr. *Camden* is decayed',[68] although Holinshed thought that Bishop Atwater died before he could complete his scheme and that no one had since taken it up.[69] Henry I reigned from 1100 to 1135 and William Atwater was Bishop of Lincoln from 1514 until 1521, so the proposed chronology is loose. William Dugdale's 1662 *The History of Imbanking and drayning of divers Fenns and marshes* goes for something in the middle when he declares that 'King Edward the second did . . . constitute John de Doncastre, and others, his Justices to clear the River of Done . . . aswell for the passage of ships from Doncastre to the River of Trent, as for drayning of the Lands adjacent', attributing the work to a king who reigned from 1307 to 1327, and adding that his son Edward III (1327–77) also took steps to keep the river clear.[70]

The idea that the course of the Trent could be moved is most famously found in Shakespeare's *Henry IV, Part One*, where Hotspur objects to the proposed division of the kingdom between himself and Edmund Mortimer:

Methinks my moiety, north from Burton here,
In quantity equals not one of yours.

> See how this river comes me cranking in,
> And cuts me from the best of all my land
> A huge half-moon, a monstrous cantle out.
> I'll have the current in this place damned up,
> And here the smug and silver Trent shall run
> In a new channel fair and evenly.
> It shall not wind with such a deep indent,
> To rob me of so rich a bottom here.[71]

Stuart Elden observes that 'This is a departure from Holinshed, and is a rich passage with several key phrases. It is clear that Hotspur thinks his share or portion ("moiety") is unfair. He points to the town of Burton-on-Trent, where the river turns northeastward.'[72] Holinshed's *Chronicles* suggest that the Staffordshire town of Burton upon Trent was to prove a significant location in the ensuing conflict:

> Kyng Henry aduertised of the proceedings of the Percys, forthwith gathered about him suche power as hee mighte make, and beeing earnestly called vppon by the Scotte, the Earle of Marche, to make hast and giue battell to his enimies, before their power by delaying of time should still too muche encrease, hee passed forwarde with suche speede, that he was in sight of his enimies, lying in camp neere to Shrewesburie, before they were in doubt of any such thing, for the Percys thought, that he would haue stayed at Burton vppon Trent, till his Counsell had come thither to him to giue their aduice what he were best to do. By reason of the Kings suddaine comming in thys sort, they stayed from assaulting the Towne of Shrewesburie, which enterprise they were ready at that instante to haue taken in hande, and forthwith, the Lorde Percie, as a Captaine of high courage, began to exhorte the Captaynes and Souldiers to prepare themselues to battell.[73]

According to this account, the battle of Shrewsbury, which the Percys lost and at which Hotspur was killed, was fought only because of a miscalculation about how long the king would remain at Burton upon Trent. Shakespeare's mention of the town thus looks like an ironic foreshadowing of the overreaching which will eventually kill Hotspur. The Trent will not be moved by him, but it will bring him down.

The Vow Breaker not only remembers another Harry Percy's role at the Siege of Leith (4.1.17) but also explicitly connects the mayor's petition to have the Trent made navigable to Hotspur's plan:

> Edward the First, from whom we bear our arms
> (Three crowns displayed in an azure field)
> First 'gan to make our river navigable.
> Small barks it bore, but not of that full weight
> That were transportable for our affairs
> In the two Edwards, the Second and Third.
> Unto the second Richard it continued,

> Till Bolingbroke began. Then Harry the Fourth
> And Percy fell at odds; in which division,
> Dividing of the land, Glendower began
> To stop the water-courses of flowing Trent.
> By that means our navigable course was stopped.
> (V.iv.30–41)

This passage surprisingly rewrites both Shakespeare's play and history by having Glendower actually begin to divert the river; it is true that he says 'Come, you shall have Trent turned' (3.1.130), but there is no indication that he is going to do it himself, or that anyone has time to do anything at all about Hotspur's idea.

By evoking Shakespeare in this way, Sampson invites us to consider the purpose and genre of his play. Julie Sanders considers that *The Vow Breaker* is in one sense 'a version of the history play that might be placed alongside other 1630s experimentation in this form such as Ford's *Perkin Warbeck*';[74] this is a suggestive comparison, because not only was *Perkin Warbeck* dedicated to the Earl of Newcastle, but it too rewrites Shakespeare, since if its hero really is Richard, Duke of York (which is hinted but never confirmed),[75] then the story told in *Richard III* cannot be true, just as *The Vow Breaker* challenges the story told in *Henry IV, Part One*, implicitly raising questions about who authorises history. But the Trent is not only a public and political river but also the place where Anne Boot happened to live, and *The Vow Breaker* is not only a history play (if indeed it is one at all). Emanuel Stelzer calls it 'a mixture of domestic play and history' and notes that the play was dedicated to a woman who had been courted in a way 'which brought about an affront to the Willoughby family, the vilification of Sir John Suckling, and opposition to King Charles ... [the] dedication of *The Vow Breaker* to Anne Willoughby explicitly references this incident';[76] Anne Willoughby, an heiress, had been pursued by the fortune-hunting Sir John Suckling and had been encouraged by King Charles to marry him, but steadfastly refused. If the play does indeed want to hint a reproach to Charles I, its task is made easier by the allusions to his grandmother Mary, Queen of Scots, who notoriously took as her third husband a man who had been implicated in the murder of her second, and the killing of Lord Darnley is also a prime example of the bleed between the personal and private which energises so much domestic tragedy of the period.

The Vow Breaker shares this interest in the interface between public and private. Griffin observes of Bateman's death that 'From the woodcuts and from other versions of the incident, it is seen that he took his own life in front of her door',[77] and Anne's body is recovered at a point which, if not liminal, is at least a crossing place: Prattle says 'drowned we found her on the riverside / Nigh Colwick ferry' (4.3.259–60). The River Trent may stand in for the River Styx as it carries Anne to her death, but it is also a real river with specific and significant geographical features. (It may be significant that Colwick ferry is close to Stoke Bardolph, where a weir built by Sir Thomas Stanhope in 1590 caused a furious quarrel with Gilbert Talbot, the future seventh earl of Shrewsbury, who claimed that it obstructed the navigation of the Trent,[78] and also involved Talbot's brother-in-law Charles Cavendish, father of the future Earl of Newcastle;[79] Stoke Bardolph would be a name likely to stick in the mind of anyone interested in the *Henriad*.)

This interplay between the mytho-historical and the private and personal is further underlined by the play's final allusion to local topography, when Queen Elizabeth decides that she would like to go and see

> The underminings and unpaced griese
> That Mortimer and Isabel did devise
> To steal their sportive dalliances in,
> Of whom your stately fortress does retain
> The labyrinth (now called Mortimer's Hole).
> (V.iv.109–113)

Michael Drayton's heroic epistle 'Mortimer to Queene Isabell' had drawn attention to this aspect of Nottingham's history by having its eponymous hero say 'whilst cleere Trent her wonted course shall keep, / For our sad fall, her christall drops shall weepe',[80] and Thomas May declared in *The victorious reigne of King Edward the Third* that

> Farre from that Castle, on the side of Trent
> A Caves darke mouth was found, of deepe descent;
> Vpon the brinke of which there grew a round
> So close a thicket, as quite hid the ground
> From sight; the Cave could be descry'd by none,
> And had remain'd for many yeeres unknowne;
> Whose hollow wombe did farre from thence extend,
> And under-ground an uncouth passage lend
> Into the Castle. This darke vault was made
> To serve the Fort, when *Danes* did first invade
> This fertile Iland.[81]

The cave has proved a refuge in times of national crisis, but it is also characterised by a 'womb' and by obvious potential as a trysting-place, perhaps with shades of Dido and Aeneas. The image of the Virgin Queen can survive being connected to the story of Edward II's adulterous queen and her lover Roger Mortimer, but if we remember either Mary, Queen of Scots or Charles I's encouragement of the fortune-hunter Sir John Suckling at this point, they might fare less well. We might also remember another Mortimer, named Edmund rather than Roger but a member of the same family, whose share of the kingdom Hotspur disputed; if so we will recall that you cannot move the Trent, but that the Trent may move you. Sampson's play may be named after Anne Boot, but its true central character is the river.

Notes

1. Patricia Griffin, 'A Critical Edition of William Sampson's *The Vow Breaker* (1636)', PhD thesis (Sheffield Hallam University, 2009), 70.
2. Julie Sanders, *The Cultural Geography of Early Modern Drama, 1620–1650* (Cambridge: Cambridge University Press, 2011), 119.
3. Griffin, 'A Critical Edition', 70.
4. Emanuel Stelzer, '*The Vow Breaker* and William Sampson's Role in "the Anne Willoughby Affair"', *Early Theatre* 20.1 (2017), 97–118, 104.
5. Griffin, 'A Critical Edition', 103.
6. Ibid., 16.
7. See https://ebba.english.ucsb.edu/ballad/36407/transcription (last accessed 21 September 2023). I am indebted to Emanuel Stelzer for pointing this out.
8. https://hrc.contentdm.oclc.org/digital/collection/p15878coll17/id/14079 (last accessed 21 September 2023). Again I owe this observation to Emanuel Stelzer.
9. Michael Drayton, *Poly-Olbion* (London: Humphrey Lownes, M. Lownes, J. Browne, J. Helme, 1612), 207–8.
10. Samuel Clarke, *A geographical description of all the countries in the known world* (London: R. J. for Thomas Newberry, 1657), 89.
11. Michael Drayton, 'To the Riuer Ankor', in *Poems* (London: Valentine Simmes for N. Ling, 1605), n.p.
12. Sanders, *The Cultural Geography*, 47–8.
13. Thomas Dekker, *Britannia's Honor shining brightly in severall magnificent shewes or pageants* (London: N. Okes and J. Norton, 1628), sig. A4r.
14. Raphael Holinshed, *The firste [laste] volume of the chronicles of England, Scotland and Irelande* (London: John Hunne, 1577), 31 and 70.
15. Thomas Malory, *Le morte darthur* (London: William Caxton, 1485), n.p., Arthur's writ runs 'on thys side trent water'.
16. Rowland Broughton, *A briefe discourse of the lyfe and death of the late right high and honorable Sir William Pawlet* (London: Richard Jones, 1572), n.p.
17. Henry Calthrop, *The liberties, usages and customes of the city of London confirmed by especiall acts of Parliament* (London: B. Allsop for Nicholas Vavasour, 1642), 2.
18. John Brydall, *Camera regis, or, a short view of London* (London: William Crooke, 1676), 70–1.
19. Drayton, *Poly-Olbion* (London: Humphrey Lownes, M. Lownes, J. Browne, J. Helme, 1612), 243. Maggie Kilgour observes of this passage, 'Britain was originally a single nation, united under its Trojan founder, Brute,

but then divided by his sons into three parts, following natural, watery boundaries . . . Drayton reminds us that water is both a symbol of unity and a principle of territorial definition'; Maggie Kilgour, 'Writing on Water', *English Literary Renaissance* 29.2 (1999), 282–305, 288.
20. Raphael Holinshed, *The firste [laste] volume*, 74.
21. Patrick Gordon, *History of Robert the Bruce* (Dordrecht: George Waters, 1615), sig. xiii3v.
22. Edward Bowles, *Manifest Truth, or an Inversion of the truths manifest containing a narration of the proceedings of the Scottish army* (London: M. S. for Henry Overton and Giles Calvert, 1646), 36.
23. Raphael Holinshed, *The firste [laste] volume*, 7.
24. John Bramhall, *A sermon preached in Yorke Minster, before his Excellence the Marques of Newcastle, being then ready to meet the Scotch Army, January 28 1643* (York: Stephen Bulkley, 1644), 22.
25. Drayton, *Poly-Olbion*, 40, 118.
26. https://lostplays.folger.edu/Black_Bateman_of_the_North,_Parts_1_and_2 (last accessed 21 September 2023).
27. William Vallans, *A tale of two swannes* (London: Roger Ward for John Sheldrake, 1590), 5.
28. James Howell, *Epistolae ho-Elianae* (London: W. H. for Humphrey Moseley, 1650), 71.
29. Holinshed, *The firste [laste] volume of the chronicles of England, Scotland and Irelande*, 1305.
30. John Speed, *The theatre of the empire of Great Britaine* (London: William Hall, 1611), 672.
31. William Habington, *The History of Edward the Fourth* (London: Thomas Cotes for William Cooke, 1640), 5.
32. Richard Baker, *A Chronicle of the Kings of England, from the time of the Romans goverment unto the raigne of our soveraigne lord, King Charles* (London: Daniel Frere, 1643), Part II, 86.
33. Richard Brome, *The Damoiselle* (London: T. R. for Richard Marriott and Thomas Dring, 1653), sig. E8r.
34. Holinshed, *The firste [laste] volume of the chronicles of England, Scotland and Irelande*, 5.
35. John Cowell, *The Interpreter* (London: John Legate, 1607), sig. Aaaa2r.
36. Cathy Shrank, 'Civility and the City in *Coriolanus*', *Shakespeare Quarterly* 54.4 (winter, 2003), 406–23, 417.
37. John Weever, *Ancient funerall monuments* (London: Thomas Harper for Laurence Sadler, 1631), 838.
38. John Brydall, *Camera regis, or, a short view of London* (London: William Crooke, 1676), 19.
39. John Stow, *A Survay of London* (London: John Windet for John Wolfe, 1598), 471.
40. Izaak Walton, *The Compleat Angler* (London: T. Maxey for Richard Marriot, 1653), 35.
41. Henry Burton, *A divine tragedie lately acted* (Amsterdam: J. F. Stam, 1636), 11.
42. Griffin, 'A Critical Edition of William Sampson's *The Vow Breaker* (1636)', IV.iii.113–36.

43. Michael Drayton, 'The Shepheards Sirena', in *The battaile of Agincourt* (London: Augustine Mathewes for William Lee, 1631), 209.
44. George Wither, *Epithalamia* (London: F. Kingston for Edward Marchant, 1613), n.p.
45. As in Edward Leigh's 1659 *England Described* where we are told that 'Trent by his due right challengeth to himself the third place among all the Rivers of England'; Edward Leigh, *England Described* (London: A. M. for Henry Marsh, 1659), 21.
46. The third on this occasion was the Arun, danced by Alethea, Countess of Arundel, Arbella's first cousin.
47. Thomas Bancroft's *Two books of epigrammes, and epitaphs* (London: J. Okes for Matthew Wallbancke, 1639), Book 1, epigram 78, 'To Trent'.
48. R. B., *Lachrymae Musarum* (London: Thomas Newcomb, 1649), 6.
49. Richard Barnfield, *Cynthia* (London: Humphrey Lownes, 1595), sonnet 4.
50. John Fletcher and William Shakespeare, *The Two Noble Kinsmen*, ed. Lois Potter (London: Bloomsbury, 2015), Prologue, 12.
51. John Cartwright, *The preachers trauels* (London: Walter Burre, 1611), 12.
52. John Hayward, *The Lives of the III Normans, Kings of England* (London: R. Barker, 1613), 302–3.
53. Baker, *A Chronicle of the Kings of England*, 57.
54. Baker, *A Chronicle of the Kings of England*, Part II, 106.
55. Nathen Amin, *Henry VII and the Tudor Pretenders: Simnel, Warbeck and Warwick* (Stroud: Amberley, 2020), 124.
56. Charles Aleyn, *The historie of that wise and fortunate prince, Henrie of that name the seventh* (London: Thomas Cotes for William Cooke, 1638), 49.
57. Francis Bacon, *The Historie of the Reigne of King Henry the Seventh* (London: J. Haviland and R. Young for Philemon Stevens and Christopher Holland, 1629), 35.
58. George Buchanan, *The History of Scotland* (London: Edward Jones for Awnsham Churchill, 1690), 237–8.
59. Margaret Cavendish, *The Life of the thrice noble, high and puissant prince William Cavendishe, Duke, Marquess and Earl of Newcastle* (London: A. Maxwell, 1667), 22.
60. Holinshed, *The firste [laste] volume of the chronicles of England, Scotland and Irelande*, 120, and 182.
61. Baker, *A Chronicle of the Kings of England*, 147.
62. Griffin, 'A Critical Edition', 3, 16.
63. Ibid., 71.
64. Sanders, *The Cultural Geography*, 45.
65. Griffin, 'A Critical Edition', 73.
66. Thomas Fuller, *The History of the Worthies of England* (London: J. G., W. L. and W. G. for Thomas Williams, 1662), 81.
67. John Potter Briscoe, 'History of the Trent bridges at Nottingham', *Transactions of the Royal Historical Society* 2 (1873), 212–21, 216. Martin Wiggins guesses 1628 as the date of composition (Stelzer, 'The Vow Breaker', 103).
68. Robert Burton, *The Anatomy of Melancholy*, ed. Angus Gowland (Harmondsworth: Penguin, 2021), 97.

69. Holinshed, *The firste [laste] volume of the chronicles of England, Scotland and Irelande*, 32.
70. William Dugdale, *The History of Imbanking and drayning of divers Fenns and marshes* (London: Alice Warren, 1662), 121–2 and 138.
71. William Shakespeare, *Henry IV, Part 1*, ed. P.H. Davison (Harmondsworth: Penguin, 1968), III.i.92–101.
72. Stuart Elden, *Shakespearean Territories* (Chicago: University of Chicago Press, 2018), 189.
73. Holinshed, *The firste [laste] volume of the chronicles of England, Scotland and Irelande*, 1138.
74. Sanders, *The Cultural Geography*, 118.
75. Gilles Monsarrat, 'John Ford's substantive accidentals in *Perkin Warbeck*', *The Library* 16.4 (December 2015), 446–57.
76. Stelzer, '*The Vow Breaker*', 97–8.
77. Griffin, 'A Critical Edition', 82.
78. Robert Boies Sharpe, *The Real War of the Theatres* (London: D. C. Heath, 1935), 74.
79. See Mary S. Lovell, *Bess of Hardwick* (London: Little, Brown, 2005), 398–401.
80. Michael Drayton, 'Mortimer to Queene Isabell', in *Poems* (London: Valentine Simmes for N. Ling, 1605), 19.
81. Thomas May, *The victorious reigne of King Edward the Third* (London: John Beale for T. Walkley and B. Fisher, 1635), sig. C3r.

Chapter 5

Ship of Fools and Slow Boat to Hell: The Literary Voyages of the Gravesend Barge

Lindsay Ann Reid

At the opening of *The Cobler of Caunterburie*, an anonymously published work of 1590 that has sometimes been attributed to Robert Greene, the first-person narrator makes a momentous decision.[1] Although he arrived at the river stairs of London's Billingsgate port intending to hire a tilt boat, he changes tack when he spots a 'crue of madde companions' perched aboard the twopenny Gravesend barge waiting for 'the tide [to] serve'.[2] He resolves to join them, 'step[ping] into the barge and t[aking] up [a] seate amongst the thickest'.[3] Their open-air journey on the Tideway commences with this 'merry' band of shipmates 'chat[ting] some of one thing and some of an other, al of myrth, [and] many of knavery'.[4] As the vessel moves eastwards, these opening 'prattles' give way, in turn, to a more formalised tale-telling exchange; the result is what has been hailed as 'a brilliant updating of the structural games of [Geoffrey] Chaucer's ... *Canterbury Tales*', with the Middle English text's celebrated pilgrims reimagined as 'divers passengers' travelling along one of early modern England's most highly trafficked waterways.[5]

While, historically speaking, the journey from Billingsgate to Gravesend that serves as the backdrop for the neo-Chaucerian storytelling antics in the *Cobler of Caunterburie* could alternatively be made aboard other vessels, as this text indicates, a common barge shuttled back and forth in near-continuous motion along this stretch of the Thames. Leaving Gravesend at low water and London at high water, the barge moved with regular irregularity at the turn of every tide. In the early modern era, the Gravesend barge also ventured now and then into the realm of imagination, and this chapter seeks to chart its most significant literary voyages.

The barge on the Thames

'Reading a city through the river that runs through it', as Sophie Watson observes, 'reveals new understandings and tells different stories.'[6] In the first half of this chapter, I want to begin exploring the underappreciated story of the Gravesend barge by situating this ferry service in the broader context of the early modern Thames. A useful starting point is a portrait of the river offered by George Turberville in a mid-Tudor poem:

> Thou stately Streame [that] with the swelling Tide
> Gainst London walles incessantly dost beate,
> Thou Thems (I say) where barge & bote doth ride,
> And snowhite Swans do fish for needefull meate.[7]

Turberville's sixteenth-century Thames is a waterway that is at once idyllically portrayed, teeming with life and activity, yet also distinctly forbidding. As the poem progresses, its depiction of the river's heaving waters ultimately morphs into a plea for the safe passage of the speaker's lady, who is journeying to London by boat. Recognising the potentially disruptive 'powre' of the river to 'weltre up and surge in wrathfull wise', the speaker therefore requests that the dread Thames 'calme [her] tyde' for his lady's sake.[8]

An apt complement to the river portrayed in Turberville's abovementioned poem is the 'silver streaming *Themmes*' that is found running towards 'mery *London*' in Edmund Spenser's later sixteenth-century *Prothalamion*.[9] Here, the Thames is likewise idealised: it is a waterway whose banks are 'paynted all with variable flowers' and whose 'gentle streame' carries swans with feathers the whitest of pure whites.[10] But the *Prothalamion*, too, laces this bucolicism with a palpable sense of trepidation. Spenser's reverential refrain 'Sweet Thames, run softly, till I end my song' hints at both the river's place of primacy within the English landscape – a major source of poetic as well as material wealth – and its inherent volatility.

The sense of awe that pervades both Turberville's and Spenser's addresses to the 'stately' – perhaps even princely – Thames is echoed in John Stow's 1598 *Survay of London*, wherein 'the most famous River of this Iland' prominently features at the work's outset.[11] Figured as a source of local and national pride, the Thames is described as moving 'with a marvelous quiet course' between its point of origin in Oxfordshire and London, whence it proceeds to break 'into the *French Ocean* by maine tides, which twise in 24. howers space doeth eb and flow . . . to the great commodity of Travellers, by the which all kinde of Marchandise be easily conveyed'.[12] In an expanded 1618 edition of *The Survay*, Anthony Munday would add to Stow's earlier work a significant amount of further detail on what he refers to as 'the commodities of the . . . River' – a waterway that he patriotically claims none 'in *Europe* is able to *exceed*'.[13] Evoking imagery reminiscent of Turberville's and Spenser's, Munday waxes poetic upon 'the infinite number of Swannes', 'the fat and sweet Salmons', and the Thames's bountiful 'store . . . of Barbels, Trowtes, Chevins, Pearches, Smelts, Breames, Roches, Daces, Gudgins, Flounders, Shrimps, Eeles, &c.'[14] Alongside this magnificent display of wildlife, he also positions 'two thousand Wherries and small Boates', as well as a panoply of larger 'Tide-Boates, Tilt-boates, and Barges, which either carry passengers, or bring necessary provision from all quarters . . . unto the Citie of *London*'.[15] A further simile added (presumably by Munday) to the again-expanded 1633 edition of this text goes even further, likening the urban riverscape to 'a very wood of Trees, disbranched to make glades and let in light: so shaded it is with Masts and Sayles'.[16]

Verbal depictions of the considerable river traffic along the Thames are reaffirmed in visual portrayals of early modern London. Boats occupy a place of primacy in John Norden's 1597 *View of London Bridge from East to Weste*, for instance – where we are also reminded of the potential hazards of river travel by the appearance of distressed passengers who have fallen out of an overturned vessel (Figure 5.1). Watercraft also conspicuously adorn the river in Norden's map of London from *Speculum Britanniae* (Figure 5.2), the map included in Georg Braun and

Figure 5.1 Detail from John Norden's *View of London Bridge from East to West* (1597). STC 18643.5. Used by permission of the Folger Shakespeare Library.

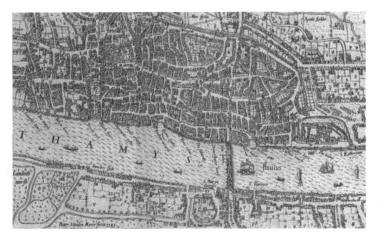

Figure 5.2 Detail from John Norden's map of London in *Speculum Britanniae* (1593). STC 18635. Used by permission of the Folger Shakespeare Library.

Frans Hogenburg's *Civitates Orbis Terrarum* (Figure 5.3), and Claes Visscher's famed panorama cityscape (Figure 5.4). The consistent presence of boats in these images reminds us that the Thames played a key role in early modern London's transport infrastructure. In an urban landscape that included only one bridge, water was often the most expedient means of circulating people and goods. It was also Londoners' primary mode of accessing and interacting with the world beyond – a fact underscored in Abraham Cowley's seventeenth-century description of 'all the liquid World [as] one extea[n]ded Thames', or a vast marine network that enables 'all the riches of the Globe beside / [to] Flo[w] in to [London] with every Tide'.[17]

Although the Gravesend barge worked alongside the multitude of other watercraft moving across and along the early modern Thames, it had, as this chapter will demonstrate, an outsized reputation that made it a common point of cultural reference. Harnessing the power of the lower Thames's celebrated tides, it left London at high water and moved downstream for twenty-some-miles to Gravesend on the river's south bank, from which point it would depart at low water to make the same journey in reverse back to London. As we learn in the opening pages of *The Cobler of Caunterburie*, travellers could catch this tidal ferry at Billingsgate, a port located a short distance to the east of London Bridge that variously appears as 'Bellyns gate' (Figure 5.2), 'Belins Gate' (Figure 5.3), and 'Billins gate' (Figure 5.4) in contemporary maps and illustrations of London. This bustling area was described by Stow as 'a large Water gate, Porte or Harbrough for ships and Boates, commonly

Ship of Fools and Slow Boat to Hell 105

Figure 5.3 Map of London entitled 'Londinum Feracissimi Angliae Regni Metropolis' from the 1635 edition of Georg Braun and Frans Hogenburg's *Civitates Orbis Terrarum* (first published 1574). MAP L85c no. 27. Used by permission of the Folger Shakespeare Library.

Figure 5.4 Detail from a 1625 imprint of Claes Visscher's *Londinum Florentissima Britanniae Urbs* (first published 1616). GA795.L6 V5 1625 Cage. Used by permission of the Folger Shakespeare Library.

ariving there with fish both fresh and salt, shell fishes, salt, Orenges, Onions, and other Fruits and Rootes, Wheat, Rie, and Graine of divers sorts'.[18] It was not only goods 'for service of the Citie, and the partes of this Realme adjoyning' that flowed through Billingsgate, however.[19] As John Taylor would report in the first half of the seventeenth century, '[a]t *Billinsgate*, are every Tyde to be had Barges, lighthorsmen Tiltboats and Wherries'.[20] The most famous of these barges was undoubtedly the one that travelled to Gravesend: it was a familiar enough feature of London's urban landscape to serve as a comprehensible unit of measurement for Thomas Deloney's Meg of Westminster, who claims she is 'not so high as *Paules* nor is [her] foot so long as Gravs-end Barge', and a journey upon it was so quotidian that it could be trivialised in Barnabe Riche's ironic characterisation of himself as an intrepid traveller who has 'sayled in *Gravesende Barge* as farre as *Billings gate*, . . . [and] gone from *S. Pankeridge* church to *Kentish* towne by lande'.[21]

In the latter part of the sixteenth century, William Lambarde's *A Perambulation of Kent* noted a market in Gravesend on Wednesdays and fairs held in the town on both Saint Paul's Day (25 January) and Saint Edward's Day (13 October).[22] The weekly market and biannual fairs were far from the only reasons why one might journey to Gravesend, however. Indeed, in *Pasquils Night-Cap* of 1612, the town is colourfully described by William Fennor as a place through which 'Men of all Countries travaile':

> *English, Italians, Turks, Moores, Spaniards, Germans,*
> *Danes, Scots, French, Irish, Muscovits, and Normans,*
> And new *Virgineans*, and of every sort,
> Some white, some blacke, some long-men, & some short.
> Som honest men, some fools, some knaves, some wise
> Passe through this Towne, of all degrees at large,
> Some thieves, some Tailors, which do still devise
> New foolish fashions to put men to charge.
> Some Cittizens, some Cuckolds there arives,
> Some queans, some Maids, som bawds, & some good wives:
> And through this Towne they travel to the ferry,
> To be convai'd by Tilt-boate, or by Wherry.[23]

The diversity of the travellers that Fennor locates in Gravesend speaks directly to the town's importance in this period as a transport hub.

In the early modern era, the Gravesend route for those travelling from London to Kent was well established. Indeed, in a memorable vignette from the fifteenth-century 'London Lickpenny', an impecunious Kentish narrator hoping to return home begs the bargeman at Billingsgate to waive his fare, only to be told: 'Here skapethe no man, by-nethe ii. pens!'[24] More than this, however, Gravesend was also a standard gateway to a variety of European destinations, as we are reminded in ballad lyrics describing the flight to the continent of Katherine Brandon, Duchess of Suffolk, with her second husband Richard Bertie:

> at Billingsgate they all did meete:
> Like people poore in Gravesend Barge,
> They simply went with all their charge.
> And all along from Gravesend towne,
> with journies short on foot they went
> Unto the Sea-coast they came downe,
> to passe the Seas was their intent,
> And God provided so that day,
> That they tooke ship and sail'd away.[25]

Indeed, the efficiency with which one might potentially (with cooperative weather and tides) reach continental Europe via Gravesend is elsewhere emphasised in an anecdote about Thomas Wolsey from Stow's *Annales of England*. Stow relates that, while on business for Henry VII in the early years of the sixteenth century, Wolsey once

> came to London about foure of the clocke, where the barge of Graves-end was ready to launch forth, both with a prosperous tide and winde ... and so passed forth with such happie spede, that he arriued at Graves-ende within little more than three houres, where he tarried no longer than his post horses were providing, and then travelled so speedily, that he came to Dover the next morning; whereas the passengers were readie under saile to Caleis, into the which passenger without tarrying he entered, and having post horses in a readinesse, ... he made such hastie speede, that he was that night with the Emperor [Maximilian I].[26]

In the early modern period, Gravesend also served as an important transfer point for those trying to reach even further-flung international locales, including the Americas. It is thus that the Algonquian woman known as Pocahontas came to be buried in Gravesend following her tragic death in transit from England back to Virginia in 1617, a fact memorialised by the modern statue of her that now stands in the town.

In thinking about the Gravesend barge's historical place on the Thames, its kinetic rhythms merit contemplation. In a letter written by Henry Wotton that prefaces John Milton's *Comus* in the 1645 edition of his *Poems*, the frequency of the ferry service becomes a point of reference: passage along another route is said by Wotton to be 'as Diurnal as a *Gravesend* Barge'.[27] The barge may have travelled predictably often, yet it also moved with a sort of capriciousness, for it was subject to the natural rise and fall of water levels in a river that, as Munday puts it, 'floweth and filleth all her chanels, twise in the day and night, that is, in euvery twelve houres once'.[28] Put otherwise, this ferry service operated in tension with the natural circadian rhythms of much other human activity. The detailed portrait of the Tideway's ebbs and flows that Munday included in his expanded version of Stow's *Survay* explains, 'These tides also differ in their times, each one comming later then other, ... wherby, the common difference between one tide and another, is found to consist of twenty foure minutes ... as experience doth confirme.'[29] This means that if a boat destined for Gravesend left London at around 9:00 a.m. on a Monday, a prospective passenger hoping to travel along the same route on Friday of that same week would find that the daytime departure had migrated to early afternoon. It also means that a good deal of the time one of the ferry's two daily departures would have happened at inconvenient or unsociable hours.

That disembarking travellers might potentially need to find an appropriate place to shelter until morning is suggested in Fynes Morison's account of a trip he undertook in 1597:

[W]ith the night-tide [we] passed in a boat [from Gravesend] to *London*, where we arived ... at foure of the clock in the morning ... This early hower ... being unfit to trouble my friends, I went to the Cocke (an Inne of *Aldersgate* streete) and there apparrelled as I was, laid me downe upon a bed.[30]

As a mid-seventeenth-century account of Mary Carleton's journey to London aboard the Gravesend barge makes clear, the search to 'finde a lodging' did not always go nearly as smoothly as it appears to have for Morison, with travellers who arrived at odd hours sometimes 'assault[ing] many Tavern doores for admittance, but finding none open'.[31] What is more, in a time before wristwatches and personal alarm clocks, a potential ferry passenger who (for one reason or another) simply arrived at the banks of the Thames at the wrong moment might be subjected to a very long wait indeed. Just how such passengers might entertain themselves while waiting for the tide to turn is coyly hinted at in *Pasquils Night-Cap* when a character named Hercules and his companions elect to 'drinke downe sorrow', spending 'all that day, and almost all the night' in Billingsgate – engaging in activities that the author pointedly says he will 'omit' – before 'at next ebbe ... ferry[ing] to *Gravesend*'.[32]

In pondering the temporal anomalies of the ferry's schedule, consider, as well, that the extent of the Thames's highs and lows were variable, with 'each tide ... not of equall height and greatnesse' (depending on the lunar cycle and other influences).[33] It was not unheard of for compounding environmental factors to bring 'the water [in] with more vehemency'.³⁴ Munday reports that 'the *Thames* ouerfloweth her bancks neere unto *London*' at times, and he also describes how the tide's movements could be altered in unpredictable ways. '[R]ough winds', for instance, could precipitate irregularities like the apparent 'chopping in of three or foure Tides in one naturall day'.³⁵ Even in the absence of such freak weather occurrences, the tides were, no doubt, not always fully cooperative. Indeed, John Sherwin's early eighteenth-century account of making the trip down the Tideway gives some sense of the difficulties that an unlucky passenger might at times encounter along this route:

> I got to *Billingsgate* by Seven, took Water at Eight for *Gravesend*, but fell short a Mile and half; the Watermen landed their Passengers at *Three of the Clock*, except my self, Wife, and Son for *John Bull* advis'd me to sit in the Boat, because I was lame, for he would strive to row to Town. We did so, and . . . in half an Hour after, he came and helped me out of the Boat over a Lime-Hoy, and had much ado to get me ashore, telling us at the same time he could not get to *Gravesend* till three Hours after, the Tide ran so strong against them.³⁶

Though the ferry to and from Gravesend was a long-standing London institution well before the dawn of the early modern era, the public barge's first origins are murky. Administrative records from the reign of Henry IV show that, by the close of the fourteenth century, it had already been custom 'time out of mind' for 'the inhabitants of the town of Gravesende . . . to ship on their own vessels all persons coming to the town and wishing to go from thence to the city of London by water'.³⁷ Legal documents produced over the course of the Tudor era indicate that successive attempts were made to better regulate the watercraft operating along this corridor. Early in the reign of Henry VIII, a Parliamentary Act took issue with perceived price gouging on the lower Thames: it thus sought to revert fares from London to Gravesend to historically agreed rates (four shillings for group hire of the entire boat, or two pence when 'ev'y p'son passing in the said barge . . . paie for hym self').³⁸

In the Marian period, another Parliamentary Act was passed in an attempt to correct the 'lack of good government and due order amongst wherrymen and watermen . . . upon the river of Thames'.³⁹ Subsequent to this, the self-governing Company of Watermen came into being, and an official confirmation of 'The prices of Fares and passages to be paid unto watermen' along the London to Gravesend route was duly printed by John Cawood. It lists rates not just for passage on the public barge (unchanged from Henry VIII's era, or indeed, from the fifteenth-century rate quoted by the bargeman in 'London Lickpenny'), but also the higher fares to be charged for the more luxurious tilt boats and wherries traversing the Tideway.[40] Company of Watermen ordinances dating from the 1560s give some sense of the relationship between these other types of boats and the barge service. Interpreting these ordinances, Henry Humphreys has speculated that 'traffic in the ferry must at this time have increased, for the owners of the barges were authorized by the corporation to appoint seven tilt boats ... to [act] as auxiliaries'.[41] He also remarks the intricacies of the payment system put in place to ensure that the tilt boats would not financially sink the common barge:

> It was stipulated that no master of a tilt boat should take of any person other than of the nobilitie or worshipful ... more than sixpence, paying out of this the accustomed fare in the barge, which was two pence, to the owner of the turn the same tide that the tilt boat was engaged, provided however that if the earnings of the barge in that turn should amount to thirteen shillings and fourpence, then the payment by the tilt boat master to the barge was to be only one penny in respect to each passenger.[42]

That the Gravesend barge did, in fact, face stiff competition from other types of watercraft in the Elizabethan era is elsewhere affirmed in a mid-seventeenth-century text, which retrospectively explains that 'oftentimes when the ... Barge had 23 Passengers, and was to stay but for one more [to reach its four shilling threshold], other Water-men that plyed at the Ferry, would take up the next Passenger at cheap rates, whereby the Barge lay long for want of a compleat number'.[43] Such practices seem to have inspired the further set of regulations agreed in 1595 where again it is reiterated that '[t]he common barge called the Gravesend barge shall serve every tide, if wind and weather will permit', transporting 'all such passengers as shall desire to go with them' for 'two pence and no more for each passenger ... or four shillings in all'.[44] The regulations proceed to outline how

> the common barge, hath been much hindered by the multitude of tilt boats, lighthorsemen, and wherries used in each of the said ferries, who, for their private gain, take upon themselves to ply and carry passengers, before the common barge be furnished and departed.[45]

Making exceptions for situations involving 'any nobleman, knight, officer, or messenger of the Queen's Majesty' as well as any 'known merchant, or alderman of London, master or warden of any company or mystery there, or justice of the peace' who might need to 'take the tide before the common barge be departed', the 1595 regulations stipulate a fine for the operator of any vessel that might solicit customers before the public barge is 'first furnished with passengers, launched forth, and gone'.[46]

The literary voyages of the Gravesend barge

The historical context laid out in the previous section of this chapter helps to illuminate the choice made by the narrator at the outset of *The Cobler of Caunterburie*. It is a decision between a smaller – more private and protected, and also more expensive – tilt boat vs a public transport experience where one might plausibly sit alongside not only a smattering of London's poorest passengers, but also the future Cardinal Wolsey or an out-of-favour duchess on her way into exile. And, notably, our narrator gambles on the vibrancy of the public barge. The same socially variegated atmosphere that attracts *The Cobler of Caunterburie*'s narrator to this vessel provokes deadly conflict rather than merriment, however, when John Browne of Ashford fatefully rubs elbows with 'a certayne Prieste' aboard the Gravesend barge in John Foxe's mid-century *Actes and Monuments*, his so-called 'Book of Martyrs'.[47] Set in the early years of the sixteenth century, the tale of this 'blessed servaunt of God' and his journey to martyrdom begins with Browne 'passing downe to Graves end in the co[m]mon Barge . . . amongest divers other passengers moe'.[48] A supercilious priest becomes offended when Browne 'saucely' dares to 'sit [too] neare unto him' in the crowded boat and aggressively 'swell[s] in stomacke agaynst him'.[49] A vocal outburst ensues, with the priest rebuking the upstart 'hereticke': 'Doest y[ou] know . . . who I am? thou sittest to neare me and sittest on my clothes.'[50] Upon disembarkation, the priest is determined to exact revenge for Browne's breach of decorum, and he hastens to the Archbishop of Canterbury to report the slight. A chance encounter on the Gravesend barge thus culminates with Browne succumbing to torture and a fiery death at the hands of church officials.

In the early modern period, the Gravesend barge's egalitarian – and officially mandated – commitment to ferrying all fee-paying passengers was sometimes the subject of explicit critique. Along these lines, the barge makes a surprising cameo appearance in Abraham Fleming's 1576 translation of Aelian's Ποικίλη Ιστορία, or *Varia Historia*. The third-century work contains an anecdote about Stratonicus. Travelling in an unknown country, the Athenian musician is pleased to receive an invitation from a local to join him under his roof – until Stratonicus disdainfully realises that this invitation lacks exclusivity, for any and all are welcome in his host's abode. Fleming's English translation of this anecdote significantly elaborates upon Aelian's late antique text: incorporating an example that must have held considerable currency for members of his anticipated sixteenth-century readership, Fleming explains that the classical Greek musician took offence when he 'sawe, now & the[n] one, now & the[n] another, & anoo[ther] too or three more (as they came) to be se[m]blably intertained, & no difference made betwene man and man, but all (lyke Graves end Barge passingers) for their penny considered'.[51]

In a letter of 2 May 1585 addressed to the future Lord Chancellor Christopher Hatton, Thomas Heneage quipped that Queen Elizabeth 'thinketh your house will shortly be like Gravesend barge, never without a knave, a priest, or a thief, &c.'[52] Heneage's words have a proverbial ring to them, and strikingly similar formulations appear both in Nicholas Breton's *Pasquils Fooles-Cap* of 1600, wherein we find a claim that '*Graves-end Barge* can never passage have, / Till it be furnisht with a Foole or Knave', and in Peter Heylyn's mid-seventeenth-century account of travel in France, in which he describes the local coaches as being 'much of a kin to *Gravesend*'s barge' since they are never lacking 'a knave or a Giglot'.[53] Allusions such as Heneage's, Breton's and Heylyn's indicate that an early modern reference to the Gravesend barge could connote seediness and 'knavery', with the barge often figuring in the popular imagination as a floating den of iniquity. It is thus that in an early Jacobean play by Thomas Dekker and John Webster, for instance, an antifeminist character derides the 'stale ... Wenches, that travaile every second tyde betweene Graves ende, and Billingsgate', while a pamphlet called *Newes from Bartholmew Fayre* situates the barge amongst a colourful array of 'Pewterers and Tinkers', 'Swearers and swinkers', 'Fencers and Fidlers', 'Joyners and Jumblers', 'Whores and whoremongers' and 'Devills of hell'.[54] As one late-seventeenth-century rhymer would put it, 'Parents and Guardians, look well to your Charge, / Let not Striplings and Girls run about at large; / Such Vermin you'l find in *Gravesend* Barge'.[55]

The conceptual link between the Gravesend barge and London's underbelly was a firmly established literary trope by the late Elizabethan era, and its dissemination may well have been assisted by John Awdelay's *The Fraternitye of Vacabondes*. This early example of so-called rogue literature appears to have been entered into the Stationers' Register in 1560–1, although the title page from the earliest extant edition – the only surviving leaf – is dated 1565. Of particular relevance to this discussion is the fact that *The Fraternitye of Vacabondes*'s wordy title page features the following dialogic verses:

> *The Upryght man speaketh.*
> Our brotherhode of Vacabondes,
> If you would know where dwel:
> In Gravesend Barge which seldom stands
> The talke wyl shew right wel.

>*Cocke Lorel speaketh.*
>Some orders of my Knaves also
>In that Bar[ge] shall ye fynde,
>For no where shal ye walke (I know)
>But ye shall see their kinde.[56]

This exchange between 'The Upryght man' and Cock Lorel thus imaginatively figures the 'seldom stand[ing]' Gravesend barge as home to the cozeners, shifters and knaves who will be taxonomised at length within the pages of *The Fraternitye of Vacabondes*.

In considering the implications of *The Fraternitye of Vacabondes*'s title page, I want to emphasise that its citation of the legendary Cock Lorel efficiently aligns the Gravesend barge with the metaphorical ship of fools popularised in Sebastian Brant's late fifteenth-century *Das Narrenschiff*. Brant's seminal work of humanist *narrenliteratur* had been translated into Latin by Jakob Locher and into English by both Alexander Barclay (in verse) and Henry Watson (in prose) in the early years of the sixteenth century. Of particular relevance is the fact that an anonymously published text entitled *Cocke Lorells Bote* was part of the broader English reception of *Das Narrenschiff*. A loose adaptation in verse that shares woodcuts with Watson's translation, *Cocke Lorells Bote* has been hailed as 'a miniature, London-specific *Ship of Fools*'.[57] The poem's eponymous shipmaster is a magnet for the inhabitants of England's capital city: 'Cocke cast a syde his hede / And sawe the stretes all over sprede / That to his bote wolde come'.[58] These are men and women 'Of every crafte', and the poem contains a long catalogue of the crew members' occupations, which include 'Talowe chaundelers', 'musterde makers', 'Sluttes drabbes', 'ratte takers', 'boke bynders', 'Parys plasteres', 'cappe knytters', 'Sylke women', 'coper smythes', 'bere brewers', 'whele wryghtes' and many more besides.[59] Each of the Londoners welcomed onto Cock's boat assumes a new 'offyce' as the motley crew morphs into 'lusty company'.[60] Again and again, *Cocke Lorells Bote* emphasises the general air of festivity and 'myrthe' aboard the ship. We hear that the crew 'banysshed ... sadnes / And toke with them ... sporte & gladnes', and, exuding a joyous sense of 'ryotte and revell', the voyagers are said to sing and dance 'full merely' as they traverse 'Englande thorowe and thorowe' duly visiting every 'Vyllage towne cyte and borowe'.[61]

The Fraternitye of Vacabondes's conflation of the humanist ship of fools with the Gravesend barge recurs elsewhere in early modern literary culture. Notably, this includes the 1591 edition of Philip Sidney's *Astrophel and Stella*. It is well known that in this posthumously published volume the poetry of the late Sidney is introduced to readers via a short prefatory piece by Thomas Nashe, who clearly tried to capitalise on this opportunity and promote his own nascent authorial brand alongside (and perhaps partially at the expense of) Sidney's. The Gravesend barge makes a fleeting appearance in Nashe's brief but symbolically rich discussion of his own, distinctly non-Sidneian, style. This signature 'stile', Nashe admits, is 'somewhat heavie gated': in a dance-based metaphor, he professes he 'cannot . . . trip and goe so lively, with oh my love, ah my love, all my loves gone' like those 'other Sheepheards that have beene fooles in the Morris time out of minde', nor does his prose 'imitate the Almond [i.e. Almain] leape'.[62] What Nashe's writing *can* allegedly do, however, is 'keepe pace with Gravesend barge' – a claim he immediately follows with the further assertion, 'I . . . care not if I have water enough, to lande my ship of fooles with the Tearme, (the tyde I shoulde say).'[63] Nashe's literary output cannot keep time with the beats of pastoral fantasy nor of choreographed social dancing. Instead, it operates in synchrony with the regular irregularity of London's best-known tideborne ferry, that local 'ship of fooles' volleying back and forth in near-constant motion to and from England's foremost city. Nashe's commentary on the unstoppable gush and capricious surges of his own unruly prose thus draws upon a familiar connection between the liquid flow of the waters naturally moving in and out of the Thames and the poetic flows of language – a connection elsewhere made more implicitly in the refrain of Spenser's *Prothalamion*, for instance. In Nashe's hands, then, this trope borrowed from *narrenliteratur* (likely under the influence of *The Fraternitye of Vacabondes*) provides a way of defining his distinctive personal style, and he articulates the case for his own authorial appeal in terms that simultaneously evoke aqueous metrical metaphors as well as the legendary mirth of Cock Lorel's zany crew and the grittiness of contemporary London's riparian landscape.

If the Gravesend barge was sometimes conceived *à la* Watson or Nashe as a veritable ship of fools, it also suggested itself to many creatives as an apt stage upon which to set fictive literary transactions. It is on board this vessel, for instance, that one 'Pasquill of Englande' (quite possibly Nashe, who mentions the barge with some frequency throughout his writings) claims to have penned the anti-Martinist tract *A Countercuffe Given to Martin Junior* in 1589.[64] Another pertinent example can be found in an ephemeral poem, undated though almost certainly written at some point between 1562 and 1584, that has been scribbled into a manuscript copy of the Middle English *Prick of Conscience*. The poem jests that 'The grave consell of gravesend barge, / Gevethe Jhon Daye a privylege large, / To put [*The Prick of Conscience*] in prynt for his gaynes' (Figure 5.5). Taking aim at the printer Day and the many financial 'gaynes' he enjoyed over the course of his career due

Ship of Fools and Slow Boat to Hell 115

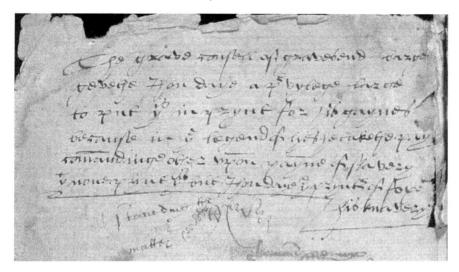

Figure 5.5 Poem about John Day written into a manuscript of *The Prick of Conscience* between approximately 1562 and 1584. Ms. E Mus. 88, fol. 94v. The Bodleian Libraries, University of Oxford.

to lucrative patents and monopolies, these lines exploit the humorous potential of hailing the Gravesend barge as a source of authority and of rendering its notoriously madcap (and questionably qualified) passengers as 'grave consell[ers]' in matters both legal and literary.[65] Such examples subtly foreshadow an equation between London's boats and its theatrical spaces that would be substantively developed in George Chapman, Ben Jonson and John Marston's 1605 satirical city comedy *Eastward Ho!*, a play wherein the carnivalesque possibilities and intertextual resonances of the waterborne journey are likewise explored to comic effect.

This conception of the Gravesend barge as an ironised stage for literary transaction – and, indeed, for the casting of literary judgement – reaches its early modern zenith in *The Cobler of Caunterburie*, a work that has been identified as 'the earliest [post-Chaucerian] attempt to write a whole collection of Chaucerian stories'.[66] In this *Canterbury Tales* adaptation, the varied personalities and social types represented by the internal narrators (a cobbler, a smith, a gentleman, a scholar, an old woman, and a conspicuously Chaucerian-sounding summoner) are carefully calibrated to recall Chaucer's 'sondry folk, by aventure yfalle / In felaweshipe'.[67] Here again the Gravesend barge serves, much as it did in historical reality, as a space wherein people of all walks of life might come into contact, and, as the unnamed narrator relates in the opening frame, the collective attention of this unlikely assemblage quickly turns to literary matters. This conversational turn is set into motion when a gentleman in their midst pulls out a copy of *Tarltons Newes*, a work with which they are all familiar enough to volunteer opinions on its quality. After sharing his own lukewarm feelings about this recently published pamphlet, the cobbler takes centre stage and redirects the group's lively conversation towards the particular merits of 'old father Chaucer'.[68] Whereas their opinions on *Tarletons Newes* were as diverse as their professional identities, the barge's passengers unanimously praise Chaucer's excellence. Prompted by the cobbler – an Elizabethan Harry Bailly of sorts – 'the whole company willingly consent[s]' to 'passe away the time till [they] come off the water' by telling one another Chaucerian-style fabliaux.[69]

The Cobler of Caunterburie's transformation of the overland journey taken by Chaucer's late medieval pilgrims into an aqueous one feels like a particularly inspired choice for a number of reasons. Chief among these, it reflects the historical reality that travel from London and Canterbury in the Elizabethan era typically involved water passage to Gravesend. To wit, the fact that most of the barge's passengers are ultimately bound for Canterbury is duly underscored within the text's frame. What is more, the neo-Chaucerian storytelling activity undertaken by *The Cobler of Caunterburie*'s cast of characters reflects the sorts of communal pastimes in which real-life passengers of the Gravesend barge – or, indeed, other forms of public transit – sometimes engaged. Indeed, we have testimony to this effect from a Jacobean-era traveller who describes a trip made 'in a wherry for the port of Graves-end': along with the 'two women and three men in [his] company', he 'past the way away by telling tales'.[70] Beyond the above, I would observe that it is not only the 'sondry' medieval personae of *The Canterbury Tales* that *The Cobler of Caunterburie* channels by bringing together 'passengers of all sortes' on the barge.[71] Rather, the Elizabethan text's designation of this socially mixed group of as a 'crue of madde companions' simultaneously evokes *The Fraternitye of Vacabondes*'s association of the Gravesend barge's patrons with the mad Londoners found on Cock Lorel's legendary boat.[72] Here, too, we find a ship whose fools are pointedly drawn from all walks of contemporary life and yet establish a remarkable (if also socially subversive) sense of onboard fraternity.

That early modern English audiences received this work with enthusiasm is suggested by the fact that *The Cobler of Caunterburie* was reprinted again in both 1608 and 1614. And that what Pamela Allen Brown has dubbed its 'riverine vein', in particular, must have struck these audiences as apt is attested by the fact that the concept was destined to be recycled more than once.[73] In 1620, for example, the anonymously written tale collection *Westward for Smelts* would feature a group of loquacious fishwives headed in the opposite direction along the Thames, and, in 1630, *The Cobler of Caunterburie* was lightly made over to become *The Tincker of Turvey*, with its neo-Chaucerian storytelling action again specifically set on the Gravesend barge.[74] The title pages for both of these framed tale collections play on the ship of fools trope: *Westward for Smelts* suggestively identifies its waterborne tale-tellers as a group of 'mad-merry ... wenches', and *The Tincker of Turvey* more effusively describes its 'Persons' as 'Mad-merry fellowes' who are 'passing from Billingsgate to Graves-End' on a 'Barge ... Freighted with Mirth' (Figures 5.6 and 5.7). *The Tincker of Turvey* also cultivates the sense that it is in dialogue with *The Fraternitye of Vacabondes* via a title-page promise that the text will enumerate 'The Eight severall Orders of Cuckolds', a claim that appears to consciously echo *The Fraternitye of Vacabondes*'s title page advertisement that readers will learn about the 'xxv. Orders of Knaves'.

In the years following *The Cobler of Caunterburie*'s debut, literary evocations of the Gravesend barge continued to appear in the works of

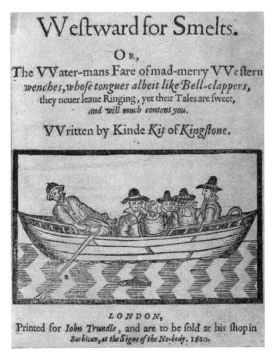

Figure 5.6 Title page of *Westward for Smelts* (1620). STC 25292. Used by permission of the Folger Shakespeare Library.

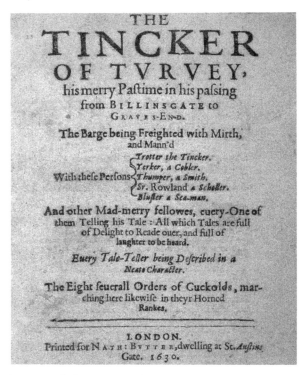

Figure 5.7 Title page of *The Tincker of Turvey* (1630). RB 81683. The Huntington Library, San Marino, California.

London's satirists, and these references often have the feel of an inside joke. This joke takes a somewhat more morbid turn in the final example that I here consider, Thomas Dekker's early Jacobean *Newes from Hell*. In this pamphlet of 1608, positioned as Dekker's response to Nashe's *Pierce Penniless*, a Lucianic journey to the underworld begins with a boat trip to Gravesend. Near the start of this text, Dekker's Knight of the Post makes for Billingsgate, intending 'when the Tide serv'd to angle for Souls & some other fresh fish in that goodly fishpond the Thames, as he passed over it, in Gravesend Barge'.[75] Apparently channelling Cock Lorel, the Post gathers a crew of companions along his way, and he specifically elects the Gravesend barge to serve as his personal 'water coach' due to the scurrilous reputation of its clientele: 'there [on the barge] he knew he should meete with some voluntaries that would venture along with him'.[76]

Heading eastward on the Tideway past Gravesend, Dekker's Post 'hoyst[s] up sayle into the Maine' and lengthily winds his way through the European continent before coming at last to 'the banck-side of

Acheron' – a place both curiously like and unlike his original point of departure.[77] *Newes from Hell*'s narrator affirms that the swarming travellers gathered 'upon the Acherontique Strond' resemble nothing so much as London theatregoers 'crowding' together 'as if . . . at a new Play', though he also specifies that they 'are not bayted by whole kennels of yelping watermen, as you are at Westminster-bridge'.[78] The Acheron's very un-London-like paucity of boisterous watermen is due to the fact that the river's legendary ferryman Charon holds something of a monopoly. '[T]here's but one boat' traversing this river, and, while 'the fare be smal', it is subject to constant inflation, 'for all things wax deare in Hell, as well as upon earth, by reason 'tis so populous'.[79]

Charon's boat in *Newes from Hell* is grotesquely constructed, 'made of nothing but the wormeaten ribs of coffins, nayl'd together, with the splinters of fleshlesse shin-bones', and 'two patcht winding sheets' form its sail.[80] It is also, as Dekker's narrator gleefully highlights, 'for al the world, like *Graves-end Barge*'.[81] Mimicking the rhythms of its equally crowded London counterpart, Charon's vessel 'sayles continually with wind and Tide', and the resemblance does not end there.[82] Death is, of course, the great equaliser, and the ferry service on the Acheron, like the public barge to Gravesend, is obliged to take any and all who can pay the fare. The mythological boatman's passengers are 'priviledged alike, for ther's no regard of age, of sex, of beauty, of riches, of valor, of learning, of greatnes, or of birth', with courtiers, lawyers, clergymen, merchants, scholars, military captains and hoards of bankrupt citizens all thrown together:

> *Will Summers* gives not *Richard* the Third the cushions, the Duke of *Guize* and the Duke of *Shore-ditch* have not the bredth of a bench between them, *Jane Shore* and a Goldsmiths wife are no better one then another. Kings & Clownes, Souldiers & Cowards, Churchmen and Sextons, Aldermen, and Coblers, are all one to *Charon:* For his *Naulum, Lucke* (the old Recorders foole) shall have as much mat, as *Sir Lancelot* of the Lake.[83]

This Gravesend-barge-as-boat-of-Charon analogy clearly tickled Dekker's fancy: not only was it retained in *A Knights Conjuring*, an expanded version of *Newes from Hell* released the following year, but Dekker would also go on to redeploy it once again (in a slightly more abbreviated form) in the opening scene of his c. 1611 play *If It Be Not Good, the Divel Is In It*.

By way of conclusion, then, I want to remark that the success of Dekker's recurring Jacobean-era joke about the Gravesend barge lies in the circularity of its imagery. No matter how slow or convoluted the itinerary, a traveller journeying to hell simply ends up in London once more – but an alter-London where the Thames is void of the plentiful swans and fish documented by early modern authors like Turberville, Spenser or Munday. The river's flows are turned 'almost as poysonous, altogether so muddy, altogether so black' as '*Moore-ditch* ... when the water is three quarters dreyn'd out', and this version of the Thames is just as bereft of watercraft as it is of aquatic life.[84] In this nightmarish alter-London of Dekker's imagination, travellers arrive at the Billingsgate of the underworld only to be denied that same choice made by our unnamed narrator when he serendipitously foregoes the tilt boat in the opening pages of *The Cobler of Caunterburie*. Stripped of their worldly belongings and markers of social distinction, the dead pile aboard a hopelessly crowded common barge. They do so not because they are enticed by the prospect of merriment or mirthful diversion, but because there is simply no alternative. And for some – the Stratonicuses amongst us or those who stridently object to being seated too near the John Brownes – a trip on this madcap ship of fools with its socially destabilising admixture of types and classes is bound to be pure hell.

Notes

1. On Greene's probable authorship of this piece, see Donna N. Murphy, 'The Cobbler of Canterbury and Robert Greene', *Notes and Queries* 57.3 (2010), 349–52.
2. *The Cobler of Caunterburie* (STC 4579; London, 1590), B1r. Throughout this chapter, I have silently regularised u/v and i/j usage in quotations from early modern texts.
3. Ibid.
4. Ibid.
5. Mike Rodman Jones, 'The Uses of Medievalism in Early Modern England: Recovery, Temporality, and the "Passionating" of the Past', *Exemplaria* 30.3 (2018), 198; *Cobler*, B1r.
6. Sophie Watson, *City Water Matters: Cultures, Practices and Entanglements of Urban Water* (London: Palgrave Macmillan, 2019), 79.
7. George Turberville, 'The Lover to the Thems of London to Favor His Ladie Passing Thereon', in *Epitaphes, Epigrams, Songs and Sonets* (London, 1567), STC 24326, D1r–D1v.
8. Turberville, 'The Lover', D1v.
9. Edmund Spenser, *Prothalamion Or A Spousall Verse* (London, 1596), STC 23088, A2r, B1v.
10. Spenser, *Prothalamion*, A2r, A3r.
11. Turberville, 'The Lover', D1v; John Stow, *A Survay of London* (London, 1598), STC 23341, B5v.

12. Stow, *Survay* (1598), B5v–B6r.
13. Anthony Munday, *The Survay of London . . . Written in the Yeere 1598. by Iohn Stow . . . Since Then, Continued, Corrected and Much Enlarged* (London, 1618), STC 23344, C5r–C5v.
14. Ibid., C7r, C5v.
15. Ibid., C7r. This replicates similar estimates made by Stow twenty years earlier in *Survay* (1598), B6r.
16. Anthony Munday et al., *The Survey of London . . . Begun First by . . . John Stow, in the Year 1598; Afterwards Inlarged . . . in the Year 1618; and Now Compleatly Finished* (London, 1633), STC 23344, B3v.
17. Abraham Cowley, *The Works of Mr Abraham Cowley* (London, 1678), 53.
18. Stow, *Survay* (1598), M1r.
19. Ibid.
20. John Taylor, *The Carriers Cosmographie* (London, 1637), STC 23740, C4v.
21. Thomas Deloney, *The Gentile Craft. The Second Part* (STC 6556; London, 1639), B2v; Barnabe Riche, *Allarme to England* (London, 1578), STC 20979, *3v.
22. William Lambarde, *A Perambulation of Kent* (London, 1576), STC 15175.5, G1v–G2r.
23. William Fennor, *Cornu-copiæ, Pasquils Night-Cap* (London, 1612), STC 10782.5, D2v.
24. I quote 'London Lickpenny' from the text in *Medieval English Political Writings*, ed. James M. Dean (Kalamazoo: Medieval Institute Publications, 1996), line 119. The poem was also known to Stow, who attributes it to John Lydgate and summarises it in *Survay* (1598), M5v–M6r.
25. Thomas Deloney, *The Most Rare and Excellent History of the Dutchesse of Suffolkes Calamity* (London, 1635), STC 6557.8.
26. John Stow, *The Annales of England* (London, 1605), STC 23337, Iii2v.
27. 'The Copy of a Letter Writt'n By Sir Henry Wootton', in *Poems of Mr. John Milton, Both English and Latin* (London, 1645), E4v.
28. Munday, *Survay* (1618), C5v–C6r.
29. Ibid., C6r.
30. Fynes Morison, *An Itinerary* (London, 1617), STC 18205, Z4r.
31. John Carleton, *The Ultimum Vale of John Carleton* (London, 1663), A4v.
32. Fennor, *Pasquils Night-Cap*, H4v.
33. Munday, *Survay* (1618), C6r.
34. Ibid.
35. Ibid.
36. John Sherwin, *The Gotham Swan: or, the Rook's Flight from Gravesend* (London, 1730), 7–8.
37. *Calendar of the Patent Rolls Preserved in the Public Record Office: Henry IV, Vol. I, 1399–1402* (London: Mackie and Co., 1903), 542.
38. Henry Humpherus, *History of the Origin and Progress of the Company of Watermen and Lightermen of the River Thames, with Numerous Historical Notes*, vol. 1 (London: Prentice and Monson, 1859), 71.
39. Humpherus, *History*, 100.
40. *The Prices of Fares and Passages to be Paide unto Watermen* (London, 1555), STC 16787.2, [A1]r.

41. Humpherus, *History*, 126.
42. Ibid.
43. Clement Oxenbridge, *The Case of the Undertakers for Reducing Postage of Inland Letters* (London, 1653), A2r.
44. Humpherus, *History*, 149.
45. Ibid., 150.
46. Ibid., 150–1.
47. John Foxe, *Actes and Monuments* (London, 1583), STC 11225, WWW4r. Foxe includes multiple versions of this same story at different points in the text; I here quote from the most detailed account.
48. Ibid.
49. Ibid.
50. Ibid.
51. Abraham Fleming, *A Registre of Hystories* (London, 1576), STC 164, Tt3v.
52. I quote from the letter as reproduced in Harris Nicholas, *Memoirs of the Life and Times of Sir Christopher Hatton* (London, 1847), 426. The original is found in the Letterbook of Sir Christopher Hatton, Add MS 15891, f. 155v, British Library.
53. Nicholas Breton, *Pasquils Fooles-Cap* (London, 1600), STC 3677.5, A4v; Peter Heylyn, *A Full Relation of Two Journeys* (London, 1656), E1v.
54. Thomas Dekker and John Webster, *West-ward Hoe* (London, 1607), STC 6540, A4r; Richard West, *Newes from Bartholmew Fayre* (London, 1606), STC 25264, A3r.
55. Robert Dixon, *Canidia, or, The Witches* (London, 1683), Gg2v.
56. I here cite the title page of John Awdelay, *The Fraternitie of Vacabondes* (London, 1565), STC 993. This same exchange continued to appear on the title pages for subsequent editions of this work reprinted later in the period.
57. Julia Boffey, 'London Books and London Readers', in *Cultural Reformations: Medieval and Renaissance in Literary History*, ed. Brian Cummings and James Simpson (Oxford: Oxford University Press, 2010), 431.
58. *Cocke Lorelles Bote* (London, 1518), STC 5456, B5v.
59. Ibid., B5v–C1r.
60. Ibid., C1v.
61. Ibid., C2r–C2v.
62. Thomas Nashe, 'Somewhat to Reade for Them that List', in *Syr. S. His Astrophel and Stella* (London, 1591), A4r.
63. Ibid.
64. *A Countercuffe Given to Martin Junior* (London, 1589), STC 19456.5, A4v.
65. A transcription appears as 'Against the Printer John Day (between 1564 and 1584)', in *Verse Libel in Renaissance England and Scotland*, ed. Steven W. May and Alan Bryson (Oxford: Oxford University Press, 2016), 202. A similar joke appears in Thomas Nashe, *A Wonderfull, Strange and Miraculous Astrologicall Prognostication for this Yeere 1591* (London, 1591), STC 11210, B4r.
66. Helen Cooper, *Oxford Guides to Chaucer: The Canterbury Tales* (Oxford: Oxford University Press, 1996), 419.

67. Geoffrey Chaucer, *General Prologue* in *The Riverside Chaucer*, 3rd ed., ed. Larry D. Benson (Boston: Houghton Mifflin, 1987), ll. 25–6.
68. *Cobler*, B1v.
69. Ibid.
70. John Taylor, *Three Weekes, Three Daies, and Three Houres Observations and Travel* (London, 1617), STC 23807, B1r.
71. *Cobler*, B1r.
72. Ibid.
73. Pamela Allen Brown, *Better a Shrew than a Sheep: Women, Drama, and the Culture of Jest in Early Modern England* (Ithaca, NY: Cornell University Press, 2003), 103.
74. Other seventeenth-century works like *A Tongue-Combat Lately Happening Betweene Two English Souldiers in the Tilt-boat of Gravesend* of 1623 and *The Graves-end Tilt-Boat* of 1699 adapted the concept by setting incidents of verbal sparring or storytelling on board Gravesend-bound tilt boats, and a barge on the Tideway is likewise the setting in John Dryden's *Of Dramatick Poesie*, a Platonic dialogue of 1668.
75. Thomas Dekker, *Newes from Hell* (London, 1606), STC 6514, C3r.
76. Ibid.
77. Ibid., D4v.
78. Ibid., E1r, D4v.
79. Ibid.
80. Ibid., E2r.
81. Ibid., D4v.
82. Ibid., E1r.
83. Ibid., D4v–E1r.
84. Ibid., E2v.

Chapter 6

Rivers, Monstrosity and National Identity in Izaak Walton's *The Compleat Angler*

Melissa Caldwell

> Nature employs her tireless force nowhere with greater power than in the waves, the ocean swell, the tides that ebb and flow, and – if we admit the truth – in the rapid river currents, since this element commands all others.
> – Pliny the Elder, *Natural History*, Book XXXI

Izaak Walton and the environment

Izaak Walton's *The Compleat Angler* uses its discourse on rivers in order to interrogate the epistemic and ontological importance of boundaries. As a site of convergence, juxtaposition and disruption, borders between land and water or between rivers and oceans are productive but also problematic spaces. In an earlier chapter in this volume, Daniel Gettings argues that rivers offered essential resources, connections to an English past and a space for community, while at the same time the frequency of flooding made them one of the most prominent sites of natural disaster in early modern England.[1] Walton's text supports a similar view of the dynamic nature of rivers, though for him their danger lies in the ways in which rivers point to the limitations of human understanding. At their most ideal, they are spaces of physical healing, psychological relief and community building. At their most fraught, they are spaces that highlight the limitation of the human understanding of nature and, by extension, humanity's place in the natural world. However, in both instances rivers and their banks reveal the wonders of creation, the value of an empirical approach to nature and the power of God. Written in a post-civil war context, these sites of connection and conflict between England and the outside world, between the known and the unknown, between the normative and the unnatural, reflect both England's borders but also its battlegrounds within: they mark a physical boundary of Englishness, while also housing strangers within the midst of England.

As Walton instructs his reader in the art of the good life and the art of angling, his discourse returns again and again to waterways and their relationship to monstrosity.

By some accounts the third most printed book in English, *The Compleat Angler* has served as the impetus for modern conservationist organisations and as a fishing manual for modern-day anglers.[2] It is strange, then, that despite the ways in which it continues to resonate with contemporary naturalists, the role of the environment in the text has been passed over in favour of discussions of the text's political, religious and moral lessons. These emphases are reasonable but they overlook the central importance of the river itself to Walton's formation of an identity and ethos for royalists during the Interregnum. An exception to this neglect is Marjorie Swann's remarks on the environmental concerns evident in *The Compleat Angler*. Interestingly, she notes that Walton lived during what climatologists have called a 'Little Ice Age' and died during an uncharacteristically bad frost.[3] Swann highlights how the text reflects this climatological reality if we pay attention to the details Walton supplies. Walton's anglers are 'governed' not by a spring shower, but by a sometimes violent rain, which is indicative of not 'a benign, predictable climate' but rather an 'unstable, threatening weather' pattern common during Walton's lifetime.[4] But as Swann notes, even scholars most invested in discussing the environment in the early modern world 'have overlooked Walton's depiction of riparian ecosystems'.[5]

The aim of this chapter is to extend Swann's observations about the importance of the environment to focus specifically on the river, its banks, and those creatures who live around and within it. The considerable changes that Walton made to the second and subsequent editions of his text suggest the importance of the habitat to the practice of the angler. In the second edition, Walton added seven chapters and increased the length of his book to about twice the size of the first edition.[6] Significantly, nearly all of the parts of *The Compleat Angler* that I will discuss below were added in the later editions. Most of Walton's changes focused on adding additional details about fish, their behaviour and, crucially, their habitat.[7] Walton's revisions sharpened the moral focus of the work along with its practical applications for the angler.[8] But they do more than that: they expand the work beyond the confines of manual or pastoral to engage in an exploration of the natural world and all its inconvenient complexity. Changes Walton made to the title of the text reflect this reframing. Whereas the 1653 edition of the text is titled *The Compleat Angler, or The Contemplative Man's Recreation. Being a Discourse of Fish and Fishing*, the second edition of 1655 revises the final part of the title to *Being a Discourse of Rivers, and Fish-Ponds, and Fish and Fishing*. The shift is instructive and reveals much about Walton's interests and focus. It is undeniable that fish, the description of their behaviour, how and where to catch them, and how to prepare them for a meal are central to Walton's manual for anglers. Nevertheless, the nature and variability of England's rivers as well as the riverbank is just as essential to Walton's other motives for writing the text – that is, the reconstitution of a physical and ideological space for royalists in exile in the years after the civil war.

First published in 1653, just four years after the execution of Charles I, Walton's text affirms his nationalism and an Englishness defined by an unwavering loyalty to a defeated royalist cause. Hardly just a fishing manual, it has often been cited as one of the fullest expressions of the *vita bona* and *vita beata* so intrinsic to the Cavalier mode. This ethos was inseparable from the monarch, for it 'entailed a vision of a nation flowing from its spring, the court'.[9] In the absence of both monarch and court, Walton turns to 'the moral geography of country life' and to a quite literal spring – the rivers of England – to replace what has been lost.[10] In this chapter I will argue that the river and its borders with land and sea are spaces where Walton affirms his own version of Englishness and yet seeks to come to terms with the fundamental uncertainty of his world. Walton offers the reader a version of Englishness that is nostalgic for the effortless overlapping values of pleasure, art and works championed by the Church of England and antithetical to the Interregnum culture in which Walton found himself in the 1650s. In *The Compleat Angler*, rivers offer Walton a calculus – and an ecology – with which to reconstitute national identity – while also bringing an awareness that the habitat of that Englishness had fundamentally changed.

Bankside borders

The Compleat Angler can be read as part of a larger phenomenon of manuals in the sixteenth and seventeenth centuries.[11] Manuals on hunting and fishing were particularly popular in the period alongside instruction manuals that codified masculinity and suggested ways in which gentlemen might perform their gentility.[12] However, Walton's text is distinctive in ways that all point to the importance of its setting, which transcends the requirements of the pastoral genre alone. Although many texts before Walton's employed the dialogue form as an entertaining way to convey informational material, Walton's localism and 'geographic preciseness' set his Platonic dialogue apart from most others.[13] Walton's Socrates is Piscator, the loquacious and affable if at times overzealous angler. The importance of time and place is clear from the opening exchange of the text. In his first remarks, Piscator claims that he has 'stretched [his] legs up Tottenham Hill' in the hopes of gaining the company of Venator the hunter, and Auceps the falconer on their way towards Ware 'this fine, fresh May morning'.[14] Compared to other discourses on the art of angling, Walton's seeks to 'create the semblance of an actual journey following the River Lea to Ware' in the Hertfordshire countryside.[15] The entire action of the five-day journey can be found on this 14-mile stretch alongside the river.[16] When the act and description of angling is temporarily interrupted by weather or by natural pause for food or drink, the 'discourse often turns to a celebration of this environment'.[17] Walton's frequent references to William Camden's *Britannia* and Michael Drayton's *Poly-Olbion* similarly suggest the importance of place for Walton. Given the detailed nature of Walton's instructions about fish and their habitats, the text demands a kind of exactitude not required of a less hybrid text. Walton's text is as animated by the empiricism of Baconian science as it is the contemplative verse of John Donne.

The most overarching theme of *The Compleat Angler* is the relationship between action and contemplation. Walton characterises the riverbanks as places of contemplation for the beleaguered royalist. Piscator elevates water to the highest place among the four elements: it is 'the eldest daughter of creation, the element upon which the Spirit of God did first move' (19). When compared to the elements of air and earth at the beginning of the text in the opening debate between Piscator, Venator and Auceps, water has the paradoxical distinction of being the most physically productive and spiritually moving of elements. And yet so integral is the art of angling that it does not even allow debate between the virtues of action and contemplation. Rather, angling from the riverside – that space where the elevated element of water and the lesser element of earth meet – is the perfect location for the merger of action and contemplation, which is to say, action *in* contemplation.

The spiritual nature of water affects the contemplative behaviour of the angler and those that he brings to the riverbank. As Nigel Smith has observed, in *The Compleat Angler* 'fishing is preaching to convert',[18] and so part of the business of being an angler involves not isolation or alienation from the world, but rather the reconstitution of community. As Piscator describes the life of the angler to Venator over the course of a few days, the hunter learns everything from how to choose and make the best fly to the nature of a variety of fish to how to prepare them for a meal. By the end of the text, Venator likens himself to Augustine in his *Confessions*, who is similarly led by a friend to rest 'free from the troubles of the world' (251). Venator admits that Piscator's teachings have been 'so useful and pleasant, that I may truly say, I have only lived since I enjoyed them and turned Angler, and not before' (251). It is a baptism by water that takes place in the transactional space of the river's edge. What is at stake in this text is not simply how to catch and eat fish, and yet it is through this activity that the individual learns contentment and a gratitude rooted in the natural world and in community. The angler's life offers a turn away from cynicism embodied by the business of the city to the ancient – and Cavalier – values of hospitality, friendship and generosity. Replacing the scoffing wit of Lucian with the light-hearted scepticism of Montaigne, Piscator attempts to lure in Venator – and the reader. *The Compleat Angler*, then, is a kind of conversion narrative wherein the reader witnesses the conversion of Venator and is likewise being asked to convert to the religion of the angler. Piscator, both a fisherman and a fisher of men, asks the reader to question their own values and see instead the greater value of recreation and pleasure that can take place not in taverns or political halls, but on the banks of England's many rivers.

Piscator looks to the riverbank as a site of contemplation and spiritual enlightenment, for 'the very sitting by the river's side is not only the quietest and fittest place for contemplation, but will invite an Angler to it' (27). Positioning himself and England's rivers in the larger context of biblical history, Walton reminds his reader that the boundary between earth and water is an important location in the Bible as the site where God reveals divine truth to the prophets of the Old Testament: 'when God intended to reveal any future events or high notions to his prophets, he then carried them either to the deserts or the sea-shore, that having so separated them from amidst the press of people and business, and the cares of the world, he might settle their mind in a quiet repose, and there make them fit for revelation' (27). Piscator connects this idea to himself, and notes that what he relates in his discourse is a product of his many hours sitting on a riverbank contemplating the nature of the river and of the various forms of life that live within it. By extrapolation, it is possible to infer that *The Compleat Angler*, as a record of this discourse, has perhaps the same claim to divine authority as the Ranters, prophets and Puritan saints of the 1640s. Yet unlike these destabilising voices, Walton's text seeks to recreate psychic if not physical stability. Indeed, one of fishing's defining characteristics for Piscator is its 'lawfulness' (39).

And so, while it is true that 'for Walton, sitting patiently by the riverbank is a form of security',[19] this idea should not be taken to suggest a kind of passivity, inaction or 'apolitical quietism'.[20] Rather, we should not overlook the subversiveness – lawful though it may be – of

Walton's text as well as the ways in which Piscator actively works to reconstitute a royalist community alongside England's rivers. It is a text that means both 'to console and confront'[21] and to act as 'a kind of recruitment tool',[22] as Walton recovers on the riverside the royalist hierarchy he has lost. For Walton, fishing is always an act of pleasure rather than necessity, and 'Piscator contrasts anglers with "money-getting men"' even as he positions himself 'as socially superior to inhabitants of the countryside who must view fish primarily as protein rather than sport.'[23] In recreating the hierarchy he has lost, Walton seeks to form a new community of like-minded royalists. As Piscator attempts to lead willing disciples such as Venator to his watery recreation, he actively attempts to 'recreate an innocent community in bad times'.[24]

The riverbank is a crucial facet of Walton's goal of carving out both a spiritual and physical space for royalists during the Interregnum. Perhaps even more than religious or political affiliation, 'men's love of the natural world' informs 'both individual identity and social order'.[25] As the border between land and water, it offers a space for quiet contemplation and for community building. It also gives Walton a space where he can engage with pastoral figures such as the Milkmaid and Coridon, which allows him both to re-enforce his social status and also to repeatedly recite – and ultimately publish – an 'anthology' of royalist poetry of Donne, Herbert, Drayton and others during the Interregnum.[26] And yet, this space is never quite as pastoral as Walton perhaps might want it to be. There are numerous interruptions to this bucolic scenery, for Walton cannot ever get away from the ways in which English history is mirrored in his perceptions about the environment. On the land, the anglers encounter 'gypsies' and 'beggars', which are probably allegories for the ship money crisis on the one hand, and indicative of religious sectarianism more largely on the other.[27]

As we will see in the next section, this tendency towards disruption at the border occurs both on land and in the water. Because Walton is fundamentally empirical in his approach to nature, he does not ignore these interruptions, but in fact incorporates them into his narrative and into his understanding of his place in post-Civil War England. This tension within the text reflects the friction between the operation of the pastoral and georgic modes Walton employs. Indeed, as we turn to Piscator's discussion of rivers and their inhabitants, his pastoralism gives way to the unruliness of nature, and divine revelation gives way to epistemic limitation as Walton confronts the reality that an individual's understanding of nature inevitably reflects his own subjectivity.

England's rivers and their monsters

As we have seen, for Walton the banks of England's rivers are the site of Piscator's pleasure and holy recreation and the means to revelation and conversion. They are also at the very juncture that connects England to the outside world. Although water in the form of either rivers or the sea is 'praised because it facilitates travel ... away from internally divided Britain',[28] these waters are also the very frontier that Walton is keen to explore in his later editions. The ocean, and its connection to the rivers of England, is often associated with a 'topography of wonder' rooted in its monstrous inhabitants,[29] yet it must be said that at times that wonder verges on horror. Walton doggedly explores the diversity and the unknown of the watery world that is source and resource for his piscatory subject. Unlike land animals, fish are more mysterious because they are harder to observe in their natural habitat. Nevertheless, Walton was eager to catalogue and classify them, with particular attention to their habitat. Similar to other collections of *naturalia* from the sixteenth century onward, Walton's catalogue of fish and their rivers surveys the idiosyncrasy and diversity therein rather than codifies universal principles.[30] Despite his love of a systematic display of learning, Walton is as interested in the 'variables' as he is in developing a method.[31]

Walton's reading of the river is closely tied to his understanding of its inhabitants. In his attentiveness to marvels and the oddities of nature, Walton follows Pliny's *Natural History*, one of his most-quoted sources. In the second edition of his text, Walton added both the discourse on rivers and also Pliny's discussion of aquatic monsters.[32] While some of Walton's revisions do add 'weight, accuracy, and authority' to his text,[33] it seems as though much of what Walton adds makes his text more *in*credible than credible. Echoing Aristotle, Pliny, Camden, as well as traditions of depicting the ocean and its dangers in medieval and early modern poetry and cartography, Walton's pastoral setting never entirely exorcises the potential dangers of the water. Even the most celebrated of England's rivers, the Thames, arrives at 'the very jaws of the ocean'. Its connection to the ocean subjects it both to physical and metaphorical inconstancy. Perhaps a nod to the realities of flooding that plagued sixteenth- and seventeenth-century England,[34] Walton describes how 'this glorious river feeleth the violence and the benefit of the sea more than any other river in Europe' (229). As the ocean affects the rise and fall of the Thames, it becomes a site of spiritual and epistemological disruption: it brings 'strange fish', or 'monsters' as Walton also calls them, begetting wonder that threatens to topple over into disbelief (231).

Just as Piscator elevates water above the other elements in terms of its divinity and spiritual force, so too does he argue for its dominance as a physical and climatological powerhouse. Walton quotes one of Pliny's most famous lines concerning water: 'Nature's great and wonderful power is more demonstrated in the sea than on the land' (32). This physical power goes hand in hand with the notion that the ocean is a repository of God's greatest works. For this idea, Walton alludes to the poetry of David in Psalm 104. The first part of the psalm focuses on how God made 'the deep' to cover the entire earth 'as a garment', stretching over even the highest mountain tops. The Flood proved that it is God who keeps the waters in their boundaries, with the implication that water is both a resource and a weapon. The second half of the psalm observes how nature displays the wonders of God. In 'the great and wide sea', there are 'things creeping innumerable, both small and great beasts. There go the ships: there is that leviathan, whom thou hast made to play therein.'[35] That water is the greatest of elements is corroborated for Walton by the fact that it is the greatest treasury of God's choicest marvels, ranging from the average fish to the greatest whale. A few pages later Piscator again invokes David, but this time when he cites Psalm 107, he adds a corrective to the psalmist's song. Discussing the strange wonders of rivers and the ocean, Piscator says, 'doubtless, this made the Prophet David say (Psalm 107:23–24), "They that occupy themselves in deep waters see the wonderful works of God": indeed, such wonders and pleasures too as the land affords not' (36).

This corrective would seem to put Pliny above David, as it is Pliny who states 'in no sphere does Nature show greater marvels' than in the water.[36] However, Pliny and David agree when it comes to the range of water's uses. Just as God can use water to destroy his creation or to illuminate his power as a creator, the qualities of water – and of rivers in particular – are variable. Aristotle, Pliny and even Camden go to great lengths to catalogue the various properties of water for good or ill. Some waters heal, while others poison or, gorgon-like, turn animate objects to stone: 'some waters being drank cause madness, some drunkenness, and some laughter to death. The river Selarus in a few hours turns a rod or wand to stone; and our Camden mentions the like in England, and the like in Lochmere in Ireland' (28).

But the wondrous nature of water is not always so dubious. Oftentimes water can be the guarantor of health in the natural and the human world. Not only are the reproductive cycles of creatures 'bred and fed in the water ... more and more miraculous', but they are also 'more advantageous to man, not only for the lengthening of his life, but for the preventing of sickness' (21). Though outside the purview of angling,

Piscator notes that England's famous baths offer 'miraculous cures' (22). The point is not just that fish and the waters whence they come are good for the individual; rather, the implications of individual health reach national and political dimensions in Walton's discussion of diet. Rooting his praise of angling in primitive Christianity, Walton looks to the Old Testament example of Moses, who 'appointed fish to be the chief diet for the best commonwealth that ever was' (21). Fish and the rivers from which they come, then, have spiritual, physical and political benefits.

Crucially, it is in the discussion of these wonders where Piscator acknowledges epistemic boundaries he will not violate. Though the text is in many ways a kind of exercise in the classification of nature and the organisation of that knowledge, Walton clearly demarcates the boundaries of Piscator's claims for the wonders of water and its inhabitants. For instance, in his observations of the Tench, 'the physician of fishes', Walton delves momentarily into the ancient lore surrounding this fish and its healing properties. Though it does not make a good meal, it is used by physicians for 'outward applications' (171). Citing Pierre Rondelet's discussion of uses of this fish in Jewish medicine, he notes that 'many of [the Jews] have many secrets, yet unknown to Christians; secrets that have never been written, but since the days of their Solomon, who knew the nature of all things' delivered these secrets from generation to generation: 'This and many other medicines were discovered by them, or by revelation; for doubtless we attained them not by study' (172). Walton's empiricism gives way to an exploration of Hermetic knowledge, but only briefly. Affirming the utility of the tench 'for the good of mankind', Piscator abruptly stops himself from 'meddl[ing]' any further, for 'there are too many foolish meddlers in physic and divinity, that think themselves fit to meddle with hidden secrets, and so bring destruction to their followers' (172).

These moments when Walton confronts the limits of empiricism are where the text becomes most fraught – that is, where Walton stops Piscator from going too far. One has the sense that Piscator is Walton's somewhat diabolical alter ego, who dares to ask the questions that Walton then must use the structure of the text to shut down. The appearance of neat classification demonstrated by the breakdown of chapters as well as the engravings Walton added of the various species of fish sits in tension with Walton's discussion of monstrosity and the unexplainable – or simply downright strange – phenomena he chooses to discuss in his later editions. At these moments in the text, Piscator turns from the marvellous to the monstrous. Asa Mittman has argued that 'Above all, the monstrous is that which creates [a] sense of vertigo, that which calls into question our (their, anyone's) epistemological worldview, highlights its fragmentary and inadequate nature, and thereby asks us ... to acknowledge the failures of our systems of categorization.'[37] Walton's discussion of monstrosity and wonder suggests his own scepticism about the degree to which he is able to classify the creatures and their habitats that he so painstakingly studies. Similar to Michael Drayton's great catalogues of England's fish in *Poly-Olbion*, a poem that without a doubt influenced Walton's work, Walton's investigation into the nature of rivers and their inhabitants 'challeng[es] the reader to think about the incredible forces of nature on display which defy human reason, a signal that there is more in the native landscape than has been discovered or can be easily imagined'.[38]

Walton chose to add his discussion of piscatory monsters just after his brief discussion of rivers in the opening chapters. Positioned so early in the text, Walton's exploration of monstrosity offers us a frame through which to read the entire discourse. Here again, he takes his cues from Pliny to introduce this topic, for his classical predecessor was similarly preoccupied with recording marvellous occurrences in nature. Laying aside his opening 'discourse on rivers', Piscator says that he 'will tell you some things of the monsters, or fish, call them what you will that ... breed and feed' in rivers (29). The apposition is tempting, as Piscator would seem to suggest the interchangeability of monster and fish. Perhaps by his later editions Walton had come to see fish existing on a spectrum of monstrosity ranging from the smallest herring to the largest whale. If we come to this conclusion, then we must further ask whether, since Walton's entire text goes on to describe these 'monsters' in detail, Walton would view his text as an exploration and categorisation of the monstrous. The rhetoric of the text in this section is instructive, as Piscator moves seamlessly from relating incredible accounts of fish in far-off places such as the Indian Ocean and the Ganges to discussing specimens collected by John Tradescant and Elias Ashmole on display at Lambeth near London (30).

It is to a description of these 'wonders' that Walton turns his attention next. The specimens in question reflect the oft-cited belief that for every animal on land, its piscatory doppelgänger existed in the sea, which explains why medieval and Renaissance maps are rife with sea monsters taking the shape of hybrid animals such as sealions, seahorses, sea unicorns and just about any other animal-fish combination conceivable.[39] For this idea specifically, Piscator quotes a poem of Guillaume Du Bartas:

> God quickened in the sea and in the rivers
> So many fishes of so many features,
> That in the waters we may see all creatures,

Ev'n all that on the earth are to be found,
As if the world were in deep waters drowned. (32)

Though Piscator admits that it may surprise his fellow Englishmen as 'islanders [who] are averse to the belief' in wonders, 'you may there see the Hog-fish, the Dog-fish, the Dolphin, the Coney-fish, the Parrot-fish, the Shark, the Poison-fish, Sword-fish' and many other such 'rarities' (30–1).

The idea that all fish are related to monstrosity in some way is frequently supported by the text's engagement with hybridity. But Walton's notion of hybridity does not simply echo the rhetoric we might observe in medieval and early modern maps or the discourse of sea monsters in Pliny or Meric Casaubon's 'Of Credulity and Incredulity'. There is a second kind of hybridity in the text in the way that the fish mirror various types of men in post-Civil War England. Throughout the medieval period, commentators often developed 'causal links between physical monstrosity, faith, and lifestyle' in their discussions of sea monsters.[40] Monstrosity was a particularly popular discourse in the late 1640s, as it was used in pamphlet literature to open up 'questions of orthodoxy, discipline, and allegiance, and the moral and religious confusions of the English Revolution',[41] and so it is not surprising to see Walton's fish take on human qualities. The French physician Ambroise Paré, whose 'On Monsters and Marvels' was popular in England, cites Rondelet, another of Walton's most cited sources in his discussion of sea monsters. Paré includes a quite literal rendition of a monk fish and a creature caught in Poland that was said to look like 'a Bishop, covered with scales, having his mitre and pontifical ornaments'.[42] The move from the monstrous to satirical was not difficult to make.

This tradition of monstrosity, which Walton clearly knew well, reflects Jeremy Cohen's seminal notion of monstrosity as a being that 'refuses easy categorization' as they are typically 'disturbing hybrids' and 'incoherent bodies'.[43] Yet Walton is nothing if he is not an adamant purveyor of natural categories. We can see a similar though much more metaphorical kind of fusion in Walton's discussion of fish. The fish that inhabit England's rivers provide sport and leisure, but they also provide moral instruction. Walton's fish reveal 'human passions, virtues, and vices, presented in a living pageant, accessible to the meanest minds'.[44] Almost every fish is given a human attribute or analogue: just as tench are the physicians of the natural world, trout are known to be generous, pikes are tyrants, salmon are king, carp are queen and so on. It is perhaps worth mentioning that fish are human-like as well in that the habitat is also singularly important to their survival and their success as a species. Walton is aware that not all waters – not even all rivers – are suitable habitats for all fish (65). Similarly, just as human diversity was explained in terms of geographic difference, there is a kind of interplay between earth, water and the fish that live in the river. Just as 'sheep in some countries differ from one another in their shape and bigness, and in the fineness of their wool; and certainly as some pastures breed larger sheep, so do some rivers, by reason of the ground over which they run, breed larger Trouts' (67–68).

Walton's most prolonged discussion of rivers occurs in chapter XIX, 'Of several Rivers, and some Observations of Fish'. While perhaps not entirely at odds with his pastoralism, Walton's catalogue of rivers, georgic in nature, at the very least complicates his pastoralism.[45] The chapter begins in a straightforward fashion with a catalogue of the most important rivers in England that he tells us is derived from Peter Heylin's 'Geography'. However, this empirical mode very quickly gives way to mythologising the peculiarities of rivers that run into the sea and anecdotes of wonder related to these places. According to Piscator, the most likely place to find 'strange fish' are in 'those rivers that run into the sea' (231). Interestingly, the mouths of rivers were among the most populated areas along a river, as settlements typically started at the mouth of a river and moved upstream.[46] And so, the mouths of rivers are the places where humans are most likely to encounter the monsters of the deep. Piscator details an incredible tale of a fish-monster that was recently dissected by a 'man of great learning and experience' who describes the fish to Piscator as follows:

> The fish was almost a yard broad, and twice that length; his mouth was wide enough to receive or take into it the head of a man; his stomach seven or eight inches broad. He is of a slow motion, and usually lies or lurks close in the mud, and has a movable string on his head about a span, or near unto a quarter of a yard long, by the moving of which, which is his natural bait, when he lies close and unseen in the mud, he draws other smaller fish so close to him that he can suck them into his mouth, and so devours and digests them. (231)

No illustration of this fish is provided and Venator and the reader are left to use their imagination to visualise this fish. However, Piscator assures Venator these kinds of monstrous fishes are not as uncommon as he might think. These and many other kinds of strange fish are very often caught 'on the mouths of our sea-rivers and on the sea-shore' (231).

This notion of the mouth of the river – that is, the border between the river and the ocean – as the site of not just wonder but the monstrous recalls Piscator's discussion of the Thames, which sits at the 'jaws of the ocean', in the opening chapter of the text. The predatory nature of the fish is notable, for it evokes the well-known description of the whale in the *Physiologus* that would perch at the surface of the ocean and lure unsuspecting sailors. Thinking that the back of the whale was an island, the sailors would disembark and start a fire. Just as the sailors would get comfortable, the whale would plunge to the depths of the ocean, taking the sailors with it. In the *Physiologus*, the whale is allegorical in nature, as it represents temptation that leads men to their eternal death in Hell. No such allegory is proffered here by Piscator; rather, the emphasis is on the wonder and strangeness – and danger – lurking beneath the surface at these borderlands. Cohen argues that 'the monster's very existence is a rebuke to boundary and enclosure'.[47] Strange fish defy the boundaries between ocean and river, even as they also defy Walton's neat categorisation. Indeed, it is telling that Walton broaches monstrosity specifically when he speaks about the nature of the river and sea. Adding these passages on water allowed Walton both to preserve and to call into question his categories. Though it is possible that Walton sees these various water dwellers on a continuum, it seems clear that there is something disturbing, something vulnerable for Walton about the borders between river and sea, between fish and monster.

Negotiating habitat and identity after the Civil War

Walton's insistence that angling is an art suggests his optimism in the possibility that humanity may assert some control over nature. Just as depictions of sea monsters on maps served to demystify them and sought to bring them to the surface to make them more accessible, so too does Walton's discussion of fish unearth the secrets of the waters.[48] Successful anglers learn to read the river: line and bait must not only be well-chosen for the angler's prey but must also 'fit the stream in which you fish' (101). Failure to understand the eccentricities of either fish or stream will result in a defeated and perhaps hungry angler. Nevertheless, even if he comes home empty-handed, angling on the banks of England's rivers is its own reward. In one of the pastoral song episodes, Walton replies to Coridon's song with his own rendition, 'The Angler's Song'. Here he affirms the benefits of the river over the sea: 'I care not, I, to fish in seas; / Fresh rivers best my mind do please, / Whose sweet calm course I contemplate, / And seek in life to imitate: / In civil bounds I fain would keep, / And for my past offences weep' (87). Unlike the unpredictability of the sea, the river offers tranquillity and a pleasure that can be held 'in civil bounds'.

Walton's attention to habitat shows the importance of environment not just for understanding fish, but also for guiding the practice of the angler. In his discussion of the river and the space of the river's edge, Walton also negotiates a new space for royalists after the civil war whose natural habitat had irrevocably changed. In the years after the death of Charles I, they become, as it were, fish out of water. Rather than see England's countryside as a place of exile, in *The Compleat Angler* Walton envisions it as a productive space where community can be reconstituted. But mapped monsters are still monsters. Even in this space of recreating hierarchy in the human world through pastoral dialogue and codifying it in the piscatory world through taxonomy, Walton never loses sight of the monsters in his midst.

Notes

1. See also in this volume, Daniel Gettings, '"Plenteous Rivers": Waterways as Resources, Threats and the Heart of the Community in Early Modern England', 42–60.
2. Julie V. Middleton, 'The Stream Doctor Project: Community-Driven Stream Restoration', *Bio-Science* 51.4 (2001), 293–6, 293.
3. Marjorie Swann, 'Literary and Environmental References in *The Compleat Angler*', *Notes and Queries* 61.3 (2014), 373–6, 375.
4. Ibid., 376.
5. Marjorie Swann, *Environment, Society and the* Compleat Angler (University Park, PA: Penn State University Press, 2023), 5.
6. H. J. Oliver, 'The Composition and Revisions of "The Compleat Angler"', *The Modern Language Review* 42.3 (1947), 295–313, 301.
7. Marjorie Swann, '"The Compleat Angler" and the Early Modern Culture of Collecting', *English Literary Renaissance* 37.1 (2007), 100–17, 103.
8. John R. Cooper, *The Art of* The Compleat Angler (Durham, NC: Duke University Press, 1968), 170 and 183.
9. Earl Miner, *The Cavalier Mode from Jonson to Cotton* (Princeton, NJ: Princeton University Press, 1971), 53.
10. Stephen H. Zwicker, *Lines of Authority: Politics and English Literary Culture, 1649–1689* (Ithaca, NY: Cornell University Press, 1993), 66.
11. Oliver, 'The Composition and Revisions of "The Compleat Angler"', 295.
12. Ibid., 296–297.
13. Raymond A. Anselment, 'Robert Boyle, Izaak Walton, and the Art of Angling', *Prose Studies* 30.2 (2008), 124–41, 127.
14. Izaak Walton, *The Compleat Angler* (New York: Modern Library Paperback, 1998), 3. All further quotations from Walton will be taken from this edition and reference will be given in the text.
15. Anselment, 'Robert Boyle, Izaak Walton, and the Art of Angling', 127.
16. John M. Adrian, *Local Negotiations of English Nationhood, 1570–1680* (Basingstoke: Palgrave Macmillan, 2011), 124.

17. Anselment, 'Robert Boyle, Izaak Walton, and the Art of Angling', 127.
18. Nigel Smith, *Literature and Revolution in England, 1640–1660* (New Haven, CT: Yale University Press, 1994), 328.
19. Ibid., 328.
20. Benjamin Guyer, 'Izaak Walton's "Holy War": *The Compleat Angler* in Polemical Context', *Sixteenth Century Journal* 47.2 (2016), 296.
21. Zwicker, *Lines of Authority*, 74.
22. Swann, "The Compleat Angler' and the Early Modern Culture of Collecting', 116.
23. Ibid., 108.
24. David Hill Radcliffe, '"Study to Be Quiet": Genre and Politics in Izaak Walton's "Compleat Angler"', *English Literary Renaissance* 22.1 (1992), 95–111, 108.
25. Swann, *Environment, Society, and the* Compleat Angler, 8.
26. Swann, 'Literary and Environmental References in *The Compleat Angler*', 2014.
27. Smith, *Literature and Revolution in England*, 329.
28. Ibid., 329.
29. Lorraine Daston and Katherine Park, *Wonders and the Order of Nature* (New York: Zone Books, 1998), 24.
30. Ibid., 159.
31. Adrian, *Local Negotiations of English Nationhood*, 129.
32. Oliver, 'The Composition and Revisions of "The Compleat Angler"', 302.
33. Ibid., 303.
34. Gettings, '"Plenteous Rivers"', 42–60.
35. Psalm 104:25–6.
36. Pliny, *Natural History*, vol. XIII, translated by W. H. S. Jones, (Cambridge, MA: Harvard University Press, 1963), 391.
37. Asa Simon Mittman and Marcus Hensel, eds, *Primary Sources on Monsters*, vol. 2 (York: Arc Humanities Press, 2018), cited in Jeffrey Andrew Weinstock, 'Introduction: A Genealogy of Monster Theory', in *The Monster Theory Reader*, ed. Jeffrey Andrew Weinstock (Minneapolis: University of Minnesota Press, 2020), 1–36, 3.
38. Andrew Hadfield, 'Drayton's Fish', in *Poly-Olbion: New Perspectives*, ed. Andrew McRae and Philip Schwyzer (Martlesham: Boydell & Brewer, 2020), 125.
39. Chet Van Duzer, *Sea Monsters on Medieval and Renaissance Maps* (London: The British Library, 2013), 9.
40. Surekha Davies, *Renaissance Ethnography and the Invention of the Human* (Cambridge: Cambridge University Press, 2016), 15.
41. David Cressy, 'Lamentable, Strange, and Wonderful: Headless Monsters in the English Revolution', in *Monstrous Bodies/Political Monstrosities in Early Modern Europe*, ed. Laura Lunger Knoppers and Joan B. Landes (Ithaca, NY: Cornell University Press, 2004), 40–66, 44.
42. Ambroise Paré, *On Monsters and Marvels*, translated by Janis L. Pallister (Chicago: University of Chicago Press, 1983), 109.
43. Jeffrey Jerome Cohen, 'Monster Culture (Seven Theses)', in *The Monster Theory Reader*, 38–58, 40.

44. Peter Harrison, 'The Virtues of Animals in Seventeenth-Century Thought', *Journal of the History of Ideas* 59.3 (1998), 463–84, 468.
45. Radcliffe, '"Study to Be Quiet"', 106.
46. Alan Everitt, *Landscape and Community in England* (Ronceverte, WV: The Hambleton Press, 1985), 48.
47. Cohen, 'Monster Culture (Seven Theses)', 40.
48. Van Duzer, *Sea Monsters on Medieval and Renaissance Maps*, 12.

III. Rivers and Money

Chapter 7

'Your Innes and Alehouses Are Brookes and Rivers': John Taylor and Free-flowing Rivers of Ale

Bill Angus

When one Henry Walker, ironmonger, wanted to thoroughly debase his subject, the self-proclaimed 'water-poet' John Taylor, he not only described his writing as a diarrhetic for the Devil himself but also completed the faecal cycle by having the Devil, his bowels now loosened, shit words back into Taylor's mouth. Walker's invective pamphlet, *Taylors physicke has purged the divel, or, The divell has got a squirt and the simple seame-rent thred bare Taylor translates it into railing poetry and is now soundly cudgelled for it* (1641), sports an informative woodcut picturing the Devil crouching over the unfortunate ferryman Taylor, who is prone in his wherry on the river, squirting diarrhoea down his throat (see Figure 7.1). Its subtitle declares 'Such is the language of a beastly railor, The Divels privi-house most fit for Taylor'.[1] Comparing Taylor to

Figure 7.1 Detail from *Taylors physicke has purged the divel* (1641). The Library grants permisson to use the image. © British Library Board. E.163.(9) fol. 1r.

William Laud the Archbishop of Canterbury, who at that time Walker claims is 'justly imprisoned by nobles in Parliament, for tormenting and corrupting the Church in this our Iland', he adds further verminous imagery when he expresses hope that 'the same noble Senatours, will serve this *furious water-Rat*, for vexing the Church upon the water'.[2]

Taylor was only an occasional contributor to religious controversies but his first published work, *The Sculler* (1612) takes a dig as it originates from the river: 'To you from fair and sweetly sliding Thames, / A popomastick sculler war proclaims', it ironically greets the 'whole kennel of Antichrist's hounds, priests, friars, monks, and Jesuits'.[3] Not quite following the stifled logic of his own extreme imagery, Walker describes how the result of Taylor's railing is that 'people flocke to my shop, exclaiming against his wicked, unsanctified, disorderly, ungodly life and conversation'.[4] Here the flow of language in the capital seems to be free and endemic, while the image of people supposedly flooding to Walker's shop to inveigh against Taylor's terrible life and writing might rather give us more than a hint of his popularity and the broad social impact of his writing. Describing him as a rat meanwhile also perhaps has the unintended effect of expressing his ubiquity. The unfortunate ironmonger in question is later convicted of having 'invented and writ divers Pamphlets, and other scandalous Bookes, to the great disturbance of his Majesty', as Taylor puts it the following year, and finds himself in the gravest of trouble.[5] But here he is still in full flow and, in employing the gloriously vile device of the Devil's outflow pipe as the source of the writer's inspiration, he implies not only that Taylor talks shite but that he does so because of the most heinous moral degradation. The range of imagery here, from the scatological to the verminous, draws upon a symbolic field often associated with the choked tributary rivers of London, principally the Fleet, whose name had acquired irony and whose stygian state was proverbial. Through all of these metaphors of filth and fluidity, this Devil's toilet poet is allowed to flow only with the worst pollution imaginable. Such imagery is meant to strike deep at the moral core of the work, but it also suggests a profound familiarity with the major metaphors and concerns of Taylor's writing: the freeflow of language and verse on any subject to hand, the unobstructed stream of goods and people along navigable rivers and the healthful imbibing of ales whose sources are the waterways of England.

The writer so intimately abused in this pamphlet had offended Walker in what we might think are fairly obscure questions of religion, but these were hardly John Taylor's trade. Born in Gloucester within shouting distance of the great trading River Severn, Taylor worked on and lived around the free-flowing waters of rivers all his life.[6] From his apprenticeship as a waterman on the Thames in London in the early 1590s, he saw himself as dedicated to the river, and if it never quite brought him prosperity it at least afforded him a liberal living, as he expresses in verse:

> ... Thames, with thee I haue decreed
> Because thou neuer faild me in my need,
> To thee, to thee againe I doe retire
> And with thee Ile remaine till life expire,
> ... Thou art my Mistresse, and oft times from thee
> Thy liberalitie hath flow'd to me.[7]

Besides its obvious commercial flow along its seaward course, the crossing of the river in London also brought much valuable traffic of various kinds in both directions. The river's 'liberalitie' flowed towards Taylor from ferrying people from the City on the north bank of the Thames across to his own neighbourhood, Bankside, on the south in the direction of the theatres, the bearbaiting and the brothels. Of the last, Taylor mentions that it was not just their customers that came and went, but the prostitutes also who, 'after they had any good trading' or what he cheekily calls 'reasonable comings in', often liked to take a boat and 'air themselves upon the water'.[8]

In those days, the Thames was London's main artery of human movement; the capital's roads were dilapidated and crowded and horse-powered transport consequently often frustratingly slow. Besides the ferries, the old London Bridge was the only other way to cross the river and the possibility of avoiding its encroaching buildings and crowds was attractive enough to the populace that in 1620 Taylor could claim that 20,000 people were either directly involved in the watermen's trade or dependent upon it.[9] Popular attitudes to such plyers of the oar at this time might be found in sympathy with some of the ironmonger's diatribe. In Thomas Overbury's *Characters* (1614) the waterman is characterised as resembling the notoriously vilified informer: one that purveys 'strange newes; most commonly lyes'. An underlying criminality is implied when this advises that 'little trust is to be given to him, for ... his daily labour teaches him the Art of dissembling; for like a fellow that rides to the Pillory, hee goes not the way he lookes'.[10] Neither does it omit the watermen's general reputation for enjoyment of both the drink and the theatre, asserting that 'The Play-houses only keepe him sober; and as it doth many other Gallants.'[11]

The common waterman might be popularly caricatured as a braggart, a liar, a drunk and a cheat but, besides the financial benefits of the everyday grinding of the oar, the job was Taylor's ticket to respectability of a kind. It afforded him advantageous associations with many of London's outstanding dramatis personae as he rowed those involved in all aspects of the theatre across and along the Thames. These included the writers Nicholas Breton and Samuel Rowlands, and most significantly Ben Jonson, whom he called his 'dear respected friend'.[12] It was first to such people that he presented himself as a maker of poetry, and they formed the principal audience for his eventual self-invention as 'the King's water-poet'. In fact, poetry was only one of the outlets for his prolific writing. Taylor may have authored around 150 separate works, including much prose, social and commercial commentary, religious diatribe of the kind much objected to by Walker, and even early versions of Yellow Pages-like business lists for public houses and for travellers to connect with the movements of London's carter community, identifying points of departure for various distant destinations. It was his journey narratives, however, that made his name, often conducted on a wager basis and involving extensive travel on the rivers which were his natural home.

Despite Walker's determined assault on his character, Taylor seems to have been regarded in most other respects as an upstanding citizen of the time: one who generally favoured the monarchy and espoused conservative religious sentiments. He became not only a member of The Company of Watermen and Lightermen of the River Thames but its clerk, and in 1613 he was appointed one of the King's Watermen, receiving 62 shillings and sixpence yearly in total for the honour. It was this that afforded him the luxury of referring to himself, somewhat dubiously, as the 'King's Water-poet'.[13] On one count, however, Taylor leaves himself open to easy criticism from judgemental contemporaries. Though seemingly a fully committed Christian believer in the style of his time, he spent what some thought to be an inordinate amount of energy in the praise, promotion and prolific partaking of alcohol, specifically in the form of traditional ales. A serious commitment to drinking has been and is of course a very widespread cultural preference for many living in the British Isles, but besides the normal options in this regard Taylor's career on the river put him in the way of some unusual opportunities to participate. Speaking of the 'mystery of Quaffing' as if it were a religious ceremony all take part in, he describes having 'oftentimes dined or supped at a great mans board, and when I have risen, the servants of the house have enforced me ... to drink, as if they had a commission under the Devils great seal, to murder men with drinking'.[14] Despite this feigned distaste, his continued interest in ale resulted in him making some curious conceptual connections between rivers, national commerce and his own attempts at poetry as a jobbing writer of his day.

After seven years of apprenticeship as a waterman and then eight years of plying his own trade on the river, in about 1605 he was appointed to the historically important post of 'Bottleman' at the Tower of London, a role he performed for ten more years. This job involved rowing out from the old fortress by the Thames to visit any passing ship that was carrying a cargo of wine up the river and asserting the Lieutenant of the Tower's right to a tribute of two large leather 'bombards' of the freight, practically involving anything from eight to sixteen gallons of wine. Bernard Capp describes the pride Taylor took in laying down a superb cellar in this way for his master and, given his apparent attitude to the drink, it is difficult to imagine that he would not have benefited from this bounty in the same way himself.[15] So for Taylor, in the act of taxing the commerce of the nation, and in service of this ancient tradition, the river then flows with wine on a daily basis. This no doubt provided one of many stimuli to the association found in his writing between the flow of river water and that of alcohol.

Besides this practical association with wine, the capital's river has an even more direct and fundamental connection with Taylor's beloved ale. This is found in the simple fact that Thames water was the actual source liquid of most London ales, especially those prepared in the vicinity of the Tower and the old city where many London breweries, or 'beere howses', had been long established on the banks of the river (see Figure 7.2). Taylor will have passed these continually in rowing to and from the Tower in the business of taxing vessels for his master's

Figure 7.2 Map of London; illustration to Braun and Hogenberg's *Civitates Orbis Terrarum*. The Library grants permisson to use the image. © British Library Board.

bombards of wine. Further upstream in the west, a canal took Thames water up to the Stag Brewery at Pimlico (which later made the famous 1970s brew Watney's Red Barrel).[16] Unfortunately, as the city grew and Thames became ever more polluted, this provision was bound to become unsafe and even as early as 1592 Thomas Nashe's *Pierce Penilesse, his supplication to the Deuil* could credibly refer to London brewers making fortunes 'by retayling filthy *Thames* water'.[17] John Grove's, *Wine, Beere, Ale, and Tobacco: Contending for Superiority* (1630) has wine represent the gentleman, beer the city dweller and ale a countryside rustic cursed 'O base Ale ... O muddy Ale'.[18] In fact, not only did the grain content of ale make it 'a nutritious source of much needed calories', as Kristen D. Burton reports, but 'because the alcohol in ale killed off bacteria present in water, ale was safer to drink than water'.[19] Those who compared it unfavourably to beer in this respect were basically correct though – the resins that beer hops contain do provide additional defence against bacterial infection.[20] The continuing association of ale with filth resounds in Walker's tirade against both Taylor and his wife, as we will see.

Taylor was to lose his post as Bottleman when succeeding Lieutenants of the Tower demanded money for its continuation, tempting him to fund this by customs fraud. He complains of 'upland tradesmen [who dare] take in hand / A wa'try business, they not understand', and asks, 'Have I not run through tempests, gusts, and storms, / And met with danger in strange various forms. / All times and tides, with, and against the stream?', declaring, 'farewell Bottles never to return. / Weep you in sack, whilst I in ale will mourn'.[21] His ensuing relative lack of employment, however, was to prompt the beginning of his literary journeying that was his main claim to celebrity, and in ale he would certainly find solace.[22]

His initial travel writing trip was to cross from Thames to Elbe and journey to Hamburg in 1616. This began with a river journey by wherry from Billingsgate to Gravesend where the passengers then repaired to an inn and took 'a Bacchanalian farewell' before heading out of the river mouth.[23] Once in Hamburg, he met the merchants of the English House whose custom it was, Capp notes, 'to welcome a stranger by making him drunk ... Taylor naturally enter[ing] into the spirit of the occasion'.[24] Taylor's wager journey to Edinburgh following in Jonson's footsteps, described in *Penniless Pilgrimage* (1618), was basically an extended pub crawl with commentary. At Holywell, he says, 'I was enforced carouse, / Ale high, and mighty, at the Blindman's House'. While 'in Barbican / There's as good beer and ale as ever twang'd', and at the Saracen's Head in St Albans, 'The jugs were fill'd and fill'd, the cups went round'. When in Manchester he is taken to the house of one

John Pinners, a man he rhymingly says 'that lives amongst a crew of sinners' where as he recounts,

> ... eight several sorts of ale we had,
> All able to make one stark drunk or mad.
> But I with courage bravely flinched not,
> And gave the town leave to discharge the shot.
> We had at one time set upon the table,
> Good ale of hyssop, 'twas no Æsop-fable:
> Then had we ale of sage, and ale of malt,
> And ale of wormwood, that could make one halt,
> With ale of rosemary, and betony,
> And two ales more, or else I needs must lie.
> But to conclude this drinking aley-tale,
> We had a sort of ale, called scurvy ale

When he finally gets to Scotland he finds all proportion given over in ale terms: for the Scots he says, 'an English gallon either of ale or wine, is but their quart'. And in these latitudes rivers are excessive too, as he says, 'though it rained not all the day, yet it was my fortune to be well wet twice, for I waded over a great river called Esk in the morning ... and at night within two miles of my lodging, I was fain to wade over the river of Annan'.[25]

Taylor's great provider being the Thames, he seems always to feel its beneficial flow beneath him and he often uses this metaphorically in writing his changing world.[26] It is a fitting vehicle: being tidal, the Thames ebbs and flows more than many rivers, as Taylor's contemporary Izaak Walton says, 'This glorious river feeleth the violence and benefit of the sea more than any river in Europe; ebbing and flowing, twice a day, more than sixty miles.'[27] The river-based wagered escapades continued in 1619 with a Bankside neighbour and vintner who had bet he and Taylor could row the Thames to Quinborough in a boat Taylor had made from brown paper, no metal or wood being allowed. The oars were made from cane with large flat dried stockfish attached and the boat floated only because of attached air-filled bladders. Half-sunk and pursued by crowds, they finally reached Quinborough where they were entertained by the Mayor.[28] Taylor's *A Very Merry Wherry-Ferry Voyage* tells the story of another wager trip in 1622 which involved him taking his wherry down the Thames to the sea and north up the coast into the River Humber, thence taking the Ouse to York. The flow of the Thames literally determines the contours of his journey as we see explicitly when he and his companion,

> ... left Gravesend, rowing down the stream,
> And near to Lee, we to an anchor came.

Because the sand were bare, and water low.
We rested there, till it two hours did flow:
And then to travel went our galley-foist,
Our anchor quickly weigh'd, our sail soon hoist.[29]

Then in his *Taylor on Tame Isis* (1632) he writes how 'down to *Cullom*, streame runs quicke and quicke / Yet we rub'd twice a ground for want of liquor'.[30] Being used to bottoming out on such shoals, this became one of his metaphors for both his own writing and for commerce in general, opposing the freeflow of riverine current. Note here also a hint of the connection between the river water and the 'liquor' that will fixate him. Increasingly, as he experienced more of the mercantile business of the country on his various travels, Taylor also used these narratives to comment on the healthy flow of commerce as an indication of the well-being of the nation, likening this to an ideal river nourishing a grateful landscape. And congruent with that fluid movement was the flow of ale between all commercial parties. When visiting the northern coal mines of Sir George Bruce on his Edinburgh odyssey, his active mind turns to thoughts of commerce and of ale as he imagines his ideal retirement as a landlord: 'I said, that I could afford to turn tapster at London, so that I had but one quarter of a mile of his mine to make me a cellar, to keep beer and bottled ale in.' Relating this to the river and trade, somewhat oddly he imagines the cataclysmic destruction of the Thames itself, musing, 'if the plotters of the Powder Treason in England had seen this mine, that they (perhaps) would have attempted to ... have undermined the Thames, and so to have blown up the barges and wherries, wherein the King, and all the estates of our kingdom were'.[31] The river flows precariously above with various precious cargoes as the ale flows from below in the industrious space of Taylor's imagination.

Ale, river water and poetry seem to continually intermingle in Taylor's mind. Water provides an elemental undercurrent to his intellectual journey as we see in his poem 'Here followeth, a laborious and effectuall discourse, in praise of the Element of all Waters fresh and salt, with their opperation; with a touch of the causes of all sorts of weather, faire and foule' from *Drinke and Welcome* (1637): 'Earth, nor Ayre, nor Fire, nor rumbling Warre, / Nor plague, or pestilence, nor famine are / Of powre to winne, where Water but commands'.[32] The following line, 'As witnesse may the watry Netherlands', gives a sense of the way his thought tends towards national interests and of how his own poetic flow can often bottom out on a clunky obstruction. Its rumination on the commercial and financial blessings of flowing waters, however, continues, 'Concerning Merchandise, and transportation, / Commerce and traffique, and negotiation /... by Navigation', through which he hopes 'To Make each Countrie have / The Goods, and Riches of each others Nation', asserting that,

> Commodities in free community,
> Embassages for warre or unity:
> These blessings, by the Sea, or some fresh River
> Are given to us, by the All-giving Giver.[33]

In this we see rivers deliver their elemental blessings, via unobstructed navigation, in the form of mutually beneficial flowing trade and the free communication of nations. His train of thought continues godwise then as he champions water as the element that brings the soul itself heaven-ordained purity, as 'a Seale and sacred Sacrament, / Which doth in Baptisme us regenerate, / And man againe with God doth renovate'. Linking this cleansing from 'sinne originall' to more mundane washings intended 'To wash our cloathes, and keepe us cleane and sweet', the business of inner piety and outer purity having been covered, his inclinations inevitably turn towards the ale, since, as water 'purges us from filth and stincke; / We must remember that it makes us drinke, / *Metheglin, Braggot, Beere*, and headstrong *Ale*'.[34] From water as pure element, we travel then through the rivers of Taylor's imagination and via both practical and pious excursions we arrive at the principal staple of life: ale. This he identifies as 'that Admired and most superexcellent Imbrewage' and asserts that it is a panacea for ills of all kinds and thus is to be 'held in high price for the nutritive substance that it is indued withall, and how precious a nurse it is in generall to Mankinde'.[35] The benefits of ale drinking are both medicinal and social – on the medicinal side, it offers a remedy against

> all melancholick diseases ... Maladies of the spleene ... *Iliaca passio* ... the stone in the Bladder, Reines or Kidneyes ... Tumors and swellings in the body ... obstructions of the Liver ... Gowt ... *Gonogra*, the Yeast or Barme ... all Impostumes ... *Sciatica passio* ... all defluxions and Epidemicall diseases ... all Contagious diseases, Feavers, Agues, Rhumes, Coughes and Catarres with *Hernia Aquosa & vertosa*.

Among its more social benefits meanwhile are listed its capacity to

> comfort a heavy and troubled minde ... make a weeping widowe laugh and forget sorrow ... set a Bashfull Suiter a wooing ... cause a man to speake past his owne or any other man's capacity, or understanding [and set] an Edge upon Logick and Rhetorick.

He betrays a personal connection when he says that it 'inspires the poore Poet, that cannot compasse the price of *Canarie* or *Gascoign* ... mounts the Musician 'bove Eccla ... makes the Balladmaker Rime beyond Reason ... puts Eloquence into the Oratour' and can make 'the Philosopher talke profoundly, the Scholler learnedly, and the Lawyer acute and feelingly'. In his irrepressible punning on Ale- and Al- words, he even suggests that what he calls the 'Turkish *Alcaron*' was 'invented by Mahomet out of such furious raptures as Ale inspir'd him withall', where ale stands in for the intervention of the angel Gabriel in inspiring holy writ.[36] He concludes, 'it is such a nourisher of Mankinde, that if my Mouth were as bigge as Bishopsgate, my Pen as long as a Maypole, and my Inke a flowing spring, or a standing fishpond, yet I could not with Mouth, Pen or Inke, speake or write the true worth and worthiness of *Ale*'.[37] Though not quite claiming to be a flowing spring of inspiration, his ink certainly runs as freely as any river on the subject of the properties of ale.

The idea that ale has all these inspirational, healing and transformative qualities is far from incredible in a world where the very rivers that supply its source liquid might also possess miraculous or metamorphic properties. In this respect, Taylor delights in describing rivers which, when 'dranke (by sheepe) doth change them black from white'; others that 'with bathing cure, blind, deafe, and lame'; one that 'makes mens haire red that doe drinke the same'; and some that '(through coldnesse) wood to stones will turne'. Other rivers meanwhile have curious otherworldly qualities and are 'at noone key-cold, at midnight hot', or will 'quench burning torches straite, and then / Dip'd in the water they are light agen'. Some are dangerous, 'banefull, full of poysn'ous harme', others again '(do with lust) make mens affections burne', or make them mad, while others are literally themselves alcoholic: he asserts that 'some makes a man ... a drunken sot'.[38] Here rivers are mysteriously pharmacological in nature, transformative and resistant, poisonous and remedious, to some extent consubstantial with the one reliable water product which not only shares these qualities but also binds trade, tradition and commercial and artistic success in Taylor's mind: the all-engrossing ale.

Thus far, the flow of both ale and river are portrayed as healthgiving manifestations of God's blessing to nations, with the underlying hint also that the writer's ink follows the beneficial flow. It is not all good news though and there succeeds a wry complaint about those who have made their money from 'sodden Water', that is ale, or rather ale-drinkers, already:

> ... many Brewers are growne Rich,
> And in estates may soare a lofty Pitch,
> Men of Good Ranke and place, and much command
> Who have (by sodden Water) purchast land:

Yet sure I thinke their gaine had not been such
Had not good fellowes vs'de to drinke too much.[39]

Apologising then for this digression into the territory of moral commentary on the alcohol trade and its beneficiaries, Taylor returns to the elemental and goes on to schematise the hierarchy of water, beginning with the clouds above and continuing downwards until he gets to the last and lowest two categories in this aquatic pantheon, those of 'Urin and strong Watermen', and in what is surely an excess of modesty places himself and his fellow tradesmen below even basic micturition.[40] When his aqueous narrative finally descends to the earth it is again the river systems which are his focus:

Springs, (in the Earth) I doe Assimulate
To veines of Man, which doe evacuate,
And drop by drop through Cavernes they distill.
Till many meetings make a petty *Rill*:
Which Rill (with others) doe make Rivolets,
And Rivolets, Brookes, Bournes and foords begets,
And thus combined, they their store deliver
Into a deeper trench, and make a River.

Once fully formed into the dominant objects of his own environment, rivers go about their business of nourishing the whole earth:

Then Rivers joyne, as *Isis* doth with *Tame*,
And *Trent* with *Owse*, and *Humber* doth the same.
These altogether doe their Tributes pay
Unto their soveraigne Ocean night and day.
These make Dame *Tellus* wombe to fructifie,
As blood in veines of men doe life supply.[41]

This imagery configures the river as both seminal fluid, seeding the womb of the earth with abundance, then more conventionally as the vascular system of the human body. But if rivers are to be imaged as carrying the lifeblood of the land, the cultural connections and resonances of blood must be considered. Through the effect of biblical imagery on influential western culture, blood is very often associated with alcohol and specifically wine, which Taylor calls 'the blood of Bacchus, Sacke and Claret'.[42] Even besides the considerable religious problem of wine at that time connected to its use in the Catholic Mass, its associations are not uncomplicated in the moral and medical economies of Taylor's world. With the obvious colour connection adopted from earlier cultures by Christianity, wine is said to be 'the blood of the Grape', as Thomas Heywood notes contemporaneously in his *Philocothonista, or, The drunkard, opened, dissected, and anatomized* (1635).[43] Heywood goes on, '*Wine* (saith one) is the blood of the Earth, and the shame of those who abuse it.'[44] It was, he asserts, the biblical Noah that first planted the vine, 'and was made drunk with the strength thereof' and he goes on to explain how 'in the dressing of it, hee moystened the rootes with the blood of sundry beasts' and that this causes various bestial responses in drunkards. They might be as 'wilde as *Lyons*, (apt for any mischiefe, or outrage) . . . dull and sortish as *Asses*, (almost voide of motion or spirit) . . . Luxurious as *Goates* (forgetting both Civilitie and manners) . . . crafty as *Foxes*, (then most subtle, either in Cheates, or Bargaines)'.[45] Although ale does not share this direct connection with blood, it nevertheless shares these same qualities. Taylor claims that it 'heates the chill blood of the Aged' as it flows like rivers in the veins of the country he describes.[46] Taylor also gives wine its place in *Taylor's Travels and Circular Perambulation* (1636), explaining, 'vines have been planted, and vineyards allowed here in *England* by the Permission of the Emperour *Probus*, at such time as the Romanes had the Government here'. Moreover, as he says, 'in the raigne of King *Iohn*, Wine was so plenty, that it was sold for twenty Shillings the Tun, which is but one penny the Gallon'.[47] In his own time, however, wine cost about twelve times more than ale.[48] No doubt this is part of the reason that the focus of his attention is on the freer flow in the veins of the nation of good old fashioned and relatively inexpensive ale.

In both *Drinke and Welcome* (1637) and *Ale-Ale-vated* (1651), ale is celebrated as superior not only to wine but also to the newfangled tipple known as 'beer', and both of these are regarded as foreign impositions, respectively of the French and the Dutch.[49] Despite these interlopers, the traditional drink of choice in Taylor's (and Shakespeare's) day was still predominantly ale. Amanda Mabillard notes usefully that Shakespeare's father was Stratford's official ale taster, a job which involved 'monitoring the ingredients used by professional brewers and ensuring they sold their ale at Crown regulated prices'.[50]

At this time beer was increasing in popularity, however, as Liza Picard explains: 'in 1574, there were still 58 ale brewers to 33 beer brewers in [London], but beer gradually replaced ale as the national drink over the course of the century'.[51] In 1577 the cleric William Harrison could claim that beer was the preferred tipple of the elite, though it was also favoured by other ranks, describing un-hopped ale as an 'old and sick men's drink'.[52] For many, this transition seemed very sudden and Walton's *Compleat Angler* quotes one complaining poetically that seemingly 'Hops and turkies, carps and beer, / Came into England all in a year'.[53] According to Taylor, the new, alien beer is acceptable only when mixed with wine, and he imagines this compromised admixture again as a watercourse merging with a river, a 'petty Brooke running into a great stream' that 'looses itself in his own current'.[54] When the inferior beer flows, it flows uselessly, and is lost in the movement of greater waters. Taylor's conclusive recommendation then is 'as many as doe love the preservation of their lives and healths, let them drinke ALE', and his vehicle for this is the river.[55]

In a Puritan age, Taylor's reputation was bound to be affected by this kind of writing. As Capp describes him, 'Taylor was no ascetic, and he never disguised his love of good food, drink, and company [insisting] "Good friendly drinking I count not evil".'[56] Regardless of his nuancing, this plays into the hands of enemies like the ironmonger Walker who employs Taylor's repute for the drink in an attempt at character assassination of both him and his family. He describes Taylor as having been 'presented to mine eyes in a tub of Lees: an infernall spirit, a Poet of Bacchus, drowned in his owne element' who is as a result 'by his distemper'd quill become a sad spectacle', that is, even his pen is drunk.[57] Walker then threatens him with 'Sodaine death ... a fearful execution to unrepentant sinners' brought on by the drink and, keeping it classy as ever, uses the example of Taylor's deceased partner drinking to excess in a section entitled 'An Exhortation to *Iohn Taylor* to repent and call to minde the example of his dead wife.' Here he sanctimoniously protests, 'in all humble manner, I doe heartily desire *Iohn Taylor* to call to minde the sad spectacle of that blacke tragedie; whilest his wife was carousing in the Taverne goblits; and let him but consider (if the like should befall him) what would become of his soule, if he repent not'.[58] In its personal cruelty, such preachment reveals its true nature, but in this case it also rehearses the false dichotomy between the tavern and the church. This suggestion is of course full of hypocrisy: as mentioned, alcohol had long been at the heart of the mass just as taverns are very often havens for believers. But Puritans especially struggled with a coherent perspective on alcohol that was complicated by the fact that Jesus' first miracle was to conjure a large quantity of good wine for a marriage feast.[59] We may also wish to note that, as determined by the ecology of the messiah's geographical locality, the alcohol here summoned accidentally establishes a religious prejudice against beer and ale that oddly favours the more potent brew, a bias that has persisted down to the present day. In this respect, Taylor impudently cites one contemporary, 'a discreet Gentleman in a solemn Assembly, who, by a politick observation, very aptly compares Ale and Cakes with Wine and Wafers'.[60]

Although he is obviously a seasoned drinker and writer on the subject, to make Taylor out to be some kind of crazed bacchanalian whose purpose is the promotion of drunken excesses is very far from an accurate critique. In fact, Taylor very often includes a warning against such extremes. In his moral writings, drunkenness was often blamed as the root cause of other vices, even to the extent of suggesting that 'brewers and vintners should be barred from all public office, on the grounds of having a vested interest in sin'.[61] He argues for harsh treatment of the dead in case of death by excessive drinking:

> If any man hang, drown, stab, or by any violent means make away his life, the goods and lands of any such person, are forfeit to the use of the King: and I see no reason but those which kill themselves with drinking, should be in the same estate, and be buried in the high ways, with a stake drove through them.[62]

He is also aware that ale in excess is bad for commercial prosperity, on both a national and personal level, and gets very personal with those who waste money on alcohol but fail to pay, or pay bare minimum for his own labour, those who 'spend most prodigally on . . . superfluous quarts and pints of the blood of Bacchus (sack and claret) . . . but upon a waterman, that hath rowed till his heart ache, and sweats till he hath not a dry thread about him . . . if he give him two pence more, he hath done a huge work'.[63] Here the waterman's labour is turning him into a man of water, however honourable in stark opposition to the excessive man of wine he has to transport. This transmutational tendency appears in other accounts of alcohol and river trade, as we will see. Rather than promoting excess, Taylor tends to turn the subject around to the more high-minded moralistic and economic implications of the consumption of alcohol, which if practiced in a controlled manner he genuinely believes to be beneficial on levels ranging from the individual to the national. A typical example of such a benefit he gives in *Drink and Welcome,* noting the commercial value that ale has brought to the town of 'Northdowne' in the Isle of Thanet which has 'ingrost much Fame, Wealth and Reputation from the prevalent potencie of their Atractive *Ale*'.[64] In addition to its many other listed healing qualities, their ale, he claims, is of 'singular force in expulsion of poison'.[65] Ale in this case is not only a panacea for many ills but even more so its abundant flow is a source of immense commercial advantage to the economy and the people of the place in question.

We have seen how Taylor praises the efficacy of ale drinking for many various members of society who may benefit from its medical and social properties. Complementing this commonwealth of ale, he also includes in *Ale Ale-vated* (1651) a ballad named 'The Exaletation *of* Ale' by his late friend Thomas Randolph which expands the community who may gain from the drinking of ale to encompass those of all religions and nations, the rich, the poor, the widow, the footman, the shepherd, the sower, the thresher, the mower, the soldier, the sailor, the tailor, the lawyer, the knave, the whore, the dwarfish, the tall, the blacksmith, the prisoner, the beggar, the carter, the courtier, the old clerk, the musician, the poet, the master philosopher, the Oxford scholar, the knight, the squire, the lord of manor or town, and even the aliens of the North Yorkshire Dales and the Picts and Scots. In Randolph's song too we find a world of benefit and commerce, as it speaks of 'Commodities store, a dozen and more, / That flow to Mankind from a pot of good ale'.[66] And we see in the imagery again that ale is tracked moving within the arteries of this nation of beneficiaries, imaged as a sailing boat in the blood stream as, 'down to the *legs* the virtue doth goe, / And to a bad *Foot-man* is as good as a *saile*, / When it fills the veins'.[67] Here also ale offers inspiration flowing for writers, in this case parodically those working up confessions or last speeches for performance at the gallows. These are once again figured as boats, now sailing the city on the inexorable tide of legal process:

> All Writers or Rimers, for such whose mishap,
> Is from Newgate up Houlbourn, to Tyburn to sail;
> Shall have suddain expression of all their confession,
> If the Muse be but dew'd with a pot of good ale.[68]

Following this metaphorical connection between sailing and drinking, Taylor's catalogue of London ale-houses, *Taylor's Travels* (1636), lists four called 'The Anker', and gives them the following epigram:

> Some men have found these Ankers very able,
> To More them safe and fast without a Cable:
> A man may Load himselfe, and Sleepe, and Ride,
> Free from Storms, Tempests, Pirats, Wind and Tide.[69]

Imaging drinking thus as taking on commercial cargo, he goes on to list twelve London alehouses sporting under the sign of the Tun or the Three Tuns:

> These Tuns proclame there's Tuns of Wine below,
> Goe in and welcome, try, and you shall know:
> There shall you see a plenteous Spring that runs
> From Pipes, Buts, Hogsheads, from the liberall Tuns.

Here the metaphor is once again of a watercourse but one that runs with 'wine' and thus the term is used perhaps with stricter echoes of its biblical sense as a collective noun for all kinds of alcohol.[70] Taylor's *Carriers Cosmographie* (1637), which listed 'the inns in London and Southwark from which carriers, wagons, and footposts set out for the provinces, [and] ... the quays where travellers could embark for coastal ports and the continent, or take boat for towns upriver', aimed at facilitating the commerce of the nation on road and river.[71] In producing these guides he ran the considerable risk of being taken for an informer. This, as we have seen, was an implication sometimes levelled at watermen in general and in this case an injurious suggestion that Taylor managed to quash by quenching: 'In some places I was suspected for a proiector ... indeed I was scarce taken for an honest man amongst the most of them: all which suppositions I was inforced oftentimes to wash away, with two or three Iugges of Beere, at most of the Innes I came to.'[72] His early version of Yellow Pages was not to be discouraged though and Taylor aims to show how, with humour and the application of alcohol, any commercial project might prosper.

The commercial advantage that most interested him was principally that concerned with the multiple benefits of navigable waterways, which seemed to Taylor to be an obvious key to trading and thus financial success for any town. As he notes, 'There is not any one town or city [in England] which hath a navigable river at it, that is poor.'[73] Taylor pointed out that 'other poets had sung the beauties of rivers ... but none before him had pressed their economic potential'.[74] His 1623 journey to Salisbury, for instance, was partly conducted in order to find out if the Wiltshire Avon could be made navigable to and from the sea, a possibility that could easily transform the economy of its hinterland.[75] This voyage was at first miserably dangerous. Off the coast of Hastings he and his companion nearly foundered on the rocks although once at Salisbury they were royally received. Back in London he was later to find it had been reported he had been drowned at sea, and Taylor was also 'stung by criticism that it was blasphemous to tempt providence by such madcap wagers' as Capp recounts.[76] These setbacks failed to deter him however and when in 1630 Charles I appointed privy councillors to investigate improvements in navigation from London to the sea, Taylor was one of the crew.[77] In 1641, he pursued inland navigation even further with an epic river and road voyage to Cirencester, Shrewsbury Bristol, Bath and Hereford, Evesham and Burford and back to London, covering 1200 miles in twenty days.[78]

The various river journeys that he undertakes are accompanied by further descriptions of physical and conceptual connections between waterways and ale. His 1623 journey recorded in *A New Discovery By Sea With a Wherry from London to Salisbury* begins of course on the river: 'We with our Wherry, and five men within her, / Along the crystal Thames did cut and curry'.[79] Again they are entertained at Greenwich, where with 'shaking hands, adieus, and drinkings store, / We took our ship again, and left the shore'.[80] At Dover an anonymous person treats them to more drink, in excess: 'Health vpon health, he doubled and redoubled, / Till his, and mine, and all our braines were troubled, / Vnto our absent Betters there we dranke'. Other victualling rests are less explicit, but he also records that they drank at a 'ragged town' two miles from Dungenness with 'Beere from the Alehouse'.[81] On arrival at Salisbury, Taylor stays, as would be usual, at a pub: 'where we brought our boat through Fisherton bridge, on the west side of the city, taking our lodging at the sign of the Kings head there'.[82] Upon arrival he is also feasted and watered by local notables. After surveying the river he informs the townsfolk 'Nature hath saued you the labour of cutting a Riuer, for I thinke you haue one there as olde as your Citie ready made to your hands, if you will bee but industrious to amend those impediments in it', and endorses trade in corn, timber and coal before informing them, 'it is well knowne what abundance of your Barley is continually made into Mault amongst you: which if you had cariage for it, might be brewed into Beere, wherewith you might serue diuers places with your Beere'.[83] Then more conceptually, he describes the process of starting such a project of clearing the river in terms of a pledge of ale: 'if one good man would begin, it would be (like a health drank to some beloved Prince at a great feast) pledged most heartily, and by God's grace effected most happily'. For Taylor, the clearing of the river is for the benefit of the whole commonwealth; both the wealthy and the needy of Salisbury will benefit. As he says, 'our River of Avon will quickly be cleansed to the honest enriching of the rich, and the charitable relieving of the poor'. He describes also a very interesting local scheme for a public brewhouse set up to raise money for poor relief that was supported by the town's charitable council, but opposed by the city's brewers.[84] Taylor's perspective on this is that the poor are deserving of such a scheme because they are more likely to spend all they have on alcohol in the first place since 'the poor man drinks stiffly to drive care away, and hath nothing to lose'.[85] Switching discourse again, Taylor declares, 'Now to turn from beer and ale to fair water, (your river I mean) which if it be cleansed, then with the profit of your Town-brew-house, and the commodity of the river, I think there will be scarce a beggar or a loiterer to be found amongst you.'[86] Prosperity here will spring from both projects, which for him are deeply moral undertakings with their sources in the management of the essentially interchangeable substances of river water and ale.

Here, as often in Taylor's writing and worldview, not only do ale and rivers dominate the discourse but they inevitably find themselves in confluence. Taking an elemental turn, both people and systems become water features in imagery which is also at once a moral critique of the system and a recommendation of material improvement in the real world. For a fan of the ale, he is curiously antagonistic of brewers when he describes them as a 'bottomless whirlpool that swallows up the profits of rich and poor'. This critique reaches a crescendo when he envisages the circular economy of the ale trade metaphorically as a vast riverine ecosystem, declaring, 'Your Inns and Alehouses are Brooks and Rivers, and their Clients are small Rills and Springs, who all (very dutifully) do pay their tributes to the boundless Ocean, the Brewhouse.'[87] In this picture, not only are the commercial conduits of alcohol imagined as watercourses, rivers and brooks of ale, but their clients are themselves bodies of flowing ale, transmuted in the riverman's fantasy into the ale itself: they are ale elementals or, as he might well have said in his oft-punning mode, 'alementals'. In a flash of Bacchic fancy, as his mind runs on the metaphor, he pays classical tribute to the culpable god, the ocean/brewhouse that is the source of both salvation and damnation in Taylor's economy of ale. Here again we see the concept of free-flow, not this time of ales flowing in the veins of the country but of the human and systemic factors depicted as the fluid alcohol itself in a natural moral economy.

Except the metaphor doesn't quite work. As always, when his writing tends towards its most poetic, his ability to work with complex concepts fails him. If the clients are streams and the pubs are rivers, surely the brewhouse/ocean should be unnaturally flowing up to them, not the other way around. It is a picture with beautiful potential that lacks confidence in its own message; the metaphor's tenor and vehicle are mismatched. Aside from his role as a writer, he of course has his own part to play in this trade as a prolific consumer, though he will later also become a purveyor in the same system. But when it comes to the first of these, despite all his apparent successes Taylor's poetry never quite flows as he wishes, unlike the rivers or the ales which sustain it.

Taylor often lamented his own 'worthless imbecility' as a poet and sometimes imaged this as being grounded on a shoal: 'though I be fast aground for my labour', he says in *Taylors Water-worke* (1614) of his poetic endeavour, 'I will attend the next high tide, and scramble up into Paul's Churchyard [the centre of London's book trade] ... I'll grabble for gudgeons, or fish for flounders in the rearward of our eminent temporizing humorists, sharp satirists, and enigmatical epigrammists'.[88] He uses this metaphor too in *The Sculler* (1612) when writing of the Pope: 'But in this matter Ile no longer trauell, / Least want of water make my Ship to grauell'.[89] Though his writing lacked poetic prowess, it was at least copious, and flowed easily over its shallow draught: he 'dashed off one of his satires on Fennor in fourteen hours, amidst other business, and when Prince Henry died he had verses ready for the press within a day'.[90]

Although he knows he is a poor poet, he nevertheless asserts his own poetic value in his *Taylor's Motto* (1621) where, as he tells it, 'on a reedy banke' by the river he is visited by the Muses who 'sate together in a ranke: / Whilst in my boate I did by water wander, / Repeating lines of Hero and Leander', and this also involves the sharing of the inspirational drink: after calling him to 'sit and chat ... They gaue to me a draught of Helicon, / Which prou'd to me a blessing and a curse, / To fill my pate with verse, and empt my purse'.[91] This draught costs him money, a refrain of his that can only again refer to alcohol.

As Capp notes, Taylor's narrative abilities 'had been honed in countless taverns and alehouses'.[92] As Bottleman he had made his living from both:

> Two strings are better to a bow than one,
> And poetry doth me small good alone:
> So ale alone yields but small means to me,
> Except it have some spice of poesy.

But his flow of writing, from poetic invective to a tiny, expurgated Bible, was to little profit: and even as early as 1614 he had declared he would give up writing, since 'even rowing paid better than poetry'.[93] One of the alehouses in which he had honed his talents appears to have been the famous Apollo room of the Devil and St Dunstan tavern at Temple Bar while drinking with Ben Jonson, someone familiar with the ebb and flow of the economics of artistic work. Capp relates how Taylor's first published work refers to Jonson as '"his dear respected friend" ... and in his latter days he reminisced how "my father Ben and I" had drunk together in the Apollo tavern'.[94] However, in private Jonson was dismissive, referring to Taylor as the 'water-rhymer' rather than the 'Water-Poet', since 'a rhymer / And a poet, are two things', and judging Taylor's popularity as a mark of the vulgarity of the public's taste.[95] Despite such snobbery, however, in 1630 Taylor's collected *Workes* were published, and as Capp remarks, 'apart from Shakespeare, only Jonson and Samuel Daniel had appeared in this format'.[96] Taylor blamed his failure to be accepted as a real poet on the belief that his verses 'being found to be of a poor man's writing ... lost their estimation'.[97] This is

I think a mistake, but it is nevertheless true that Taylor never found acceptance in the hierarchical ecosystem of letters in his day. Unlike the easy confluence of ale and the river, his place flowing in the cultural veins of the nation was never certain despite his popularity and his many achievements.

One artistic problem was that, as Capp says, 'Taylor showed little interest in structure, and very often his own personality was the only unifying thread . . . virtually merging the author with his subject-matter.'[98] He was his own subject really, but in terms of narrative structure he often flows like the river himself and describes himself in such terms. Praising his welcome on one of his journeys by the Mayor of Hull, he himself flows in superfluity: 'Their loves (like Humber) overflowed the banks, / And though I ebb in worth, I'll flow in thanks'.[99] His poetry also went with him in physical form on his river journeys, as to York in 1622 where he took along a load of his own pamphlets. Not only did the printed matter move with the commerce of the river, but more so becomes itself the substance of further stories flowing along the ancient waterways with their travellers. This may also have been seen by his contemporaries as abject and vulgar self-promotion. And as ever, the ale and river combination is not far from the riverman's writing process, as in 1634 when commissioned to devise the Lord Mayor's pageant in which two watermen and two sailors land a boat of cloth cargo, whereupon 'being overjoyed [they] pike their oars, and every [one] of them drinks his can as a health, tossing them up' before the barge is carried aloft 'as the foremost pageant in the show through the city'.[100] Here the trade of London's river water is blessed in ale in this celebration and confirmation of the incommensurable necessity of both.

When Taylor inevitably became an innkeeper himself he did his best to combine his poetry and pamphleteering with his being a publican. In 1647, during the Civil War, he took on The Crown in Covent Garden, just 700 yards from his beloved Thames and less than half a mile from his old haunt the Devil and St Dunstan tavern.[101] The Crown was of course an unashamedly royalist name for a pub at that time and even more obviously he changed the name to the Mourning Crown after Charles I's execution in 1649 until this was suspected of being a seditious move. Then he altered it again, this time to the Poet's Head, and hung his own portrait outside as the sign.[102] Often featuring in his latter writings, the pub then consummates the marriage of ale and poetry, both of which now flow quite literally, though in different ways, from the poet's head.

Ultimately, despite his wish for an abundantly flowing national prosperity, as we saw with the ironmonger Walker's assault on his character, Taylor was himself a partaker in the religious controversies that would be the great divider and devastator of the England he loved. Unwittingly perhaps, like many others, he helped to set the scene as the tide of public and political opinion flowed ever more surely towards and through civil conflict. The religio-political controversies Walker taxes him with are, however, thankfully rare in his demotic canon, and neither is he quite the bibulous bacchanalian Walker takes him to be. The self-described water-poet cannot quite claim to live up to that ideal, despite his more respected drinking pals. His verse is in some respects written in water and, for all the respect some contemporaries gave him, his poetry might as well be written in invisible ink. But in fact, more than being a mere water-poet by virtue of the medium of his specialism, he can claim to be an ale-poet, not simply because he sings the praises of ale but because he is somehow comprised of it. With due deference to Capp's description of him as a 'Cultural Amphibian', I would say rather that he bears the indelible stamp of his liquid origins.[103] Just as much as the water, ale is his element. It's in his blood we might say. Although his trivial verse is written on the ever-moving surface of the river, Taylor the riverman's real message is nonetheless eloquent and lasting. The health of the national body comes through the ample current of its river veins carrying its bountiful commerce, of which, for Taylor at least, ale may be its best example. On these metaphorical and material rivers he situates his plea for health and prosperity through the flow and consumption of a traditional drink throughout an ever more ideologically obstructed nation.

Notes

1. Henry Walker, *Taylors Physicke has Purged the Divel. Or, the Divell has Got a Squirt, and the Simple, Seame-Rent, Thredbare Taylor Translates it into Railing Poetry, and is Now Soundly Cudgelled for it. by Voluntas Ambulatoria* (1641), https://ezproxy.massey.ac.nz/login?url=https://www.proquest.com/books/taylors-physicke-has-purged-divel-divell-got/docview/2240939585/se-2 (last accessed 20 August 2023).
2. Walker, *Taylors Physicke* (my italics).
3. John Taylor, *The Sculler Rowing from Tiber to Thames with His Boate Laden with a Hotch-Potch, Or Gallimawfry of Sonnets, Satyres, and Epigrams. with an Addition of Pastorall Equiuocques Or the Complaint of a Shepheard. by John Taylor* (1612), https://ezproxy.massey.ac.nz/login?url=https://www.proquest.com/books/sculler-rowing-tiber-thames-with-his-boate-laden/docview/2240889740/se-2 (last accessed 20 August 2023).
4. Walker, *Taylors Physicke*.

5. John Taylor, *The Vvhole Life and Progresse of Henry Walker the Ironmonger. First, the Manner of His Conversation. Secondly, the Severall Offences, and Scandalous Pamphlets the Said Walker Hath Writ, and for which He is Now a Prisoner in New-Gate. Thirdly, the Forme of the Inditement which is Laid Against Him, by the Kings Sergeants at Law, and His Learned Counsell. Fourthly, His Conviction by the Iury. Fiftly, His Recantation, and Sorrow for the Publicke Wrong He Hath done His Majesty and the Whole Kingdome. here are also Many Remarkable Passages Concerning the Offence, and Apprehending the Said Henry Walker, with a True Relation of His Severall Escapes and Rescues from the Hands of Justice* (1642), https://ezproxy.massey.ac.nz/login?url=https://www.proquest.com/books/vvhole-life-progresse-henry-walker-ironmonger/docview/2240942177/se-2 (last accessed 20 August 2023).
6. Here the River Severn usefully splits into three accessible streams; Elizabeth I granted Gloucester the status of customs port when Taylor was two years old.
7. John Taylor, *In Praise of Hemp-seed*, in *The Works of John Taylor, the Water-poet* (London: James Boler, 1630), 75.
8. John Taylor, *All the Workes of John Taylor the Water Poet*, Vol. II (London, 1630; facsimile reprint Menston, Yorkshire: Scholar Press, 1973), 37.
9. Bernard Capp, *'Water-Poetry': The World of John Taylor the Water-Poet 1578–1653* (Oxford: Oxford University Press, 1994), 8. An indication of expenditure involving watermen might be seen in the detailed account that the Cecil family kept of the money they spent on a visit to the theatre, as Tim-Christoph Tröger notes, to attend 'an unspecified performance in 1639, they spent seven shillings in total "for a play and boat hire for the young ladies, the nurse, and others"'. See Tim-Christoph Tröger, 'Playgoing in Early Modern London after Shakespeare (1616–1642)' (Thesis, Georg-August-Universität Göttingen, 2016), 241, https://d-nb.info/1114497290/34 (last accessed 23 August 2023). By 1559 set prices, the fare across for a sole passenger was 1d., while longer-distance journeys would be more (the fare was greater against the tide). London to Greenwich was 8d. with the tide and 12d. against. A labourer might earn 6d. a day at this time.
10. Sir Thomas Overbury, *New Characters (drawne to the life) of several persons in several qualities* (1614), n.p., https://www.eudaemonist.com/biblion/overbury/ (last accessed 23 August 2023).
11. Ibid., n.p.
12. John Taylor, *All the Workes of John Taylor*, 16, 31.
13. Capp, 'Water-Poetry', 11–12.
14. John Taylor, *A New Discovery By Sea With a Wherry from London to Salisbury* (London: Edw. All-de., 1623), 26.
15. Capp, 'Water-Poetry', 15.
16. John Bickerdyke, *The Curiosities of Ale & Beer: An Entertaining History* (London: Swan Sonnenschein, 1889), 123.
17. Thomas Nashe, *Pierce Penilesse, his supplication to the Deuill* (1592), n.p. http://www.luminarium.org/renascence-editions/nashe1.html (last accessed 3 August 2022).
18. John Grove, *Wine, Beere, Ale, and Tobacco: Contending for Superiority, A Dialogue.* (London, 1630), n.p.

19. Kristen D. Burton, '"The Citie Calls For Beere": The Introduction of Hops and the Foundation of Industrial Brewing in Early Modern London', *Brewery History* 150 (2013), 6–15, 7.
20. Ibid., 7.
21. John Taylor, *Taylors Farevvell, to the Tovver-Bottles* (1622), https://ezproxy.massey.ac.nz/login?url=https://www.proquest.com/books/taylors-farevvell-tovver-bottles/docview/2240927446/se-2 (last accessed 20 August 2023).
22. Capp, 'Water-Poetry', 17–18.
23. Ibid., 86–7.
24. Ibid., 18.
25. John Taylor, *The Pennyles Pilgrimage, Or the Money-Lesse Perambulation, of John Taylor, Alias the Kings Majesties Water-Poet how He Trauailed on Foot from London to Edenborough in Scotland, Not Carrying any Money to Or Fro, neither Begging, Borrowing, Or Asking Meate, Drinke Or Lodging. with His Description of His Entertainment in all Places of His Iourney, and a True Report of the Vnmatchable Hunting in the Brea of Marre and Badenoch in Scotland. with Other Obseruations, some Serious and Worthy of Memory, and some Merry and Not Hurtfull to be Remembred. Lastly that (which is Rare in a Trauailer) all is True* (1618), n.p., https://ezproxy.massey.ac.nz/login?url=https://www.proquest.com/books/pennyles-pilgrimage-money-lesse-perambulation/docview/2240938081/se-2 (last accessed 20 August 2023)
26. Alexander Pope called him the 'swan of Thames' in his *Dunciad*, with some irony: see Alexander Pope, *The Major Works* (Oxford: Oxford University Press, 2006), *Dunciad III*, 19–20, 492.
27. Izaak Walton, *The Compleat Angler* (Boston: Little, Brown & Co., 1867), 266.
28. Capp, 'Water-Poetry', 23.
29. John Taylor, *A Verry Merry Vvherry-Ferry-Voyage: Or Yorke for My Money Sometimes Perilous, Sometimes Quarrellous, Performed with a Paire of Oares, by Sea from London* (1622), 3, https://ezproxy.massey.ac.nz/login?url=https://www.proquest.com/books/verry-merry-vvherry-ferry-voyage-yorke-my-money/docview/2240896179/se-2 (last accessed 20 August 2023).
30. John Taylor, *Taylor on Tame Isis* (London, 1632), fol. 5v.
31. John Taylor, *The Pennyles Pilgrimage*, n.p.
32. John Taylor, *Drinke and Welcome* (London: Anne Griffin, 1637), 16–17.
33. Ibid., 16–17.
34. Ibid., 17. Italics original.
35. Ibid., 6.
36. Ibid.
37. Ibid.
38. Ibid., 22.
39. Ibid., 18.
40. Ibid., 20.
41. Ibid., 21. Here he taps into the concept of rivers as 'the arteries of the global body'; see Albrecht Classen, 'Waterways as Landmarks,

Challenges, and Barriers for Medieval Protagonists: Crossing Rivers as Epistemological Hurdles in Medieval Literature', *Amsterdamer Beiträge zur älteren Germanistik* 78 (2018), 441–67, 445.

42. John Taylor, 'Jacke A Lent His Beginning and Entertainment: with the mad prankes of his Gentleman-Vsher Shroue Tuesday that goes before him, and his Foot man Hunger attending', in *All the Workes of John Taylor*, 117.
43. Thomas Heywood, *Philocothonista, or, The drunkard, opened, dissected, and anatomized* (London: Robert Raworth, 1635), 3. In fact it is anthocyanin that makes red wine red while haemoglobin makes blood red. Although not the business of this chapter, some evidence suggests the former is good for the latter.
44. Ibid., 88.
45. Ibid., 2.
46. Taylor, *Drinke and Welcome*, 9.
47. John Taylor, *Taylor's Travels And Circular Perambulation, through, and by more then thirty times twelve Signes of the Zodiack, of the Famous Cities of London and Westminster. With the Honour and Worthinesse of the Vine, the Vintage, the Wine, and the Vintoner; with an Alphabeticall Description, of all the Taverne Signes in the Cities, Suburbs, and Liberties aforesaid, and significant Epigrams upon the said severall Signes* (London: A. M., 1636), 10–11.
48. Jeffrey L. Singman, *Daily Life in Elizabethan England* (Westport, CT: Greenwood Press, 1995), 137.
49. John Taylor, *Ale Ale-vated into the Aletitude* (London, 1653), 11, 13–14, https://quod.lib.umich.edu/e/eebo2/A95518.0001.001?rgn=main;view=fulltext (last accessed 20 September 2023).
50. Suggestion has also been made that Anne Hathaway was an 'alewife'; see Amanda Mabillard, 'Shakespeare's Drinking', *Shakespeare Online*, http://www.shakespeare-online.com/faq/shakespearedrinking.html (last accessed 10 August 2022).
51. Liza Picard, *Elizabeth's London* (London: Phoenix Press, 2003), 187. This was especially the case in urban centres; see Burton, '"The Citie Calls For Beere"', 10.
52. William Harrison, *Description of Elizabethan England* [1577] (LaVergne, TN: Kessinger Publishing, 2010), 48–50.
53. Walton, *The Compleat Angler*, 192.
54. Taylor, *Drinke and Welcome*, 11–12.
55. Taylor, *Ale-Ale-vated*, 16.
56. Capp, 'Water-Poetry', 130.
57. Walker, *Taylors Physicke*.
58. Ibid.
59. John 2:1–11.
60. Taylor, *Drinke and Welcome*, 9.
61. Capp, 'Water-Poetry', 130.
62. Taylor, *A New Discovery*, 30.
63. John Taylor, *The True Cause of the Watermen's Suit Concerning Players* (1613 or 1614), in https://archive.org/stream/worksofjohntaylo00tayl/worksofjohntaylo00tayl_djvu.txt (last accessed 20 August 2023).

64. Taylor, *Drinke and Welcome*, 7.
65. Ibid., 9.
66. Taylor, *Ale-Ale-vated*, 24.
67. Ibid., 21.
68. Ibid., 25.
69. John Taylor, *Taylor's Travels and Circular Perambulation*, 16.
70. Ibid., 58.
71. Capp, 'Water-Poetry', 37.
72. John Taylor, *The carriers cosmographie* (London: A[nne] G[riffin], 1637), 2.
73. Capp, 'Water-Poetry', 111.
74. Ibid., 30.
75. The scheme came to nought until after the Restoration; see ibid., 111.
76. Ibid., 27–8.
77. Ibid., 30.
78. Ibid.
79. Taylor, *A New Discovery*, 1.
80. Ibid., 5.
81. Ibid., 12.
82. Ibid., 36.
83. Ibid., 23.
84. *The History of Parliament: The House of Commons 1604–1629*, ed. Andrew Thrush and John Ferris (Cambridge: Cambridge University Press, 2010), http://historyofparliamentonline.org/volume/1604-1629/constituencies/salisbury (last accessed 10 August 2023).
85. Taylor, *A New Discovery*, 28.
86. Ibid.
87. Ibid.
88. Capp, 'Water-Poetry', 60, 56.
89. John Taylor, 'Epigram 3', *The Sculler*, (1612), https://quod.lib.umich.edu/e/eebo/A13493.0001.001?rgn=main;view=fulltext (last accessed 20 August 2023).
90. Capp, 'Water-Poetry', 60.
91. John Taylor, *Taylor's motto Et habeo, et careo, et curo* (London: E. Allde for J. Trundle & H. Gosson, 1621), STC 23800, sigs. 5v–D6r.
92. Capp, 'Water-Poetry', 86.
93. Ibid., 17.
94. Ibid., 43.
95. Ibid., 75–6.
96. Ibid., 29–30.
97. Ibid., 77.
98. Ibid., 88.
99. Taylor, *A Verry Merry-Wherry-Ferry Voyage*, 20.
100. Capp, 'Water-Poetry', 33.
101. The Crown was in Crown Alley, which was later renamed Phoenix Alley and is now Hanover Place. See ibid., 38–9, 155.
102. Ibid., 155.
103. Ibid., 49, with a nod to Charles Darwin.

Chapter 8

The Rose and the Riverside

Cecilia Lindskog Whiteley

Playing was suspended at the Rose playhouse at the end of the 1580s due to the Marpelate controversy, and the capital was forced for a time to bid farewell to the regular sight of Tamburlaine, Tom Stukeley and other 'proud Tragedians'.[1] With the temporary closure, London's citizens lost their access to Bankside's only theatre and also to its 'ritualised, philosophical version' of the violence and sex which was the contemporary brand of the South Bank.[2]

The loss was not simply a matter of entertainment: rather, entertainment was economy, then as now. The watermen, who 'have their maintenance by rowing in Boats on the River of *Thames*',[3] complained about their members' loss of income, and the impact the ban would have on their 'poore wives and Children'.[4] Merely two years after the theatre's establishment, the Rose and the watermen had become intimately connected in a symbiotic relationship, each benefiting from the other and both in their own way reliant upon the 'the Ancient and famous River of Thames'.[5] The playhouse derived its ability to stage plays from its location 'across' the river, away from the jurisdiction of the Mayor of London. For their part, the watermen depended upon the fare of pleasure-bent Londoners crossing over to the 'dangerous, seedy, exciting, liberated Surrey side' of the river, customers drawn mainly from 'the more affluent north bank'.[6] Carol Chillington Rutter points out that the establishment of the theatrical industry on the Bankside brought a 'need for water transport' and worked to 'great profit' for the watermen.[7] The river was an essential part of the playgoing experience, just as it was an integral part of life in early modern London: it provided transport routes and prosperity, and was a natural barrier, boundary and border that delineated London. At the same time, the river also marked the authority of the Mayor of London, which stretched into the water itself but no further,[8] meaning that city authorities' opposition to theatrical performance was rendered impotent south of the river. As such, the Thames functioned to protect illicit behaviour on its opposite shore, creating a dichotomy of sorts between the strait-laced city and the permissive Bankside. The river was a site of liminality as well as demarcation, and movement across this border, between the two banks, signified more than a fare for the watermen.

In this chapter, I consider how the Thames is figured as an ambivalent space, simultaneously allowing and thwarting movement. I look at how the river provided theme, backdrop and extratheatrical special effects in one of those temporarily suspended plays, George Peele's *The Battle of Alcazar* (1588). I argue that the setting of the Rose is mobilised by Peele to anchor his paradoxical protagonist Stukeley in the ambivalent Bankside space, allowing playgoers to both applaud and censure the English mercenary and wannabe Catholic king of Ireland. This is made possible by the littoral space around the Thames, an inescapable presence in, as well as around, the Rose, where the river facilitated movement as well as pretence, but where lasting social mobility remained stigmatised. The centrality of river space in *The Battle of Alcazar* is contrasted with the treatment of social mobility in relation to the ferryman Phao in John Lyly's *Sappho and Phao* (1584), another play performed adjacent to the river but on the opposite side, and in which a ferryman is brought on stage.[9]

The consideration begins with Peele's play, which appears to have been written partly in order to capitalise on the success of *Tamburlaine* (1587), Marlowe's runaway success that also appeared at the Rose, and which charts the fortunes of an ambitious shepherd seeking the 'sweet fruition of an early crown'. Peele's play shares a stage and a riverside vicinity with *Tamburlaine*, but where Marlowe fetishises the proper names of rivers – the Nile, the Ganges, Euphrates – so as to denote the vastness of Tamburlaine's ambitions and achievements, Peele draws on less famous though no less real rivers to craft a closeness between Morocco and Bankside. Rivers wind through much of Peele's play; the rivers of real battlefields are alternately conflated with and pointedly differentiated from the Thames, in a play that was originally written for the Rose, which is to say, to be staged in a space where London's riverscape provided an inevitable 'undertow to theatrical performances'.[10] Through the explicit invocation of this riverside setting, the play invites its audience to relate themselves more closely with its ambivalent protagonist. My reading will suggest that Peele foregrounds the littoral Thames as a space of ambivalence and hybridity, movement and the transgression of boundaries, which is very much embedded in its early modern historical reality. Yet at the same time, in *The Battle of Alcazar* Peele also cautions against overtly transgressive infringements, his Bankside redolent not only of the hybrid river space, but also of warnings against excessive violation of boundaries and rules.

After tracing the rivers of Peele's play and exploring its productive symbiosis with its Bankside performance space, the chapter turns briefly to a companion piece of sorts, Peele's poem *A Farewell to Drake and Norris* (1589), which invokes the Thames in similar terms to *The Battle of Alcazar*. A reading of this poem underlines the class-based social structures implied in the spatial demarcation provided by the river, a second undertow in *The Battle of Alcazar* and in *Sappho and Phao*. The chapter then concludes with a reading of Lyly's play, considering the ferryman Phao as neither an appendage to Sappho nor from the perspective of his incipient relationship with the virginal female monarch, but instead focusing on his transformation in terms of ambition and social mobility, noting that his disappointed aspiration leads him to abandon his ferry. As a waterman of sorts, Phao facilitated movement, but while it was possible to traverse rivers and navigate between different cultural spaces in early modern life, Lyly shows how social mobility can never be more than transitory performance. In this sense, the lesson of Lyly's play applies equally to Peele's protagonist, Stukeley, whose ambitions rival those of Tamburlaine and who finds validation for them in his littoral origin. Like Phao, Stukeley discovers that make believe and self-fashioning do not extend beyond the river space, but when any of Peele's or Lyly's characters attempt to cross the river in a more lasting manner, they all falter at the riverbank.

Attending a performance of *The Battle of Alcazar* at the Rose meant crossing the Thames for most playgoers. In operation from 1587, Henslowe and Cholmley's venture was the first playhouse on Bankside. Prior to this, London's purpose-built open-air playhouses were located in Shoreditch, north of the wall, and in Newington Butts, quite a distance to the south. The Newington Butts playhouse appears not to have been in regular operation, perhaps because of the relative distance from the city proper, but Shoreditch sites such as the Theatre and the Curtain were veritable success stories. In the Rose, Henslowe and Cholmley attempted to replicate this success in a new location. The river was vital to their project. In jurisdictional terms, it functioned much like the wall that separated Shoreditch's playhouses from the authority of Mayor of London, but with one crucial difference: whereas the wall was a man-made barrier obstructing movement, the river was a waterway that facilitated it. The Rose was located only a few steps from London Bridge, the only bridge spanning the Thames in London at the time, and could be reached by boat from any of the many water stairs.

Easily accessible, the Rose likely also benefitted from the pull of other forms of entertainment available on the Bankside: cockfighting, bear baiting and brothels, alongside many drinking establishments. Clearly, playacting could hold its own against this plethora of pleasures of the South Bank, for in fairly short order the Rose was followed by the establishment of the Swan, the Globe and the Hope, making Bankside London's first theatre district.

Londoners crossed the river in search of pleasures and entertainments which were not generally on offer on the more strictly regulated northern side. The place of the stage, to borrow Steven Mullaney's phrase, was located 'across the natural barrier of the Thames', and as such situated 'on the margins of society'.[11] A pilgrimage into this pleasure land meant encountering tokens of the transgressive nature of the space about to be entered and the activities about to be undertaken. The city's authorities marked the limit of their own jurisdiction with a grim reminder of the ultimate consequence of violating order: the gatehouse on the southern end of London Bridge was adorned with the severed heads of traitors executed for their crimes. Visible to all those who crossed the river on foot or by horse, and to anyone who alighted from a boat near the Rose, playgoing was preceded by symbols of the violence and power of the state.[12] It was also preceded by the sensory experience of the river itself, and, as Julie Sanders notes, 'the sonic, olfactory, and haptic, as well as optic, experience of it would have struck the imagination forcefully'.[13] The Rose was located in a riverscape that intruded upon the playgoing experience in the form of sensory backdrop and mental framework.

Peele appears to be drawing upon this inescapable presence of the Thames in *The Battle of Alcazar*. Like all plays, it will have been intended for performance on tour as well as in London, but as Tiffany Stern writes, London was literally the theatres' backdrop and 'part of the plays' context'. Just as the carnivalesque South Bank became a 'feature' of the plays performed there, so did the river.[14] Peele's play was situational in another sense, for, as critics from Peter Berek to Lisa Hopkins and Daniel Vitkus have noted, *The Battle of Alcazar* also bears clear signs of the stylistic and topical influence of Marlowe's *Tamburlaine*.[15] Known to have been performed by the same company at the same playhouse as Marlowe's play, and on the basis of the many verbal parallels, Peele appears to have been attempting to replicate the 'huge commercial success' enjoyed by the Scythian shepherd.[16] In other words, there is benefit in considering *The Battle of Alcazar* as a very timely and localised work: Peele crafted a play for an intended audience and group of actors, to be staged at an intended venue, the Rose. In this light, it is not surprising that Peele draws upon the location and associations of this playhouse as part of the context of the play, not least of all the dominant river on whose banks it lay.

The subject matter of *The Battle of Alcazar* seems to have been ideal to appeal to a Rose audience. The real-life battle of El-Kasr el-Kebir in 1578 was well known to audiences of the period, and had immediate relevance to the historical moment at the time of Peele's writing. The *casus belli* was a struggle over the Moroccan crown, passed from brother to brother. The old king's son, Mulai Mohammed el-Meslokh (Peele's Muly Mahamet), took the crown from his uncle Abd el-Malek (Abdelmec) in 1574, and, after he reclaimed it in 1576, Mulai Mohammed enlisted the help of Portugal to regain it. Sebastian I, in his turn, sought the backing of Spain and the Catholic Church, while Abd el-Malek was supported by the Ottoman Empire. As such, the conflict developed into a showdown of the major military powers of the Mediterranean. In the end, the ambitious, overreaching upstart faction was resoundingly trounced, while both aspiring Moroccan kings lost their lives, as did Sebastian. So far, so Tamburlainian, and eminently suitable for Peele's own offering for the Rose.

Domestic interest in the battle of El-Kasr el-Kebir was piqued owing to its European geopolitical consequences. Sebastian's death improved the position of Philip II of Spain, who acquired the Portuguese crown; his increased strength may even have contributed to his planned invasion with the Armada in 1588, a failed maritime campaign that formed the immediate historical backdrop and a political context for Peele's play. There was also curiosity about the 'desert debacle' of El-Kasr el-Kebir owing to the participation of the English mercenary, Captain Thomas Stukeley.[17] Stukeley may have been aiming to invade Ireland with an Italian fleet to establish himself as Catholic king in that English colony before he was persuaded by Sebastian to support the Portuguese campaign instead; indeed, this is made explicit backstory in Peele's play. With such significant links to political and historical happenings directly affecting matters in London, it is hardly surprising that the battle itself was news as well as sensation 'almost from the moment it happened'.[18] Adding to this interest, wider cultural transformations taking place were exerting an influence on dramatic fare in the capital, something that is perhaps most clearly reflected at the Rose. As Vitkus notes, trade relations with the Ottoman Empire and North Africa became increasingly important from the 1570s onwards; the Levant Company was established in 1581, and by 1588, English trade consuls could be found in Aleppo, Damascus, Alexandria, Cairo, Tunis, Tripoli in Syria and Tripoli in North Africa. A consequent preoccupation with Mediterranean cultural and mercantile influx is found in a number of late sixteenth-century plays, not least among them *Tamburlaine*.[19] Goran Stanivukovic notes that early modern drama was a 'cultural conduit' bringing 'the distant Mediterranean to London audiences', and this type of fare seems to have had a particular allure at Henslowe's Bankside playhouse in the late 1580s.[20]

Beyond the style and subject matter of *The Battle of Alcazar* aligning well with the repertory of the Rose, the play's treatment of transgression and treason were also marked by its performance location 'across' the river and in view of the gatehouse of London Bridge. As the first theatrical representation of 'Moors' in early modern English drama,[21] Peele's play was staged for playgoers who had been confronted on their way to the performance with the decapitated heads of criminals who had suffered the ultimate punishment for their crimes. As Stern points out, these severed human heads were 'black in appearance, having been parboiled and coated in tar',[22] and as such resembled the visual of blackened actors on stage.[23] Referring to *Othello*, Stern has suggested the ways in which such spectacles would have resonated with Shakespeare's audience, and Peele harnesses similar early modern connotative equivalences between dark skin and damnation.[24] A link between skin colour and behaviour is explicitly invoked in the prologue, where the Presenter describes Muly Mahamet as 'Blacke in his looke, and bloudie in his deeds', words which would resonate more resoundingly with a playgoer who had recently been confronted with the grisly visages of London Bridge.[25] Through the twin impact of the authorised voice of the presenter and the sight of authorised violence on top of London Bridge's gatehouse, Muly Mahamet becomes proleptically figured as villainous and treacherous. Contextualised in the physical space of the playhouse alongside the early modern Thames, those disturbing links between skin colour and morality that are so unpalatable to later audiences can be seen to have drawn upon the Rose as performance venue for additional effect, harnessing the anxieties about transgression that were part of the cultural context of the the playhouse's riverside setting.

While the opening of *The Battle of Alcazar* seems to draw obliquely upon this riverside setting for effect, the play's final act explicitly invokes the Thames. In what may be a piece of contrafactual positioning, Stukeley casts himself as a native of London Bridge:

> Hark friends, and with the story of my life
> Let me beguile the torment of my death.
> In Englands London Lordings was I borne,
> On that brave Bridge, the barre that thwarts the Thames. (V.i.1326–9)

With his final breath, Stukeley lays claim to being a Londoner, one born atop the same mighty flow of water that would have been audible to the playgoers as they listened to this dying lament. But as Vitkus notes, the historical Stukeley was born in Devonshire around 1525,[26] where his family had their seat.[27] Indeed, while John Yoklavich claims that Peele based his Stukeley on a wide selection of contemporary sources, his selection of material is interesting: any hint of the persistent rumours of his possibly being an illegitimate son of Henry VIII is notably absent, instead replaced with the claim of his being a creature of the river.[28] With this in mind, Peele's origin story seems a case of artistic liberty, yet another way to foreground the play's performance location and its associations both with the Thames and with playacting. Stukeley dying on the banks of a Moroccan river receives an additional dimension when performed against the sounds and smells of a river; in writing for the Rose, Peele could utilise this backdrop.

The notion of Stukeley straddling the Thames is the alpha and omega of his character in Peele's play: it is the origin that he lays claim to and the cradle that he attempts to reclaim in his moment of death. Although he declaims against the importance of birthplace earlier in the play, stating that 'To be begot or borne in any place, / [is] a thing . . . / That might have been performed elsewhere' (II.ii.418–20), this disavowal comes in the context of a national, and specifically English, origin, whereas his dying speech is more precise and less historically accurate. It is London Bridge and the Thames that Stukeley constructs as an alternative origin. While Brian Lockey has argued that the speech constitutes a somewhat ambivalent reassertion of national identity by Stukeley at the end of his life, it is not merely England that the renegade captain is associating himself with and harking back to, but explicitly the littoral space of the Thames and London Bridge, the site of hybridity and ambiguity that symbolises the challenging of settled identities.[29]

Both conduit and border between licit and illicit London, London Bridge was also the likely means by which some of the playgoers had ventured to the Rose to hear *The Battle of Alcazar*. Described as 'a continual street, well replenished with large and stately houses on both sides' in *The Survey of London*, the bridge mimicked the urban thoroughfares to the north of the river.[30] It was marked by the nascent capitalism that fed the emerging theatre industry, with Stern noting that its buildings counted merchants and moneylenders among their inhabitants.[31] As such, the bridge is a product of early modern London, and testament to its economic links with Morocco and countries beyond, the city constituting a kind of 'huge intake zone' in incorporating the world beyond.[32] Crossing London Bridge on horseback required payment of a toll, so that it was marked out from other London streets to its north; the gatehouse with its grisly displays of state punishment demarcated it architecturally to the south. It was a space in-between, suspended between the north bank of order and authority and the south bank of transgression and excitement, between London as the capital of the emergent English nation and the tantalising possibilities of foreign exchange: a strange space in which to be born, but fitting for the character that Peele makes of Stukeley. A figurative child of this transgressive river space, he claims for himself a privileged position of alterity and hybridity that he believes will allow him to define himself, to range the world and rise to a crown. It is a self-fashioning project that is encapsulated by Stukeley's dying speech, and one that was 'marked ... and destinate' (V.i.1363–4) to fail, because the notion of social mobility was like playacting: another illusion on offer in illicit Bankside.

In the Rose, Stukeley's invocation of London Bridge called up a space with which the playgoers were equally familiar. If they had not crossed it on their way to the playhouse, they had seen it from one of the boats or wherries. The resituation of Stukeley in his dying moments works not only to draw upon the riverside for sensory special effects and to bring a sense of proximity of the Mediterranean to London, but also to bring Stukeley closer to his audience. At the time of hearing the 'story of [his] life', playgoers occupied the same space that he depends upon – that has, in a manner, created him. In a very real, extratheatrical sense, Stukeley the character can playact his dying moments only because of the river's function as border, just as the playgoers are able to be 'beguiled' by the performance because of the liberty afforded by the Thames. We have already seen how this space was acknowledged to be a separate jurisdictional and cultural sphere to London: the 'liberty' designation can be extended to the additional lenience of behaviour that was not only allowed on the Bankside, but which formed the basis for the area's identity.[33] This permissive space is where Stukeley spent his 'golden days' and 'younger carelesse years' (V.i.1330), a halcyon time that received its gilded sheen from his having the freedom to enjoy the pleasures on offer. Crossing the river made playgoers temporary children of London Bridge themselves, just as the character of Stukeley was, each performing their own part within the entertainment economy that flourished south of the river – and which must remain 'across' the river.

In a poem written in the aftermath of *The Battle of Alcazar*, Peele calls upon this river space as a site of fiction, drama and myth-making and constructs a brief presence for the Rose north of the Thames. *A Farewell Entitled to the famous and fortunate generals of our English forces: Sir John Norris & Sir Francis Drake Knights, and all their brave and resolute followers. Whereunto is annexed: a tale of Troy* (1589) was written for the occasion of the English Armada setting sail in 1589, placing it firmly within the same historical context that formed the basis of the currency of *The Battle of Alcazar*.[34] The bulk of the text is made up of the legend of London as the new Troy. Hopkins has identified the Aeneas myth as foundational to expansionist English imperial ambition in a number of early modern dramatic texts, not least *The Battle of Alcazar*, and claims that this classical myth is mediated though Marlowe; with its explicit yoking together of proto-imperial nationalism and the 'Troynovant' story, *A Farewell* seems to be another text in which Peele avails himself of a Marlovian appeal.[35] At the same time, the introductory poem maintains a focus on the Thames as a space for transformation and theatre that Peele established in his play:

> bid stately Troynovant adieu,
> Where pleasant Thames from Isis' silver head
> Begins her quiet glide, and runs along,
> To that brave Bridge the barre that th'warts her course[.] (4–7)

The language replicates Stukeley's dying description of his origin. London Bridge is once again central, along with the Troynovant myth with its dramatic connotations – connotations that were established in plays frequently performed at the Rose, which is to say, in this space which derived its identity from the river and all that it made possible. Peele proceeds to re-emphasise this connection in the poem, imploring the sailors to

> Bid Theatres and proud Tragedians,
> Bid Mahomet's Poo, and mighty Tamburlaine,
> King Charlemaine, Tom Stukeley and the rest
> Adieu (20–3)

Per Peele, a significant part of leaving London is leaving behind its dramatic scene. The inexorable 'quiet glide' of the Thames towards the wider sea is different from the turbulent river space inhabited by Stukeley and his peers, and progress means departure from playacting.

A Farewell is figured as a river journey away from the London it lauds, while the readers left behind can continue to enjoy 'all the lovely British Dames' (17) and the fictional inhabitants of dramatic London whom the sailors must renounce. There is a definite sense of imagined loss in this enforced separation, the poet envisaging that the adieus cause a sense of involuntary separation. For the current consideration of the Rose and the riverside, this implied loss points to another perceived contemporary link between the playhouse, its riverside identity and dramatic output at the time. Notably, all the tragic figures invoked by Peele in *A Farewell* belonged to the Rose. Tamburlaine and Tom Stukeley have already been identified with extant plays known to have been performed there. King Charlemaine seems to be a reference to the protagonist of a now lost play about the Carolingian emperor: the role was likely played by Edward Alleyn, Philip Henslowe's son-in-law and the lead actor at the Rose.[36] As for 'Mahomets Poo', this appears to relate not to a dramatic character, but to a specific piece of theatrical property (poo generally considered to be short for 'poll', or head), the prophetic idol of Mohammed that appears in Robert Greene's *Alphonsus, King of Aragon* (1587), which is yet another play that was performed at the Rose.[37] In *A Farewell*, Peele highlights the dramatic offering of the Rose as emblematic of London as a theatrical space.[38]

In making these four plays representative of London's dramatic scene, there was perhaps also a sense of (self-)promotion at work for Peele. *A Farewell* belonged to a different class of literary output to a stage play, and unlike the majority of the plays written in the 1580s, it was printed and available for purchase on the strait-laced northern side of the river.[39] Peele's full name and his academic qualification – 'Master of Arts in Oxford' – appeared on the title page underneath a Latin inscription reworked from Ovid's *Tristia*.[40] Stage plays, unlike poetry, did not typically feature the name of their author: Peele claims for himself a more respectable literary identity on this title page. However, the poem simultaneously functions as a promotion of Peele's theatrical endeavours, and those of the Rose. Stern has noted that the Bankside playhouses struggled to advertise their offering on the London side of the Thames, but *A Farewell* is a piece of promotion of sorts, one that elevates its product through the print medium and the more socially elevated form of poetry rather than drama, as well as with reference to the classical and nationalist subject matter.[41] Perhaps most importantly for considerations of the river as emblematic of dramatic space, it is an instance where Bankside is allowed to enter London proper, both in the poem, where it is markedly the south and not the north bank that comes to represent the capital, and through its presence in bookstalls north of the river. The Latin inscription from Ovid on the title page points the way: *Tristia* opens with Ovid anticipating that the book he is writing is allowed to enter the city space (in this case Rome) from which the poet himself is exiled: 'Little book, you will go without me – and I grudge it not – to the city, whither alas your master is not allowed to go!'[42] Ovid's poetry will allow him a form of entry to the city from which he is barred, just as *A Farewell* allows Peele metaphorical entrance to London as a poet. With the poem, Tamburlaine, Charlemaine, the prophetic head of Mohammed and Tom Stukeley all cross London Bridge and 'enter' safeguarded civic space with *A Farewell*, a feat that in itself carried heavy symbolism. But as in Ovid's *Tristia*, such an incursion carries inherent danger.

While Stukeley and his dramatic brethren in *A Farewell* have the ability to cross the Thames in printed form, and while he claims a similar ability for himself in Peele's play by virtue of his supposed origin 'On that brave Bridge, the barre that thwarts the Thames', he is ultimately unable to achieve a lasting foothold beyond this river space. This is symptomatic of the alterity of the river space itself, which is simultaneously boundary and transport route, signifying possibility as well as the strictures circumscribing it. In both *A Farewell* and *The Battle of Alcazar*, the permissive river space is circumscribed by the 'bar', a word which puns, describing both its shape and its function as an instrument of confinement; but it is also shaped by the 'thwarting' of this 'bar', which as a transitive verb in early modern English referred to the movement of crossing (*OED* cites Shakespeare's *Pericles*, IV.iv.10), but which also, very recently at the time of Peele's writing, had taken on its primary modern sense of opposition (*OED* gives Richard Mulcaster's *Positions* in 1581 as the first use). In other words, the Thames bridge that links Bankside with London also ensures that overreaching is penalised. Hubris and treachery are struck down and, in early modern London, often converted into cautionary examples and displayed on top of London Bridge.

The edge of the river was a particularly loaded site, charged with the dual context of spectacle and violence. It is within this context that Peele coined the new compound 'river shore' (*OED* gives *The Battle of Alcazar* as the first use). Muly Mahamet acknowledges this in a curiously Freudian attempt to assure Sebastian of his faithfulness:

> And that thy Lords and Captains may perceive
> My mind in this single and pure to be,
> As pure as is the water of the brook,
> My dearest son to thee I do engage,
> Receive him Lord in hostage of my vow,
> For even my mind presageth to my self,
> That in some slavish sort I shall behold
> Him dragged along this running river shore,
> A spectacle to daunt the pride of those
> That climb aloft by force, and not by right. (III.iv.931–40)

This 'presage' would have been redolent with dramatic irony for an audience who knew Muly Mahamet to be perfidious and untrustworthy. They had heard the Presenter explain how he 'usurps upon' (I.i.11) his uncle in the Prologue, and many knew the story before even entering the playhouse. If a punishment was to be extracted for attempting to climb above one's station, it was fitting that it be bestowed on Muly Mahamet whose only triumph came from 'ambitious tyranny' (I.i.34) and murder, which is to say, from transgressive, traitorous acts similar to those presumably committed by those to whom the tarred and boiled heads that oversaw the path to and from the playhouse once belonged. These displays of authorised violence were situated along the boundary of the city authorities' jurisdiction as cautions and *memento mori* of a sort. Michael Taussig notes that a border can be conceived, not 'as the farthermost extension of an essential identity spreading out', but instead as its 'core', with identity (spatial as well as social, in this case) acquiring 'its satisfying solidity' because of 'the turbulent forces . . . that the border not so much contains as emits'.[43] As a site of demarcation where permissibility and order met, the 'river shore' in early modern London and in Peele's dramaturgy is an eminently fitting location for spectacles of violence, whether in actual or 'ritualised' form.

Both the shores of the Thames and of the Moroccan rivers of Peele's play take on this fetishistic quality, making attempts to ford them, to establish more than a transient presence on the opposite bank, a matter of tantalisation as well as anxiety. In *The Battle of Alcazar*, the rivers of the battlefield prove to be nigh on uncrossable, entrapping characters in situations where they are unable to realise their expansionist ambitions and instead cannot flee their fates. The Portuguese army is slaughtered en masse when they are caught between a river and Abdelmec's forces. Stukeley is ambushed by two of his own soldiers and mortally wounded on the banks of the same river. After he has delivered his dying speech, he crawls offstage to die at the side of Sebastian, who has also been defeated when attempting to ford the river.[44] The villain of the piece, Muly Mahamet, meets his fate offstage in a way that parallels Sebastian, defeated by his inability to cross the river. However, whereas Sebastian's demise by the river is described as a warrior's end – his corpse is found 'even among the thickest of his Lords, . . . Wrapt in his colours [and] done to death with many a mortal wound' (V.i.1410–13) – Muly Mahamet dies in ignominy:

> Seeking to save his life by shameful flight,
> He mounteth on a hot Barbarian horse,
> And so in purpose to have passed the stream,
> His headstrong steed throws him from out his seat,
> Where diving oft for lack of skill to swim,
> It was my chance alone to see him drowned. (V.i.1430–5)

The bystander narrates a fate which is at once spectacular and antispectacle: the death itself is withheld from the audience of the playhouse, yet the lone witness describes it in dramatic terms. For a character who had deliberated upon the riverbank as a site for spectacular death in punishment earlier in the play, this seems a suitably punitive end. It also links the fetishised border of the river shore with the riverside Rose, making both fitting locations for the spectacle of violence.

As Peele is at pains to remind his audience, the riverside space was not only a threat to Muly Mahamet, but to the play's 'Londoner'. Much as Stukeley attempted to fashion for himself permissibility for his transgression by claiming to be a child of this turbulent space, he also meets his fate on the river shore. Like Muly Mahamet, he aspires to 'win a crowne' (II.iii.457). If he had truly been content to be simply 'King of a mole-hill' (II.iii.464) rather than setting his aim at being 'king of Ireland' (II.iii.463), he could have continued to roam the vicinity of London Bridge and enjoy the pleasures of pretence in Bankside. Linking Stukeley and Muly Mahamet, Peele provocatively calls on his audience to register their own potential transgressions and mark the limits of their social mobility. Thames-side London and the South Bank in particular allowed for transgressions of behaviour and morality, for exploration of foreign cultures and exchange, and for playacting. All social classes were brought together in pursuit of illicit pleasures, cohabiting the same carnivalesque space 'across' the river, but this permissibility did not extend to the permanent transgression of class boundaries. Even as he lays claim to a London Bridge origin with the hybridity that this offers, Stukeley also recognises that he never had the potential to transcend the pretence of the Bankside to reach the realities of his ambition: his youth in riverside London was the 'height of Fortunes [sic] wheel' (V.i.1331), as high as he could reach. Like Marlowe's famous band of 'overreachers', the higher aspirations of Peele's Stukeley doom him, just as Muly Mahamet and Sebastian are doomed for their unwarranted ambition and 'pride'. The river facilitates movement but not mobility.

A near-contemporary play to *The Battle of Alcazar*, John Lyly's *Sapho and Phao* (1584), also utilises the crossing of water as a symbol for social mobility and a conduit for anxieties related to social hierarchy.[45] Lyly's play appeared at the first Blackfriars theatre. Located on the London side of the Thames, Blackfriars was one of two theatres within intramural London where plays were performed at this time, something that was possible because of the district's historical separation from the jurisdiction of the mayor and the city authorities. A smaller indoor space that staged plays in the evenings, the cultural geography of the Blackfriars district also differed from the Rose and Bankside. It was home to many of the capital's more affluent inhabitants and had long-established links to courtly culture. At the same time, Julie Sanders has shown that Blackfriars was also diverse and not without traces of anxiety about transgression.[46] Whereas Bankside had the infamous Clink prison, Blackfriars had Bridewell, a former royal palace turned house of correction – as good an illustration as any of the perils of stepping out of line. And notably for this consideration of the symbiosis between the river and drama, the Thames again 'provided a particularly resonant adjacent locale' for playwrights working in and for this space.[47]

The story of Queen Sappho falling in love with the lowly ferryman Phao is eminently suitable for a consideration of social (im)mobility in a playhouse marked both by its vicinity to the Thames and its courtly connections. Lyly drew on classical sources for the plot, in which Phao is granted beauty as a gift by Aphrodite and attracts the attention of Queen Sappho. Their love is mutual and Phao leaves his ferry in favour of life at court, but is ultimately rejected when Sappho remembers that even a queen cannot overcome class boundaries without consequences. Rather than returning to his own riverine space, Phao exiles himself because of the discontent that he now feels with his former situation as ferryman.

While the tone and style of the plays differ, it is not difficult to see a basic parallel between Lyly's Phao and Peele's Stukeley of London Bridge. Both protagonists are preoccupied with social standing and both, for their own reasons, move away from their littoral origins, trading contentment for the possibility of social mobility. Stukeley was happy in hindsight in a position where he could vacillate between the two banks of the Thames, but was drawn away from that permissive space by his 'discontented humour' (V.i.1334). Phao likewise begins the play with contentment, aware and satisfied with his own lack of ambition and social elevation:

> Thou art a ferryman, Phao, yet a free man, possessing for riches content and for honours quiet. Thy thoughts are no higher than thy fortunes, nor thy desires greater than thy calling. Who climbeth, standeth on glass and falleth on thorn. Thy heart's thirst is satisfied with thy hand's thrift, and thy gentle labours in the day turn to sweet slumbers in the night. (I.i.1–7)

He is aware of the perils of ambition and happy to draw a distinction between himself and the Queen, whom he has yet to meet: 'As much as it doth delight thee to rule thine oar in a calm stream as it doth Sappho to sway the sceptre inter brave court' (I.i.7–9). This blithe acceptance changes drastically once Phao has been made beautiful: 'O Venus, in thinking thou hast blessed me thou hast cursed me, adding to a poor estate a proud heart and to a disdained man a disdaining mind' (II.i.3–5). Phao is no longer content with his lowly station: he deserts his ferry in favour of a position at court, much as Stukeley left behind littoral London in search of 'right royal pay' and, eventually, a crown. We have seen how this ambition leads to Stukeley's downfall; in Phao's case, thwarted aspiration and disappointed love – and in a courtier courting a reigning queen, the two are much the same – join to preclude a return to the contentment he once enjoyed: 'A ferry, Phao? No, the stars cannot call it a worser fortune. Range rather over the world, forswear affections, entreat for death' (V.iii.14–16). Once Phao finds social mobility denied to him, he rails against fate and his former profession both: 'I must now fall from love to labour, and endeavour with mine oar to get a fare, not with my pen to write a fancy' (V.iii.11–13). Rejected by the queen, Phao has been cast out of the position of temporary ease and aristocracy which he had enjoyed since Sappho brought him to court and he disdains the thought of attempting to return to his life as a ferryman.

While the sounds of the Thames would not have been audible to playgoers inside the Blackfriars theatre in the same way that those at the Rose would have heard the river as an audible backdrop to *The Battle of Alcazar*, all Londoners would have been familiar with the English equivalent of Phao, London's watermen. The notion of a queen elevating one of these riverside labourers, even temporarily, would have carried more significance to an audience in daily contact with their own watermen, and whose queen shared many similarities with the on-stage poetess regent. Perhaps this was part of the reason for Lyly's selection of the myth. As was his custom, in *Sappho and Phao* he reworked a classical narrative into a text that could – and often is – read as an elaborate compliment to Queen Elizabeth I.[48] The story as it came down to Lyly was somewhat different from the plot in the hands of the playwright. Classical Phaon was a crabby old man who used his gift of beauty and youth to attract several paramours. Sappho pursued him one-sidedly and when he rejected her, the Queen killed herself in despair. Such an outcome could of course not be staged in Blackfriars or at court, where *Sappho and Phao* was performed in front of the Queen. The reworked resolution of the love story functions as an elaborate compliment to Elizabeth and aligns particularly well with the theme of self-mastery that is found in Lyly's *Campaspe* (1583) too, also performed at Blackfriars and at court. In the altered narrative, authority and agency are reassigned from Phao/Phaon to Sappho, with the Queen ending the play in a triumph of sorts, as a regent displaying her ability to overcome her emotions for the betterment of the nation, much as Alexander did in *Campaspe*. However, Lyly also makes alterations to Phao beyond what would be required to sustain a compliment to Elizabeth. His path from contentment to despairing self-imposed exile is markedly different from Phaon's hedonistic selfishness. It was necessary to make the attraction between the Queen and the ferryman mutual in order for the theme of self-sacrifice to be valid, but this theme would not have been undercut if Phao had returned to his littoral life after he was dismissed from court. That he finds himself unable to resume his oars and regain his sense of contentment seems to relate to the fact that his ambitions have been awakened and thwarted. Once shunned, the potential of social mobility was thrust upon him only to be withdrawn, in an illustration of the ultimate futility of aiming to venture further than between the two shores.

Originally belonging to playhouses on opposite sides of the river, Stukeley and Phao can both be read as characters who draw upon the proximity of the Thames for additional relevance. They each mediate the ambivalent river space in ways that denote the anxieties and opportunities that pertain to it. Excessive, transgressive, elusive and exhibitionist, Stukeley typifies the southern bank of the river and the fare on offer at the Rose. While he revels in the riverside, his ambition cannot be contained by the boundaries imposed upon him and he meets an end of spectacular violence, fitting for South Bank's reputation and the theatrical fare offered there. Phao, on the other hand, is disappointed in his attempts to establish himself away from the water, in a courtly coded space: like London's watermen, the classical ferryman is required to facilitate theatrical performance, but neither is invited to establish a foothold outside of their sphere. As can be seen in *Sappho and Phao* and *The Battle of Alcazar* both, early modern rivers and waterways suggest the possibility of social mobility that is ultimately 'thwarted' by the reimposition of order once the bank is reached.

Notes

1. George Peele, *A Farewell Entitled to the famous and fortunate generals of our English forces: Sir John Norris & Sir Francis Drake Knights, and all their brave and resolute followers. Whereunto is annexed: a tale of Troy* (London: Gabriel Cawood, 1589), vol. 1, 20.
2. Tiffany Stern, *Making Shakespeare: From Stage to Page* (London: Routledge, 2004), 20.
3. John Stow, *The Survey of London* (London: Nicholas Bourn, 1633), 649.
4. Quoted in Carol Rutter, *Documents of the Rose Playhouse* (Manchester: Manchester University Press, 1984), 65. Rutter notes that the watermen's petition is undated and may relate to this particular closure or to a different one at a later date. She also suggests that Henslowe may have organised the petition in preparation for any kind of playhouse closure, as it would

have been 'the sort of permanently useful appeal [he] might have held in reserve to issue ... whenever his playhouse was threatened'. Whatever the immediately precipitating factor for and the organisational force behind this document, it does point to a confluence of interests between the watermen and Henslowe's theatrical operations on the Bankside, as Rutter also notes (63–4).

5. Stow, *The Survey of London*, 14.
6. Stern, *Making Shakespeare*, 20.
7. Rutter, *Documents of the Rose Playhouse*, 64.
8. Stow, *Survey of London*, 20–1.
9. This chapter relies on the dating in Martin Wiggins and Catherine Richardson, eds, *A Catalogue of British Drama, 1533–1642, Volume II: 1567–1589* (Oxford: Oxford University Press, 2012).
10. Julie Sanders, *The Cultural Geography*, 20.
11. Steven Mullaney, *The Place of the Stage: License, Play, and Power in Renaissance England* (Chicago: University of Chicago Press, 1988), 8.
12. Stern, *Making Shakespeare*, 8.
13. Sanders, *Cultural Geography*, 18.
14. Stern, *Making Shakespeare*, 18 and 15.
15. Peter Berek, '*Tamburlaine*'s Weak Sons: Imitation as Interpretation before 1593', *Renaissance Drama*, NS 13 (1982), 55–82; Lisa Hopkins, 'Marlovian Models and Itinerant Identities: Dido, Tamburlaine, and the Discourse of Colonialism', *Marlowe Studies* 5 (2015), 61–77; Daniel Vitkus, 'Rogue Cosmopolitans on the Early Modern Stage: John Ward, Thomas Stukeley, and the Sherley Brothers', in *Travel and Drama in Early Modern England: The Journeying Play*, ed. Claire Jowitt and David McInnis (Cambridge: Cambridge University Press, 2018), 128–49.
16. Daniel Vitkus, *Turning Turk: English Theatre and the Multicultural Mediterranean, 1570–1630* (Basingstoke: Palgrave Macmillan, 2003), 67.
17. John Yoklavich, 'Introduction', in *The Dramatic Works of George Peele*, vol. II (New Haven and London: Yale University Press, 1961), 218–92, 230.
18. Emily Bartels '*The Battle of Alcazar*, the Mediterranean, and the Moor', in *Remapping the Mediterranean World in Early Modern English Writings*, ed. Goran V. Stanivukovic (Basingstoke: Palgrave Macmillan, 2007), 97–116, 97.
19. Vitkus identifies not only the two *Tamburlaine* plays, but also *The Jew of Malta* as examples of Marlowe mediating this cultural influx from the Mediterranean (*Turning Turk*, 23). All three of these plays have been associated with the Rose and Strange's or the Admiral's Men, and these two companies in turn were closely associated from 1590.
20. Goran Stanivukovic, 'Introduction: Beyond the Olive Trees: Remapping the Mediterranean World in Early Modern English Writings', in *Remapping the Mediterranean World*, 1–20, 3.
21. The epithet 'Moor' is contradictory in Peele's play, as Bartels notes: 'on the one side is the "brave Barbarian", Abdelmec, and on the other, the "black" and "barbarous" Muly Mahamet ... There is a striking – but, in early discriminatory discourse, familiar – nonequivalence in these descriptive markers'; see Bartels, '*The Battle of Alcazar*', 107.

22. Stern, *Making Shakespeare*, 9.
23. Bartels, 'The Battle of Alcazar', 98. Similar encounters are likely to have taken place for playgoers at the Theatre and the Curtain, who entered Shoreditch via one of the gates in the city's wall. Like the gatehouse on London Bridge, these were frequently topped with decapitated heads. Plays staged in one of the intra-mural liberties, in Blackfriars or Paul's playhouse, on the other hand, did not require such close encounters.
24. Black make up, paint or masks were worn by actors appearing in Black roles, but also by actors playing devils; see Stern, *Making Shakespeare*, 9.
25. George Peele, *The Battle of Alcazar*, in *The Dramatic Works of George Peele*, vol. 2, ed. John Yoklavich (New Haven and London: Yale University Press), 16. All further quotations from the play will be taken from this edition and reference will be given in the text.
26. Vitkus, 'Rogue Cosmopolitans', 135.
27. Peter Holmes, 'Stucley, Thomas (C. 1520–1578), Soldier', *Oxford Dictionary of National Biography* (2004), online ed.
28. Yoklavich, 'Introduction', 165.
29. Lockey, 'Elizabethan Cosmopolitan', 31.
30. Stow, *Survey of London*, 30.
31. Stern, *Making Shakespeare*, 7.
32. Vitkus, *Turning Turk*, 26.
33. Stern notes that the government of Surrey, the county south of the Thames which encompasses the Bankside area, was 'particularly weak', and that this applied to Southwark to an even greater degree; see *Making Shakespeare*, 13.
34. I use the 1589 edition of the poem available on Early English Books Online for all quotations. Spelling has been silently modernised.
35. Peele himself claims in the dedication that he has 'annexed an olde Poeme of myne owne, *The tale of Troy*' to the more topical verses addressing the expedition. Regardless of whether the epic poem was composed years prior to the laudatory verses to the counter Armada or not, Peele clearly felt that the two were suitable to be paired together. He recommended *The Tale of Troy* as fitting recreational reading for the voyage, also claiming a measure of fame for himself among the soldiers setting out. Hopkins traces the Aeneas myth and the second Troy through Marlowe's *Tamburlaine* and *Dido, Queen of Carthage* to *The Battle of Alcazar* and a number of later plays which perpetuate the connection, but were written long after Peele published *A Farewell*, and therefore cannot have formed part of the cultural connotations on which he draws in the poem. The *Tamburlaine* plays and *The Battle of Alcazar* both appeared at the Rose, while *Dido* was an indoor play, most likely performed at Blackfriars; we will consider the river connections of Blackfriars below.
36. *The Catalogue of British Drama* lists this as a lost play (#808) on the basis of the reference in *A Farewell* alongside an inventory of costumes worn by Edward Alleyn and compiled by his brother John Alleyn, which includes a cloak for Charlemagne.
37. Matthew Dimmock, *Mythologies of the Prophet Muhammad in Early Modern English Culture* (Cambridge: Cambridge University Press, 2013), 101–9.

38. In line with the association between the Rose and an interest in Mediterranean matters, it is interesting to note that all four of the plays highlighted by Peele in this poem also deal in various ways with Mediterranean expansion and encounters between northern European and Mediterranean cultures, notions that, according to Vitkus, became preoccupations of early modern drama in the wake of the expanding trade between England and these regions.
39. Aaron T. Pratt points out that only five plays from the 1580s were printed during the decade and that the overwhelming majority of surviving plays composed in that decade were printed between 1592 and 1594. A partial exception to what appears to have been a rule was John Lyly, who alone accounted for two of the five plays printed in the 1580s (Aaron T. Pratt, 'Printed Playbooks, Performance, and the 1580s Lag', *Shakespeare Studies* 45 (2017), 51–9, 53–4): one of these was *Sappho and Phao*, discussed below.
40. The title page reads, '*Parue nec inuidio sine me (liber) ibis ad arma, / Hei mihi, quod domino non licet ire tuo.*' This is the first two lines of the poet's lament in exile.
41. Stern mentions the use of flags on top of playhouse roofs, the pasting of play bills across the intramural city (a slightly later practice) and the practice of what might be called early modern flash mobs, groups dispatched into the streets of London with drums and trumpets to shout the name of the play being performed that day as methods by which the playhouses attempted to gain attention for their offering (*Making Shakespeare*, 15).
42. Ovid, *Tristia, Ex Ponto*, translated by A. L. Wheeler (Cambridge, MA: Harvard University Press, 1924), 1.1.1–2.
43. Michael Taussig, *Mimesis and Alterity: A Particular History of the Senses* (Abingdon and New York: Routledge, 2018), 112.
44. Brian C. Lockey points out that Stukeley's death speech seems to stand for Sebastian as well, the Portuguese king being killed off stage, and that this choice allows for the possibility of perpetuating the 'Sebastianismo' myth in which the Portuguese king had survived the battle and would return to reclaim his throne and redeem his country in the mould of the once and future English King Arthur; see Brian C. Lockey, 'Elizabethan Cosmopolitan: Captain Thomas Stukeley in the Court of Dom Sebastian', *English Literary Renaissance* 40.1 (2010), 3–32, 31.
45. *Sapho and Phao* appeared several years before *The Battle of Alcazar*, but Peele is almost certain to have been familiar with it. Lyly's play was performed at the first Blackfriars playhouse and at court in 1581 or 1582. Around the same time, the Children of the Chapel also performed Peele's first play, *The Arraignment of Paris*. Both Lyly and Peele wrote for the Children of the Chapel in the early 1580s.
46. Julie Sanders, '"In the Friars": The Spatial and Cultural Geography of an Indoor Playhouse', *Cahiers Élisabéthains* 88 (2015), 20–33.
47. Sanders, '"In the Friars"', 25.
48. David Bevington, 'Introduction to *Sappho and Phao*', in John Lyly, *Sappho and Phao*, ed. David Bevington (Manchester: Manchester University Press, 1991), 141–95, 154–6. All quotations from the play will be taken from this edition and reference will be given in the text.

Chapter 9

'As Water Mill, Made Rags and Shreds to Sweate': Fluvial Bodies and Fluminous Geographies

Jemima Matthews

To grace his goodly Queen, Tames presently proclaimes,
That all the Kentish Floods, resigning him their names,
Should presently repaire unto his mighty Hall,
And by the posting Tides, towards London sends to call
Cleere Ravensburne (though small, remembred them among)
At Detford entring. Whence as down she comes along,
She Darent thither warnes: who calles her sister Cray,
Which hasten to the Court with all the speed they may.
And but that Medway then of Tames obtain'd such grace,
Except her country Nymphs, that none should be in place,
More Rivers from each part, had instantly been there,
Then at their marriage, first, by Spenser numbred were.
– Michael Drayton, *Poly-Olbion*[1]

In *Poly-Olbion* Michael Drayton depicts the River Darent who, along with her sister Cray, 'hasten[s] to the Court'. In Song 18, these two sisters are welcomed by a masculine Thames and, like all the 'Kentish floods', they 'resign him their names'. Once the personified tributaries reach the 'mighty Hall' of Thames it becomes 'fluminous', a word that Thomas Blout defined in 1656 as 'Full of rivers'.[2] By contrast 'fluvial' is defined by the *Oxford English Dictionary* as 'Of or pertaining to a river or rivers; found or living in a river.'[3] Drayton's personified rivers, Darent and Cray, are fluvial in both these senses, belonging to a river and taking up residence in a larger river they possess qualities which are simultaneously human and fluvial: 'hasten[ing] ... with all the speed they may'. The word 'tributary' only came to be used for a stream in 1616 in William Shakespeare's *Cymbeline*.[4] However, Drayton's poem playfully anticipates this usage depicting the tribute of these tributaries to the Thames. The female fluvial bodies in the river belong to a courtly riverine community which includes the Thames and the Queen herself. Their names are simultaneously catalogued and 'resign[ed]', 'remembred' and also lost. Architect and water theorist Cecilia Chen speaks of communities 'convened by water' and the etymology of 'convened' suggests a form of meeting or assembly. Drayton depicts a community 'convened by water' but the one that he figures as a fluvial community and a fluvial meeting.[5] Despite being insistently fluvial, water, in the sense of material wetness or material flow rather than personification, is entirely absent from this moment of excessive riverine meeting. The sisters are instead part of a confluence of flow, obligation and connection.[6]

In the 1970s the River Darent, a tributary of the Thames, was not full of rivers and a Kentish flood but was instead at risk of drying up. In its present state it is still subject to dangerously low water in periods of drought such as that experienced in the summer of 2022. The Darent River Preservation Society (DRiPS) notes that this chalk stream is one of only '210 in the world ... 190 of which are in England'.[7] A further notice on the homepage of their website reads:

> URGENT – ACTION PLEASE
> We are receiving reports related to **fish in distress** in the Darent due to low flows and the increased temperatures.
> These have been reported to the Environment Agency.
> If you witness dead fish or fish in distress, please report your incident directly to the EA on their emergency number – 0800 807060 – providing as much detail as you can.
>
> PLEASE, please try to reduce your **water consumption** as much as you can, and ask your friends and neighbours to do the same. River levels are dropping every day. A lot of our residents still remember how whole sections of the Darent dried out during the 70s, 80s and early 90s. The whole ecology of the river is in danger again. Please don't assume we can manage without it. These days we understand that everything in nature is interconnected. Absolutely nothing can be independent, even us.
> Or we should probably say, ESPECIALLY us.[8]

Here local inhabitants are warned to be both watchful and mindful. They are asked to keep an eye out for dead or floating bodies or associated 'distress'. They are asked to be considerate in their water usage and to ask their own community to mirror their behaviour. It encourages them to perform a mode of what Owain Jones has termed 'hydrocitizenship', or the 'recognition of the need for a more ecologically integrated approach to water management, which involves communities of place as proactive stewards of their local water environments'.[9]

A close observer of rivers in the summer of 2022 might have noticed other strange objects appearing in the waters. In the widespread drought experienced in the summer of 2022, hunger stones began to appear in rivers across Europe.[10] These stones are designed to remind the viewer of earlier droughts and earlier moments in time when the waters receded revealing the matter under the water. In doing so they are designed to forecast famine.[11] These stones are sometimes marked with dates recording moments of low water and sometimes they are marked with phrases directed at the viewer themselves. For example, a stone in the River Elbe carved with the date 1616 reads 'If you see me then weep.'[12] Instead of being 'fluminous' these stones record moments of receding waters, and predict the social ramifications of these changes in water level for local communities. The sudden revelation of these visual records of moments of low water within the river to a viewer on the banks is intriguing. They create new communities across time and space linking temporal moments by shared water level rather than by chronology.

The water level of a river, whether low or high, or indeed any alteration of the river system with an impact on flow, could have serious repercussions for early modern river users and inhabitants. Whilst these could be the result of extreme weather or natural changes over time, a particular early modern preoccupation was the impact human intervention might have on the alteration of flow or water level in a local area. In this chapter poetic petitions by watermen John Byshop and John Taylor concerning the distress of river workers in the upper reaches of the Thames are considered alongside a poem praising the erection of a paper mill on the river Darent near Dartford. Watermen asserted that accidents on the Thames between Maidenhead and Oxford were caused by mills and their associated structures such as weirs and locks.[13] Byshop is an important figure in the wider debate and his petition is located in this bitter history of conflict between navigation and the milling industry.[14] Byshop's petition contains a poetic survey of the obstacles in the river and a catalogue of the goods and men lost because of what Taylor later defined as the acts of 'private persons'.[15] I want to contrast this poetic petition concerning the upper reaches of the Thames to a different kind of mill poetry concerning a paper mill on the Darent, a tributary of the Thames in Kent. Thomas Churchyard published *A Sparke Of Frendship and Warme Goodwill* in 1588 in support of John Spillman, defending and simultaneously advertising his watermill and its alteration of the local landscape.[16] Whilst these poems are site-specific and concern very different stretches of the Thames and Darent respectively, this comparative study charts the confluence and divergence in the material and linguistic riverscapes presented by these writers. All three poets address their work to the Queen and all three construct their argument around the idea of the ideal riverine community. These poets all frame the river's 'work' as a service to the state but the labour these writers each have in mind is incompatible. This chapter considers how river water is worked and reworked by these writers, these two different industries, and the models of riverine community that they set up or reject.

Although this chapter does not concern Drayton, I began this chapter with *Poly-Olbion* because of the way in which he catalogues his embodied rivers. His mode of engagement with rivers and river personification is distinctly early modern. On the other hand, DRiPS's appeal on their homepage in 2022 presents a river requiring local and national action and whose waters trouble, distress or even kill those that swim in its waters. In Byshop's petition we see the meeting point of poetic chorography and an appeal for intervention in the river. Byshop depicts bargemen desperately labouring within a new and threatening environment. He describes the dead bodies of bargemen and catalogues the names of the dead. The bargemen are put in danger and their bodies broken, Byshop suggests, because of the alterations caused by locks, weirs, mills and floodgates. Bodies are remembered in Byshop's poem as they were in the personification of *Poly-Olbion* and they are also broken by the force of the water. In the three texts discussed in this chapter the authors all show a deep awareness of the 'interconnected' nature of human bodies and river water as well as a clear sense of the impact of alterations in the landscape which redirect the flow of river water not only within the local landscape but also across the 'aqueous terrain' of the page.[17]

All three texts show an awareness of the potential 'distress' changes in flow might cause. For waterman Byshop, the distress is not piscine but is instead the human distress of wives and children of the men drowned by the altered river. Nevertheless, the poem by Thomas Churchyard in defence of the paper mill on the Darent and its alteration of the surrounding riverscape is couched in terms which self-consciously reframe the alterations and their impact. Despite their opposing views, both writers make surprisingly similar assertions concerning public good, charitable work and the universal right to water. Churchyard's poem is calculated to rework the terms of riverine debate and in so doing reframe what Andrew McRae has previously described as incompatible frames of reference.[18] This chapter traces the entangled histories of bodies, river-water, paper and sweat, charting how these poems map fluvial geographies of location and dislocation.

Byshop vs churchland: De/constructing river community

Mill dams were substantial structures made from 'timber and rubble' and 'stretched the full width of the main stream'.[19] The danger was caused by the alterations which the mills created in the environment. After the dissolution of the monasteries, mills at Dartford became crown property and were leased to Spillman in 1588 when he converted them into paper mills.[20] Spillman commissioned Thomas Churchyard to publish a poetic tract in favour of the mill. It has been argued that this was partly designed to protect Spillman from competition by bolstering a petition to the Queen to give Spillman monopoly on the 'raw materials' for production of paper.[21] Churchyard printed a poem and a letter entitled *A Sparke of Friendship* in 1588. The subsequent granting of the patent on 7 February 1589 appears to indicate that they were successful. Furthermore, David Linton has noted the striking similarity between the poem and the language of the patent.[22] Churchyard's poem makes extravagant claims about the constructive contribution the paper mill made as a site of cultural production and the positive definitions of the alterations which the mill made to the local community and landscape.[23]

The extent to which they correspond in their arguments is striking given that they have opposite motivations and are writing on behalf of very different communities. Both writers appeal to the Queen (whether directly or indirectly) asserting the importance of *her* river as part of *her* realm. Churchyard positions his appeal to Elizabeth as one of national importance and which facilitates mutual benefit: 'The glory then, and honor of this deede, / is hers, and ours, shall be the gayne therein'.[24] David Linton points out that Churchyard's text created a series of audiences: he writes on behalf of Spillman, to the Queen in a letter and poem addressed to Raleigh but printed publicly.[25] Models of community are thus built into the verse structure of the poem.

By contrast, Byshop addresses his petition to the Queen directly and attempts to draw her attention to 'weares mylles and Floudgates vnlawfullie erected . . . contrarie to your highnesses godlie statutes'.[26] His main concern is for the 'drowninge of men w[i]thin her streame' and his repeated use of the word drowning creates a disconcerting rhythm embedded in the structure of the poem itself.[27] Their drowning is repeatedly remembered with each iteration in a pattern that models sinking, emerging and re-immersive motion. Byshop suggests the obstructions are an act against the Queen; by association, this also places the responsibility for the human cost of those structures within her jurisdiction. The text suggests that the Thames is unique in this way:

> no place els w[i]thin the land
> such wronges done to o[u]r gratyous quene
> And yet those lockes and weares do stande[28]

Churchyard instead refigures the mill 'a service to the state' and conflates this with the mill structure itself: a 'stately work most rare'.[29] One stanza in particular maps out its construction:

> The mill it selfe, is sure right rare to see,
> the framing is, so queint and finely done,
> Built all of wood, and hollowe trunkes of tree,
> That makes the streames, at point device to runne,
> Nowe up, nowe downe, now sideward by a slight,
> Now forward fast, then spouting up on height,
> As Conduites colde, coulde force so great a heate,
> That fire shoulde flame, where thumping hammers beat.[30]

The description of the construction of the mill in Churchyard's text is as a mechanical hydraulic feat of engineering. The way in which the mill manages water and generates power is emphasised. Water is the force to 'drive the mill'.[31] Nevertheless, water is still passive until mobilised and set in motion by Spillman and his mechanics. *Sparke Of Frendship* creates an energy narrative of water but it is one in which water itself is controlled, rechannelled and harnessed through the design of one man. The mechanisms in the mill serve as 'extensions of the identity of the workers' as hammers seem to beat on their own.[32] By contrast, Byshop emphasises the vulnerability of the men and the force of the artificial alterations of the environment and repeats his accusations concerning the 'extorc[i]on of Myllers'.[33] The individuals, Byshop insists, can be personally blamed because they have 'drownde those symple men'.[34] In addition to the catalogue of deaths in the river, McRae notes that the poem pays attention to the woeful destitution caused. Byshop centralises female bereavement and the economic hardship inflicted on the families of watermen: 'mannie wofull widowes and fatherless children daylie do befall' and '[t]heir wives be left remedilesse'.[35] Re-engineered water is figured here as creating geographies of dislocation. To reroute is to defamiliarise water's connective power.

The first encounter with water in Byshop's poem is one that seems to be driven not by the redirected river water itself alone but by the tears of the orphaned children: 'One farmer have a lock in store / that hath made many a child to weepe'. Byshop completes the rhyme scheme with: 'Their mothers beg from dore to dore / their Fathers drowned in the deepe'.[36] These tears in their end position in the line then, through the drop down to the start of the next line, seem to drive the mothers onwards door to door. This inverted familial structure creates a circular motion where the father's death in the 'deepe' at the end of the final line of the stanza and the child's tears which they 'weepe' are connected through their rhyme both to each other and to the subsequent circulation of the mother's wandering door to door, which they both enclose. By encountering the watery death of the fathers last and the impact of their deaths first, the drowning appears to be prefigured, remembered and repeatedly re-membered. The 'store' or retention of water at the start of the stanza which is geographically located in one place leads to an outpouring elsewhere in the stanza and elsewhere in the river system. Viewed together this structure constructs a water world out of balance and one in which, like Spillman's mill, water is driven in different directions within the confines of a stanza, the page, the mill and the river beyond. The visible working of water in Byshop's poem is depicted by the struggling bargemen attempting to navigate a steep lock, or drowning in the deep, the weeping children, the circulating wives and the 'woeful' wife who is later described 'wringing' her hands before being presented with five shillings for the death of her husband. In so doing the poem continually presents misplaced work or seemingly wasted labour just as Byshop argues the millers misplace water in redirecting it for their private trade. Families are not re-membered but dismembered by this altered landscape and I want to return to this idea of a dismembered riverscape and dismembered community at the end of the chapter.

One of the most interesting points of comparison between the two poetic petitions by Churchyard and Byshop is the different ways in which both texts construct home. Both industries capitalise on a mobile workforce who treads the tricky early modern divide between worker and vagrant, or one who strays and roams out of bounds. McRae notes that 'Conservative discourse on vagrants typically represents domestic travel as random and profoundly unsettling.' Whilst river improvers tried to harness a new model to 'endors[e] circulation', watermen such as Byshop and Taylor were vulnerable to accusations of vagrancy.[37] Byshop figures the mills as devices whose capacity to redirect or refigure water in turn renders women and children masterless and placeless: 'Their mothers beg from dore to dore / their fathers drowned in the deepe'.[38] Instead, Churchyard suggests that the mill makes a home for its workers by providing them with employment. In truth though this industry was dependent on a mobile workforce of ragpickers many of whom were female. Crucially, 'a 1601 complaint written by the Lord Mayor and Aldermen in response to a letter from the Privy Council' about Spillman states that he

> Began to offer wrong to the charters of the city authorizing great numbers of poor people, especially girls and vagrant women, to collect rags, etc. within the city liberties, who under pretence of that service, ranged abroad in every street, begging at men's doors, whereby the discipline of the city was weakened.[39]

Moreover, Heidi Craig draws on the *OED* in order to define 'rag' not only as a piece of cloth but as 'a disreputable or contemptible person; a person of low social class' suggesting an interesting overlap between the material goods and the ragpicker carrying them. In fact the very movement of the women through the streets is problematic and, 'in the specification that women begged at "men's doors"', the complaint carries an 'insinuation of prostitution'.[40] Churchyard himself repeatedly compares the mill to a dwelling: firstly it is 'a paper mill . . . Where Spillman may, himself and household dwell'; secondly there is also a comparison to a country estate: 'with workmanship set forth, / so surely built, and planted in the ground. / That it doth seeme, a house of some estate'.[41] Churchyard figures Spillman as a benevolent landlord of a manor with obligations to the landscape and tenants. The poem could be read as an early precursor of the country house tradition. Devices such as this serve to naturalise Spillman's claim but they also collapse the frenetic movement of the female workforce from house to house into the revolutions around, or to and from, a single abode. The energy narrative of rags is reframed from simply a network of circulation from the mill to the community into a circulation within the mill's own water system and hydro-community.

Water ethics

Churchyard gestures to the wider landscape of the river in his description of water as an 'element which every creature needes . . . whereby a world of people daylie live'.[42] Here he maps a trajectory from an element to world, micro to macro, water to local community. It is perhaps surprising that water is represented by both authors as something which should be free to all. The mills Byshop is concerned with are not necessarily paper mills, but these two writers who should be potential opponents surprisingly seem to share this particular form of water ethics in common. Moreover, this admission by Churchyard appears to stretch the point too far exposing an underlying contradiction in his claim. Despite the 'world of people' who 'daylie live' by the river, Churchyard is only interested in those who do so through their positive contribution to the mill. This contribution is figured as energy in terms of their labour or their supply of raw materials for the paper-making process. Most importantly the mill is figured as itself a charitable work:

> Spillman, Help-man, so rightly call the same:
> For greater help, I gesse he cannot giue,
> than by his help, to make poore folke to liue.[43]

Chapter 1 in this volume emphasised the connection between water and charity. In this poem charity is transferred from its traditional association with the home and the estate to the working mill. The assertion that there are six hundred workers at the mill and that 'many heads, and handes may thrive thereby' is part of an attempt to figure the mill itself as sustaining and mobilising this self-contained community.[44] Churchyard repeatedly emphasises the spiritual qualities of water, suggesting by association that they are little worlds and that the millers and mill owners are in turn godlike. Byshop also focuses on the power of the landowners, indicating that a typical owner of a lock 'hath no mercie at all / On those that come his lock[e]s w[i]thin / The streame is so stronge w[i]th such a fall / He cares not whether the[y] sinke or swyme'.[45]

For Byshop the key issue is the economic harnessing of something which should be free.[46] Instead Churchyard appears to pre-empt this accusation and neatly sidesteps it by suggesting that prior to the construction of the paper mill, 'Water ranne, in waste and vaine a way, / Nowe profit yeeldes, and brings in poundes and pence'.[47] There is an insistence here that the use of the water for the mill, and the way in which it channels the water, does not displace other uses but merely deploys what was previously a wasted energy source. Churchyard is setting up a distinction between these working waters artfully deployed using Spillman's artificial management of water and the 'natural' state of the water.[48] Chen observes that,

> whereas useful waters easily find articulation within human practices, 'useless' waters (waters that exceed anthropocentric ideas of service) are less intelligible, as agents of troublesome, unpredictable, and transformational energies – energies that are integral to risky processes of becoming, including but certainly not limited to death.[49]

Service is certainly encoded into the models of water management and water community based on flow, obligation and connection found in these texts. Byshop figures artificial alterations as a risky strategy that increases the likelihood of death. Churchyard figures the hydraulic feat of engineering upon which the community is dependent for subsistence as the key force sustaining life.

Byshop's appeal was repeated in the seventeenth century in *Taylor Tame on Isis* a pamphlet by waterman John Taylor, discussed in more detail in the next chapter.[50] Taylor surveys the obstacles and state of the river above Staines. Taylor's account is important in relation to the way in which 'use' (both as a term and as a concept) is deployed in all three texts. Taylor, like Churchyard, suggests that water is a free gift from God. However, instead of thereby associating the work of a miller with godly labour, as Churchyard does, Taylor positions the miller as 'abus[ing]' God's gift by constructing it anew:

> Shall it to spoyle and ruine be let to runne?
> Shall private persons for their gainful use
> Ingrosse the water and the land abuse?
> Shall that which God and nature gives us free,
> For use and profit in community,
> Be barr'd from men[51]

Taylor protests that millers should not be allowed to 'spoile the public for a private trade'.[52] His use of 'ingrosse' appears to conflate multiple meanings of the term 'engross'. Engross could mean 'To write in large letters; chiefly, and now almost exclusively, to write in a peculiar character appropriate to legal documents; *hence*, to write out or express in legal form'; 'To buy up wholesale ... or as much as possible, of (a commodity) for the purpose of "regrating" or retailing it at a monopoly price' and 'To gain or keep exclusive possession of; to concentrate (property, trade, privileges, functions) in one's own possession (often with the notion of unfairness or injury to others); to "monopolize".'[53] The debate turns on right and proper 'use' and what constitutes an abuse in the riverine environment. This, it seems, depends on who is making the definition and in whose interests they are acting. What is at stake is the notion of community, but these writers show community can be redefined by the opponents of the debate.

Jonathan Sawday asserts that water 'was the single most reliable source of power known to early-modern communities, providing the foundations upon which so much social, communal, and urban life depended'.[54] There is merit to this sweeping statement and yet it seems necessary to examine in more detail the nature of the communal function of water, as not only could it 'foun[d]' communities and modes of 'hydrocitizenship', but its 'micropolitics' could create divisions.[55] Mills were 'only maintained by the constant exercising of contested economic and legal power'.[56]

Human cost

Byshop evokes the cost of water which is calculated in terms of the payment of five shillings for the life of a man drowned in a lock indicating the substitution and monetisation of a human life. It also appears in the extortion of millers, which leads to 'poor men' having to make payment to millers for water in the stream, a resource Byshop argues should be free. Finally, it appears in the loss of goods worth thousands of pounds in the water and the danger of going up steep locks, which leads to the breaking of cables. Again according to Byshop these cables cost an extraordinary price. The measurements included in the poems of Byshop and Churchyard seem hyperbolic but they draw attention to the role of measurement and calculation of cost in riverine and littoral communities which I discuss elsewhere.[57]

Churchyard's poem sees various raw materials jostle for space within the confines of the mill, and the catalogue of practices deployed within the mill sends materials and water in different directions. Byshop's poem features items tossed around by the force of the water, but in his text it is the bodies of bargemen which are thrown around and 'drown in the deep' including 'a mans braines knocked out' in stanza 16.[58] The lives lost are commemorated at the end of Byshop's poem by the list of those who have died in the Thames. Byshop catalogues the names of the men drowned. Lists render the past 'thing-like' as Kelly Wisecup has observed.[59] Byshop draws on the shock of this technique illustrating that the men are 'thing-like' once submerged in water. This catalogue of the human cost of altering the ecology of the river is unsurprisingly absent from Churchyard's description of a 'merry mill' on the Darent.[60] Yet the threat of this human cost appears in disconcerting moments and fragmented images in Churchyard's text when we least expect it. The toil and labour of production at the mill site is full of violence and force: thumping, beating, stamping, washing, spouting and so on. All this work, both human and non-human as well as the resultant energy, is, however, turned into an articulation of the spiritual value of human endeavour.

Churchyard insists that the goods produced within the mill are embedded in trade and circulation nationally and internationally. The mill then, in Churchyard's construction, is part of the national economy, not one which is siphoned off for private use. By contrast in Byshop's petition the re-scripted river provokes 'discomfort and to the exceeding losse and spoile of their goodes and commodities', and he repeats the assertion that 'both Corne and Malte they still distroye'.[61] By emphasising these two commodities, staple essentials to daily living, Byshop situates the river's role as a conveyor of necessities in a similar fashion to Churchyard's description of the way in which paper distribution facilitates the economy. Both writers signal how re-engineered water flow intersects with food security.[62] Churchyard aligns the movement of corn from rotting in the ground to grinding in the mill and finally posits a parallel between the production of bread with the production of paper, juxtaposing them in the same stanza. The rotting grain and the redeployed rags which are used to produce paper are mapped onto similar trajectories. Churchyard insists that paper passes 'through many a hand and head' and that it 'passe like drosse, that of self is nought / til it be tried, by skill and thoroughly wrought'.[63] The transformation of these unremarkable materials is described as a 'quasi-magical process'.[64] Crucially, Churchyard does not specify the role of inland waterways in the conveyance of paper within his discussion – it is implied but, perhaps intentionally, not specified. McRae has illustrated how the discourse of river improvement was modelled on the circulation of blood in the body.[65] Churchyard simultaneously invokes but avoids explicitly stating a comparison to inland navigation which river improvers relied upon.

Both poets valorise the labour which they advocate. Churchyard characterises the mill system as one large labour force:

> The myll goes round, the workmen moyle and sweate,
> the streame goes streaight, that earst ranne all at large,
> The wheeles conveyes the Water diuers wayes,
> the hammers thump, the stamp but seldome stayes:
> The ragges and clowts, becomes as white as snowe,
> and all these knackes, the master needes must knowe.[66]

Alongside the sweating workmen, Churchyard personifies all aspects of the process of converting the raw materials to paper as labouring towards the finished product: 'as Water mill, made rags and shreds to sweate. / Of whose thick froth, a creame or crude should rise, / that shoulde take shape, and strength by breath of skyes'.[67] In Churchyard's poem then the river is a rich source of sites of cultural production and the circulation of the hydraulic system of the mill itself facilitates the circulation of paper and commerce which it generates. The troublesome bodies of the female ragpickers are conspicuously absent. Yet human energy and skilled workmanship replace riverine energy and value. The human and the non-human materials stand in for the fluvial and the fluvial does not exist unaided in the world of this poem.

Dismembered riverscapes

In Byshop's text he depicts a grotesque moment of consumption in which the dead bodies of the bargemen are unceremoniously buried: 'Then beinge drowned they bury them there'. The result is that scavenging animals 'doe them finde / their fleshe they eat and all do teare / w[hi]ch contrary is to mankind'.[68] In McRae's reading, 'The sins of the propertied are thereby aligned with a dehumanising realisation of eternal placelessness, which is disturbing in spite of its rhetorical excess.'[69] The image is certainly designed to shock and repulse the reader who might miss the way the passage maps out a larger pattern in which the alterations in the landscape mark the working body as disposable. In Byshop's text the families are figured as homeless and in their death the bargemen and their families are positioned as liminal, thing-like, yet the image of a buried then exhumed and dismembered bargeman's body is disconcerting in other ways when we view it alongside Churchyard's mill-scape.

Churchyard also includes a grotesque moment of consumption: 'and who may boast, they are with paper fed, / Straunge is that foode, yet straunger made the same'.[70] The families who gain subsistence from work in the mill are here imagined to be consuming paper, the product of their labours is aligned with their own ingestion and digestion. The food is 'Straunge', playing on the etymology of this word: it is simultaneously a food that is strange unto their blood, as they consume a foreign body, and a substance made by the German 'straunger' Spillman.[71] Helen Smith and Elaine Long have noted the extensive use of paper not only as writing materials but blue paper for example was used as the wrapping for sugar, whilst other papers were used to wrap food, or even bodies when deployed in medicinal work.[72] In both poems, riverine work is envisaged as an inhuman act of consumption and digestion despite the fact that in one instance the poem seeks to defend or even advertise the powers of altered riverine flow and the other seeks to dehumanise it with a view to provoking intervention. Meanwhile, the rags which provided one of the raw materials for paper were scavenged by ragpickers from the refuse of households and even from dead bodies. Heidi Craig notes that executioners would remove linen from a corpse, preventing the valuable resource being buried with the subject.[73] Byshop's poem is not aimed at a paper mill specifically, but his grotesque image of the inhuman rending and consumption of 'flesh' can be situated in relation to this larger set of cultural practices connected to paper mills as well as wider associations with 'flesh'. As Helen Smith has observed, writers such as Bacon noted that the greasy texture of early modern paper bore a close affinity to skin.[74] In contemporary theory the surface of the skin was understood through a comparison to a 'fishing net' which enabled the passing of sweat and 'excrements' through its porous surface.[75] Fishing nets in turn were one of a number of raw materials Spillman was given a monopoly on the collection of for use in his paper mill, suggesting an overlapping set of cultural associations which I argue inform both Churchyard and Byshop's dismembered riverine bodies. The description of a drowned body by physician Alexander Read (considered in Chapter 2 in this volume) further reinforces that rivers recomposed and distorted human flesh in unsightly and distressing ways. The imagery associated with Falstaff, explored in my own work elsewhere, also indicates that submerged bodies are reframed in the early modern imagination either as raw material or raw matter.[76] These bodies are all simultaneously rendered human, inhuman, riverine and terrestrial after violent contact with the waters.

Paper was made from recycled rags; former clothing or domestic linen would be redeployed as 'wiping rags' for 'household or bodily uses' until they 'became too weak and tattered', at which point ragpickers would collect and sort them into different qualities of linen. Many of these ragpickers were women. As well as linen, paper could be made from 'old ropes, sails, canvas, and off-white linen, hemp and cotton' though these tended to 'produce coarse papers for wrapping, pasteboard, and other uses apart from printing and writing'.[77] To this we might add, as Joshua Calhoun notes, that once a book or paper reached the end of its life it 'might have been used as toilet paper, reused as fertilizer for flax plants, which were then harvested and converted into linen underwear before once again providing pulp for paper'.[78] Calhoun notes the 'network of flecks and fibers embedded in' many early modern pages.[79] This includes

> bits and pieces of vegetable fibers that made their way into clothing (during flax processing) and then into paper and flecks of organic matter, presumably from riparian flora upstream, that were too small to be filtered out of the papermaker's vat.[80]

He tells us also that the flecking of paper could also be affected by seasons and weather patterns. Not only might the paper show the traces of river ephemera in its warp and weft; the water itself shaped and informed the paper made during the paper-making process:

> ... rivers that provided water for paper mills were not always pristine, especially in the spring (when they ran muddy) or when the river banks were populated upstream. The stuff vat, the pot of macerated fibres used to make sheets of paper, was about ninety-nine percent water, so it is no surprise that silty, muddy, or polluted water would render sheets of paper darker.[81]

The paper produced in Spillman's mill then was a material product of the Darent's specific chalk stream and thereby subject to seasonal changes and human intervention. The paper of Byshop's petition and Churchyard's printed verse each capture and record the state of the water at the time of their composition. For each of their respective waters then, they record fluminous temporal compositions.[82] Nevertheless, as well as providing the basis for its existence, 'whereby a world of people daylie live', Churchyard states, 'Water too, that Papers enmy is' because whilst it formed the essential ingredient to bind the multifarious matter into a single sheet it could also destroy the finished product if the paper came into contact with water again.[83] The next chapter looks at how Leland's manuscripts might be 'mangled' and 'defaced' by coming into contact with a 'wet' landscape.[84] The sweating working bodies in Churchyard's poem are understood as symbiotic with the product and process of the mill itself where rags were repeatedly scoured. In contemporary understandings of sweat it was part of the elimination of 'harmful impurities'.[85] In Churchyard's reading then the working bodies and the rags themselves are cleansed through the process of papermaking at the paper mill on the Darent but the sweating bodies also threaten the finished product. As I have noted elsewhere there is a 'collective concern' in the early modern period for the 'impact contact with water might have on the body: how it might reshape, affect, transform the body, rendering it vulnerable'.[86] Working in riverine waters, whether in the challenging upper reaches of the Thames or the proto-industrial waters of the Darent, made the early modern working body uniquely vulnerable. Vulnerable because it was inherently porous, as a fisherman's net, and easily broken, knocked or drowned. Whilst working bodies are repeatedly remembered by these texts they are also dis-membered again and again.

Conclusion

This chapter has taken the reader on a journey tracing the entangled histories of bodies, river-water, paper and sweat, showing how these poems map fluvial geographies of location and dislocation. Through my 'fluvial-methodology' we have been able to chart the movement of water from the directed flow across the page and within the landscape to its rechannelled force within a watermill, or water vat, and finally to water and its silty signification as marks in the fabric of the page itself or how water's force reconfigures the raw materials of an early modern body.[87] It has been possible thus to trace how Byshop and Churchyard delineate a set of energy narratives formed across space and time. These poems reveal their writers to be political and establish that though their water politics are differently inflected they both rely on similar devices and a surprisingly similar set of water ethics. McRae suggests that the disputes between navigation and mills were provoked by incompatible frames of reference: local versus national and property versus circulation.[88] Churchyard's support for the mill is not directly to emphasise local priorities or property rights, as McRae's argument implies that it would be. As David Linton points out, Spillman's pursuit of the patent indicates that he was in favour of an advantageous monopoly on the trade.[89] Despite this, however, the arguments made by Churchyard in support of Spillman have to be couched using assertions of public good, charitable work and universal right to water as a necessity. This is because, I argue, these are the same terms which are deployed to the opposite effect in Byshop's petition and writing against re-scripting waterways. Churchyard (and presumably Spillman) shows an awareness of contemporary debate concerning mills, weirs and locks, which was especially prevalent between 1570 and 1590 and can be usefully understood in relation to Stefania Barca's concept of 'energy rent' explored in Chapter 2 in this volume. Churchyard has to work hard to deflect each of the issues raised by those who opposed mills and he does so through assertions which centralise the role of the water in local economies and communities. In every instance, however, he substitutes human art, skill and labour for riverine force or flow. The anthropocentric re-scripting of water then, is both literal device and literary device, and in so doing, Churchyard's writing reframes the terms of the debate. This reframing reveals a crucial difference in these writers as well as surprising similarities. The crucial difference is that Churchyard figures that essential 'element', water, as energy and power rather than as a transportation network. It establishes connections between humans but it does so through the transfer of energy from human to human or human to machine not as a mode of geographical connection uniting communities spatially. The only instance that disrupts this pattern is the lifecycle of corn discussed earlier. At a very basic level, in one model of right use of water the human subject moves on water; in the other water is moved. One model of circulation is replaced with another. In one the safe transfer of goods or the loss of goods or workers is monetised as rivers are envisaged as 'facilitat[ing] economic growth'.[90] In the other the movement of water is itself monetised.

When water is monetised in these texts it is often simultaneously materialised and therefore in that process it becomes full of stuff. The bodies in these poems jostle with a large array of goods within riverine waters. Whilst Byshop's poem is full of drowning or at risk human and non-human materials, Churchyard's waters are crammed with human and non-human stuff to the point of rhetorical and material excess. Both Byshop and Spillman, via Churchyard, attempt to make their labour matter by re-materialising watery labour. The mode of narration deployed by Churchyard and Byshop utilises the space of the page to depict both water's motion and its rearticulation through human intervention. They each create poetic hydro-narratives which rely on the space and time of the page. In so doing they create communities linked or disrupted by water level and flow across time and space. For these poets the little room of the stanza and its set of interlinked rooms provide the architecture through which to think with, and rethink, water's scriptive capacity to convene hydro-communities. Both writers construct and deconstruct the idea of the ideal community. They explore bodies that fragment and watery modes of dismemberment. Memory is non-linear both in terms of how it works at the level of the poetic line as well as through time. Chen has argued that, 'unlike the abstract and dislocated idea of resource, the waters that join us in relation are articulated with space and time'.[91]

As this chapter has shown, both Byshop and Churchyard utilise the space of the page. They rechannel water across and within the page and they direct their reader to engage with its flow from the vantage point of their own local politics. Their poetic and practical work relies on a comparison of past, present and future water levels and flows. In so doing they delineate riverine communities within their texts and attempt to convene a new riverine community with their readers. Yet their texts also map out complexly unique fluminous temporal compositions which are products of the particular moment of their submersion.

Notes

1. Michael Drayton, *Poly-Olbion*, https://poly-olbion.exeter.ac.uk/the-text/full-text/song-18/ (last accessed 22 September 2023).
2. Thomas Blount, *Glossographia; or, A dictionary interpreting all such hard words, whether Hebrew, Greek or Latin . . . as are now used in our refined English tongue* (London, 1656), Wing B3334, Sig.R3^r.
3. *OED*, 'fluvial', adj. 2.
4. *OED* observes that the first instance is in William Shakespeare's *Cymbeline*: *a*1616 W. Shakespeare *Cymbeline* (1623), iv.ii.36: 'Th'emperious Seas breeds Monsters; for the Dish, Poore Tributary Riuers, as sweet Fish': *OED*, 'Tributary', adj and n., 2.
5. Cecilia Chen, 'Mapping Waters: Thinking with Watery Places', in *Thinking with Water*, ed. Cecilia Chen, Janine MacLeod and Astrida Neimanis (Montreal: McGill–Queen's University Press, 2013), 274–98, 275.
6. It is interesting to consider this confluence of flow, obligation and connection in relation to the mode of 'bioregionalism' that Todd Borlik argues Drayton advances in *Poly-Olbion*: Todd Andrew Borlik, 'Bioregional Visions in *Poly-Olbion*', in *Poly-Olbion: New Perspectives*, ed. Andrew McRae and Philip Schwyzer (Martlesham: Boydell & Brewer, 2020), 89–111.
7. Darent River Preservation Society homepage, http://www.darent-drips.org.uk/ (last accessed 22 September 2023).
8. Ibid. (bold in original).

9. Stephen Scott-Bottoms and Maggie Roe, 'Who Is a Hydrocitizen? The Use of Dialogic Arts Methods as a Research Tool among Water Professionals in West Yorkshire, UK', *Local Environment* 25.4 (2020), 273–89, 274.
10. I am grateful to my postdoctoral research assistant Dr Eliza Cubitt for alerting me to the recent emergence of hunger stones.
11. For a discussion of famine and rivers in the context of early colonial Bengal, see Ujjayan Bhattacharya, 'Rivers, Inundations, and Grain Scarcity in Early Colonial Bengal', in *A Cultural History of Famine: Food Security and the Environment in India and Britain*, ed. Ayesha Mukherjee (Abingdon: Routledge, 2019), 94–111.
12. https://www.telegraph.co.uk/world-news/2022/08/15/can-see-weep-drought-hit-river-elbe-reveals-hunger-stones-1616/ (last accessed 22 September 2023)
13. BL Lansdowne MS 44/39; for a discussion of John Byshop's poetry see Andrew McRae, 'Fluvial Nation: Rivers, Mobility and Poetry in Early Modern England', *ELR* 38.3 (2008), 506–34.
14. Cf. Fred S. Thacker, *The Thames Highway: A History of the Inland Navigation* (London: Fred S. Thacker, 1914), 45–58.
15. John Taylor, *Taylor on Thame Isis* (London, 1632), STC.23803, Sig.B^v.
16. Thomas Churchyard, *A Sparke Of Frendship and Warme Goodwill* (London, 1588), Sig.D^v.
17. For a discussion of the 'aqueous terrain' of the page in the context of riverine and oceanic writing, see Jemima Matthews, 'Maritime Ephemera in Walter Mountfort's *The Launching of the Mary*', in *Practices of Ephemera in Early Modern England*, ed. Callan Davies, Hannah Lilley and Catherine Richardson (Abingdon: Routledge, 2023), 173–90, 175; for a discussion of the river Thames and an 'aqueous season' of court performance, see Matthews, 'Inside Out and Outside In: The River Thames in William Shakespeare's *The Merry Wives of Windsor*', *Shakespeare* 15.4 (2019), 410–27.
18. Andrew McRae, *Literature and Domestic Travel in Early Modern England* (Cambridge: Cambridge University Press, 2009), 27.
19. David Gordon Wilson, *The Thames: Record of a Working Waterway* (London: Batsford, 1987), 19.
20. David Linton, 'Reading Metacanonical Texts', in *Other Voices, Other Views: Expanding the Canon in English Renaissance Studies*, ed. Helen Ostovich, Mary Vera Silcox and Graham Roebuck (New York: University of Delaware Press, 1999), 21–45, 25; Rhys Jenkins, *Paper Making in England, 1495–1798* (London: Association of Assistant Librarians, 1958), 7.
21. Jenkins, *Paper*, 8–9; Linton, 'Reading', 25–6.
22. Churchyard, *Sparke*, STC.5257; cf. Linton, 'Reading', 25–6; Jenkins, *Paper*, 10–11.
23. Chen has noted that even now, 'the pulp and paper industry [are] among the many industries that involve a large quantity of water': Chen, 'Mapping', 280.
24. Churchyard, *Sparke*, Sig.D2^v.
25. Linton, 'Reading', 25.
26. BL Lansdowne MS 44/39.

27. Ibid.
28. Ibid.
29. Churchyard, *Sparke*, Sig.D2^v.
30. Ibid.
31. Ibid., Sig.D2^r.
32. For a discussion of how materials extend the identity of workers in another maritime community see my discussion of Walter Mountfort's *The Launching of the Mary*: Matthews, 'Maritime Ephemera', 273–89.
33. BL Lansdowne MS 44/39.
34. Ibid.
35. Ibid.; McRae notes this kind of language but not its connection to Churchyard's writing: *Literature and Domestic Travel*, 45.
36. BL Lansdowne MS 44/39.
37. McRae, 'Fluvial', 520.
38. BL Lansdowne MS 44/39; cf. McRae, *Literature and Domestic Travel*, 45.
39. SP 12/279 f.165, cited in Heidi Craig, 'Rags, Ragpickers, and Early Modern Papermaking', *Literature Compass* 16.5 (2019), 1–11, 7.
40. Heidi Craig, 'English Rag-women and Early Modern Paper Production', in *Women's Labour and The History of the Book*, ed. Valerie Wayne (London: Bloomsbury, 2020), 29–46, 36.
41. Churchyard, *Sparke*, Sig.D^r; D4^v.
42. Ibid., Sig.D4^r.
43. Ibid., Sig.D^r.
44. Ibid., Sig.D2^v.
45. BL Lansdowne MS 44/39.
46. Cf. McRae, *Literature and Domestic Travel*, 27.
47. Churchyard, *Sparke*, Sig.D2^v.
48. However, there is also a comparison to be drawn between these working waters and the hydraulic feats of engineering used in elite displays in England and throughout Europe. In these displays the sheer extravagance of wasting water is a key component of the power of the display in elite settings. For a discussion of the use of water in displays at court, see Matthews, 'Inside Out and Outside In', 413–16. I am also grateful to Rosamund Paice for a discussion about water management and waste in her forthcoming work on Baroque gardens.
49. Chen, 'Mapping', 277.
50. Taylor, *Taylor on Thame Isis*, in *Works Of John Taylor the Water Poet Not Included In the Folio Volume Of 1630* (London, 1870), 9–27.
51. Taylor, *Taylor on Thame Isis*, Sig.B^v.
52. Ibid., Sig.B6^v.
53. *OED*, 'engross', v. 1a; 3a; 4b.
54. Jonathan Sawday, *Engines of the Imagination: Renaissance Culture and the Rise of the Machine* (Abingdon: Routledge, 2007), 34.
55. Cf. Mark S. R. Jenner, 'From Conduit Community to Commercial Network? Water in London, 1500–1725', in *Londinopolis: Essays in the Social and Cultural History of Early Modern London*, ed. Paul Griffiths and Mark S. R. Jenner (Manchester: Manchester University Press, 2000), 250–72, 251; Jemima Matthews, *Habitat and Habitation: The River Thames 1550–1650* (forthcoming).

56. Stuart Oliver, 'Liquid Materialities in the Landscape of the Thames: Mills and Weirs from the Nineteenth Century', *Area* 45.2 (June 2013), 223–9, 228.
57. Matthews, *Habitat and Habitation* (forthcoming). I am also grateful for discussion of this with Marine Bellago in the context of eighteenth-century practices.
58. BL Lansdowne MS 44/39.
59. Kelly Wisecup, 'Encounters, Objects and Commodity Lists in Early English Travel Narratives', *Studies in Travel Writing* 17.3 (2013), 264–80, 276; for a discussion of the role of lists in a maritime context and a detailed examination of Wisecup's argument, see Matthews, 'Maritime Ephemera', 180–1.
60. Churchyard, *Sparke*, Sig.D3^r.
61. BL Lansdowne MS 44/39.
62. For a discussion of 'food security' see Ayesha Mukherjee, ed., *A Cultural History of Famine: Food Security and the environment in India and Britain* (Abingdon: Routledge, 2019).
63. Churchyard, *Sparke*, Sig. D2^v.
64. Helen Smith, '"A Unique Instance of Art": The Proliferating Surfaces of Early Modern Paper', *Journal of Northern Renaissance* 8 (2017), 1–39, 28.
65. McRae, 'Fluvial', 506.
66. Churchyard, *Sparke*, Sig.E^r.
67. Ibid., Sig.D2^r.
68. BL Lansdowne MS 44/39.
69. McRae, 'Fluvial', 519.
70. Churchyard, *Sparke*, Sig. D^v.
71. Alexandra Halasz, 'Strange Food Paper', *EMLS* 20.1 (2018), 1–21, 8.
72. Smith, 'A Unique', 15; Elaine Leong, 'Papering the Household', in *Working with Paper: Gendered Practices in the History of Knowledge* (Pittsburgh: University of Pittsburgh Press, 2019), 32–45, 35.
73. Craig, 'Ragpickers', 5–7.
74. Smith, 'A Unique', 27, 33.
75. Helkiah Crooke, *Mikrokosmographia. A Description of the Body of Man, together with the Controversies and Figures thereto Belonging / Collected and Translated out of all the best Authors of Anatomy, especially out of Gasper Bauhinus and Andreas Laurentius, by Helkiah Crooke* (London: W. Iaggard, 1616), 73, cited in Mieneke te Hennepe, 'Of the Fisherman's Net and Skin Pores: Reframing Conceptions of the Skin in Medicine 1572–1714', in *Blood Sweat and Tears: The Changing Concepts of Physiology from Antiquity into Early Modern Europe*, ed. Manfred Horstmanshoff, Helen King and Claus Zittel (Leiden: Brill, 2012), 523–548. For a further discussion of the relationship between water and skin, see Matthews, 'Inside Out and Outside In'; Matthews, 'Maritime Ephemera', 185–9; Matthews, *Habitat and Habitation* (forthcoming).
76. Matthews, 'Inside Out and Outside In', 421–3.
77. Craig, 'Ragpickers', 3–11, 3.
78. Joshua Calhoun, *The Nature of the Page* (Philadelphia: University of Pennsylvania Press, 2020), 60.
79. Calhoun, *Nature of the Page*, 53.

80. Joshua Calhoun, 'The Word Made Flax: Cheap Bibles, Textual Corruption, and the Poetics of Paper', *PMLA* 126.2 (March 2011), 327–44, 332.
81. Calhoun, 'The Word Made Flax', 332.
82. In a discussion of future research trajectories at the end of a conference paper on paper making, Heather Woolf noted the rich possibilities of extending Calhoun's work to examine water composition of individual paper sheets: Heather Woolf 'Director's seminar – Heather Woolfe (Folger Library): "Papermakers and paper projects in Early Modern England, 1580–1640"', 9 March 2022.
83. Churchyard, *Sparke*, Sig.D4^r, Sig.D^r; for a discussion of paper's vulnerability to water and sea air, see Matthews, 'Maritime Ephemera', 177–9.
84. See Chapter 10 in this volume.
85. Michael Stolberg, 'Sweat: Learned Concepts and Popular Perceptions, 1500–1800', in *Blood Sweat and Tears*, 503.
86. For a discussion of the body and water, see Matthews, 'Inside Out and Outside In', 422.
87. For a discussion of my 'fluvial-methodology', see Matthews, *Habitat and Habitation* (forthcoming).
88. McRae argues that '[s]uch contested zones brought popular perceptions of circulation into collision with property-owner's assumptions of rights of containment and exclusion'; see *Literature and Domestic Travel*, 27.
89. Linton, 'Reading', 25.
90. McRae, *Literature and Domestic Travel*, 49.
91. Chen, 'Mapping', 276.

IV. Ecocritical Approaches

Chapter 10

'Insatiable [Gourmandize] Thus All Things Doth Devour': Reading the Threat of Human Greed along the Rivers of Early Modern England

Emily J. Naish

William Harrison's preface to the 1587 publication of Raphael Holinshed's *Chronicles* – titled, in this edition, 'A Description of Britain' – makes many apologies for its imperfections and the imperfections of its sources. Preceding the 'Description', his dedicatory letter to Sir William Brooke sees Harrison admitting the fact he has 'never travelled 40. miles foorthright and at one journey in all my life'.[1] Harrison must, therefore, make use of the sometimes less-than-perfect works of his predecessors, such as the manuscript notes of the Henrician antiquarian John Leland, which are 'utterlie mangled, defaced with wet and weather, and finallie unperfect through want of sundrie volumes'.[2] These apologies continue into the 'Description' itself: having dealt with the grand matters of England's history of invasion, religion, languages and giants, he expresses concern that the tract he produces is 'not correspondent to mine intent'.[3] He has neither the experience nor the sources to write as comprehensive a 'Description of Britain' as he has hoped. The anxiety about incompleteness leads Harrison to another apology as he begins to describe England's rivers:

> And even so it happeneth in this my tractation of waters, of whose heads, courses, length, bredth, depth of channel (for burden) ebs, flowings and falles, I had thought to have made a perfect description under the report also of an imagined course taken by them all.[4]

In his dissatisfaction with his own experience and his sources, Harrison produces two rivers. There is the (unattainable) 'perfect description', which attempts to lay out the course of English rivers accurately and comprehensively. Then there is the 'imagined course': the journey a writer must take when all knowledge (drawn either from personal experience or other manuscripts) fails.

Harrison's attempts at a 'perfect description' produce a journey along England's waterways that is not entirely smooth. His reader encounters many of the frustrations faced by those who relied upon unobstructed waterways around the country for their income, such as watermen. The reader travelling along these parts of the river runs into difficulties with certain human interventions: there might, for example, be tolls in place, producing a financial obstruction. But there are also parts of the river that suffer from too little human intervention: a lack of proper maintenance along the river leads waterways to become choked with weeds, sands and gravel. In the 'perfect description', such frustrating details paint a journey along the river that is far from idyllic; rather it is marred by the competing interests of watermen and landowners. However, for the most part, the topographical nature of Harrison's 'Description' results in what could be framed as the 'imagined course': a vision of English rivers that move freely through the land without either physical or financial blockage. The text flows freely where the water may not.[5]

It is the 'perfect description' and the 'imagined course' – and writing and cartography that moves between them – with which this chapter is concerned. Using the framework of ecocriticism, it aims to understand poetic and cartographic depictions of rivers that elude the frustrations of everyday water travel: what can these falsely free-flowing rivers tell us about the early modern relationship to the natural world? The chapter is structured in three parts. It begins with an outline of the socio-economic contexts within which these representations of rivers were produced. Rivers – in providing fresh water and fish, and in enabling mobility around the country and overseas – represented many anthropocentric opportunities. However, there were often frustrations: not only the physical and financial blockages that appeared along the river (outlined briefly above), but also the threat of burst banks. Flooding (fuelled by the biblical associations) provided a vividly unnerving image in the early modern imagination, leading to understandable nervousness about overflow. The chapter will then turn to early seventeenth-century river poetry, homing in on a comparative study between Michael Drayton's *Poly-Olbion* (1612 and 1622) and *Taylor on Tame Isis* (1632) by John Taylor (1578–1653), waterman and self-titled 'Water Poet'. The chapter will consider the ways in which Drayton's poetry seemingly ignores the grievances of watermen such as Taylor, and instead excitedly celebrates the many opportunities that the river could offer. However, *Poly-Olbion* is comprised of more than just Drayton's poetry: there are also cartographic etchings by William Hole and explanatory notes (called 'Illustrations') by John Selden. In the final section of this chapter, I will focus on Hole's etchings, which appear to expose anxieties about the destructive potential of overflowing water. This will lead to a conclusion that considers the reasons for this mesh of celebration and anxiety: the river represented potential for human expansion; however, there are moments where these early modern writers reconfigure the human relationship to the river, understanding the devastating impact of greed and excess.

The centrality of the river to urban life in sixteenth-century England is illustrated well by the London-esque capital city of Amaurot in Thomas More's *Utopia* (1516). Amaurot, the 'most worthy of all' the Utopian cities, has been built around a stretch of the Anider, a river whose source lies eighty miles above Amaurot, and which flows right to the sea.[6] The Anider, Hythloday explains, brings a constant supply of fresh water to the city: the tide flows in every six hours, bringing an influx of 'brackish' salt-water; this drives fresh water further along the river to where the city lies; and as the tide withdraws, the whole river is once again fresh.[7] There is a second river, whose spring arises within the city: should Amaurot be besieged and Anider's source be poisoned, the citizens still have access to clean water from this second river. Those citizens whose houses are far from the second river have cisterns to collect rainwater. Every inhabitant thus has easy access to clean, fresh water, even during times of war. The river also does not present an obstacle to the citizens: there is a stone bridge connecting one bank to the other, enabling movement between each side. And this bridge does not prevent incoming sea-ships from reaching the heart of the city, as it lies at the furthest point from the river's mouth. The river is depicted as even more central in Ambrosius Holbein's visual representation of the city. Holbein depicts Utopia as a circular island with the river curving round in a circle so that it runs through every city. At the base of the island, the cyclical river is interrupted by an estuary, where river becomes sea. The only key feature missing from Holbein's representation is the bridge that allows Amaurot's inhabitants to cross from one side to the other. This is perhaps omitted to better portray his *memento mori*: shaped this way, the island forms a skull.[8] The easily accessible flow of water is essential to the ideal Amaurot's success as a capital city. This is, most directly, because it ensures fresh water – to drink, wash and cook – for all citizens. But, for the purpose of this chapter, I want to focus on the benefit of mobility, both within the city and further afield. The river enables the movement of trade between Amaurot and other cities of the same nation, exploration of new lands via access to the sea, and (thanks to the bridge) it does not restrict the movement of the inhabitants around the city. More, in writing his Utopian capital as dependent on (and built around) a free-flowing river, recognises its role in stimulating urban development via the movement of goods and people.

Like its imagined offspring, the sixteenth-century River Thames enabled mobility within London and to other English counties, whilst also connecting the city to countries overseas. Within London, the two halves of the city were connected by London Bridge, which, according to Harrison, was 'the most chieflie to be commended' of all the bridges along the course of the Thames.[9] Harrison's reasons for commendation are both architectural and economic. The bridge was imposingly large ('three scorefoot in heigth' with the arches 'full twentie in distance one from another') and impressively built ('situat upon twentie arches', each made of 'excellent free squared stone').[10] Of greater significance to the everyday Londoner, the bridge provided free movement across the river as 'a co[n]tinuall street, well replenished with large and statelie houses on both sides'.[11] This movement was, as we saw in *Utopia*, seen to be crucial for a developing urban economy, and these 'large and statelie houses' were predominantly occupied by shops, further contributing to the city's wealth.[12] Amidst all these successes, however, the real-life London Bridge was not quite as perfect as the Amaurot bridge: being so far downstream it presented a hindrance to shipping and consequently trade. More, in fact, alters the position of the Utopian bridge, placing it further inland, making it less disruptive.[13]

Nonetheless, the Thames bustled with boats. The Agas map (c. 1561) depicts a great range of vessels going both across and along the river, a detail captured on the map as they are steered in different directions.[14] To the west of the bridge, there are mostly smaller crafts, navigated by a waterman transporting either one or two passengers or occasionally some goods. Harrison suggests there are as many as 2,000 of these 'wherries and small boats, wherby three thousand poore watermen are mainteined'.[15] These boats represent another option for travelling around London and, simultaneously, an income for the watermen.

Looking again at the Agas map but now to the east of London Bridge, we find grander sea-going ships, sails billowing in the wind and apparently ready for their journey. Harrison does not make reference to ships going overseas (nor the problem of the bridge obstructing trade); however, he does describe 'huge tideboats, tiltbotes, and barges, which either carrie passengers, or bring necessarie provision from all quarters of Oxfordshire, Barkeshire, Buckinghamshire, Bedfordshire, Herfordshire, Midlesex, Essex, Surrie, and Kent, unto the citie of London'.[16] Whilst the wherries provide transport around the city, these bigger boats arrive in from other counties from both the east and the west, bringing in people, along with goods that cannot be produced locally, the perfect stimulant for a thriving market economy. Such movement would not be possible without the river: it has been estimated that water transport was more than ten times cheaper than that by land.[17] Without the river, the city would not have been able to thrive in the way it did, either in terms of its wealth or its population. It is no wonder that the sixteenth-century capital clusters around the central flowing water.

Outside of the city, the river provided additional benefits in the form of an 'aboundance of all kind of fish'.[18] Fish – that could be caught in the river, but also in the fens and at sea – were a vital part of the early modern economy.[19] They could be sold at the market, and were thus a source of income, but they were also a staple part of the early modern diet.[20] Harrison suggests that without access to fishing, 'manie a poore man' would become 'undone'.[21] As well as providing food and income for England's poor, the seventeenth century saw writers – in particular, John Dennys (d. 1609) and Izaak Walton (1593–1683) – begin to praise angling as a recreational activity. Fish are, of course, a central motif in Christian symbolism, and angling is, by its nature, a quiet and contemplative sport: it was thus argued that the activity could bring men closer to God.[22] The Thames of Harrison's 'Description' therefore appears very attractive indeed for all manner of people: there is a great variety of fish, including 'fat and sweet salmons', as well as 'barbels, trouts, chevins, pearches, smelts, breames, roches, daces, grudgings, flounders, shrimps, [e]tc'.[23] There are in fact so many fish that Harrison goes on to suggest that 'this famous river complaineth commanlie of no want, but the more it looseth at one time, the more it yeeldeth at another'.[24] The river, it seems, will always provide more.

The only fish in the Thames that is in short supply is the carp:

> Onelie in carps it seemeth to be scant, sith it was not long since that kind of fish was brought over into England, and but of late to speak of into this streame, by the violent rage of sundrie landflouds, that brake open the heads and dams of divers gentlemens ponds, by which means it became somewhat partaker also of this said commoditie, whereof earst it had no portion that I could ever heare.[25]

Carp – a foreign species to England, likely introduced around the late fourteenth or early fifteenth century – were, by the end of the sixteenth century, a particularly popular fish, bred in artificial ponds on the estates of landed gentry.[26] Husbandry manuals, such as Richard Surfleet's translation of *Maison rustique, or, The country farme* (1600), encouraged the creation of such ponds: the 'good householder', *Maison rustique* suggests, 'shall not esteeme a little of Fish, seeing that of them he may make both provision for his table, and great gaine unto his purse'.[27] This endorsement of fishponds is followed by extensive advice on proper maintenance to ensure fish would stay alive and continue to breed, and to ensure the pond did not dry up.[28] However, water did not always behave as expected. Returning to Harrison, we find the water has surged, causing the ponds to overflow. And as the water from the artificial ponds poured into the Thames, so did the carp, causing gentlemen to lose the commodities they had attempted to introduce. This demonstrates one way in which human attempts to impose will over nature could go awry: exploitation of the river could result in unforeseen consequences.

This experience of small-scale overflow was clearly frustrating for the pond owners; however, tidal surges (vividly described by Harrison as 'the violent rage of sundrie landflouds') could become something rather more fearful. In the following paragraph, Harrison describes the 'daily triall, that each tide is not of equall heigth and greatnesse' on account of the changes of the moon.[29] Indeed, the river might rise so significantly that 'the Thames overfloweth hir banks neere unto London', particularly in the winter months of January and February.[30] Such larger surges could be worsened by 'some rough winds out of the west or southwest' or perhaps 'some other extraordinarie occasion'.[31] In these cases, the effect could be catastrophic. On the morning of 30 January 1607, the southwest of England and Wales suffered what has been named the worst flooding in the history of Britain, as a huge surge of both salt and freshwater along the Bristol Channel and the lower River Severn caused flood defences in five counties (Devon, Somerset, Gloucestershire, Glamorgan and Monmouthshire) to burst.[32] The affected area spanned 570 km of coastline, and 2,000 human lives were recorded as lost, along with the lives of thousands of farm animals.[33] For the god-fearing early modern population, such extreme flooding recalled the biblical flood, as revealed by a flurry of pamphlets produced in the wake of the event. Images such as the frontispiece of *A true report of Certaine wonderfull overflowings of water* (see Figure 10.1) demonstrate the profound anxiety caused by flooding, as well as highlighting what is lost: human lives of course; animal lives (and therefore food and milk for consumption and wool for trade); as well as material possessions such as homes.[34] Perhaps most importantly of all, the church is lost to the flood, with only its steeple emerging from the waters. In another pamphlet, the flood was framed as 'God's warning to his people'.[35] Interventions put in place by landed gentry would not cause such extreme flooding; however, it is unsurprising that Harrison frames the overflowing ponds with some nervousness. These smaller floods could perhaps be seen as echoes of those that are more destructive and damning.

Flooding was not the only source of discontent along the river. Harrison describes how the river has become 'choked of late with sands

'Insatiable [Gourmandize] Thus All Things Doth Devour' 217

Figure 10.1 Frontispiece to William Iaggard's *A true report of Certaine wonderfull overflowings of water* (1607). © British Library Board 1103.e.58.

and shelves, through the penning and wresting of the course of the water for commodities sake': both activities required to establish a fishpond.[36] This problem is, Harrison suggests, 'easilie remedied, if good order were taken for the redresse thereof': the river simply requires some maintenance to keep it flowing freely, although Harrison's complaint suggests maintenance was not being done.[37] A more difficult issue to resolve was that of financial blockages, in the form of 'the fine or paie set upon the ballasse', or even temporal blockages.[38] On arrival at a weir, for example – built by a mill-owner to aid the milling of grain – a waterman could be forced to wait for days before the miller would release water, allowing the boat passage (for a more detailed discussion of conflicts between watermen and mill-owners, see Chapter 9).[39] The interests of landowners thus conflicted with the needs of watermen travelling around the country, making the transport of goods via the river more difficult.

From this one compact passage about the Thames, we can see that rivers represented many things to many people: they enabled mobility around the city of London and to other parts of the country; the rivers themselves held fish for consumption and sale at the market; angling was growing as a recreational activity; and, for the enterprising landlord, they represented an opportunity to create additional income through the collection of tolls. However, these various competing interests around the river had the potential to clash: the mobility of the watermen (and, by extension, the goods they transported along the river) could be hindered by the economic expansions of landowners, and vice versa. Similarly, a *lack* of human intervention could also create a blockage through a build-up of sand and weeds. On the other hand, human interventions on the river could impact the environment, as attempts to redirect water resulted in overflowing banks. It is little wonder, then, that the river – with all its exciting opportunity for development, as well as its different frustrations – was such a rich spring for the imagination of the early modern poet.

The opportunity for economic development along the river translates into buoyant optimism in much sixteenth- and seventeenth-century poetry. Taking what we can frame as the 'imagined course', rivers become celebrated figurative representations. Leland's *Cygnea Cantio* (1545) takes on the voice of a dying swan, who uses its last journey along the Thames to highlight the impressive development along the river's banks and the accomplishments of Henry VIII. For Edmund Spenser (and other Tudor poets), the joining of rivers could result in marriage: river marriages appear in three of Spenser's poems, namely *Colin Clout Comes Home Againe* (1595), Book IV of the *Faerie Queene* (1596) and the posthumously printed *Mutabilitie Cantos* (1609).[40] In Ben Jonson's country-house poem 'To Penshurst' (1616), the willingness of nature to bend to the desires of humankind causes fish to swim into nets and leap onto land of their own accord. And Michael Drayton – in writing the poetic rivers of *Poly-Olbion* topographically, that is describing long courses of rivers across many counties – suggests a falsely smooth course for those travelling by water. These celebratory representations seem a world apart from the everyday frustrations and difficulties that Harrison so neatly highlights.

The poetry of John Taylor – a waterman by trade – stands somewhat apart from these representations.[41] Like his predecessors, Taylor's poetry has moments of buoyant optimism, highlighting the economic importance of the river in early modern England, for both rural productivity and urban development; however, far more frequently, Taylor uses his poetry to complain about the state of England's waterways. Taylor can be seen, like Harrison, to write two rivers: the idealistic imagined course, and the frustrating perfect description. This dichotomy is particularly stark in his 1632 *Taylor on Tame Isis*. Taylor begins this poem by taking a topographic approach to describe the course of the Isis (which later becomes the Thames) from its spring in the Gloucestershire Cotswolds right down to the Kent shore. Through this half, Taylor poetically swoops along the course of the river, eluding any complaints about choked waterways through the nature of his writing. And as he writes this topographical description, he paints a scene of thriving rural productivity that centres around the Isis, with mills, driven by the force of water, and large meadows, watered by the river.[42]

This idyllic vision of the river's course is only minorly disturbed as Taylor describes the course of the Tame. This journey is not so easy: Taylor writes that the stream progresses with 'strange meanders' and without any other 'Brooke or River waiting him upon'.[43] Unlike along the Isis, there are no references to milling, which is unsurprising: if we trace its course along satellite images, it is a comparatively minor stream. Taylor has referred to the rivers as male (the Tame) and female (the Isis) throughout the poem, but he draws more strongly on this anthropomorphism as the two rivers draw closer to one another: the Tame now begins 'Bewailing *Isis* absence, and his fate'.[44] Tame's grief comes to a crescendo of despair at the point of union:

Poore *Tame* all heauie and disconsolate,
Unnavigable, scorn'd, despis'd, disgrac'd,
Having in vaine so many paces pac'd;
Despairing and quite desperate with these harmes,
He hurles himselfe unwares in *Isis* armes.[45]

The union should be a happy one: Taylor depicts the confluence of the two rivers as a marriage of man and wife, with the Tame and the Isis being 'closer [than] the bark be to the tree / . . . / They rise and fall together'.[46] But despite their intimacy, the wedding is troubled: the Tame does not quietly join with his bride, but instead 'hurles himselfe unwares in *Isis* armes' as the river curves back on itself like an elongated and backwards S. The strange course of the river as it draws closer to Isis causes it to become 'unnavigable', and therefore 'scorn'd, despis'd, disgrac'd'. The unnavigability threatens the ideal of free-flowing water that Taylor has depicted. However, it does not last long: once the two rivers are joined together (and Tame has abandoned his 'strange meanders'), 'pleasantly the river takes free way'.[47] Taylor continues with his topographical approach as the river runs through London and to the coast.

This ripple of threat to Taylor's ideal of free-flowing rivers foreshadows that which causes him greater grief in the second half of the poem: the excess of human interventions along the Isis (see also Chapter 9). To explain why these interventions are so disruptive, Taylor first tells his reader about the wealth of reasons that free-flowing water is essential. This is something that he has already mentioned in passing when describing Gloucestershire's mills and meadows, but he now expands on the river's uses: the meadows feed the cattle, who in turn provide dairy products to feed people; the river is full of fish; other 'beasts' and 'fowles' breed along the banks; water ensures the growth of trees which provide fuel; there are even apparent medicinal benefits, with the river 'bear[ing] the lame and weake'; and breweries use water in the process of brewing beer.[48] And then there are those whose trade is directly linked to flowing water: seamen, navigators, fishers, bargemen and watermen (all positions that, whilst essential to the economy, were not respected in seventeenth-century society).[49] These tradesmen and their families, Taylor suggests, '[i]n number more than hundred thousands are, / Who doe their Prince and Country often serve'.[50] Without the free-flowing river, there are a great number of people, serving king and country, who 'might goe sterve [die]'.[51]

However, despite the importance of these tradesmen and their reliance on the river, there are, in Taylor's words, 'private persons [who] for their gainfull use, / Ingrosse the water and the land abuse'.[52] London, in Taylor's view, is not too problematic. The stretch of river that causes him the most grief requires us to travel back upstream, past the meeting of Tame and Isis, to a strip of river running two miles from Oxford to Iffley (a small village in Oxfordshire). Along this short stretch of water, Taylor comes across constant obstructions:

> And there a new turne pike doth stand amisse,
> Another stands at *Stanford*, below that,
> Weeds, shelves, and shoals all waterlesse and flat;
> At *Newnham* lock there's plac'd a fishing weare,
> A gravell hill too high, scarce water there;
> At *Abington* the shoales are worse and worse,
> That *Swift ditch* seemes to be the better course,
> Below which towne near *Sutton* there are left
> Piles that almost our Barges bottome cleft;
> Then *Sutton* locks are great impediments,
> The waters fall with such great violence,
> Thence down to *Cullom*, streame runs quicke and quicke
> Yet we rub'd twice a ground for want of liquor.
> The Weare of *Carpenter's* sans fault I thinke,
> But yet neare *Witnum* towne a tree did sinke,
> Whereas by fortune we our Barge did hit,
> And by misfortune there a board was split.[53]

The complaints continue over several pages in much the same vein. There are some sections of water, such as the 'Weare of *Carpenter*', that are not too troublesome, but for the most part, the journey along is depicted as difficult for both watermen and their boats. There are three complaints that stand out. There are 'weeds, shelves, and shoals', which damage Taylor's boat, even causing a split board. Then there are turnpikes that 'stand amisse', which result in the collection of tolls. And finally, there are locks that should make the river more navigable, but at Sutton, in fact they cause the 'waters [to] fall with such great violence'. Taylor comes to a concluding question: 'Shall *Thames* be barr'd its course . . . / To spoile a publike for a private Trade?'[54] The cause of the public is frustrated by individual greed. The poem ends with a call for improvements along the river. Here, the language becomes damning: 'Shame fall the doers, and Almighties blessing / Be heap'd upon their heads that seeke redressing'.[55] The needs of the public simply must be prioritised over individual expansion.

For Taylor, then, the main trouble that people might encounter in relation to the river is obstruction, most literally of the flow of water, and (in turn) of trade and the livelihoods of many English workers. We might then expect *Poly-Olbion* – attuned, as it is, to contemporary issues relating to the natural world, and yearning, as it does, for a lost golden age – to make similar complaints about the state of England's waterways.[56] However, Drayton's waterways run free: there is, in fact, no mention of obstruction, either along the course of the Thames or through the rest of the poem. Like the first half of *Taylor on Tame Isis*, Drayton's topographic rivers are described as if traced along a map. Indeed, far from obstructing movement as in Taylor's poetry, the rivers provide a navigational route for Drayton's Muse. At the beginning of the poem, before she begins her arduous journey through England and Wales, the Muse is seen 'hovering while she hung / Upon the Celtick wastes'.[57] The description stays focused on the coastline until the Muse climbs to the clifftops, where

> her selfe she firmlie sets
> The Bourns, the Brooks, the Becks, the Rills, the Rivilets,
> Exactlie to derive.[58]

This attention to the edge of the land suggests that she waits for her entry into England to be granted. Yet from the clifftop, she can observe 'The Bourns, the Brooks, the Becks, the Rills, the Rivilets', all words that can be defined as brooks or streams. It is this network of waterways that allow her to derive: to 'derive' here means 'to conduct (a stream of water or other fluid) *from* a source, reservoir, main stream, etc. *to* or *into* a channel, place, or destination'.[59] The water, it seems, will let her into and through the land. She is able to enter when the sea (given the epithet of Neptune) comes 'cutting in' to the land, thus beginning her journey through Cornwall.[60] As the Muse continues, the rivers are so prominent that they cannot be ignored: she follows the Camel, then the Tamar with its various tributaries, the Dart, and finally the Exe. And it is because of the rivers that the Muse is conducted through the first song.

Throughout the poem, the rivers are a thread of navigation and connectivity for the Muse (and the reader). The River Avon, associated as it is with the Bristol area, appears first in the third song; however, it later makes appearances in the fourth, ninth, twelfth, thirteenth and fourteenth songs as it flows through Wales and the nearby counties of Staffordshire, Warwickshire and Gloucestershire. The same can be said for the Severn: the river divides Bristol and Wales, yet also appears in the fourteenth song as the Muse leaves Wales and enters Gloucestershire. This easy spanning across songs and county borders suggests a journey that is very different from that which we took with the real-life waterman Taylor.

This broad topographical approach to describing the course of a river, as we saw earlier, is one that Taylor also takes in the first half of *Taylor on Tame Isis*. But in *Poly-Olbion*, as we home in on the same stretch of water that so troubles Taylor, we find a rather different representation of the river. There are some points of comparison, particularly in the use of literary devices, namely prosopopoeia and the river marriage metaphor. However, the effect is completely contrasting: whilst Taylor's description of the winding Tame and the obstructions along Isis is a source of complaint, Drayton continually finds cause for celebration along the course of both rivers.

The entirety of the fifteenth song anticipates the forthcoming marriage of the two rivers: Drayton flits between describing the course of each river, before poetically marrying the pair towards the close of the song. The celebratory tone is set in the opening lines: 'Now Fame had through this Ile divulg'd, in every eare, / The long-expected day of Mariage to be neere'.[61] The excitement about the nuptials appears to have rippled throughout England: 'every eare' has heard the good news. There are two causes for this celebration along the rivers. Drayton, like Taylor, celebrates the role of the rivers in rural productivity: the course of Tame produces 'soyle throughout so sure', and, as a result, good grain and well-fed sheep.[62] The agricultural benefits of both the Tame and the Isis are mentioned again later in the song, but only briefly: what is more pervasive is Drayton's other source of celebration, namely his appreciation for the aesthetic value of the two rivers. As Drayton again praises the agricultural benefits provided by the Tame, he also describes the flowers along its bank: the manly Tame

> Should not be drest with Flowers, to Gardens that belong
> (His Bride that better fitte) but onely such as sprong
> From the replenisht Meads, and fruitfull Pastures neere.[63]

Drayton proceeds to name these flowers: there are primroses, the 'azur'd Hare-bell', whose 'lushious smell' is intermingled with 'Woodbind' (or honeysuckle), lilies and daffodils.[64] Then, '[t]o sort these Flowers of showe, with th'other that were sweet', there are cowslips, oxlips, columbines, 'yellow King-cup' (marsh-marigolds), crow-flowers, 'Clover-flower' and daisies.[65] These are, as Drayton acknowledges, not flowers that we expect to find beautiful. Yet here, the many different colours mingle with the 'lushious smell' that Drayton describes, providing a glut of sensory imagery. The fields surrounding Tame may be agriculturally essential, but, for Drayton, their beauty is an even greater triumph.

The banks of the Isis are similarly described as adorned with many heavily scented flowers; however, here I want to focus on Drayton's description of the movement of the water. The river '[c]omes tripping with delight, downe from her daintier Springs'.[66] To trip, in its older sense, is to 'move lightly and nimbly on the feet; to skip, caper; to dance'.[67] Applied to the river, the tripping could be problematic: it perhaps suggests the water moves quickly or unpredictably. Yet Drayton's anthropomorphism of the river (unlike Taylor) provides good reason for the river's speed: why should she not be 'trip with delight' on her wedding day? The speed of the water is mentioned again as 'From *Oxford*, *Isis* hasts more speedily, to see / That River like his birth might entertained bee'.[68] But, again, this passes without any frustration: in fact, the increased speed after Oxford appears counter to Taylor's description, where the river becomes excessively choked. The speed of the river is not mentioned again, not even as the Tame curves strangely around just prior to the union. Instead, quite contrary to Taylor's description of the meandering Tame, as the two rivers are finally wed, 'wise Charwell here was thought / The first to cheare the guests'.[69] This summarises Drayton's depiction of this stretch of river, and indeed of many of *Poly-Olbion*'s other rivers: there is much that should be celebrated.

However, whilst Drayton's poetic rivers are written in this celebratory tone, when we look at the cartographic etchings by William Hole, there appears to be some anxiety. The anxiety here is not about obstruction; rather the rivers seem ready to overflow onto the land. As in the poetry, the etched rivers are unignorably prominent, as even minor streams and tributaries are mapped out with overt and decisive lines. The cartographic etching for the eighteenth song, which focuses on Kent, provides a good example of this: small streams begin to look like fractures in the land. By the nature of being wider, the larger rivers in the north of Kent, such as the Thames and Medway, become more disquieting. In counties such as Cambridgeshire, represented in the twenty-first song, the multitude of rivers that flow through the land look particularly dramatic, and the county appears riven by these different streams. The rivers perhaps even seem threatening, as though the water might spill onto the land.

As we return to the confluence of the Tame and the Isis (now paying attention to Hole's etching; see Figure 10.2), the nymphs have, in fact, come out of the river to celebrate the wedding on land. This is unusual: the nymphs are normally confined to their respective river, stream or forest. Granted, the celebration is not represented in very watery terms: two of the nymphs scatter leaves and petals across the ground (which do somewhat resemble droplets of water); another pair makes garlands from the riverside flowers; and, of course, there is music and dancing, as the new couple watches the festivities unfold. But these are still river nymphs breaking out of their usual habitat and making use of the surrounding plains. The water is no longer threatening to overflow: it appears to have actually happened.[70]

As the water reaches the coast, the tearing effect on the cartographic etchings only intensifies further. On the east coast, the river mouths become so wide that the land seems to fray at its seams. There is potential to read these gaping river mouths within the contexts of the history of invasion that Harrison covers in his 'Description': the wide river mouths could be read as inviting foreign raiders.[71] It is through an opening in the land, of course, that Drayton's Muse enters the coast, and whilst she may be a friendly presence, those with nefarious intentions could do the

'Insatiable [Gourmandize] Thus All Things Doth Devour' 225

Figure 10.2 Cartographic etching for Song 15 of Michael Drayton's *Poly-Olbion* (1612/1622). Image used courtesy of the University of Sheffield Library, Special Collections and Archives.

same. But as well as attacks and invasions from other countries, it seems as though the land and the sea are at war, and perhaps here the water might win. This idea is one that Drayton also presents in the poem: the sea is repeatedly given the epithet of 'Neptune', the violent Roman god of the seas, and at times his behaviour becomes rapacious.[72] Read alongside these frayed edges of the landscape, the anxiety only seems to worsen.

In examining *Poly-Olbion* as a collaborative work (comprised of a long poem, cartographic etchings and illustrative notes), the largely celebratory nature of Drayton's rivers is complexified. The rivers may be both beautiful and essential to agricultural productivity; however, as we look at the etchings, we are reminded of the threatening undercurrent of potential destruction. We might ask why Drayton himself did not make an open complaint against human interventions or the lack thereof on the river: he was certainly not shy about entering into contemporary socio-economic debates, as demonstrated in his poetic handling of England's forests.[73] One simple answer might be that *Poly-Olbion* (which Drayton began writing in the 1590s) was being produced a good four decades before *Taylor on Tame Isis*: it could be there were simply fewer blockages.[74] However, if we read *Poly-Olbion* within the framework of ecocriticism, it does seem particularly fitting that Drayton would give less attention to the plight of the human waterman, with greater concern directed at the damage caused to the natural world. Concern about the coastline – ruled, in *Poly-Olbion*, by the tyrannical Neptune – is not unique to Drayton: the metaphor of an appetitive sea eating away at the coastline is also used by Spenser and Shakespeare.[75] Overflowing rivers, however, are more unusual, making Hole's cartographic etchings particularly compelling. These seem to suggest an atypical nervousness about rivers that could – as the nymphs do in song fifteen's etching – burst free. Nature does not always behave in accordance with humanity's expectations or desires, and therefore humankind cannot always control nature.

Despite their differences, a thread of human greed runs through all three works examined in this chapter, and (following this thread) we can return to Drayton's poetry where we find a particularly poignant concern about England's rivers. The forests – while lamenting the increased deforestation in England – turn to the rivers to give a word of warning:

> How happie floods are yee,
> From our predestin'd plagues that priviledged bee;
> Which onelie with the fish which in your banks doe breed,
> And dailie there increase, mans gurmandize [greed] can feed?
> But had this wretched Age such uses to imploy
> Your waters, as the woods we latelie did enjoy,
> Your channels they would leave as barren by their spoile,
> As they of all our trees have lastlie left our soile.[76]

Nestled amidst the many celebratory lines about England's rivers, this warning is jarring. But perhaps it is unsurprising in the face of insatiable human greed: after all, it is human greed that caused Taylor so much grief; it is human greed that causes fishponds to burst their banks; and here, it is human greed that threatens the river's endless yield of fish. The threat never quite materialises within *Poly-Olbion*: as in Harrison's description of the Thames, the supply of fish is thought to be boundless. However, in the next line, the warning comes again: 'Insatiable Time thus all things doth devour: / What ever saw the sunne, that is not in Times power?'[77] The trees ultimately conclude that the rivers will 'out-liv[e] manie a day', but the conclusion rings somewhat hollow: how could the rivers be the only part of the landscape to escape 'Insatiable Time', or, indeed, humankind's insatiable gourmandize?[78]

The assurance that the rivers will continually yield more fish seems even more unbelievable when read alongside Taylor and Harrison: although Harrison does suggest the supply of fish is endless, he also references the 'insatiable avarice of the fishermen'.[79] And when we take into account Hole's etchings, the warning seems even more pressing: the nymphs that represent the natural world, in their excitement about the wedding nuptials, become unruly. The unpredictability of nature in the face of the insatiability of human greed begins to seem particularly sinister, and an ecocritical reading of all three works reveals the ways in which greed and excess wreak havoc on England's rivers, threatening to leave 'barren' that which was the cause for so much celebration.

Notes

1. Raphael Holinshed, *The First and Second volumes of Chronicles* (London, 1587), fol. 2r. All references are to this edition.
2. Ibid., fol. 2v.
3. Ibid., 45.
4. Ibid.
5. Andrew McRae, 'Fluvial Nation: Rivers, Mobility and Poetry in Early Modern England', *English Literary Renaissance* 38.3 (2008), 506–34, 511.
6. Thomas More, *Utopia*, ed. by George M. Logan, trans. by Robert M. Adams, 3rd edn (Cambridge: Cambridge University Press, 2016; 7th repr. 2022), 47.
7. Ibid.
8. Malcolm Bishop, 'Ambrosius Holbein's Memento Mori Map for Sir Thomas More's *Utopia*: The Meanings of a Masterpiece of Early Sixteenth Century Graphic Art', *British Dental Journal* 199.2 (2005), 107–12, 108.
9. Holinshed, *The First and Second volumes of Chronicles*, 47.
10. Ibid.
11. Ibid.
12. Walter Besant, *The History of London* (London: Longmans, Green, and Co. 1893), 57–8.
13. Sarah Rees Jones, 'Thomas More's "Utopia" and Medieval London', in *Pragmatic Utopias: Ideals and Communities 1200–1630*, ed. Rosemary Horrox and Sarah Rees Jones (Cambridge: Cambridge University Press, 2004), 117–35, 124–5.
14. Janelle Jenstad et al., *The Agas Map*, digital reproduction of *Civitas Londinum* (c. 1561), Map of Early Modern London, https://mapoflondon.uvic.ca/agas.htm (last accessed 17 August 2022).

15. Holinshed, *The First and Second volumes of Chronicles*, 47.
16. Ibid.
17. Evan T. Jones, 'River Navigation in Medieval England', *Journal of Historical Geography* 26.1 (2000), 60–82, 61.
18. Holinshed, *The First and Second volumes of Chronicles*, 46.
19. Andrew Hadfield, 'Drayton's Fish', in *Poly-Olbion: New Perspectives*, ed. Andrew McRae and Philip Schwyzer (Martlesham: Boydell & Brewer, 2020), 112–31, 113.
20. Whilst the sale of corn and cattle by far dominated the sixteenth-century market, 'thirty or more' market towns specialised in the sale of fish: see Joan Thirsk, *The Agrarian History of England and Wales, 1500–1640*, 8 vols (Cambridge: Cambridge University Press, 1985), IV, 495. For the importance of fish as a foodstuff see Julie Sanders, *The Cultural Geography of Early Modern Drama, 1620–1650* (Cambridge: Cambridge University Press, 2011), 55–6.
21. Holinshed, *The First and Second volumes of Chronicles*, 46.
22. Hadfield, 'Drayton's Fish', 118.
23. Holinshed, *The First and Second volumes of Chronicles*, 46.
24. Ibid.
25. Ibid.
26. Christopher K. Currie, 'The Early History of the Carp and Its Economic Significance in England', *The Agricultural History Review* 39.2 (1991), 97–107, 101–3.
27. Charles Stevens and John Liebault, *Maison rustique, or, The countrey farme*, translated by Richard Surfleet (London, 1616), 505.
28. Ibid., 508–9.
29. Holinshed, *The First and Second volumes of Chronicles*, 46.
30. Ibid., 46–7.
31. Ibid., 47.
32. John Emrys Morgan, 'Understanding Flooding in Early Modern England', *Journal of Historical Geography* 50 (2015), 37–50, 37; Kevin Horsburgh and Matt Horritt, 'The Bristol Channel Floods of 1607 – Reconstruction and Analysis', *Weather* 61.10 (2006), 272–7, 272.
33. Edward A. Bryant and Simon K. Haslett, 'Catastrophic Wave Erosion, Bristol Channel, United Kingdom: Impact of Tsunami?', *The Journal of Geology* 115.3 (May 2007), 253–69, 254–5.
34. See William Iaggard, *A true report of Certaine wonderfull overflowings of water* (London, 1607).
35. William Jones, *Gods warning to his people of England* (London, 1607).
36. Holinshed, *The First and Second volumes of Chronicles*, 46. To pen a river is 'to dam [it] up', whilst to wrest its course refers to forcing a change of the water's direction. See *OED*, 'Penning', v. 1, 3.; *OED*, 'Wrest', v. There is not a specific river-related definition, but meanings often refer to some means of force (I. 1. a; I. 1. c; 2. a.), and always to a change of direction, literally or figuratively.
37. Holinshed, *The First and Second volumes of Chronicles*, 46.
38. Ibid.
39. Charles Hadfield, *British Canals: An Illustrated History*, 5th edn (London: David & Charles, 1974), 18–20.

40. Jack B. Oruch, 'Spenser, Camden, and the Poetic Marriages of Rivers', *Studies in Philology* 64.4 (1967), 606–24.
41. Taylor was not the only waterman-poet (another such poet was the late sixteenth-century John Byshop). However, Taylor has become the most famous. For an examination of Byshop's poetry, see McRae, 'Fluvial Nation', 518–19 and Chapter 9 of this volume.
42. John Taylor, *Taylor on Tame Isis* (London, 1632), fol. 5v. See also Chapter 7, in which Bill Angus discusses Taylor's depictions of flow in relation to ale.
43. Taylor, *Taylor on Tame Isis*, fol. 6r.
44. Ibid.
45. Ibid., fol. 6r–6v.
46. Ibid., fol. 6v.
47. Ibid., fol. 7r.
48. Ibid., fol. 8r–8v.
49. Taylor complains of 'unlawful abuses' against watermen following his poem: ibid., fol. 14v.
50. Ibid., fol. 8v.
51. Ibid.
52. Ibid.
53. Ibid., fol. 9r.
54. Ibid., fol. 13v.
55. Ibid.
56. For *Poly-Olbion*'s attention to contemporary environmental issues, see esp. Todd Borlik, *Ecocriticism and Early Modern Literature: Green Pastures* (New York: Routledge, 2011), 75–104; Andrew McRae, 'Tree-Felling in Early Modern England: Michael Drayton's Environmentalism', *The Review of English Studies* 63.260 (2012), 410–30; Sukanya Dasgupta, 'Drayton's "Silent Spring": *Poly-Olbion* and the Politics of Landscape', *The Cambridge Quarterly* 39.2 (2010), 152–71. For *Poly-Olbion*'s perceived nostalgia, see Clare McEachern, *The Poetics of English Nationhood, 1590–1612* (Cambridge: Cambridge University Press, 1996), 138.
57. *The Works of Michael Drayton*, ed. by J. William Hebel, 5 vols (Oxford: Shakespeare Head Press, 1931–41), II.1.43–4.
58. Ibid., II.1.77–9.
59. *OED*, 'Derive', v. I. 1. a.
60. Drayton, *The Works of Michael Drayton*, II.1.81.
61. Ibid., II.15.1–2.
62. Ibid., II.15.35; 15.37.
63. Ibid., II.15.145–7.
64. Ibid., II.15.149–54.
65. Ibid., II.15.155–62.
66. Ibid., II.15.67.
67. *OED*, 'Trip', v. I. 1. a.
68. Drayton, *The Works of Michael Drayton*, II.15.119–20.
69. Ibid., II.15.209–10.
70. See Sharon Garner, 'Curls to Curled Waves: Romance and Ecomaterial Assemblages in Michael Drayton's *Poly-Olbion*', in McRae and Schwyzer, *Poly-Olbion*, 132–44. Garner follows an ecomaterial approach to examine

the agency of *Poly-Olbion*'s non-human elements, tracing the ways in which history physically impacts the landscape within the poem. Garner's approach could be applied here: the narrative of the river marriage causes the nymphs in Hole's etchings to encroach onto the land.

71. Holinshed, *The First and Second volumes of Chronicles*, 5–8.
72. Drayton, *The Works of Michael Drayton*, 2.87–95. See also Bernhard Klein, 'Maritime Olbion; Or, "*th'Oceans Island*"', in McRae and Schwyzer, *Poly-Olbion*, 145–65.
73. See McRae, 'Tree-Felling in Early Modern England'.
74. See Jones, 'River Navigation'.
75. See Edmund Spenser, *Faerie Queene*, ed. by Thomas Roche, Jr and C. Patrick O'Donnell, Jr (London: Penguin Books, 1978; repr. in Penguin Classics, 1987), 5.2.30.4–5; William Shakespeare, *The Complete Sonnets and Poems*, ed. Colin Burrow (Oxford: Oxford University Press, 2002), 509: the ocean here is described as 'hungry'.
76. Drayton, *The Works of Michael Drayton*, 2.137–44.
77. Ibid., 2.145–6.
78. Ibid., 2.147. Andrew Hadfield discusses another moment in *Poly-Olbion* in which the lines 'hint at possible imbalance, the dangers of overfishing which have become so much more obvious in recent years' ('Drayton's Fish', 114; see also 126–8 for a discussion of the passage cited here).
79. Holinshed, *The First and Second volumes of Chronicles*, 46.

Chapter 11

Powtes, Protest and (Eco)politics in the English Fens
Esther Water

Wetlands have long been rendered in Western literary tradition as environments mired in malevolence. This environmental framing traces back to Dante's 1320 narrative poem *The Divine Comedy*, in which the marshy Styx 'ghast pool' forms part of Upper Hell.[1] In 1629, Queen Elizabeth I's archivist William Lambarde encouraged large-scale drainage of the East Anglian Fens due to what was in his eyes their hellish and repugnant nature. An influential tract written by a commentator titled only H.C., described the area as 'water putred and muddy, yea full of loathsome vermin; the earth, spuing, unfast and boggie'.[2] This view of the riverine Fens landscape as miasmic, rough and rude was also shared by an anonymous traveller who in 1635 described the fenlanders, as 'debauched, lazy and intemperate' and 'half fish, half flesh, for they drink like fishes, & sleep like hogs'.[3] What these views obscure is not only the biodiversity which formed a basis for the wealth and abundance of the watery Fens, but also the resilience of the fenlanders who maintained a livelihood and customary way of life for centuries that was directly twinned to the dynamic Fens wetland ecosystem.

From the late sixteenth century, pressure to instigate flood mitigation measures, in conjunction with a burgeoning view of the Fens as an untapped resource, led the English Crown to explore schemes for large-scale drainage of the Fens. The ensuing comprehensive control of the Fens would drastically alter the Fens landscape and significantly decrease the fenlanders' access to common resources which were critical to their survival. The resultant rebellion, rioting and general revolt by the fenlanders against the changes not only indicate the lengths to which the fenlanders would go to protect their livelihoods and Fens culture, but also signify a clash of ideologies between the fenlanders and the Crown. The satire *The Devil is an Ass* by Ben Jonson and the battle ballad 'The Powte's Complaint' by Penny of Wisbech are two texts which give insight into the perspective of those opposed to the Crown's proposals. The environmental and cultural battle over the Fens foregrounds contemporary disputes between modern states and local peoples and demonstrates the longevity of some of the ideological positions held.

Encompassing an area of 3,850 square km, the Fens are situated between East Anglia and the eastern Midlands and arc around the Wash, a large, coastal bay on the east coast of England. The term 'fen' refers to an inland, minerotrophic freshwater wetland comprised of peat, while a coastal wetland of marine silt is a marsh: collectively these are commonly referred to as 'the Fens'.[4] The low-lying landscape of the Fens creates a natural basin and therefore the Fens play a central role in regulating the drainage of several major rivers in the region, including the Great Ouse, the Nene and the Welland. Viewed on a map, the many rivers and waterways of the Fens look like a vast, dendritic network of brilliant blue capillaries, whose role is to contain, absorb and slowly release water from regular flooding events. It is this absorptive capacity which gives the Fens its uniquely fluid and dynamic character. In turn, the riverine Fens system contributes to the ecological abundance and diversity of the Fens, which has enabled human occupation and use, in, or on the margins of, the Fens.

The Fens have been centres of human settlement for centuries, indicating the ability of fen-dwelling communities to adapt to their watery environment. Archaeological records show that settlement on the margins of the Fens dates back to the Bronze Age.[5] The Domesday survey of 1086 notes there were fifty villages close to the Wash, occupying the higher land in the silt marshes and by the fourteenth century the Fens was one of the most thriving and prosperous agricultural areas in England due partly to the lands in common contained within the Fens.[6] This long, interrelated history of occupation and use extends into the sixteenth and seventeenth centuries and suggests that regular flooding was accepted as a normal process and part of Fens life.[7] The inherent, fluid dynamism of the landscape was managed through small-scale, local flood management structures and schemes, alongside which customs developed to manage the inevitable changes that came with the regular inundations of water.

The flow and flux of water contributed to the rich ecological diversity and beauty of this riverine land and waterscape.[8] Michael Drayton's 1622 poem 'Holland Fen'[9] focuses on this through enumerating the abundance of species within the Fens. The poem, which sits within the Herculean topographical and chorographical poem *Poly-Olbion*, was in effect an environmental and cultural nationwide survey of England.[10] 'Holland Fen' provides a window into the ecological diversity of the Fens in the early modern period, and Drayton's concern for their destruction reveals an ecopolitical stance which permeates the text.[11]

For current-day Fens rewilders and conservationists, the poem provides a broad, indicative, baseline measure against which current biodiversity might be measured. Drayton wrote of

> My various Fleets for Fowl: O, who is he can tell
> The species that in me for multitudes excel!
> The Duck and Mallard first, the Falconer's only sport
> (Of River-flights the chief, so that all other sort
> They only Green-fowl term), in every Mere abound,
> That you would think they sat upon the very ground,
> Their numbers be so great, the waters covering quite,
> That raised, the spacious air is darkened with their flight. (51–8)[12]

The evocation of a wide-open sky, which is obscured from sight by numerous birds, gives contemporary readers an opportunity to imagine the abundance of green-fowl, which was the term for immature birds considered too young to hunt.[13] That a specific term existed for birds banned from being killed suggests an intimacy with the local environment and points to a set of customs that regulated the use of resources on the Fens. The meres, on which the birds lived, were also significant for their abundance of fish and eels, which provided a year-round food source for the fenlanders.[14] The natural occurrence of winter flooding contributed to the existence of the meres and to one of the early modern fenlanders' most valuable resources – an abundance of grass. When water overflowed the existing rivers and waterways, it left rich silt soil deposits which in turn fertilised the grass in 'common waste' areas and allowed for near year-round grazing of livestock such as cattle, sheep and horses in intercommon areas.[15] Resources for fuel and shelter were also harvested from the Fens. Reeds and sedge were cut for fuel or roof thatching, and peat was a valuable fuel source which could be used locally or sold.[16] The Fens then, provided a diverse array of seasonal resources and thus possibilities for fenlanders to exist in their environment. The uniqueness of this environment is evocatively celebrated by Drayton in 'Holland Fen':

> She by the Muse's aid shall happily reveal
> Her sundry sorts of Fowl, from whose abundance she,
> Above all other Tracts, may boast herself to be
> The Mistress, and (indeed) to sit without compare. (21–24)[17]

Trade with local and regional markets was a key aspect of fenlanders' livelihoods, and suggests their ability to look outwardly for opportunities to maintain their lives. The monasteries (established in the Fens from the eighth century) provided a local market for food and resources and the reliability of demand from large landowning monasteries was central to the medieval prosperity of the Fens.[18] The monasteries were also key players in early, local water management schemes. They undertook drainage projects to reclaim land, and then, in a bid to gain revenue, claimed tithes from local communities who were held responsible for maintaining the water management structures.[19] Records show the significance over time of the Fens rivers and waterways as conduits for travel. Prehistoric log boats (commonly dugout canoes from a single oak trunk) and sewn plank boats have been found at several wetland sites throughout the region.[20] Fenlanders regularly traded with urban centres, which demonstrates the way in which the local Fens economy was integrated within a broader national economy.[21] Despite exterior narratives which portrayed fenlanders living in extreme poverty and ill health, the Fens had one of the fastest-growing populations in the sixteenth century,[22] which suggests that fenlanders were able to adapt to variable ecological conditions.

Systems of customary practice, as noted in Drayton's 'Holland Fen', were key to the ongoing relationship between the Fens and fenlanders. Eric Ash notes that the socio-economic structure of Fens culture was based on a process called 'intercommoning' which generated elaborate customs for access and use within and between villages, particularly for communal 'common waste' areas, including the riverine commons.[23] In this way, the Fens' unique environment contributed to shaping the fenlander's culture. Ash argues that the ability to negotiate and compromise to maintain common livelihoods shows the historically cooperative nature of the fenlanders.[24] This, he notes, may have been compounded by the more equal distribution of wealth in the Fens, and less hierarchical social structure than that which existed in areas such as the Midlands, which practised more conventional forms of farming.[25] However, fenlander culture came under threat due to large-scale drainage and land reclamation plans promulgated by the Crown.

Existing local legal governance structures dating back to 1252 were also critical in mediating fenlanders patterns of use of the Fens, and indicate a historical level of support from the Crown for the fenlanders.[26] In 1258 Commissions of Sewers, which were quasi-legal bodies, were set up to manage disputes,[27] and in 1532, under King Henry VIII the Statute of Sewers further elaborated the power and responsibilities of the commissioners.[28] Commissioners were mostly wealthy local landowners and members of the sociopolitical elite, many of whom also served as justices of the peace and as members of Parliament.[29] Their role included conserving existing relationships and arrangements, which involved maintenance of the existing drainage network.[30] For women, access to the commons was particularly important for maintaining their livelihood resilience, which potentially explains women's significant role in protesting against changes to the commons.[31] The 1548 Fen Charter contained seventy-two articles which codified management of the commons and established that no foreigners could use the fen.[32] This can be seen as conferring rights to the fenlanders, and is also Crown acknowledgement of the unique relationship the fenlanders had with their local environment. The legal mechanisms also reflect the deeply embedded customary use protocols indicated in Drayton's 'Holland Fen', and thereby indicate a confluence between legal and customary frameworks. These were profoundly entrenched, leading to a sense of stability for the fendwellers. The plans for large-scale drainage and land reclamation ruptured these foundational rights and led to a sense of destabilisation. The anger that courses through the protest ballad 'Powtes Complaint' indicates the extent of reactions to the proposed changes.

From the 1540s, customary arrangements and relationships came under pressure through multiple, intersecting external factors. The dissolution of the monasteries under Henry VIII's Reformation after 1536 saw the monasteries' wealth transferred to the Crown, and formerly monastic land either granted to favourites or sold.[33] The creation of new ownership structures transformed patterns of use, with many landowners taking advantage of the social, economic and religious changes to enclose what was previously 'common' land.[34] This effectively removed the right of commoners to utilise what were commonly managed resources. Disrupting patterns of use in the Fens further, many of these new landowners did not have a relationship to the Fens. Consequently, there was limited consideration of customary rights and obligations (for example maintenance of flood management structures), which therefore complicated the traditional management of the Fens.[35] The period around 1600 saw cooling climatic conditions and rising seas which made the Fens more flood-prone. In the beginning of King James I's reign, a series of floods surged over existing coastal embankments and the water inundated farms and villages, drowning large numbers of people and livestock.[36] Existing flood management structures and strategies, which were arbitrated and managed by Commissioners of Sewers, became overwhelmed.[37] The Commissioners of Sewers appealed to the Crown for help, but the Privy Council's ability to broker solutions on a piecemeal basis were largely ineffective, due to internecine conflicts among the commissioners, and the challenge of dealing with large-scale, complex and compounding water management issues.

The Crown's shifting priorities during Queen Elizabeth I's reign (1558–1603) catalysed new ways of thinking about the Fens. Elizabeth's outward-facing reign[38] enlarged the Crown's purview and the concept of 'commonwealth' was developed and promulgated as Elizabeth attempted to cohere disparate parts of her kingdom into a united whole. The ensuing discourse, coupled with a growing awareness of the need for strategic security, was pivotal in the Crown's approach to management of the Fens.[39] The Fens shifted into the Crown's focus as a source of valuable strategic and economic resources.[40] Compounding this interest was the Crown's large landholdings in the Fens.[41] Large-scale development of the Fens would yield potentially lucrative dividends for the Crown's coffers, a factor not unnoticed by King James I, who sought to shore up the Crown's dwindling finances. He saw the Fens as a possible source of revenue and would not 'let them lie waste and unprofitable'.[42]

The shift to considering large-scale drainage of the Fens sat within the broadening and intensifying of the Crown's interests in natural resources, an aspect of a state building project that was characterised by the quantification and exploitation of the environment through state control.[43] Tied to this, the Crown's focus on technological and entrepreneurial innovation played into proposals for large-scale drainage. This was achieved through the policy of granting royal patents to 'projectors', people who had money, expertise (or ideally both) and who could generate lucrative financial benefits and returns (for the elite) from existing resources.[44] Projectors were not perceived as apolitical, however. By the end of the sixteenth century, projectors had acquired a reputation as 'deceiving charlatans' and 'greedy opportunists' who leveraged their connections at court to obtain monopolies, characteristics that were highlighted in Ben Jonson's popular 1616 satire *The Devil is an Ass*, which lampoons projectors and their avarice.[45] In 1601, a bill for general drainage was presented to Parliament which was referred to as the General Drainage Act. This act enabled landowners and some commoners to make legal agreements with anyone, namely Crown-sponsored drainage projectors, who could drain their land in return for financial compensation.[46] The Act was, arguably, a method of state formation which privileged landowners and encouraged local elites to support Crown interests.[47] Its effect was to subsume local commoners' interests, and rights to the commons, into the Crown's control.

The development of flood mitigation and land reclamation technology by the Dutch also contributed to plans to drain the Fens.[48] The Crown engaged Dutch engineer Cornelius Vermuyden and Dutch-Anglo surveyor and engineer Humphrey Bradley (who assisted on an extensive survey of the Fens) in order to design and construct large-scale flood management systems with the view of also increasing agrarian production. However, Vermuyden found in the English Fens that river regulation was more complex than the polder, canal and sluice construction he was accustomed to in the Netherlands. The drainage works he helped instigate impeded river flows and subsequently caused unintended flooding on land adjacent to rivers. As the peat surface of the Fens dried it shrank and lowered the land which also exacerbated the potential for flooding from rivers.[49] It is estimated that the large-scale drainage works reduced common lands to one-third of their former size.[50]

While *Poly-Olbion* provided a literary map of England, the developing science and art of mapping presented a new way for viewing and understanding the world and for managing the Fens. In 1520, only a limited percentage of the English population had seen a map.[51] In 1579, Christopher Saxon created a detailed atlas of England and Wales, rendering the land as something completely seen and therefore knowable.[52] This enabled the whole nation to be comprehended, and therefore maps and surveying became critical tools in the management and control of disparate parts of the kingdom. This included the Fens, which were surveyed separately by commission of the Privy Council in 1589 by surveyor engineer Humphrey Bradley.[53] The exercise of surveying is alluded to in *The Devil is an Ass* when Fitzdotterel claims, 'We have viewed it. And measured it within, all by the scale!' (2.3.54–5).[54] This source of new geographic knowledge played into an ideology of nationalism and imperialism, and the attendant colonising forces that come with that.[55] The omniscient view provided by accurate maps had implications for the Fens. In an early modern form of surveillance, their territory was marked, calculated and visible. The maps made it possible for the Crown to understand the scope of a natural resource that was available for development and exploitation.

Dominant negative portrayals of Fens and fenlanders, coupled with the influence of Protestant beliefs which emphasised the value of hard work, also encouraged the Crown's growing narrative of landscape improvement and change. In contrast to the glowing words which Michael Drayton used to describe 'Holland Fen', one traveller in 1635 described the Fens as 'unhealthful, raw and muddy' where 'the climate is so infinitely cold, & watery' and the fenlanders' homes as 'poor, and mean'.[56] The occupants of the Fens were also characterised by contemporary writers in disparaging tones, and described as 'lazy, and intemperate' and 'superstitious heathens'.[57] As noted by James Boyce, abundant access to common resources was assumed to encourage fenlanders towards paganism and savagery.[58] Therefore, plans to drain the Fens not only hinged on economic concerns, but also ideologically became a redemptive mission of human salvation, through forcing the fendwellers into hard, honest labour, and to relinquish their herder/hunter-gatherer lifestyle.[59] Accordingly, the Fens became a dominion over which the Crown's ideology was exerted in order to tame the land and people. Bradley described the Fens as 'a vague, deserted empire' and portrayed the region as a *terra nullius*, which 'With good regulation, the drained land will be a regal conquest, a new republic and complete state.'[60] Potentially anticipating resistance to this grand vision, Bradley wrote, 'really the greatest impediments to all good drainage projects lie in the minds and in the imaginations of men, and not in the facts [of nature] themselves'.[61] Drayton's celebratory 'Holland Fen', Jonson's satire *The Devil is an Ass* and Wisbech's protest ballad 'The Powte's Complaint' responded to the proposed drainage projects by influencing people's imaginations, but the projects ultimately went ahead unimpeded.

Eventual legislative changes brought about large-scale drainage and attendant impacts, including widespread alterations to the ecology of the Fens. The General Drainage Act made it possible for drainage projectors to negotiate legal agreements with landowners, including a majority of commoners, to drain their land in exchange for renumeration which could include a percentage of profits from land they reclaimed.[62] In this new arrangement, no formal role was given to the Commissions of Sewers.[63] This early modern form of neoliberalism, while potentially seen as delivering efficiencies, circumvented the long-standing governance structure of the commissions, and therefore removed a key mechanism with which fenlanders could negotiate for their rights.

Resistance to the General Drainage Act and the proposed large-scale draining of the Fens came from multiple fronts and was not limited to the fenlanders who depended on the commons for their livelihood. Peregrine Bertie, Baron Willoughby de Eresby, who was both a prominent lord and landowner from Willoughby Lincolnshire (close to Holland Fen and the Witham River), stated his concerns in a letter to the Earl of Essex, in which he criticised the General Drainage Act. He wrote that the law 'pretendeth to enable and relieve a multitude of poor men for Her Majesty's service and the commonwealth's good', but he suspected that 'instead of helping the general poor, it would undo them and make those that are already rich far more rich'.[64] His protest reflects the perception that only the nation's elite would gain from exploiting the Fens.[65] This concern, which included disquiet towards projectors facilitating this wealth transfer, was not confined to letters. It was also brought into the public arena through theatre.

Julie Sanders notes the way in which Jonson's comedic satire *The Devil is an Ass* touches on Jacobean anxieties about the long-standing grievance of fen drainage, and highlights the way in which the play invites Londoners (to whom it was performed) to see themselves within the play's events.[66] *The Devil is an Ass* was first staged in the fall of 1616, in the same year Jonson received a royal pension from King James I and his play reflected widely held views about projectors.[67] As a form of protest, it was partially successful in that it offended an important ranking person (possibly one of the King's favourites, Sir Robert Carr or the Earl of Argyll), which caused the play to be withdrawn from the repertory by royal command.[68] The play was published in 1631, a timing which Todd Borlik contends was in effect a further deliberate intervention in the long-standing public debate over the widescale changes to the Fens.[69]

The Devil is an Ass is a caustic commentary on projectors and large-scale land reclamation projects. Here, the fraudster Merecraft manipulates the feckless Fitzdotterel (whose name links him to a species of plover found in the Fens which is easily caught) with a scheme that will swindle 'citizens, commoners, and aldermen' of their finances and then 'blow 'em off again, / Like so many dead flies, when 'tis carried' (2.1.42–4).[70] Fitzdotterel, oblivious that Merecraft intends to con him also, believes in the lie that he will be made a wealthy Duke – the dubiously titled Duke of Drowned Land. He declaims to his perceptive wife, 'You know I am not easy to be gulled. / I swear, when I have my millions, else I'll make' (2.3.39–40),[71] and promises his wife she will become a duchess. His wife admonishes him for believing in false spirits, but undeterred, Fitzdotterel resists his wife's wise counsel, exclaiming that:

> This man defies the Devil and all his works!
> He dos't by engine and devices, he!
> He has his winged ploughs, that go with sails,
> Will plough you forty acres at once! And mills
> Will spout you water ten miles off! All Crowland
> Is ours, wife; and the fens, from us in Norfolk
> To the utmost bound of Lincolnshire! (2.3.48–54)[72]

Fitzdotterel's optimism and (clearly foolish) belief in the efficacy of the technologies described to him, adds to the sense of ludicrousness about the proposed venture. The audience, it is clear, is invited to register this.[73] The play not only comments on the contested terrain of Fen drainage, but also implicates the Crown in this foolishness through describing the king's involvement in the spurious project through Merecraft who makes the royal sham clear:

> The thing is for recovery of drowned land,
> Whereof the Crowne's to have his moiety,

If it be owner; else, the Crown and Owners
To share that moiety, and the recoverers
T'enioy the tother moiety, for their charge. (2.1.45–9)[74]

Here, Jonson makes explicit the common arrangement in which the king benefits from sharing in the profits from monopolies and projects.[75] Accordingly, the play suggests that the Crown was not a neutral arbiter in the question of whether large-scale Fens drainage should go ahead, a contentious factor that possibly heightened overall objections to drainage of the Fens. By the 1630s, the ongoing objections to drainage were contributing to what would be the eventual dissolution of Charles I's personal rule.[76] This suggests the significance of the play as a politically charged protest text.

Overall, ideologically the play's concerns centre primarily on a moral aversion to human greed, embodied in the role of projectors and the Crown, rather than concern for the fenlanders themselves or the environment they lived in. Possibly this is reflective of more London-centric concerns, in which questions of the Crown's power and decision-making share centre stage. As such, the play may be more of what Borlik describes as a 'techno-sceptical satire' which 'promotes a shallow rather than deep ecology'.[77] Notwithstanding this, it can also be viewed as an important, ecologically engaged text within the body of early modern English drama.[78] The play's concerns, and others, also rippled out from the Fens where fendwellers themselves protested vigorously against the Crown's proposals to drain their 'vast and queachy soil'.[79]

Fenlanders' close connection to place, reflected in their diverse livelihoods which relied on local, seasonal ecologies and was mediated through unique Fens culture, came under direct threat from the 'great designe' on a scale that was unprecedented. Accordingly, the fenlanders fought hard, and sometimes violently, for protection of their watery way of life and ties to their riverine place. Yi-fu Tuan frames this relationship to place as an affective bond between people and locations of significance, which develops over time.[80] This affective bond linking fenlanders to the Fens over millennia is evidenced by the long-standing use rights in addition to customs which developed and grew over hundreds of generations. Ideologically, the fenlanders' key relationships were with their environment, each other and local institutions that managed those relationships, which included customs stipulating customary use. Boyce implies this made the fenlanders indigenous to the Fens.[81] Framed within this context, the Crown's attempts at widespread and incursive change can be viewed as a form of colonisation including the associated violence implied by the term. Resistance to this is reflected in multiple strategies employed by fenlanders which included using courts and lobbying Parliament. The rousing ballad 'The Powte's Complaint', which may have been used in the fen riots, and to galvanise action, is another.

The ten-verse ballad the 'Powte's Complaint'[82] is significant for how it reflects fenlanders' relationship to place and its expression of environmental concerns through the voice of the 'powte'. The early modern term 'powte' refers to a freshwater fish that is a member of the cod family, and commonly known as a burbot (*Lota Lota Gadidae*).[83] This long, sinuous eel-like fish with a distinctive goatee-like chin barbel, is nocturnal and a voracious predator. The latter characteristic potentially suggests that the creator of the ballad deliberately chose the powte as a fierce, emblematic presence, which those protesting the destruction of the Fens could draw on for encouragement. The ballad protests against the prospect of large-scale fens drainage and the resulting desiccation of the landscape to accommodate newly introduced 'Essex-calves' and 'horned Beasts and Cattel' (12, 19).[84] It invokes curses against those involved in large-scale drainage and appeals to an array of deities for assistance in repelling incursions into Fens territory, calling upon the god of wind, 'God Eolus, we do thee pray' to stymie the projectors in their work and 'send a blast, that they in haste may work no good conclusion' (29, 32).[85] The narrating powte also calls upon the 'Bretheren of the water and let us all assemble / To treat upon this matter, which makes us quake and tremble' (1–2).[86] This call for assembly suggests a form of affiliation, in which the plight of the powte is inextricably linked to human fate.

As a protest song, the 'Powte's Complaint' not only references fenlanders' attitudes of resistance towards the planned large-scale drainage, but also reflects a broader concern for their livelihoods and sense of place. Protest and resistance in the Fens were not uncommon; the riverine, watery landscape made land travel difficult, and therefore local knowledge was crucial for navigating the aqueous terrain. Accordingly, the landscape was a refuge for outlaws and over time became a haven for the anti-drainage provocateurs, the 'fen tigers'.[87] The ballad exhorts people to protest against the 'Essex Calves' (calf was slang for 'fool' in early modern English and potentially also refers to Essex nobility involved in large-scale drainage as a business venture), and calls rousingly to 'drive them out by Battel', thereby referencing some of the more violent measures which fenlanders, many of them women, could (and did) undertake to fight for their rights.[88]

These Fen riots, in which fenlanders assembled to forcefully protest, were vigorously sustained throughout the seventeenth century and aimed primarily at the Crown, projectors and foreigners employed to work on the drainage projects.[89] Protest was often local and varied. In one instance, hundreds of mostly female protestors threw stones at exchequer commissioners whose job was to communicate an order dividing the commons. In another event, two thousand of the 'common sort' of people gathered to protest through much of one night, milling around bonfires in a cacophony of ringing bells, banging drums and firing of muskets.[90] Direct action is also recorded in a lawsuit from April 1629, which describes how the villagers of Torksey 'filled up the ditches and drains, made to carry away the water, burned up working tools and other materials of the Realtor and his workmen' and 'set up poles in the form of gallows, to terrifie the workmen and threatened to break their arms and legs, and beat and hurt many of them and made others flee away'.[91] Events like this occurred throughout early modern Fens communities as fenlanders sought to exert what power they could. But while this widespread resistance suggests fenlanders were a homogeneous group united in fighting large-scale drainage works, as livelihoods came under increasing pressure conflict among the fenlanders themselves escalated, for example when changes in drainage in one area had adverse downstream effects on another area.[92]

Potentially, the 'Powte's Complaint' served as a common rallying cry to remind fenlanders of their collective cause. And while in this way it gives voice to the concerns of the fenlanders, in effect the narrating powte also decentres the human voice and amplifies the concerns of the environment. But more so, the voicing of camaraderie from the powte's perspective, 'for we shall rue it if't be true that Fenns be undertaken' (3), appears to articulate an amphibious kinship between Fen aquatic species and humans, in which the two are inextricably linked.[93] Viewed from an outsider perspective, this close connection de-civilises the human and potentially also played into narratives from the Crown, of fendwellers as half-fish and therefore sub-human – a species apart. Overall, the 'Powte's Complaint' subverts the idea that humans have the right to dramatically change the Fens environment, and the rioting and resistance recommended by the powte reveal the length to which fenlanders would go to protect the environment which contained and enabled their livelihoods and way of life.

Despite sustained resistance, however, in the long term, the fenlanders were not successful. By the mid-nineteenth century, most of the original Fens were destroyed and therefore a culture and way of life based on and around waterways was irrevocably devastated also. The shift to large-scale agriculture largely replaced livelihoods that worked with the dynamics of the local riverine environment, and a mostly egalitarian society was superseded by a more hierarchical structure in which a few people controlled the land while the majority were reduced to landlessness and wage labour.[94] The majority of the original Fens is now some of England's most productive monocultural farmland, but the cost is the annihilation of what was one of England's most biodiverse areas.[95] Many groups are now working to rewild small pockets of extant Fens, in a bid to reverse the damage and within the aegis of an ecological imaginary based on regeneration, resilience and open-ended 'forward restoration'.[96] Konik horses and highland cattle now range freely over large areas of Wicken Fen,[97] and the boom of bitterns can be heard again in Bourne North Fen.[98] The aspirations for increased biodiversity links these measures directly to 'Holland Fen', which spoke to the ecological complexity and diversity of an early modern Fen. If we could trace an arc from Drayton's time to the present, a corresponding, contemporary version of his poem might be an ode to the species returning to the Fens: exquisite, iridescent emperor dragonflies darting along 'slamps',[99] rivers and other waterways; great crested newts; golden-bloomed grey longhorn beetles; vibrant wildflowers – yellow rattle, meadow rue and devils-bit scabious; congregations of swallows and martins assembling before their autumnal journey south; and a dusk sky filled with a vast murmuration of starlings.[100] In this way, the aspirational, regenerative efforts of current day re-wilders connect to the ecological abundance articulated in 'Holland Fen'.

Within the context of environmental degradation, *The Devil is an Ass* remains a humorously topical text in relation to understanding how human avarice maps onto both anthropological and ecological terrain. As a protest song[101] the popular, grassroots 'The Powte's Complaint' potentially rallied support in Fens' communities and contributed to direct action taken by fenlanders (although it is not possible to quantify the extent of this). Its present-day currency is the way in which the ballad foregrounds contemporary environmental and social concerns. Ideologically, the battle between the Crown and fenlanders over the Fens reveals two divergent groups fighting over a resource. The Crown's claims sat within a wider project of large-scale development, and the fenlanders' claims within centuries of occupation and use and the right to maintain this use. The wide-scale drainage of the Fens largely subsumed the fenlanders into a mainstream economy and way of life, and decimated a unique Fens culture. Within this debate is a third entity – the Fens themselves. 'The Powte's Complaint' gives voice to the powte, a species that was once common in the Fens but has not been sighted in England since 1969.[102] While the song still seeps into the present through inclusion by current-day folk musicians,[103] the powte's absence from the Fens creates a form of silence. Ideologically, this highlights urgent, contemporary questions regarding the rights of the powte, the Fens and other ecologies to exist and thrive.

Notes

1. William J. Mitsch and James G. Gosselink, *Wetlands*, 5th edn (Oxford: Wiley, 2015), 8.
2. Eric H. Ash, *The Draining of the Fens: Projectors, Popular Politics, and State Building in Early Modern England* (Baltimore: Johns Hopkins University Press, 2017), 181. Ash describes the author of this comment as a 'knowledgeable, anonymous commentator' and cites the source as the following: H. C., *Discovrse*, fols. A3v, C3r.
3. Quoted in Ash, *The Draining of the Fens*, 17.
4. Ash, *The Draining of the Fens*, 23. Mitsch and Gosselink note that peat-accumulating wetlands receive some drainage from surrounding mineral soils and usually support marshlike vegetation (*Wetlands*, 711). Further information on peatland classification can be found on the International Peatland Society website, https://peatlands.org/peatlands/types-of-peatlands/.
5. William A. Boismier, Edmund Taylor and Yvonne Wolframm Murray, *Excavations at Stanground South, Peterborough: Prehistoric, Roman and Post-Medieval Settlement along the Margins of the Fens* (Oxford: Archaeopress, 2021), 19.
6. Ash, *The Draining of the Fens*, 27–8.
7. The perceived benefits of flooding are contained in a c. 1646 record of the Bishop of Ely (linked to one of the largest monasteries in the Fens), who described the profits of flooding when he stated that meadows are 'not hurtfully surrounded but are better and more fruitfull by being sometymes overflowne and surrounded': see Julie Bowring, 'Between the Corporation and Captain Flood: The Fens and Drainage after 1663', in *Custom, Improvement and the Landscape in Early Modern Britain*, ed. Richard W. Hoyle (London: Routledge, 2016), 239.
8. Not all early written accounts valued the Fens. Early written records of St Guthlac, who chose the Fens as a site of pilgrimage in 669 CE, focused on the wild and pestilent elements of the Fens (possibly in part to enhance a narrative of hardship and deprivation which was central to the endeavour of true pilgrimage). As noted by James Boyce, Guthlac was possibly afflicted by malarial fever which was also rife in the Fens. James Boyce, *Imperial Mud: The Fight for the Fens* (London: Icon Books, 2021), 10.
9. Todd Andrew Borlik, *Literature and Nature in the English Renaissance: An Ecocritical Anthology* (Cambridge: Cambridge University Press, 2019), 448.
10. *Poly-Olbion: New Perspectives*, ed. Andrew McRae and Philip Schwyzer (Martlesham: Boydell & Brewer, 2020), 2–4; María Vera-Reyes, 'Michael Drayton's Topographies: *Ideas Mirrour* (1594) and *Poly-Olbion* (1612–1622)', *English Studies: A Journal of English Language and Literature* 102.8 (December 2021), 1002–23, 1005.

11. Sukanya Dasgupta, 'Drayton's "Silent Spring": "Poly-Olbion" and the Politics of Landscape', *The Cambridge Quarterly* 39.2 (June 1, 2010), 152–71, 171.
12. Michael Drayton, 'Holland Fen', in Borlik, *Literature and Nature*, 448–52, 448.
13. Borlik, *Literature and Nature*, 449.
14. Ash, *The Draining of the Fens*, 33; Boyce, *Imperial Mud*, 105.
15. Ash, *The Draining of the Fens*, 32; Boyce, *Imperial Mud*, 22; Michael Chisholm, 'Navigation and the Seventeenth-Century Draining of the Fens', *Journal of Historical Geography* 32.4 (January 1, 2006), 731–51, 740.
16. Ash, *The Draining of the Fens*, 33; Boyce, *Imperial Mud*, 107; Ian D. Rotherham, *The Lost Fens: England's Greatest Ecological Disaster* (Cheltenham: The History Press, 2013), 11.
17. 'Holland Fen', in Borlik, *Literature and Nature*, 448.
18. Boyce, *Imperial Mud*, 14. In turn, the abundance of resources in the Fens contributed to the wealth of the Fens monastic houses. Ely, Ramsey, Thorney and Crowland were among the wealthiest monasteries in England. The monastic centres also served as hostels for travellers and farmed the land, grazing both cattle and sheep, in addition to managing fishponds and other small industries. Ash, *The Draining of the Fens*, 27; Rotherham, *The Lost Fens*, 68; Annie Proulx, *Fen, Bog & Swamp: A Short History of Peatland Destruction and Its Role in the Climate Crisis* (London: HarperCollins, 2022), 61.
19. Rotherham, *The Lost Fens*, 104, 68.
20. Ibid., 62.
21. In the early modern period, a burgeoning dairy industry provided milk, butter and cheese for local communities and urban centres such as Cambridge, Peterborough, Norwich and London. Goods were taken to these markets via the region's inland rivers and waterways, which were the most extensive in northern Europe at the time. Ash, *The Draining of the Fens*, 32.
22. Ibid., 34.
23. Ibid., 35. Within the Fens, 'common waste' areas enabled smallhold farmers and landless fen-dwellers to maintain livestock through access to the abundant grass on the common waste, whose fertility was partly due to regular flooding from rivers. The habitat of waterfowl, fish, eels, reeds and sedge formed part of a seasonal, riverine commons, which was also tightly managed.
24. Ibid.
25. Ibid., 34.
26. 'Jurats' are recorded in 1252 as having the power to control the ditches of Romney Marsh, and the earliest recorded river engineer was Girard Fossaruis – Gerard of the Drain. Jeremy Purseglove, *Working with Nature: Saving and Using the World's Wild Places* (London: Profile Books, 2019), 97.
27. Boyce, *Imperial Mud*, 26.
28. Ash, *The Draining of the Fens*, 38; Boyce, *Imperial Mud*, 26.
29. Ash, *The Draining of the Fens*, 38.

30. Ibid., 7 and 41.
31. Women's right to reasonable estovers (the right to collect wood) was enshrined in 1215 in Magna Carta; Boyce, *Imperial Mud*, 104.
32. This included regulations on when to harvest and mow, in addition to regulation on fallow times, and provided a structured system of governance that was maintained through penalties and local arbitration; Boyce, *Imperial Mud*, 25.
33. Ash, *The Draining of the Fens*, 45–6.
34. Boyce, *Imperial Mud*, 29.
35. Ash, *The Draining of the Fens*, 45–6.
36. Ibid., 45 and 47.
37. Ibid., 49.
38. Elizabeth's reign included a growing focus on international trade, the 'discovery' of new lands (already occupied by indigenous people), and the strengthening of a naval fleet in order to develop new opportunities and protect existing resources.
39. Chisholm, 'Navigation and the Seventeenth-Century Draining of the Fens', 731.
40. An increase in domestically produced crops would reduce dependence on imported food, and drained fenlands provided possibilities for building and supplying merchant ships and men-o-war through the production of hemp and flax whose fibres were used in making canvas, rope and twine; Chisholm, 'Navigation and the Seventeenth-Century Draining of the Fens', 732.
41. Ash, *The Draining of the Fens*, 8.
42. Quoted in Boyce, *Imperial Mud*, 39.
43. Ash, *The Draining of the Fens*, 5; Malcom Hebron, *Key Concepts in Renaissance Literature* (New York: Palgrave, 2008), 231.
44. Ash, *The Draining of the Fens*, 63.
45. Ibid.
46. Ibid., 62.
47. Ibid., 63.
48. Land reclamation was carried out in the Dutch Republic from the twelfth century, with both salt and freshwater lakes pumped of water in order to convert them to polders, offering not only flood protection but also new, arable land; see E. F. J. de Mulder, A. J. van Bruchem, F. A. M. Claessen, G. Hannink, J. G. Hulsbergen and H. M. C. Satijn, 'Environmental Impact Assessment on Land Reclamation Projects in The Netherlands: A Case History', *Engineering Geology* 37.1 (January 1994), 15–23, 15. By 1400, the Dutch had further sophisticated the technology of windmills for grinding corn, which were then adapted to pump water; see R. J. Hoeksema, 'Three Stages in the History of Land Reclamation in the Netherlands', *Irrigation and Drainage* 56, Suppl. 1 (December 2007), 113–26, 116. This new technology, of what Ben Jonson termed 'winged ploughs' (2.3.50) in *The Devil is an Ass*, sped up the rate of drainage and between 1565 and 1615 the Dutch reclaimed over 100,000 acres of land from marsh in the Dutch Republic; see Boyce, *Imperial Mud*, 35; Rotherham, *The Lost Fens*, 103. The Dutch expertise in this area led to the extensive export of knowledge, technology and organisational skills in land reclamation, and

their experience was widely sought after for large-scale drainage projects in northern Germany and other European countries; see Boyce, *Imperial Mud*, 35.
49. Carolyn Merchant, 'Hydraulic Technologies and the Agricultural Transformation of the English Fens', *Environmental Review: ER* 7.2 (July 1983), 165–78, 170.
50. This resulted in a cascade of negative effects. Less land resulted in less fodder and therefore fewer animals survived the winter. Accordingly, less manure was available for replenishing existing soil and consequently overall, soil fertility and crop yields declined. Merchant, 'Hydraulic Technologies and the Agricultural Transformation of the English Fens', 170.
51. D. K. Smith, *The Cartographic Imagination in Early Modern England: Re-writing the World in Marlowe, Spenser, Raleigh and Marvell* (New York: Routledge, 2008), 41.
52. Ibid., 9.
53. Ash, *The Draining of the Fens*, 57.
54. Ben Jonson, *The Devil is an Ass*, in Ian Donaldson, Martin Butler, David L. Gants, Eugene Giddens, David M. Bevington and Karen Britland, eds, *The Cambridge Edition of the Works of Ben Jonson Online* (Cambridge: Cambridge University Press, 2014).
55. Lesley Cormack quoted in Smith, *The Cartographic Imagination*, 48.
56. Quoted in Ash, *The Draining of the Fens*, 17.
57. Ash, *The Draining of the Fens*, 17; Todd Andrew Borlik, 'Magic as Technological Dominion: John Dee's Hydragogy and the Draining of the Fens in Ben Jonson's *The Devil Is an Ass*', *Neophilologus* 105.4 (December 2021), 589–608, 589.
58. Boyce, *Imperial Mud*, 150.
59. Ash, *The Draining of the Fens*, 8–9.
60. Quoted in Ash, *The Draining of the Fens*, 58.
61. Quoted in Ash, *The Draining of the Fens*, 58.
62. Ash, *The Draining of the Fens*, 62; Todd A. Borlik and Clare Egan, 'Angling for the "Powte": A Jacobean Environmental Protest Poem', *English Literary Renaissance* 48.2 (2018), 256–89, 257.
63. Ash, *The Draining of the Fens*, 63.
64. Quoted in Ash, *The Draining of the Fens*, 61.
65. Sanders, *The Cultural Geography*, 26.
66. Julie Sanders, *Ben Jonson's Theatrical Republics* (Basingstoke: Palgrave Macmillan, 1998), 107, 109 and 114.
67. Robert C. Evans, *Jonson and the Contexts of his Time* (Lewisburg: Bucknell University Press, 1994), 62 and 70.
68. *Conv.*, l.355 quoted in Sean McEvoy, *Ben Jonson, Renaissance Dramatist* (Edinburgh: Edinburgh University Press, 2008), 141.
69. Borlik, 'Magic as Technological Dominion', 604.
70. Ibid., 602; Sanders, *Ben Jonson's Theatrical Republics*, 118; Jonson, *The Devil is an Ass*.
71. Jonson, *The Devil is an Ass*.
72. Ibid.
73. Sanders, *Ben Jonson's Theatrical Republics*, 114.

74. Jonson, *The Devil is an Ass*.
75. Leah S. Marcus, *The Politics of Mirth: Jonson, Herrick, Milton, Marvell, and the Defense of Old Holiday Pastimes* (Chicago: University of Chicago Press, 1986), 100.
76. Sanders, *Ben Jonson's Theatrical Republics*, 122.
77. Borlik, 'Magic as Technological Dominion', 605.
78. Ibid., 590.
79. 'Queachy' refers to mushy or damp soil, as shown in the footnotes in Drayton's 'Holland Fen', in Borlik, *Literature and Nature*, 448.
80. Yi-fu Tuan, *Topophilia: A Study of Environmental Perception, Attitudes, and Values* (New York: Columbia University Press, 1990), 4.
81. Boyce, *Imperial Mud*, 126 and 150.
82. William Dugdale's 1662 version of 'The Powte's Complaint'. As noted by Borlik and Egan, there are four different manuscripts of the document in the British Library. Borlik and Egan, 'Angling for the "Powte"', 284–5.
83. Ibid., 259; Martin A. Stapanian, Vaughn L. Paragamian, Charles Madenjian, James R. Jackson, Jyrki Lappalainen, Matthew J. Evenson and Matthew D. Neufeld, 'Worldwide Status of Burbot and Conservation Measures', *Fish & Fisheries* 11.1 (March 2010), 34–56, 35.
84. Dugdale, 1662 version of 'The Powte's Complaint'. Borlik and Egan, 'Angling for the "Powte"', 284–5.
85. Dugdale, 1662 version of 'The Powte's Complaint'. Borlik and Egan, 'Angling for the "Powte"', 284–5; Borlik, 'Magic as Technological Dominion', 594.
86. Dugdale, 1662 version of 'The Powte's Complaint'. Borlik and Egan, 'Angling for the "Powte"', 284–5.
87. Rotherham, *The Lost Fens*, 27.
88. Ash, *The Draining of the Fens*, 142; Boyce, *Imperial Mud*, 45; Borlik and Egan, 'Angling for the "Powte"', 282–3.
89. Ash, *The Draining of the Fens*, 145; David Underdown, *Revel, Riot, and Rebellion: Popular Politics and Culture in England, 1603–1660* (Oxford: The Clarendon Press, 1985), 136.
90. Boyce, *Imperial Mud*, 37–8.
91. Boyce, *Imperial Mud*, 42. In a direct echo of this event, direct action also occurred in 1972 when naturalist William Bunting led a team known as 'Bunting's Beavers' in preventing wholesale peat extraction on the bog at Thorne Moors by damming drains used for excavation. Purseglove, *Working with Nature*, 85.
92. Bowring, 'Between the Corporation and Captain Flood', 255.
93. Dugdale, 1662 version of 'The Powte's Complaint'. Borlik and Egan, 'Angling for the "Powte"', 284–5.
94. Underdown, *Revel, Riot, and Rebellion*, 24.
95. Borlik and Egan, 'Angling for the "Powte"', 258.
96. Francine M. R. Hughes, Peter A. Stroh, William M. Adams, Keith J. Kirby, J. Owen. Mountford and Stuart Warrington, 'Monitoring and Evaluating Large-Scale, "Open-Ended" Habitat Creation Projects: A Journey Rather than a Destination', *Journal for Nature Conservation* 19.4 (January 2011), 245–53, 245.

97. https://www.rewildingbritain.org.uk/rewilding-projects/wicken-fen (last accessed 15 September 2022).
98. https://www.theguardian.com/environment/2021/may/23/hares-cranes-bitterns-small-triumphs-in-the-battle-to-rewild-britains-landscape (last accessed 15 September 2022).
99. A slamp is a 'boggy strip of land bordering Fen riverbanks'; see Robert Macfarlane, *Landmarks* (Harmondsworth: Penguin Books, 2015), 52.
100. https://www.nationaltrust.org.uk/wicken-fen-nature-reserve/features/wildlife and https://nt.global.ssl.fastly.net/wicken-fen-nature-reserve/documents/wicken-fen-research-and-recording-newsletter---june-2017.pdf (last accessed 23 October 2022).
101. The song 'The Powte's Compaint' is included in the University of East Anglia's project of protest songs from 1600 to the present day: 'Our Subversive Voice', https://oursubversivevoice.com (last accessed 15 September 2022).
102. Martin A. Stapanian, Vaughn L. Paragamian, Charles Madenjian, James R. Jackson, Jyrki Lappalainen, Matthew J. Evenson and Matthew D. Neufeld, 'Worldwide Status of Burbot and Conservation Measures', *Fish & Fisheries* 11.1 (2010), 34–56, 37; T. Worthington, P. S. Kemp, P. E. Osborne, A. Dillen, J. Coeck, M. Bunzel-Drüke, M. Naura, J. Gregory and K. Easton, 'A Spatial Analytical Approach for Selecting Reintroduction Sites for Burbot in English Rivers', *Freshwater Biology* 57.3 (2012), 602–11, 603.
103. See The Shackleton Trio, *Fen, Farm & Deadly Water*, Bandcamp (2018). https://www.shackletontrio.co.uk/ (last accessed 15 September 2022).

Chapter 12

Shakespeare's Waterways: Premonitions of an Environmental Collapse

Sophie Chiari

> Sweet Swan of Avon! What a sight it were
> To see thee in our waters yet appear,
> And make those flights upon the bankes of Thames
> That so did take Eliza and our James!
> – Ben Johnson, 'To the memory of my Beloved the Author, Mr William Shakespeare'

Ben Jonson's memorial poem published in the First Folio seven years after his death contains lines which famously link Shakespeare to the River Avon but which hardly obliterate the paradoxical absence of the Avon in his works. Of crucial importance to Stratford, the river was an artery for trade and a source of power and must have fed the imagination of the young William. England was then as much a fluvial as a maritime nation: no less than the sea, rivers contributed to England's development and wealth. It is certainly no coincidence that river poetry flourished in sixteenth-century England and celebrated the country via its aquatic network. In John Leland's nationalistic *Cygnea cantio* (1545),[1] for example, the poem's speaker is a swan which floats down the Thames (i.e. the Isis, in the poem) and which voices his observations on places observed along the banks. Similarly, William Camden's chorographic poem, 'De connubio Tamae et Isis', which appeared in fragments throughout his monumental *Britannia* (1586),[2] focuses on rivers and describes the courses of the Tame and the Isis as well as their confluence and merging in the Thames.[3]

These two examples testify to a general enthusiasm for sources of freshwater in both literary and political terms. According to the pre-scientific thought of the time, it was frequently assumed that watercourses were fed by the sea, through underground channels, before running back to the sea ('All rivers have recourse unto the sea', *Edward III*, 18.1.93):[4] they were thus believed to be part of a constant cycle nourishing both oceans and rivers. In the early Middle Ages, Isidore of Seville (560–636 CE) had already described the world's hydrologic cycle in his *Etymologiae*. Summarising western knowledge about the circulation of waters, he explained that the water of the oceans produced the rivers from below the land:

> The reason why the sea has no increase in its size, even though it receives all the rivers and springs, is partly because its own huge size is not affected by the waters flowing in; then again, it is because the bitter water consumes the fresh water flowing in; or because the clouds themselves draw up and absorb a great deal of water; or because the winds carry away part of the sea, and the sun dries up part; finally, because it is percolated through certain hidden openings in the earth, and runs back again to the source of springs and fountains.[5]

This 'reverse hydrologic cycle',[6] which, since Aristotle, had implied that the subterranean source of rivers was the sea, remained a vivid belief in Shakespeare's time and beyond.[7] The playwright must therefore have been familiar with 'contemporary theories of the natural circulation of water: that it was drawn from the sea through underground channels, issuing as springs which initiated the flow of rivers'.[8] At the heart of this conception are concerns with soil and soil moisture, with freshwater ecosystems; however, water scarcity and sustainability cannot be seen as compelling issues here, since in the reverse hydrologic cycle, fresh water never stops flowing. Does that mean that Shakespeare's contemporaries were not able to sustain what we would call, today, an 'eco-minded vision' of their watercourses?

Having long focused on the poetic and pastoral power of river images in Shakespeare's time, independently of their deeper ecological significance, literary criticism has seldom addressed this question. This difficulty actually illustrates a fundamental human reticence: as Bergson argues, the intellect is, by essence, averse to the 'fluid continuity of the real',[9] and it is thus prompt to solidify things with which it comes into contact.[10] Yet the waterworld of early modern England, primarily made of streams, rivers, channels and brooks, was one of the kingdom's most strategic networks in terms of economy, exchange and transportation.[11] So how can we think more accurately about early modern fresh water?

In the present chapter, I argue that, beyond their poetic power, Shakespearean allusions to waterways may point to a shifting environment and reflect what were then new environmental issues involving the general welfare of the population. By shedding light on three environmental issues in Shakespeare's plays and involving the waterscape of the period, that is the exploitation of rivers, ditch digging and the increasing pollution of fresh water, I unpack the specific implications of the use of fresh water in order to put forward an early modern aesthetics of collapse rather than one of rejuvenation and progress as has long been implied in literary criticism dealing with sources and streams.

An instrumentalist approach to rivers

'There are also in this Iland great plentie of fresh riuers and streams, ... and these throughlie fraught with all kinds of delicate fish accustomed to be found in riuers', William Harrison writes in his wide-ranging *Description of England* published as a preface to Raphael Holinshed's *Chronicles* (1577 and 1587).[12] Incidentally, the same Harrison writes a first-hand report on the extraordinary powers of the baths at King's Newnham, Warwickshire, which were then said to turn plants, wood and so on to stone.[13] Whether Shakespeare was already familiar with these beliefs or whether he read such news in Harrison's text, it is impossible to say; but Claudius, in *Hamlet*, jeeringly compares the people to 'the spring that turneth wood to stone' (4.7.20) in that they '[c]onvert' Hamlet's 'guilts to graces' (4.7.21).

The transformative powers of the English springs are, in this case, brought to an exceptional degree: they are related to medicinal waters and are meant to convey the impressive charisma of a prince loved by the Danes, no matter how he behaves. In most other occurrences in the literature of the period, however, these powers are linked to the rivers' productivity – a rather understandable concern if one remembers that Wednesdays, Fridays and Saturdays were fish days in Elizabethan England. As Liza Picard makes clear, 'so was the whole of Lent and various other days': fish days thus amounted to 'almost a third of the year'.[14] No wonder if waterways and their riverside pasturages were usually praised for being 'fruitful' (*Hamlet*, 1.2.80), that is, for their utilitarian dimension, rather than for their beauty or their rich riparian ecosystems. In line with this, Commissions of Sewers then 'managed flood defence, drainage and navigation on a local and regional scale'.[15] As John Emrys Morgan puts it, '[w]ater management' was therefore 'deeply woven into the social fabrics of communities'.[16]

Rivers were then quite shallow and floods were thus part of rural life: when rivers overflowed their banks, especially at the awkward time of the season of growth, all the surrounding crops were under threat.[17] Shakespeare seems to have been alert to this particular issue, signalled time and again in his plays and poems. Flooding is always seen as a hazard, and never as a way of improving hay crops, for example, whereas a number of husbandry manuals of the period are keen to stress that the overflowing of riverside land helps husbandmen to 'better yeerely ...

yeelde his gayne'.[18] An expert in soil improvement, Hugh Platt asserted in the second part of his *Jewell house of art and nature* (1594) that 'when those common waters run downewardes, alongst the vallies, whether they be flouds, rivers, or springs', they prove 'generative' and make the ground profitable.[19] Poets such as Michael Drayton also regarded floods, especially spring floods, as positive events enriching the soil:

> Through all the partes, dispersed is the blood,
> The lustie spring, in flower of all her pride,
> Man, bird, and beast, and fish, in pleasant flood,
> Rejoycing all in this most joyfull tide.[20]

Shakespeare, by contrast, does not seem to have prized or praised flood water, though he was fully aware of its agricultural potential: in *Antony and Cleopatra*, the annual Nile floods make the soil especially fertile ('The higher Nilus swells / The more it promises: as it ebbs, the seedsman / Upon the slime and ooze scatter his grain, / And shortly comes to harvest', 2.7.17–23). This fertility, however, is deceptive as it goes hand in hand with the sterile self-indulgence of the two title characters, unable to leave a long-lasting imprint: their world is one of impermanence and dissolution. I have argued elsewhere that, in the play, the Nile actually stood 'for the nothingness of existence (*nihil*)' and came to 'symbolis[e] the river Lethe (2.7.107), the stream of oblivion in the underground'.[21]

If throughout most of the canon the playwright considers the natural sphere, which is vividly particularised in his plays and poems, as deeply interconnected with the human one, he tends to promote tamed landscapes and contained waterscapes, predicated on 'loss and profit, ownership and remuneration'.[22] It is with such considerations in mind that, in *Venus and Adonis*, the poet observes that 'Rain added to a river that is rank / Perforce will force it overflow the bank' (l. 71–2) and that, in *A Midsummer Night's Dream*, the lines he devotes to Titania's speech on ecological disasters include allusions to inundations and agricultural failures:

> Therefore the winds, piping to us in vain,
> As in revenge, have sucked up from the sea
> Contagious fog; which falling in the land
> Have every pelting river made so proud
> That they have overborne their continents.
> (2.1.88–92)

Contagious fogs, overflowing rivers, drowned fields and rotting corn are all part and parcel of the natural turbulences afflicting the mortals' daily lives and economic survival. Much has already been said on the passage's possible echoes to the calamities that plagued England during the summer of 1594 and that of 1596: in both cases, the heavy rains caused floods and wrecked bridges.[23] Be that as it may, this example suggests that, in Shakespeare's personal and fragmented geography, features of the English waterscape are used to characterise exotic countries. Even a Roman play like *Julius Caesar* includes a channel and flooding metaphor overtly reminiscent of the Thames, given the context: 'weep your tears / into the channel, till the lowest stream / Do kiss the most exalted shores of all' (1.1.58–60).

Shakespeare's imaginary was thus informed by his own knowledge of streams and sources. The playwright was well aware of the fact that riverbanks were dangerous places: because most of England's rivers were then untamed (i.e. neither sluiced nor disciplined in any sort of way), 'coroners' records from the sixteenth century show that as many as 53 per cent of all accidental deaths were caused by drowning'.[24] In 2021, Steven Gunn discovered a coroner's report into the drowning of a Jane Shaxspere, in 1569. The girl (who was just two-and-a-half years old), the report explains, was picking flowers when she fell into a millpond near Stratford: the similarities between her case and Ophelia's drowning in *Hamlet* are intriguing, to say the least.[25] Whether the girl was the playwright's young cousin or not, he had probably heard of the case, which must have imprinted itself upon the imagination of the young William who was five at the time of the tragedy.

Yet in his plays, fresh water remains a wealth and a necessity more than a hindrance: most daily activities (household chores, animal cure, fishing practices for example) then depended upon the presence of fresh water, and the intrinsic worth of the land was closely connected to its irrigation. As he is about to die poisoned, King John associates his beloved kingdom with its rivers (5.7.38), and when King Lear says that he intends to give Goneril a very large amount of land, he proudly highlights the abundance of watercourses in what he offers her:

> Of all these bounds even from this line to this,
> With shadowy forests and with champains riched,
> With plenteous rivers and wide-skirted meads,
> We make thee lady.
> (1.1.63–6)

Here, Lear still reasons as a powerful sovereign: the '[en]rich[ing]' fields alluded to promise fertile soil and good crops (something he will utterly disavow later on by asking nature to make her daughter's womb sterile), while the 'shadowy forests' hint at pleasant hunting grounds. His vision of nature is a highly instrumentalist one. Unsurprisingly therefore, the old man's chorography is organised around woods and watercourses; it conventionally emphasises the place of rivers which, as dynamic elements of landscape, provide structural lines in his map. Here Shakespeare may also wink at his native Warwickshire, irregularly divided by the Avon into two very different sorts of landscapes: the woodland (i.e. the 'shadowy forests') at the north on the one hand, and fertile pasturelands ('champains') on the other .[26]

While a number of plays contain quick allusions to the compelling characteristics of watercourses, Shakespeare always blends, in his descriptions, the small and touching details of river life with more pragmatic hints at the fluvial economy of the time. When the eponymous hero of *Timon of Athens* praises the natural resources of the earth, he includes water ('Within this mile break forth a hundred springs', 4.3.413) as part of his daily necessities, while Caliban, in *The Tempest*, regrets having shown his master

> ... all the qualities o' the isle,
> The fresh springs, brine-pits, barren place and fertile:
> Cursed be I that did so!
> (1.2.338–40)

Against all odds, fresh water is here depicted as a tradeable good. Indeed, having been taught human language, Caliban is now perfectly able to differentiate between 'the useful or commodifiable and the useless or uncommodifiable'.[27] This means that, with the arrival of the settler Prospero, fresh water has suddenly become a tradable commodity.

Besides, watercourses, when navigable (be they natural or improved), allowed the transportation of provisions,[28] which explains why, for many contemporaries, 'rivers were for carrying trade'.[29] At the turn of the seventeenth century, England and Wales already had 'about 950 miles of navigable waterways'.[30] John Stow notes that London's main artery, the Thames, easily transported a variety of goods to London.[31] In 'A Lover's Complaint', Shakespeare (if, in spite of its controversial attribution, the poem is indeed his) implicitly questions and reverses this function by having a deceived maid throw 'amber', 'crystal' and 'beaded jet' in 'a river' after having realised how vain these favours are: exported goods are here returned to and swallowed by the waterway which initially transported them. Elsewhere, the importance of river traffic transpires in the plays, even when there is no direct mention of the Thames: barges appear in such plays as *Antony and Cleopatra*, when Antony first glimpses Cleopatra on her royal barge on the river Cydnus, *Pericles* which features a barge in the play's last act, or *All is*

True (i.e. *Henry VIII*), when, in Act 2, Vaux is supposed to accompany Buckingham to the river, where a barge is waiting to take him to his death. While the word could designate 'small seagoing vessels' (*OED* †1.a), it had mainly referred, since the early sixteenth century, to 'flat-bottomed freight-boat, chiefly for canal- and river-navigation' (*OED* 2) and it was generally connected to the navigation of the Thames.

Fresh water control and diversion

Even more significant is Shakespeare's use of sluices, which systematically combines the idea of regulation (of a volume of water) or control with a metaphorical context connoting excess. Much has already been said on *The Winter's Tale* where the verbal form of the word ('she has been sluiced in's absence', 1.2.195) reflects Leontes's perverted imagination in rather crude terms. Beyond the sexual double entendre, one also realises that, for the playwright, causing fresh water to flow out is likely to be a negative, not to say dangerous, action. This can also be observed in both narrative poems,[32] in which eyes are compared to sluices – the eyes being those of Venus and Lucrece, in accordance with the 'leaky vessels' theory developed by Gail Kern Paster and applied to the eminently porous feminine body of the early modern era.[33] When the gates (or the eyes) are closed, the situation is in control. However, when they are opened in spite of common sense, water threatens to smash everything in its path. The desperate Venus, towards the end of *Venus and Adonis*,

> . . . vailed her eyelids, who like sluices stopped
> The crystal tide from her two cheeks fair
> In the sweet channel of her bosom dropped.
> But through the flood-gates breaks the silver rain,
> And with his strong course opens them again.
> (l. 956–60)

References to overflowing in the poem systematically refer to unrestrained passion.[34] Once again here, lacking any sense of inhibition, Venus proves unable to refrain her flood of tears. While the aqueous metaphors pervading the poem as a whole are worth commenting upon and point to fantasies of incontinence (as opposed to deprivation), it is equally rewarding to un-metaphor the poet's lines in order to approach in more nuanced and perceptive ways his eco-material environment. What this recurrent imagery suggests, in this perspective, is Shakespeare's familiarity with sluices and his interest in controlling the flow of waterways in order to make them profitable.

This comes as no surprise, given his own entrepreneurial trends as well as the new importance then given to the control of rivers, the better to exploit them. During the post-medieval era, some rivers were indeed canalised for boat traffic. The Exeter Ship Canal, for example, was completed in 1567. Andrew MacRae makes it clear that

> [c]anals were not unknown in early modern England. Mill-leets and irrigation channels were common enough, while the sixteenth-century Exeter Ship Canal (one of the earliest of its kind) employed a similar principle on a greater scale, enabling river traffic to bypass a troublesome stretch of the River Exe. But these were relatively minor achievements, all geared toward the improvement of existing rivers for particular purposes, rather than the creation of entirely new routes.[35]

Contrary to the word 'channel', 'canal' does not crop up in Shakespeare, which does not mean that the playwright never alludes to canals in his works. In *The Merchant of Venice*, Belmont, where Portia lives, is implicitly situated on the Brenta[36] – the river-cum-canal which was already beginning to be lined with beautiful villas in Shakespeare's time, and which is mentioned no fewer than eight times in Fynes Moryon's *Itinerary* (1617).[37] It was known to locals as the continuation of the Grand Canal: being part of an extensive canal system, it stretched all the way across the Po Valley from Venice. This location may well testify to Shakespeare's interest in tamed waterscapes – an interest further corroborated by his utterly negative take on natural floodings.

Directing the movement of water, channels and diversions of all kinds then allowed proponents of river improvement to represent an emerging water industry as orderly and purposeful. Part of the hydraulic technology of the period, 'conduits' (a term then referring to aqueducts and to destination fountains),[38] are mentioned nine times by Shakespeare if we include *Sir Thomas More* where, in a passage actually written by Anthony Munday and marked for deletion, an apprentice called Robin tells his fellow Harry, 'Faith, Harry, the head drawer at the Mitre by the Great Conduit called me up, and we went to breakfast into St Anne's Lane' (Scene 4a).[39] The Great Conduit was an underground channel in London which brought drinking water in the City from Tyburn to Cheapside. In more canonical works such as *2 Henry VI*, London's water resources are also part and parcel of the cityscape. In a passage intended to parody the accession celebration of Henry VI,[40] Jack Cade commands indeed that 'the Pissing Conduit run nothing but claret wine this first year of our reign' (4.6.3–4): woven into the play's urban life, the Little (or 'Pissing') Conduit evokes an actual London place located at the west end of Cheapside (just outside the north corner of St Paul's churchyard) and which ran a very thin stream. On a different note, in *The Rape of Lucrece*, the poet alludes to 'ivory conduits coral cisterns filling' (l. 1234) as he portrays his heroine in tears. While conduits are here pipes for the conveyance of water and are not inherently poetic devices, Shakespeare turns them into metaphoric objects fit to convey Lucrece's despair. While these examples cannot be said to reflect 'the repeated addition of conduits over the sixteenth century' in London,[41] they nonetheless reveal something about the shift towards a new water technology in the capital and about the way Shakespeare found surprising reservoirs of metaphors in his changing environment.

Clearly, whether commodification of water could help improve access to freshwater supplies and conserve water as a resource was already an issue in his time. The topic of fresh water diversion is especially enlightened in two plays, namely in *1 Henry IV*, where it serves a political agenda, and in *Coriolanus*, when the titular character contemptuously refers to an 'officer' ready to turn a 'current in a ditch' and make the senators' channel 'his' (3.1.94–8). In both plays, the issue is alluded to at the very core of the plot, in Act 3.

In *1 Henry IV*, Hotspur's proposal to change the course of the River Trent shows how he plans a new channel for one of the natural boundary lines and illustrates what was, by the era's own standards, Hotspur's progressive nature (especially when compared to the more conservative Glendower):

> Methinks my moiety north from Burton here
> In quantity equals not one of yours.
> See how his river comes me cranking in
> And cuts me from the best of all my land
> A huge half-moon, a monstrous cantle, out.
> I'll have the current in this place dammed up,
> And here the smug and silver Trent shall run
> In a new channel fair and evenly.
> It shall not wind with such a deep indeed,
> To rob me of so rich a bottom here.
> (3.1.88–102)

Shakespeare's source, Holinshed, does mention the Trent but he never evokes its diversion. According to William M. Jones, the playwright may have had this idea by associating the River Trent of his source with the name of one of his famous contemporaries, Aconcio of Trent who, in 1566, had regained 600 acres from the Thames with the approval of Parliament. These manipulations of water flow seem minor compared with major drainage schemes such as those carried out in the southern Fenland in the seventeenth century (as described in Chapter 11), yet they betray the utilitarian, not to say ecophobic, vision Shakespeare's contemporaries had of fluvial areas. Aconcio's success was such that 'he entered [into] partnership with Elizabeth's Italian tutor, Giovanni-Baptista Castiglione' for his drainage operation and that Elizabeth herself sent him 'to Berwick-on-Tweed as consultant on new fortifications to be constructed' in this 'Scottish-border town'.[42] This hypothesis suggests, if anything, Shakespeare's interest in bold entrepreneurs aiming at changing the course of rivers.

No wonder then if, in *Coriolanus*, the playwright seems to have had in mind a project which aimed at bringing fresh water from the River Lea to Central London between 1608 and 1613.[43] Coriolanus compares the tribunes to the monstrous Hydra:

> O good but most unwise patricians! Why,
> You grave but reckless senators, have you thus
> Given Hydra here to choose an officer
> That with his peremptory 'shall', being but
> The horn and noise o' th' monster's, wants not spirit
> To say he'll turn your current in a ditch
> And make your channel his?
> (3.1.90–6)

Coriolanus's jibe looks like an attack on the management of crucial resources by an ignorant urban rabble. Somewhat ironically, Shakespeare actually reverses an actual situation by making plebeians entrepreneurs ready to use common space for private wealth and, therefore, willing to sell water. Indeed, throughout the play, Coriolanus fears that the people will usurp, despoil and redirect the senators' wide river into a narrow 'ditch'. Here the word suggests a polluted cesspool. But there is more to it. London was looking for ambitious projects to boost its supply of water in an era of increasing commodification of space. In 1582, Peter Morris (sometimes spelt Morice or Moritz), a Dutch engineer, had built a system of waterwheels and pumps in the Thames, which marked the beginning of the water industry.[44] A few years later, another water infrastructure system started to be constructed: it was called the 'New River', and consisted of a thirty-eight-mile canal running under London's main streets and bringing water from springs (the Chadwell and Amwell springs) in Hertfordshire. It was originally designed by Edmund Colthurst in 1604: this former army officer from Bath had received a royal charter specifying that two-thirds of the water would be used to flush the streets for free.[45] The significant point for present purposes is that, while *Coriolanus* was being written and staged between late 1608 and early 1610, it looked as if the New River would be shut down. In his compelling analysis of 'the hydrocommons' in the tragedy, Randall Martin makes clear that, 'at the time of the play's fist performance . . ., it seemed as if parliamentary resistance to royal authority . . . would succeed in rejecting' the takeover of a most precious city resource.[46] The construction of the New River was stalled between 1605 and 1609. Construction then resumed, this time under the supervision of Hugh Myddelton, a rich goldsmith,[47] before halting again for almost two years. In May 1610, a group of landowners even petitioned the House of Commons to stop the New River's construction. Indeed, '[t]hough partly an aqueduct elevated above the ground, the proposed canal for conveying the water would primarily be a trench dug through the estates of up to three hundred landowners'.[48] In 1611, James I finally intervened in Myddelton's favour: accepting to bear half the cost of the project in return for half its profits, the king definitely promoted an ethically dubious commodification of public space.[49]

Ditches and drainage issues

Geographically, socially and economically, the Thames was the nation's most prominent river. Joseph P. Ward observes that '[t]he City's ceremonial occasions acknowledged the river's central role in metropolitan life' and explains that '[d]uring the annual Lord Mayor shows and the occasional royal procession, the Thames served as something of a ceremonial thoroughfare in metropolitan London, as its streets were far too narrow for the purpose'.[50] Yet, in Shakespeare's time, splendour was never far from squalor: the Thames and its '[p]oor tributary rivers' (*Cymbeline*, 4.2.36) were already under threat, subject to serious damage from human activities. The menace of water pollution is hinted at in several texts of the period and present, for example, in *Richard II*, where a metaphorical stream goes 'through muddy passages' (5.3.60) and becomes 'defiled' (5.3.61) as a result, or in *1 Henry IV*, where the 'bubbles in a late-disturbèd stream' (2.4.59) are not necessarily to be associated with the lovely, natural gassy bubbles usually found in freshwater streams, as they conjure up, in Lady Percy's anxious speech, unfortunate events to come. These bubbles, as a result, rather suggest human pollution. In *2 Henry 6*, the Captain despitefully says to Suffolk:

Ay, kennel, puddle, sink; whose filth and dirt
Troubles the silver spring where England drinks,
Now will I dam up this thy yawning mouth
For swallowing the treasure of the realm.
(4.1.71–4)

'[T]he silver spring where England drinks' pointed out here is oddly reminiscent of addition V in *Sir Thomas More*, where one reads the following line: '*Troubled the silver channel* of the Thames' (9.10; italics added). So, when Shakespeare evokes 'filth and dirt' in connection with a 'silver spring', it is tempting to imagine that he had the Thames in mind. While the mention of a spring, that is '[s]omething resembling a flow of water emerging naturally out of the ground, esp. in being refreshing or revitalizing' (*OED* I.1.b.), traditionally evokes purity, this purity is soiled here. The Captain puns on the word 'pool' implicit in Suffolk's family name (de la Pole) and, blaming him for the loss of French possessions, he sullies England's source which is suddenly turned into a mere ditch.

The word 'ditch' comes from the Old English *dic*: it is a long, narrow and open hole dug in the ground. By extension, the term has also extended to natural channels since the end of the sixteenth century. Ditches generally evoke muddy places and stagnant water, something which horrified James. The Fens, in particular, were perceived as permanently flooded, and in response the king 'implemented the General Drainage Act of 1600 which was meant to aid in draining the Fens'.[51] Yet the authorities were not the only ones to blame: the theatre industry of the period was involved in the ecocidal process which consisted in draining low-lying lands to produce new pastures and new ground for the rampant urbanisation of London's whereabouts. As Todd Andrew Borlik reminds us, '[t]he Rose and Globe stood . . . on top of reclaimed marshland', and the audience of the time 'would have caught', coming there, 'a whiff of smoke from the neighbouring glassworks',[52] which, incidentally, adopted seacoal as their main source of fuel at the beginning of the seventeenth century, soon becoming major polluters of the Thames.

Not very far from this riverine site of industrial transition, the River Fleet (which was scoured out to no avail in 1502, 1606 and 1652) entered the Thames at what is now Blackfriars Bridge: all sorts of industries poured waste into this waterway which thus quickly became known as a ditch infested by rats and which functioned as a sewer like many other small rivers.[53] Generally speaking, the word 'ditch' appeared in connection with drainage issues and riverine pollution in the literature of the period. While Shakespeare, contrary to Jonson,[54] does not directly allude to the Fleet, he does refer to ditches in his plays. In *1 Henry 4*, Moorditch, the filthy channel outside the city walls, between Bishopsgate and Cripplegate (London), is mentioned: 'What say'st thou to a hare, or the melancholy of a Moor-ditch?' (1.2.88). This ditch was actually draining the swampy ground of Moorfields. In *Coriolanus*, the eponymous hero warns against the danger of turning currents into 'ditches' (3.1.97) as he blames patricians and senators alike for their submission to the multitude.

This use of ditches testifies to an intimate knowledge of water and to first-hand contact with the surrounding waterscape: Tim Ingold precisely emphasises bodily engagement with the environment as central to place-making.[55] This bodily engagement is what characterises the characters of *The Merry Wives of Windsor*, so much so that some of its characters (Ford – who occasionally disguises himself as Master Brook – as well as Mistress Ford and Shallow) are named after fluvial features. In Act 3, Mistress Ford orders her servants John and Robert to take the buck basket in which Falstaff has hidden himself under a heap of dirty linen, to carry it among the whiteners, and to 'empty it in the muddy ditch close by the Thames' (3.3.12–14). The muddy waters of the English realm were then raising serious health concerns and, despite its resolutely comic tone, Shakespeare's comedy alerted its audience to the condition of rivers which tended to become open sewers as they crossed the cities. This anxiety must have been all the more shared as most English individuals were then 'demonstrably adverse to filth and nastiness' and meant to keep 'both linens and skin sweet and clean', contrary to prevailing ideas on early modern hygiene and to the biased perception, in particular, that all European, sixteenth-century societies repudiated the use of water.[56] In the Folio version of the play, Falstaff complains about his disagreeable contact with water and alludes to his 'transformation' by the Thames:

> If it should come to the ear of the court how I have been transformed, and how my transformation hath been washed and cudgelled, they would melt me out of my fat, drop by drop, and liquor fishermen's boots with me. (4.5.88–91)

The waters are so corrosive that they can re-dimension Falstaff's grotesque body by making its grease melt down. 'By indicating that immersion in the Thames has the capacity to physically refigure Falstaff's body this aqueously inflected Folio description indicates the cultural currency of contact with water', Jemima Matthews writes.[57] In this context, Falstaff becomes yet another infectious commodity transported by the river. Wendy Wall convincingly explains that Falstaff's 'transformation' recasts 'him into manageable domestic goods'.[58] In fact, his feminised (and impure) sweating body is as liquid as the river itself and it almost dissolves in the watery space of the play. Matthews notes that Falstaff's belly 'becomes synecdochical of the riverscape itself'.[59] Mistress Ford's characterisation of Sir John as 'this unwholesome humidity' (3.3.37) is thus particularly apt. Even his belly mimics the very contents of the river, replete with waste and impurities. The whitening process of the women, as a result, seems bound to failure, devoted as it is to an object which cannot be properly cleaned. In the same line of ideas, the 'foul shirts and smocks, socks, foul stockings, greasy napkins' (3.5.84) of the wives working on the adjacent riverbank also designate, by extension, the dirty liminal space of the banks.

Fluid dynamics in Shakespeare

'Earth is neither nature, nor a machine. It is not that we should try to puff some spiritual dimension into its stern and solid stuff', Bruno Latour wrote in 2014, 'but rather that we should abstain from de-animating the agencies that we encounter at each step.'[60] Shakespeare can certainly help us in that way. From his own anthropocentric perspective, no matter how utilitarian they are, rivers still generate emotions: from play to play, he keeps telling us a tale of transformative and animate water, which can, at times, be eco-conscious from our own twenty-first century perspective. His water flows create changing habitats and frequently rise above their banks; they can be 'slow' (*The Rape of Lucrece*, l. 1738), silvery (*Richard II*, 3.2.103), 'pelting' (*A Midsummer Night's Dream*, 2.1.91) or 'proud' (*King John*, 2.2.23); they can carry 'remorse and innocency' (*King John*, 4.3.110), be 'shallow' (*The Merry Wives of Windsor*, 3.1.16) or 'wild' (*All Is True*, 3.2.198). Endowing them with an impressive variety of moods and traits, the playwright obviously sought to engage with streams in multiple ways, sometimes highlighting a sense of connection to the natural world, sometimes perceiving them as an economic commodity. Granted, in his plays and poems, nothing looks like Jonson's nauseating scatological sketch of London's sewage and waste in his 'Famous Voyage' – narrative poetry probably allowing for more detailed accounts of ecocidal practices when compared to drama, less prone to expose so bluntly the vexing problems caused by human exploitation. Neither crudely satirising the gross contamination of English rivers, nor extolling their 'celebratory nature' as Michael Drayton somewhat did,[61] Shakespeare indirectly hints at transcorporeality, consumption and environmental issues. As a result, his references allow us to trace the transformation of early modern rivers, whose flows were increasingly reworked by humans. To put it simply, Shakespeare's rivers can actually be called rivers of the Anthropocene – rivers, in other words, increasingly denatured by the pressing demands of the early modern society.[62]

Disturbingly, perhaps, for today's readers and audiences in search of a more fundamental conception of nature, the playwright's waterways are seldom sources of harmony. The truth is that, traditionally conceived as veins allowing the kingdom to subsist, the early modern English fluvial network did not simply nourish the earth: it also reflected the unruly nature of landscape and the profound mutations of the Elizabethan and Jacobean societies. As sites of contestation, rivers happened to be generative as much as decaying aqueous spaces, both destructive and transformative for the early modern society. River-borne trade in London's economy developed at an accelerated pace around 1600 and still increased at the end of the seventeenth century. With the advent of mercantile water industries, the Thames was no longer freely available to the people. As a consequence, the use of fresh water (generally contaminated and making people sick if they drank it) shed light on the growing tensions between the various categories of the English population, from the poor to the elite. Shakespeare reflects, in his plays and poems, the crucial social and economic importance of waterways and he pays particular attention to their regulation, probably in connection with his own entrepreneurial interests. However, he is not blind to the beauty of untamed springs. His texts thus suggest a somewhat ambivalent stance towards the (ab)use of fresh water. While he never explicitly denounces the industrialisation and the over-exploitation of waterways in the name of productivity and at times betrays an interest in the taming of waterscapes, he also points to some of the dire consequences of these phenomena. Hinting at the deterioration of waterways, he underlines the tensions between the poetics and the politics of water. In so doing, he adumbrates an early modern aesthetics of riverine collapse, one in which rivers, despite their beauty, generate pain, disagreement, dissension and pollution. In his own lucid way, he was already paving the way for narratives of habitat destruction and perhaps also for the redefinition of waterways as rich, life-sustaining ecosystems, neither reducible to a basic means of sustenance nor to an idealised natural space of 'pristine wilderness'.[63]

Notes

1. John Leland, *Cygnea cantio* (London: Reyner Wolfe, 1545). On Leland's text, see Emily J. Naish's chapter, '"Insatiable [Gourmandize] Thus All Things Doth Devour": Reading the Threat of Human Greed along the Rivers of Early Modern England', in the present volume, 211–30.
2. William Camden, *Britannia sive Florentissimorum Regnorum, Angliae, Scotiae, Hiberniae, et Insularum Adjacentium ex Intima Antiquitate Chorographica Descriptio* (London: Ralph Newberry, 1586).

3. On the poems by John Leland and William Camden, see Robert Imes, 'Writing Geography: Traversing Early Modern English Chorographies' (doctoral thesis, University of Saskatchewan, 2020), 1–6, https://harvest.usask.ca/bitstream/handle/10388/13004/IMES-DISSERTATION-2020.pdf?sequence=1&isAllowed=y (last accessed 6 August 2022).
4. All Shakespeare quotations come from *William Shakespeare: The Complete Works*, ed. Gary Taylor and Stanley Wells (Oxford: Oxford University Press, 1988).
5. Isidore of Seville. *The Etymologies of Isidore of Seville*, edited and translated by S. A. Barney, W. J. Lewis, J. A. Beach and O. Berghof (Cambridge: Cambridge University Press, 2005), Book XIII; xi.21–xiii.11, 276.
6. On the notion of 'reverse hydrological cycle', see Christopher J. Duffy, 'The Terrestrial Hydrologic Cycle: An Historical Sense of Balance', *WIREs Water* 4.4 (July/August 2017), n.p., https://wires.onlinelibrary.wiley.com/doi/full/10.1002/wat2.1216 (last accessed 22 September 2023).
7. See the frontispiece of Johannes Herbinius's *Dissertationes de admirandis mundi cataractis supra & subterraneis* (1678), commented upon in detail in Duffy, 'The Terrestrial Hydrologic Cycle', n.p.
8. Andrew McRae, 'Fluvial Nation: Rivers, Mobility and Poetry in Early Modern England', *English Literary Renaissance* 38.3 (2008), 506–34, 512.
9. Henri Bergson, *Creative Evolution*, translated by Arthur Mitchell (London: Macmillan, 1911), 48–9.
10. On this argument, see Tim Ingold and Cristián Simonetti, 'Introducing Solid Fluids', *Theory, Culture & Society* 39.2 (2022), 3–29.
11. Navigation on the Thames was reaching such proportions in the mid-sixteenth century that, in 1555, an Act of Parliament formalised the trade of watermen, 'by Reason of the rude, ignorant and unskilful Number of Watermen' who were then exercising their profession. The text of the Act, 'Anno secundo & tertio Philippi &Mari. An Act touching Watermen and Bargemen upon the River of Thames', is available online: https://vlex.co.uk/vid/thames-watermen-act-1555-808183929 (last accessed 6 August 2022).
12. William Harrison, *An Historicall Description of the Iland of Britaine, An Electronic Edition* (London, 1577, 1587), ed. Henry Ellis, Perseus Digital Library, coll. Renaissance Materials, Book 1, Chap. 18, 'Of the aire, soile, and commodities of this iland', https://www.perseus.tufts.edu/hopper/text?doc=Perseus%3Atext%3A1999.03.0083%3Abook%3D1%3Achapter%3D18 (last accessed 2 August 2022).
13. William Harrison, *An Historicall Description of the Iland of Britaine*, Book 2, Chap. 23, 'Of baths and hot welles': 'The fourth place where baths are, is kings Newnam, and within certeine miles of Couentrie, the water wherof (as it is thought) procédeth from some rocke of allume, and this I vnderstand by diuerse glouers which haue béene there, and also by mine owne experience, ... The said water hath a naturall propertie also following it which is rare, for if a leafe, or sticke of ash, oke, &c: doo fall into the same, within a short space, such store of fine sand (comming no doubt out of the earth with the water) will congeale and gather about it, that the forme being reserued, and the inner part not lightlie altered, it will seeme to become an hard stone, and much like vnto that which is ingendred in the kidneis of a man, as I haue séene by experience', n.p., https://www.perseus.tufts.edu/

hopper/text?doc=Perseus%3Atext%3A1999.03.0083%3Abook%3D2%3Achapter%3D23 (last accessed 10 August 2022).
14. Liza Picard, 'Food in Elizabethan Literature', *British Library. Discovering Literature: Shakespeare & Renaissance* (2016), n.p., https://www.bl.uk/shakespeare/articles/food-in-elizabethan-england (last accessed 10 August 2022). While the Elizabethan diet was ruled by the calendar, the necessity of eating fish can be qualified: 'But "fish" included veal, game and poultry, and if you really couldn't do without beef you could buy a "flesh-eater's licence", or get round the rules in other ways', Picard writes (n.p.).
15. John Emrys Morgan, 'The Micro-Politics of Water Management in Early Modern England: Regulation and Representation in Commissions of Sewers', *Environment and History* 23.3 (2017), https://www.research.manchester.ac.uk/portal/files/55190754/1391.pdf (last accessed 1 August 2022).
16. Yet, as Morgan points out, 'floods at the right time, in the right place and for the right duration could be immensely beneficial to farmers'; '[t]he primary use of flood-liable land', he adds, 'was as grazing'. See Morgan, 'Flooding in Early Modern England: Cultures of Coping in Gloucestershire and Lincolnshire' (PhD thesis, University of Warwick, 2015), 48, https://wrap.warwick.ac.uk/79945/1/WRAP_THESIS_Morgan_2015.pdf (last accessed 4 August 2022).
17. Flooding seldom has positive consequences in the Shakespearean canon. Even the rebellion of Henry, Second Duke of Buckingham, fails in *Richard III* because of the flooding of the River Severn: 'by sudden floods and fall of water, / Buckingham's army is dispersed and scattered' (4.4.441–2).
18. Conrad Heresbach, *Foure books of husbandry*, translated by Barnaby Googe (London, 1577), fols 20v, 43v.
19. Hugh Plat, *Diverse new sorts of soyle not yet brought into any publique use, for manuring both of pasture and arable ground* [Part 2 of *The jewell house of art and nature*] (London: Peter Short, 1594), 24.
20. Michael Drayton, 'The Shepheard's Garland, Fashioned in nine Eglogs. Rowlands Sacrifice to the nine muses' (1593), in J. William Hebel, ed., *The Works of Michael Drayton*, 4 vols (Oxford: Blackwell, 1931), I, 45–94, 47.
21. Sophie Chiari, 'Overflowing the Measure: Cleopatra Unbound', *Actes des congrès de la Société française Shakespeare* 37 (2019), par. 6, n.p., http://journals.openedition.org/shakespeare/4397 (last accessed 5 August 2022).
22. Charlotte Scott, *Shakespeare's Nature: From Cultivation to Culture* (Oxford: Oxford University Press, 2014), 152.
23. Sidney Thomas, 'The Bad Weather in A Midsummer Night's Dream', *Modern Language Notes* 64.5 (May 1949), 319–22.
24. Karen V. Lykke Syse, 'Ideas of Leisure, Pleasure and the River in Early Modern England', in *Perceptions of Water in Britain from Early Modern Times to the Present: An Introduction*, ed. Karen V. Lykke Syse and Terje Oestigaard (Bergen: University of Bergen, 2010), 35–57, 36. See also E. Towner and J. Towner, 'Developing the History of Unintentional Injury: The Use of Coroners' Records in Early Modern England', *Injury Prevention* 6 (2000), 102–5.
25. There are, of course, other well-known hypotheses about the inspiration for Ophelia, including the story of Katharine Hamlet, who drowned in the River Avon, not far from Stratford upon Avon, in 1579. On Gunn's

new hypothesis, see 'The Shakespeare Blog', http://theshakespeareblog. com/2011/06/more-ophelia-contenders-jane-shaxspere-v-katherine-haml et-and-margaret-clopton/ (last accessed 4 August 2022).
26. On this see Peter Ackroyd, *Shakespeare: The Biography* (London: Chatto and Windus, 2005), 6–7: 'The countryside around Stratford was divided into two swathes. To the north lay the Forest of Arden, the remains of the ancient forest that covered the Midlands; these tracts are known as the Wealden . . . Beyond the Wealden, in the south of the county, lay the Fielden. In Saxton's map of Warwickshire, issued in 1576, this region is almost wholly devoid of trees except for those growing in groves and small woods.'
27. John Gillies, *Shakespeare and the Geography of Difference* (Cambridge and New York: Cambridge University Press, 1994), 143.
28. The demand for coal, in the early modern seventeenth century, 'encouraged the development of both the Tyneside coal fields and the attendant shipping trades, which transported the coal three hundred miles along the coast and up the Thames to London'. See Ward, 'The Taming of the Thames', 57.
29. Ibid., 74.
30. Max Satchell, 'Navigable Waterways and the Economy of England and Wales: 1600–1835' (2017), 4, https://www.campop.geog.cam.ac.uk/ research/projects/transport/onlineatlas/waterways.pdf (last accessed 4 August 2022). Satchell adds that '[b]y 1760 this had increased to 1400 miles' and in 1835, 'the total waterways network was around 4,000 miles – with most of the increase due to canal building'.
31. John Stow, *A Survey of London*, ed. C. L. Kingsford, 2 vols (Oxford: Clarendon, 1911), II, 199–201.
32. In *The Rape of Lucrece*, see l. 1076.
33. Gail Kern Paster, *The Body Embarrassed: Drama and the Disciplines of Shame in Early Modern England* (Ithaca, NY: Cornell University Press, 1993).
34. Nancy Lindheim, 'The Shakespearean Venus and Adonis', *Shakespeare Quarterly* 37.2 (Summer 1986), 190–203, 202.
35. McRae, 'Fluvial Nation', 525.
36. See Murray J. Levith and Albert Bandura, *Shakespeare's Italian Settings and Plays* (New York: St. Martin's Press, 1989), 18.
37. Fynes Moryson, *An itinerary* (London: John Beale, 1617), STC (2nd ed.), 18205.
38. Leslie Tomory, *The History of the London Water Industry, 1580–1820* (Baltimore: Johns Hopkins University Press, 2017), 20.
39. See Appendix A in Taylor and Wells, *William Shakespeare: The Complete Works*.
40. Stephen Longstaffe, '"A short report and not otherwise": Jack Cade in *2 Henry VI*', in *Shakespeare and Carnival: After Bakhtin*, ed. Ronald Knowles (Houndmills: MacMillan, 1998), 13–35, 17.
41. Tomory, *The History of the London Water Industry*, 28.
42. William M. Jones, 'The Turning of Trent in *1 Henry IV*', *Renaissance News* 17.4 (Winter 1964), 304–7, 306.
43. For an extended analysis of this particular issue in *Coriolanus*, see Randall Martin, 'Ecocritical Studies', in *The Arden Research Handbook of Contemporary Shakespeare Criticism*, ed. Evelyn Gajowski (London: Bloomsbury, The Arden Shakespeare, 2020), 189–204.

44. Tomory, *The History of the London Water Industry*, 14.
45. Su Mei Kok, '"How Many Arts from Such a Labour Flow": Thomas Middleton and London's New River', *Journal of Medieval and Early Modern Studies* 43.1 (Winter 2013), 173–90, 174.
46. Martin, 'Ecocritical Studies', 200.
47. In 1617, he acquired a lease for silver, copper and lead mines in Wales from the Mines Royal Society 'and made a fair profit on the venture, enough to offset the losses he was experiencing in building the New River at the time'. See Tomory, *The History of the London Water Industry*, 52.
48. Kok, '"How Many Arts from Such a Labour Flow"', 174.
49. Ethically dubious because on grounds of urban development, the project entailed the privatisation of water which, so far, had been a common good. More generally, on Myddelton's enterprise in connection with environmental degradation, see Bruce Boehrer, *Environmental Degradation in Jacobean Drama* (Cambridge: Cambridge University Press, 2013), esp. chapter 1.
50. Ward, 'The Taming of the Thames', 57.
51. Martha Lynn Russell, '"The King's Highway": Reading England's Road in *The Pilgrim's Progress*, Part I', in *Reading the Road, from Shakespeare's Crossways to Bunyan's Highways*, ed. Lisa Hopkins and Bill Angus (Edinburgh: Edinburgh University Press, 2020), 238–51, 248.
52. Borlik, *Literature and Nature*, 21.
53. Tomory, *The History of the London Water Industry*, 28.
54. 'On the Famous Voyage', the final poem in Ben Jonson's book of *Epigrammes* (c. 1612), famously narrates a journey up the polluted Fleet Ditch from Bridewell to Holborn. On the poem's 'excremental fixation' (19), see for example Bruce Boehrer, 'Horatian Satire in Jonson's "On the Famous Voyage"', *Criticism* 44.1 (Winter 2002), 9–26.
55. Tim Ingold, *The Perception of the Environment: Essays on Livelihood, Dwelling and Skill* (London: Routledge, 2000).
56. Susan North, *Sweet and Clean? Bodies and Clothes in Early Modern England* (Oxford: Oxford University Press, 2020), 284.
57. Jemima Matthews, 'Inside Out and Outside In: The River Thames in William Shakespeare's *The Merry Wives of Windsor*', *Shakespeare* 15.4 (2019), 410–27, 415.
58. Wendy Wall, *Staging Domesticity: Household Work and English Identity in Early Modern Drama* (Cambridge: Cambridge University Press, 2002), 116–17.
59. Matthews, 'Inside Out and Outside In', 421.
60. Bruno Latour, 'Agency at the Time of the Anthropocene', *New Literary History* 45.1 (Winter 2014), 1–18, 14.
61. I am referring here to Naish's chapter in this volume (Chapter 10), which notably analyses the literary treatment of rivers in Drayton's *Poly-Olbion* (1612).
62. I am alluding to Jason M. Kelly, Philip Scarpino, Helen Berry, James Syvitski and Michel Meybeck, eds, *Rivers of the Anthropocene* (Oakland: University of California Press, 2018).
63. Timothy Morton, *The Ecological Thought* (Cambridge, MA: Harvard University Press, 2012), 5.

Conclusions: Rivers of Life and Death

Lisa Hopkins and Bill Angus

We explained at the outset that this book is divided into four sections: 'Conceptualising the River', 'Writing the River', 'Rivers and Money' and 'Ecocritical Approaches'. In fact those classifications are largely artificial because each of the four flows into others as surely as rivers converge and flow into the sea. Esther Water explores writing about the Fens as well as the fens themselves, noting how the fens are 'evocatively celebrated by Drayton in "Holland Fen"' (263); Sophie Chiari notes not only the degradation of early modern waterways but literary inscriptions of it and argues for 'an early modern aesthetics of collapse' (251–2). Moreover, just as the rivers themselves moved, so their meanings moved. In the classical world rivers had been figured as deities in their own right; the early modern period played with this idea through the literary modes of chorography (reference to which opens and closes Brice Peterson's chapter) and personification, as Jemima Matthews shows in her discussion of Drayton's *Poly-Olbion* (188), and unexpected floods or fluctuations could also be read as indications of divine displeasure. The popular genre of chorography, of which Drayton was a leading exponent, often focused on rivers because they shaped and demarcated the land. Lisa Hopkins notes that 'Trent divided the north from the south' (86) and Rebecca Welshman observes that 'Conflicts often took place near rivers because they marked the edge of a contested territory and were natural borderlands' (61).

It was not only poets who wrote about rivers, though; Welshman's interest in real battles is complemented by Cecilia Lindskog Whiteley's exploration of fictional battles staged in plays close to the river such as the Globe and the Rose. She argues that 'Merely two years after the theatre's establishment, the Rose and the watermen had become intimately connected in a symbiotic relationship' (168), while Lindsay Ann Reid argues for 'an equation between London's boats and its theatrical spaces' (115). On the most basic level, river transport was the most likely means for audience members to reach the bankside theatres, and this underlines the centrality of rivers to early modern transport, traffic and trade: Sophie Chiari notes that 'the waterworld of early modern England, primarily made of streams, rivers, channels and brooks, was one of the kingdom's most strategic networks in terms of economy, exchange, and transportation' (251), and also observes how often Shakespeare mentions barges, while Emily J. Naish points out that water transport was far cheaper than land-based equivalents.

As well as offering transport, rivers could also be a source of power, particularly for mills, as explored by Daniel Gettings and Jemima Matthews. The practical and cultural importance of rivers led to the development of distinctively riverine communities, as explored here by Daniel Gettings, and also gave prominence to the watermen discussed by Bill Angus and Lindsay Ann Reid. And it was not only men whose lives might be shaped by the river: Esther Water notes that 'For women, access to the commons was particularly important for maintaining their livelihood resilience, which potentially explains women's significant role in protesting against changes to the commons' (235), while Daniel Gettings notes the importance of rivers for domestic laundry, and Jemima Matthews considers the treatment of female ragpickers and of women whose husbands had drowned. There were of course also non-human inhabitants of the river, notably fish; Sophie Chiari points out that fish days accounted for nearly a third of the year, Emily J. Naish explores the importance of fish to the economy, Daniel Gettings discusses riverine communities' reliance on fish and Melissa Caldwell considers Izaak Walton's *The Compleat Angler*. Esther Water notes conceptual connections between the local fish and the dwellers in the Fens themselves.

Caldwell also intriguingly argues that all fish were potentially connected to monstrosity (Rebecca Welshman notes the occasional appearance of whales in the Thames), suggesting that the inhabitants of rivers could, like rivers themselves, be important not only literally but also metaphorically. As Welshman puts it, 'The Thames ran through the lives and workplaces of poets, playwrights and publishers alike, and offered an ever-present living metaphor familiar to audiences and readers' (63). Lindsay Ann Reid notes that '*The Fraternitye of Vacabondes*'s title page['s] citation of the legendary Cock Lorel efficiently aligns the Gravesend barge with the metaphorical ship of fools popularised in Sebastian Brant's late fifteenth-century *Das Narrenschiff*' (113), and Brice Peterson observes that 'The depiction of a soul as a ship carrying treasures figures grace as an economic exchange: the soul receives treasures from God, which it then "returns again"' (32). Peterson's discussion of rivers as metaphors for grace might remind us that in the classical world rivers demarcated not only geographical but also spiritual territory: the River Styx was the border between life and death, and could be crossed only if the ferryman was paid. The early modern period did not believe in the Styx, but it did not forget it, and something of the same suggestion of the uncanny could accrue to early modern figurings of rivers. Melissa Caldwell observes that 'As a site of convergence, juxtaposition and disruption, borders between land and water or between rivers and oceans are productive but also problematic spaces' (124), and this was all the more so because rivers could bring death to communities as well as feeding and watering them: Daniel Gettings notes the frequency of death by drowning and he, Sophie Chiari, Esther Water and Emily J. Naish all note the devastation caused by flooding. Naish also notes, however, that 'Rivers – in providing fresh water and fish, and in enabling mobility around the country and overseas – represented many anthropocentric opportunities' (212). Her word 'anthropocentric' is a suggestive one because rivers might not only be personified but might also be figured as almost symbiotic with humans: Brice Peterson suggests that 'spiritual rivers of grace cause physical rivers of tears to flow within and issue from believers' (31) and Lisa Hopkins notes in her discussion of William Sampson's *The Vow Breaker* that 'Even before the River Trent itself is mentioned in Sampson's play, there is a note of watery imagery' (88) in the description of the characters who live on its banks. Bill Angus reminds us of the imagined ale, brewed from muddy river water, running in the veins of John Taylor.

The importance of rivers made them an early site for human intervention; Hopkins, Welshman and Chiari all note discussions about changing the course of the Trent and Esther Water traces hotly contested debates about the draining of the Fens. Human activity had already had visible effects on many English rivers: Bill Angus points to 'the choked tributary rivers of London, principally the Fleet, whose name had acquired irony and whose stygian state was proverbial' (144), and Chiari too traces the degradation of early modern waterways. Daniel Gettings notes that 'The charges by county governments against those who disrupted the flow of the rivers ... were framed in terms of community disruption both through breach of the peace but also through the disturbance of an ancient order' (52); what they could not know was that they were also contributing to man-made climate change. We are being terrifyingly reminded of that now, and also of its roots in the early modern period: Jemima Matthews notes that 'In the widespread drought experienced in the summer of 2022 hunger stones began to appear in rivers across Europe' and that 'a stone in the river Elbe carved with the date 1616 reads "If you see me then weep"' (189). We do see it and we do weep. We should also remember that what early modern people knew and thought about rivers still affects us now, in both our physical geography and in the ways we conceive of the bodies of water that flow through our world and continue to give it form.

Notes on Contributors

Bill Angus is a senior lecturer in English at Massey University, New Zealand. He has written extensively on early modern drama and material culture. His books with Edinburgh University Press include *Metadrama and the Informer in Shakespeare and Jonson* (2016), *Intelligence and Metadrama in the Early Modern Theatre* (2018), *Reading the Road, from Shakespeare's Crossways to Bunyan's Highways* (2019), co-edited with Lisa Hopkins, and his last monograph, *A History of Crossroads in Early Modern Culture* (2022). His latest edited collection, *Poison on the Early Modern English Stage*, co-edited with Kibrina Davey and Lisa Hopkins, was published in 2023.

Melissa Caldwell is a professor of English at Eastern Illinois University. Her research interests include the literature, philosophy and religion of seventeenth-century England; adaptation studies with a focus on literary adaptation; and war literature, both in the seventeenth and the twenty-first centuries. Her publications include '"The Isle Is Full of Noises": The Many Tempests of Margaret Atwood's *Hag-Seed*' (*Comparative Drama*, 2023), 'Poetry after Descartes: Henry More's Adaptive Poetics', in *Adaptation before Cinema* (2023) and *Skepticism and Belief in Early Modern England* (2017).

Sophie Chiari is Professor of Shakespeare Studies at Université Clermont Auvergne (UCA), France. She is currently working on soil studies in connection with Shakespeare and his contemporaries. She has written numerous essays on ecocritical issues in early modern English literature, and she has recently co-edited with Janet Clare a special issue of the *Journal of Early Modern Studies* on *The Circulation of Cosmographical Knowledge in Early Modern Europe* (vol. 12, 2023). Her most recent books include *Shakespeare and the Environment: A Dictionary* (2022), *Shakespeare's Representation of Weather, Climate* *and Environment* (2019) and As You Like It: *Shakespeare's Comedy of Liberty* (2016).

Daniel Gettings is a final year PhD candidate at the University of Warwick in the Department of History. His PhD thesis focuses on exploring the relationship between early modern English people and water across a broad range of areas including food and drink, religious beliefs, work and the environment.

Lisa Hopkins is Professor Emerita of English at Sheffield Hallam University and co-editor of *Shakespeare*, the journal of the British Shakespeare Association, of Arden Studies in Early Modern Drama and of Arden Early Modern Drama Guides. Her most recent publications are *The Edge of Christendom on the Early Modern English Stage* (2022) and *A Companion to the Cavendishes*, with Tom Rutter (2020). She also works on detective fiction and her book *Ocular Proof and the Spectacled Detective in British Crime Fiction* was published by in 2023.

Cecilia Lindskog Whiteley is a doctoral candidate in English Literature at Uppsala University, Sweden. She is currently completing her thesis on the ways in which the establishment of the first permanent playhouses in London created new possibilities for drama in the 1580s. She has published a number of other pieces on early modern literature in journals and edited collections, including essays on Shakespeare and the urban, early modern city comedy, and the Jacobean macabre. Her most recent essay was 'Cold Maids and Dead Men: Gender in Translation and Transition in Hamlet', in *Disseminating Shakespeare in the Nordic Countries* (2022).

Jemima Matthews is a lecturer in early modern English literature at King's College London and co-director of the Shakespeare Centre London. She is a recipient of the King's Artist award for her project 'Silt and Other Matters'. She has published on 'Maritime Ephemera in Walter Mountfort's *The Launching of the Mary*', in *Practices of Ephemera in Early Modern England* (2023) and 'Inside Out and Outside In: The River Thames in William Shakespeare's *The Merry Wives of Windsor*' (*Shakespeare*, 2019).

Emily J. Naish is a PhD student at the University of Sheffield. Her thesis takes a historicist-ecocritical approach to examine the works of canonical Renaissance writers such as Shakespeare, Spenser and Sidney alongside Michael Drayton's *Poly-Olbion*. Most recently, she has presented her research at Renaissance Society of America (grant awarded), the Society for Renaissance Studies, and the Association for the Study of Literature and the Environment. Emily has been a postgraduate coordinator for Sheffield Centre for Early Modern Studies since 2021 where she is involved with organising the Early Modern Discussion Group. She is also an editorial assistant at *Green Letters*.

Brice Peterson is an assistant professor in the English Department at Brigham Young University. He studies knowledge taxonomies in early modern English literature, specifically how knowledge is represented, organised and interrogated. His research examines four specific knowledge domains (theology, medicine, gender and genre) to decipher how poets and playwrights rethink religious doctrines, medical theories, gender assumptions and generic conventions. His essay 'Diagnosis, Medical Ethics, and Moral Authority in *The Pardoner's Tale*' is forthcoming in *The Chaucer Review*. His work has also been published in *Studies in Philology*, *Early Modern Women: An Interdisciplinary Journal*, *Studies in English Literature, 1500–1900* and *American Literature and the New Puritan Studies* (2017).

Lindsay Ann Reid is a senior lecturer in English at the University of Galway. Her research primarily focuses on the reception of classical and medieval literature in early modern England. She is the author of two monographs, *Shakespeare's Ovid and the Spectre of the Medieval* (2018) and *Ovidian Bibliofictions and the Tudor Book* (2014).

Esther Water is currently studying a Master of Creative Writing at Massey University. Her previous studies include a Bachelor of Resource Studies (Environmental Management, majoring in Human Ecology and Development) and a Master of Applied Science. Esther has worked and kayaked on rivers for the last thirty years in both Aotearoa/New Zealand and overseas. Her long relationship with rivers has influenced her current research which focuses on ecopoetics, New Zealander's relationships with rivers and the rights of rivers.

Rebecca Welshman is an independent scholar, and Honorary Fellow of the University of Liverpool (2014–17). She works on interdisciplinary projects in the humanities concerning literature and landscape. Her PhD (University of Exeter, 2010–13) focused on nineteenth-century literature and archaeology, and she is particularly interested in 'the literary archaeology of place' – the study of texts in the context of geography, history and environment. Her most recent publication '"The Invisible

Operator": Plague, Corruption, and Conspiracy in Renaissance Drama' appeared in *Pandemics and Epidemics in Cultural Representation* (2022). Other publications include an edited collection of essays by the Victorian author and naturalist Richard Jefferies (2019), 'Archaeology', in *Thomas Hardy in Context* (2013), and a chapter about archaeology and literature in *Mysticism, Myth and Celtic Identity* (2013). Most recently she has been working on new interpretations of the topography of the battlefield of Hastings.

Index

Aelian, 111–12
alcohol, 11–12, 145–9, 270
   benefits of, 151–2, 156–7
   dangers of, 156
   drunkenness, 155–6
   and riverine metaphor, 150–5, 157–60
   types of, 154–5
Alleyn, Charles, 91
Anderson, Anthony, 25
Anyan, Thomas, 24
aquatic inhabitants, 130–6, 215–16, 270
   folkloric, 89–90, 133–6, 224
   as anthropomorphic metaphor, 134–5
   as political metaphor, 67–8, 241
Awdelay, John, 10, 112–14, 116–17

Baker, Richard, 87, 90, 92
Bancroft, Thomas, 90
Barclay, Alexander, 113
Barnfield, Richard, 90
the body, 199–200
   as a metaphor for waterways, 153, 157–8, 198
   as a site of contest, 62, 73–5
   waterways as metaphors for the body, 30–1, 73, 88, 153–4, 256, 258, 262–3
Bowles, Edward, 86
Bradley, Humphrey, 237
Brant, Sebastian, 113, 270
Braun, Georg, 103–4
Breton, Nicholas, 112, 146
Brome, Richard, 87
Buchanan, George, 91
Burton, Henry, 88
Burton, Robert, 93
Bydall, John, 87
Byshop, John, 13, 189–201

Camden, William, 22, 127, 250
Carleton, Mary, 108
cartography, 4, 13–14, 26, 28, 103–5, 130, 133–4, 214–15, 224–6, 237
Cartwright, John, 90
Cawood, John, 109
Chapman, George, 115
Churchyard, Thomas, 13, 190–203
chorography, 21, 35, 85, 190, 232–3, 250, 255, 269
Clitherow, Margaret, 4
Cobler of Caunterburie, 101–20
Cocke Lorells Bote, 113
Coleridge, Samuel Taylor, 66
Colthurst, Edmund, 259

Cotton, John, 25
Cowell, John, 87
Crooke, Helkiah, 30

dangers of rivers, 11, 14, 90–1, 102, 197, 225–6
  drowning, 50–1, 88, 91, 103, 179, 189–94, 196–200, 254, 271
  flooding, 6, 8–9, 15, 44, 48–50, 64–5, 130, 212, 216–17, 235, 252–4, 271
Dante, 231
Day, John, 11, 114–15
Dekker, Thomas, 11, 112, 119–20
Deloney, Thomas, 106
Dennys, John, 215
devotional poets, 35–8
Drayton, Michael, 2, 14–15, 22, 6, 66, 85, 89, 90, 96, 126, 133, 187–8, 190, 212, 219, 221–7, 232–3, 237, 253, 263, 269
drought, 188–9, 271–2

Eucharist, 26–7, 35–6

faith and waterways, 151
  as gods, 1–3, 269
  as grace, 8, 21–7, 270–1
  as virtues, 26, 31
  as destiny, 32–3
  as punishment, 48–9
  as great works, 131
the Fens, 14–15, 93, 231–44, 261, 269–70
  ecology of, 232–4, 238–40, 243–4
  inhabitants of, 231–5, 237–8, 240–1
  riots, 240–2

Field, Richard, 63
Fiennes, Celia, 46
Flemming, Abraham, 111–12
Foxe, John, 10, 111
Fuller, Thomas, 93

Gardiner, Ralph, 46
Gordon, Patrick, 86
Greene, Robert, 101
Grove, John, 148

Habington, William, 87
Harrison, William, 43, 212–19, 224–7, 252
Hasted, Edward, 55
Harvey, William, 25
Hayward, John, 90
Herbert, George, 8, 22–3, 28–31, 36
Heylyn, Peter, 112, 135
Hieron, Samuel, 25
Hogenburg, Frans, 104
Hole, William, 14, 212–13
Holinshed, Raphael, 85–7, 94, 212, 252
Howell, James, 86
hunger stones, 188–9, 270–1

improvement, 53–4, 92–5, 190–203, 212, 217, 232, 234, 236–44, 256–62
  negative impacts of, 189–90, 192–203, 212–13, 215–18, 220–1, 226–7, 237, 242–4, 264
Isidore of Seville, 250–1

Jones, William, 48–9
Jonson, Ben, 4, 14–15, 85, 115, 146, 161, 219, 231, 236–40, 243–44, 250, 261, 263

Lambarde, William, 106
Lanyer, Aemilia, 8, 22–3, 25–8, 35–6
legal management of rivers, 43–8, 52, 53–4, 109–10, 234–8, 252, 264, 271
  taxes, 147–8
Leland, John, 22, 212, 218, 250
Livy, 73
London Bridge, 5, 64, 65, 103–5, 145, 170–1, 173–8, 180, 214
Lyly, John, 13, 169–70, 180–3

management of rivers, 50
Marlowe, Christopher, 3, 169, 171, 176
Marston, John, 115
medical properties of rivers (including the mystical), 131–2, 152, 220, 252
Milton, John, 3, 22, 35, 107
More, Thomas, 213
Morison, Fynes, 108, 257
Morris, Peter, 260
Munday, Anthony, 103, 107–9, 257

Nashe, Thomas, 10, 113–14, 118, 148
national identity, 125–6, 174, 237
nature as divine, 23–4
Norden, John, 103

oak, 62, 70–1
Overbury, Thomas, 145
Ovid, 66, 177–8

paper making, 198–200
Paré, Abroise, 134
Peele, George, 12–13, 169–83

phenomenology of grace
  sensory, 25–8, 33–5
  as emotion, 29–32, 36
phenomenology of rivers, 7, 171, 174, 182, 223
Platt, Hugh, 253
Pocahontas, 107
pollution of waterways, 46, 56, 144, 148, 260–4

Riche, Barnabe, 106
rivers as a resource, 9, 11, 13, 15–16, 43–8, 225–6, 233, 236, 254
  access to, 195–7, 257–60
  food, 46–7, 85, 103, 127–8, 131–2, 212, 215, 220, 252, 271
  power, 44–5, 192, 195–6, 202, 217, 270
  water, 43–4, 147–8, 194, 212–13, 220, 252–3, 255, 257–60, 271
rivers as borders, 4–5, 9, 11, 13, 52, 61, 70–1, 84–7, 124–5, 168–171, 269
  national borders, 22, 68–9, 124
  spiritual borders, 3–4, 11, 88, 95–6, 119–20
rivers as contemplative spaces, 126–9, 136–7
rivers as infrastructure, 4, 10, 11, 15, 101–10, 116, 145, 170–1, 180–1, 212–15, 251, 255, 269–70
  economic infrastructure, 32, 92–3, 102–3, 145, 150–1, 157–60, 197–8, 202, 213–15, 219, 234, 264
  military infrastructure, 70, 91
  sanitation, 45–6, 53, 69–70, 234–5, 261–3

rivers as meeting places, 52–3, 116
rivers as permissive spaces, 169, 175–80
rivers as sites of battle, 9, 61–8, 91–2, 179
rivers as sites of entertainment, 5–7, 113, 129, 162, 168–83, 260
rivers
  Allier, 67
  Amazon, 2
  Anider, 213
  Annan, 149
  Avon, 61, 87, 222, 250, 255
  Avon (Wiltshire), 158–60
  Blackwater, 2
  Brenta, 257
  Calder, 4
  Camel, 222
  Cray, 187–8
  Danube, 4
  Darent, 56, 187–90, 197, 201
  Dart, 222
  Don, 93
  Eastern Cleddau, 7–8
  Elbe, 148
  Esk, 149
  Euphrates, 2, 90, 169
  Exe, 222
  Fleet, 144, 271
  Forth, 9, 61
  Ganges, 2, 133, 169
  Great Ouse, 14
  Humber, 85–6, 89, 149, 153, 162
  Indus, 2
  Lea, 16, 63, 127, 259
  Liger, 67
  Lugg, 71
  Medway, 2, 56, 70, 187
  Nene, 14
  Nile, 2, 7, 169, 253
  Orinoco, 2
  Otterburn, 9
  Ouse (Yorkshire), 4, 149, 153
  Po, 90
  Rede, 9, 61
  Rubicon, 3
  Segre, 67
  Severn, 7, 61, 64, 65, 85, 87, 144–5, 216, 222
  Sherbourne, 52
  Shirebrook, 4
  Swilgate, 61, 64
  Tamar, 4, 222
  Tame, 153, 219–23, 250
  Thame, 2
  Thames (Isis), 1, 2, 3, 4, 5–7, 10, 11, 12, 13, 16, 43–4, 56, 62–4, 67–71, 86, 87, 90, 101–20, 130, 135–6, 144–63, 168–83, 191–2, 195–6, 201, 214–27, 254, 255–6, 258–9, 260–4, 270
  Tiber, 7
  Tigris, 2
  Trent, 9–10, 65–6, 83–97, 153, 258–9, 271
  Tweed, 2, 86, 259
  Tyne, 2
  Ure, 61
  Volga, 3
  Welland, 14
  Western Cleddau, 7
  Wye, 68
The Rose playhouse, 168–83, 269
Rosinus, Johannes, 65
Rowlands, Samuel, 146
royalism, 125–6, 128–9, 137, 162
Russell, Lucy, 35

Sampson, William, 9–10, 83–97, 271
Saxon, Christopher, 237
scatological imagery, 143–4, 263
Shakespeare, William, 7–8, 9, 15–16, 63, 89, 154, 250–64
  1 Henry 4, 15, 65, 93–4, 258, 260, 261
  All is True, 255–6, 263
  A Midsummer Night's Dream, 253, 263
  Antony and Cleopatra, 6, 7, 66–7, 253, 255–6
  Coriolanus, 15, 258–62
  Cymbeline, 7, 187, 260
  Edward III, 66
  Hamlet, 252, 254
  Henry IV, Part Two, 69–70
  Henry VI, Part Two, 64, 257, 260–1
  History of Henry VI, 64, 74
  Julius Caesar, 7, 254
  King John, 263
  King Lear, 42, 254–5
  Merchant of Venice, 257
  The Merry Wives of Windsor, 7, 16, 51, 62, 67–73, 262–3
  Othello, 61
  Pericles, 255–6
  The Rape of Lucrece, 62, 73, 258, 263
  Richard II, 64, 260, 263
  Romeo and Juliet, 74
  The Tempest, 15, 255
  Timon of Athens, 255
  Troilus and Cressida, 61
  Venus and Adonis, 63, 253
  The Winter's Tale, 256
Sheldon, Richard, 21, 26
Sherwin, John, 109
Sidney, Philip, 113–14

Sir Thomas More, 257, 261
social orders, 111, 112–13, 129, 148, 154, 158, 161–2, 234, 264
  mixing, 111–12, 116, 119–20, 180
social mobility, 180–3
Sparke, Thomas, 24
Speed, John, 87
Spenser, Edmund, 2, 22, 35, 63, 102, 218–19
Stow, John, 102–3, 104–6, 255
Strange's Men, 12–13
Surfleet, Richard, 215

Tasso, Torquato, 66
Taylor, John, 7, 11–12, 13, 14, 106, 143–63, 189, 195–6, 212, 219–24, 226–7, 271
The Tinker of Turvey, 117–18
tolls, 212, 217, 221
Traherne, Thomas, 8, 22–3, 31–5, 37
Tryon, Thomas, 43
Turberville, George, 102

Vallans, William, 86
Venner, Tobias, 43
Vergil, Polydore, 92
Visscher, Claes, 104

Walker, Henry, 143–4, 155
Walton, Izaak, 11, 87, 124–37, 149, 215, 270
water cycle, 31, 153, 250–1
watermen, 12–14, 118–19, 145–6, 156, 158, 162, 168–9, 182, 189, 192, 193, 212, 214, 219, 226, 269
  Company of Watermen, 109–10, 146
Watson, Henry, 113

Webster, John, 112
Weever, John, 87
Westward for Smelts, 116–17
White, John, 26, 27
Wisbech, Penny of, 14–15, 231–2, 238, 241–4
Wither, George, 89
Wotton, Henry, 107